VMware vRealize Orchestrator Cookbook

Master the configuration, programming, and interaction of plugins with Orchestrator to efficiently automate your VMware infrastructure

Daniel Langenhan

BIRMINGHAM - MUMBAI

VMware vRealize Orchestrator Cookbook

First published: February 2015

Production reference: 1240215

Published by Packt Publishing Ltd.
Livery Place
35 Livery Street
Birmingham B3 2PB, UK.

ISBN 978-1-78439-224-6

www.packtpub.com

Credits

Author
Daniel Langenhan

Reviewers
Burke Azbill
Christophe Decanini
Steffen Oezcan
Brian Ragazzi
Earl Waud

Commissioning Editor
Dipika Gaonkar

Acquisition Editors
Rebecca Pedley
Greg Wild

Content Development Editor
Pooja Nair

Technical Editors
Tanvi Bhatt
Pramod Kumavat
Mitali Somaiya

Copy Editors
Deepa Nambiar
Stuti Srivastava
Neha Vyas

Project Coordinator
Suzanne Coutinho

Proofreaders
Simran Bhogal
Stephen Copestake
Safis Editing
Ameesha Green
Paul Hindle

Indexer
Tejal Soni

Production Coordinator
Conidon Miranda

Cover Work
Conidon Miranda

Foreword

If there is something I did right from the beginning of my IT career, it was automation and integration. Coming from a development background, it was natural for me to script or develop small tools to automate most of the manual tasks our team had to accomplish. This was in the mid 90s and required using a combination of scripting and programming languages, tools such as network boot and floppy disks, and performing low-level operations such as dumping PC BIOS to extract the information required by an installation process.

Since then, IT has evolved and now provides application programming interfaces to get information and perform remote operations. Simpler scripting languages were released to make these easily consumable, and virtualization provided the agility that was missing to automate a lot of data center operations.

Streamlining these operations as modular, reusable, highly available workflows is what VMware vRealize Orchestrator brought to the equation.

After being used prominently by service providers to build their public cloud offerings and the enterprises for their private cloud, Orchestrator is now fast becoming a core component of several VMware Software-defined Data Center capabilities such as self-service provisioning, custom service authoring, DevOps, and automatic remediation. The Orchestrator workflows powering these can be leveraged to design your own custom automation and integrations.

VMware vRealize Orchestrator Cookbook guides system engineers in understanding how to best design workflows to orchestrate data centers. It walks them through all the important Orchestrator features using real-world use cases presented as recipes, explaining how these work, and providing directions to aid further development.

My colleague Burke Azbill and I have been working with Orchestrator for the last 8 years, enabling our customers in their journey to the software-defined data center. We can definitely say that if we had had a copy of this book back then, it would have saved us hundreds of hours; even today, with all the experience we have, it is still a much-needed reference.

We have worked with Daniel Langenhan for the last 6 years, and we are delighted that he has managed to share so much of his knowledge and experience acquired by delivering Orchestration solutions to our customers; the result is that you can now unleash the power of Orchestrator.

We wish you the best in your workflow designs and deployments.

Christophe Decanini and **Burke Azbill**

Consulting Architects

VMware Global Center of Excellence

@vCOTeam / vCOTeam.info

About the Author

Daniel Langenhan is a virtualization expert with formidable skills in architecture, design, and implementation for large multitier systems. His experience and knowledge of process management, enterprise-level storage, and Linux and Windows operating systems have made him and his business a highly sought international consultancy in the Asia Pacific and European regions for multinational clientele in the areas of finance, communication, education, and government. Daniel has been working with VMware products since 2002 and has been directly associated with VMware since 2008. He has a proven track record of successful integrations of virtualization into different business areas while minimizing cost and maximizing reliability and effectiveness for his clients.

Daniel's expertise and practical approach to VMware have resulted in the publication of the following books:

- *Instant VMware vCloud Starter, Packt Publishing*
- *VMware View Security Essentials, Packt Publishing*
- *VMware vCloud Director Cookbook, Packt Publishing*

He has also lent his expertise to many other publishing projects as a technical editor.

I would like to thank my wife, Renata, for her endless efforts and patience. I also like to express my gratitude to my reviewers for improving this book. A special thank you goes out to Christophe Decanini and Burke Azbill who have been committed to make Orchestrator a successful product since they started working on Orchestrator.

About the Reviewers

Burke Azbill has been a technology professional since 1996 and holds certifications from Cisco, Citrix, ITIL, Linux Professional Institute, Microsoft, Novell, and VMware. He joined VMware in 2007 as part of the acquisition of Dunes Technologies from Lausanne, Switzerland, where he had begun his work with Orchestrator. Burke is the founder and contributor of `http://www.vcoteam.info` as well as a leading contributor to the VMTN communities for Orchestrator. During his tenure at VMware, Burke has trained hundreds of employees on Orchestrator, built many integrations for customers and partners, and worked in various roles in the VMworld Hands-on Labs. He has coauthored *vCloud Architecture Toolkit, VMware Press*, and he has reviewed *Automating vSphere with VMware vCenter Orchestrator, VMware Press* and *VMware vSphere for Dummies, For Dummies*.

Christophe Decanini is a consulting architect at VMware, Inc. He joined VMware in 2007 as part of the acquisition of Dunes Technologies. Based in Gland, Switzerland, Christophe is an Orchestrator expert, supporting VMware customers, partners, and field resources globally.

Christophe has worked on several important contributions to Orchestrator, including product features that participated in making Orchestrator a successful product. He has presented orchestration solutions at conferences such as VMworld and is a main contributor to the `www.vcoteam.info` blog and the official VMware Orchestrator community.

Christophe has reviewed and contributed to books that cover Orchestrator, including *VMware vCloud Architecture Toolkit, VMware Press*. He was awarded the vExpert designation for several years and is now a VMware CTO ambassador.

He has 20 years of experience in IT automation and holds a VMware Certified Professional 5 - Data Center Virtualization (VCP5-DCV) certification and a Bachelor's degree in computer science. You can follow Christophe on Twitter at `@vCOTeam`.

Steffen Oezcan is a data center technologist based in Germany with more than 10 years of experience within the IT industry. What started as a career in data center administration moved swiftly into IT consulting and training with the focus on Microsoft and VMware-based virtualization technologies. He combines his deep technical and excellent educational skills to deliver the best solutions to his clients, who span across many industries in EMEA.

Steffen holds several advanced certifications, including VMware Certified Advanced Professional 5-Data Center Administration (VCAP5-DCA) and VMware Certified Advanced Professional 5-Data Center Design (VCAP5-DCD). In the last 5 years, he has become a well-known VMware Certified Instructor (VCI) Level 2, teaching classes across EMEA for vSphere, vRealize Operations Manager, Horizon View, and vCloud Networking and Security. In this role, he received the VCI Achievement Award for his outstanding contribution and the best instructor evaluations in EMEA, presented on VCI Day at VMworld Europe 2013.

Since 2010, he has been working as a freelance IT consultant and technical instructor, currently focusing on virtualization technologies, cloud enablement, and data center automation.

Brian Ragazzi is an advisory solution architect at EMC with more than 15 years of experience in the IT industry. He is a lead architect at EMC Enterprise Hybrid Cloud and specializes in Software-defined Data Center and IT automation. Brian can be found online at `http://brianragazzi.com`.

Earl Waud is a virtualization development professional with more than 9 years of focused industry experience, creating innovative solutions for hypervisor provisioning, management, and automation. He is an expert in aligning engineering strategy with organizational vision and goals and delivering highly scalable and user-friendly virtualization environments.

With more than 20 years of experience in developing customer-facing and corporate IT software solutions, he has a proven track record in delivering high-caliber and on-time technology solutions that significantly impact business results.

Earl lives in San Diego, California. He is blessed with a beautiful wife, Patti, and three amazing daughters, Madison, Daniella, and Alexis.

Currently, Earl is a senior systems engineer with Intuit Inc., which is a company that creates business and financial management solutions that simplify the business of life for small businesses, consumers, and accounting professionals.

Earl can be reached online at `http://sandiegoearl.com`.

Thank you to my wonderful family for allowing me to spend some of our precious family time reviewing this book. I love and appreciate you, and I know I am truly blessed that you are my family.

www.PacktPub.com

Support files, eBooks, discount offers, and more

For support files and downloads related to your book, please visit `www.PacktPub.com`.

Did you know that Packt offers eBook versions of every book published, with PDF and ePub files available? You can upgrade to the eBook version at `www.PacktPub.com` and, as a print book customer, you are entitled to a discount on the eBook copy. Get in touch with us at `service@packtpub.com` for more details.

At `www.PacktPub.com`, you can also read a collection of free technical articles, sign up for a range of free newsletters, and receive exclusive discounts and offers on Packt books and eBooks.

`https://www2.packtpub.com/books/subscription/packtlib`

Do you need instant solutions to your IT questions? PacktLib is Packt's online digital book library. Here, you can search, access, and read Packt's entire library of books.

Why subscribe?

- Fully searchable across every book published by Packt
- Copy and paste, print, and bookmark content
- On-demand and accessible via a web browser

Free access for Packt account holders

If you have an account with Packt at `www.PacktPub.com`, you can use this to access PacktLib today and view 9 entirely free books. Simply use your login credentials for immediate access.

Instant updates on new Packt books

Get notified! Find out when new books are published by following `@PacktEnterprise` on Twitter or the *Packt Enterprise* Facebook page.

Table of Contents

Preface

Orchestrator started its life as Dunes at a small company in Lucerne, Switzerland. In 2009, VMware bought Dunes and then introduced Orchestrator into vSphere 4.0 as vCenter Orchestrator. Orchestrator's first stage debut was with VMware Lifecycle Manager, which used Orchestrator to automate the virtual infrastructure life cycle. Orchestrator itself never really received the spotlight until the recent launch of VMware vCloud Automation Center (vCAC). In the beginning, vCAC used Orchestrator only as an extension, but with version 6.1, it became the central tool for automation.

In October 2014, VMware renamed vCenter Orchestrator (vCO) to vRealize Orchestrator (vRO) to align with their new strategies. vRO is not a new product; it is just the new name of vCO.

With version 6.2 of vCAC, the product has been renamed to vRealize Automation.

Due to the massive renaming bonanza that VMware undertook during the writing of this book, we will simply refer to vRO/vCO as Orchestrator. Even after the renaming, you will still find reminisces of Dunes and vCO in vRealize Orchestrator; have a look in some of the error messages or in the API.

The nice thing about Orchestrator that still astounds people is that Orchestrator is licensed with vCenter, which means that it comes free with vCenter (as well as vRealize Automation). Also, there are no extra licensing fees for any VMware distributed plugins.

A lot of third parties such as F5, Cisco, and so on have developed plugins for Orchestrator, making it possible to push the automation further.

Orchestrator comes in four versions that differ only in the way they are installed but not in their content or their abilities. The version most people don't know about is the one that is automatically installed (but not activated) with vCenter. The second is the one that is integrated with vRealize Automation. Then, there is a Windows-based installation, and last but not least, the shrink-wrapped Linux appliance. This book covers all of these and also dives into their little specialties.

Best approaches to reading this book

You might think that depending on which version or installation of Orchestrator you use, things will be different. Well, they're not. Have a look at the following figure:

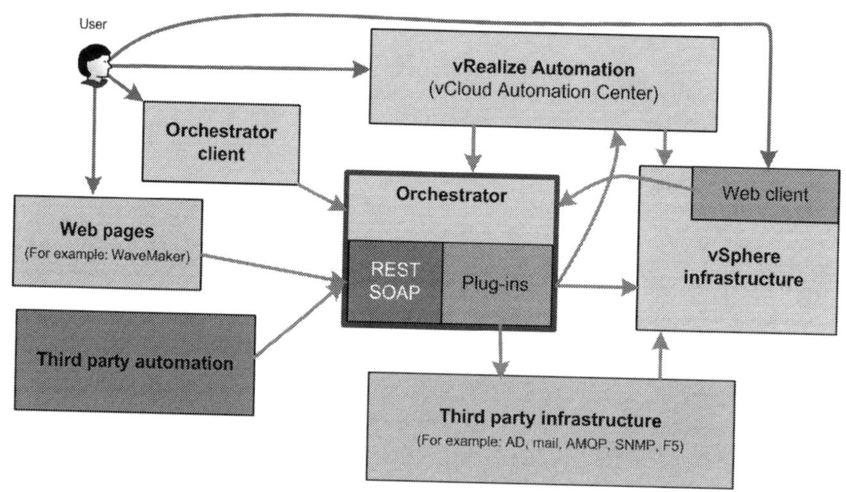

Orchestrator is the central part of any automation effort.

If you plan to use vRealize Automation, it is best to read the introduction to *Chapter 7, Working with VMware Infrastructure*, first before diving deeper. vRealize Automation just leverages Orchestrator workflows and plugins. Check out *Chapter 1, Installing and Configuring Orchestrator*, to understand how to access Orchestrator and then follow the vSphere Automation path.

If you plan to automate your vSphere infrastructure, you can dive straight into *Chapter 1, Installing and Configuring Orchestrator*, and then check out the introduction in *Chapter 7, Working with VMware Infrastructure*, as well as the first recipe for vCenter in the same chapter.

You should definitely read all the chapter introductions as they contain valuable information for beginners as well as advanced readers.

If you are new to Orchestrator, start at *Chapter 1, Installing and Configuring Orchestrator*, and then move on to *Chapter 5, Basic Orchestrator Operations*, and finally *Chapter 3, Visual Programming*. This will give you a very good start.

What this book covers

Chapter 1, Installing and Configuring Orchestrator, shows you how to install, configure, and access the various Orchestrator installation types.

Chapter 2, Optimizing Orchestrator Configuration, dives into more specialized setups, such as clusters, and how to tune the Orchestrator appliance.

Chapter 3, Visual Programming, introduces and dives into the visual programming of Orchestrator.

Chapter 4, Working with Plugins, showcases how to use the different plugins of Orchestrator with detailed examples.

Chapter 5, Basic Orchestrator Operations, teaches you how to operate Orchestrator, working with user management, packages, and more.

Chapter 6, Advanced Operations, dives into more advanced operations such as language packs, resources, and policies.

Chapter 7, Working with VMware Infrastructure, teaches you how to automate the vSphere infrastructure as well as use Orchestrator workflows in vRealize Orchestrator.

What you need for this book

This book covers a lot of ground and discusses the interactions with a lot of other infrastructure services such as AD, e-mail, the vSphere infrastructure, and vRealize Automation.

You can use this book with Orchestrator versions 5.0, 5.1, and 5.5 as well as with the renamed version, vRealize Orchestrator (5.5.2.x, 6.0, and newer).

The requirements differ from chapter to chapter. For *Chapter 1, Installing and Configuring Orchestrator*, and *Chapter 2, Optimizing Orchestrator Configuration*, you just require some space on your virtual infrastructure to deploy Orchestrator and maybe a working vCenter. Everything in *Chapter 3, Visual Programming*, can be accomplished with only the Orchestrator appliance; however, it's more fun with a vCenter around. *Chapter 4, Working with Plugins*, will require some more infrastructure such as e-mail, AD, REST, SOAP, SNMP, and AMQP. *Chapter 5, Basic Orchestrator Operations*, and *Chapter 6, Advanced Operations*, require mostly only Orchestrator and a working vCenter structure. For *Chapter 7, Working with VMware Infrastructure*, you will require a fully operational vCenter. A vRealize Automation installation is only needed if you are planning to use this product.

Some readers might not have all the resources or infrastructure to rebuild or play with some of the recipes; however, I'm sometimes in the same boat. As a consultant, I travel a lot, so while writing this book, I used this little mini lab. It isn't fast or fancy but it does the trick.

My mini lab consists of a laptop with Windows 7 Pro and VMware Workstation 10 on an Intel i7 quad core (3.4 GHz) with 8 GB RAM. My base VMs look like this:

Name	Content	Virtual hardware
ADDNS	AD, DNS, MS SQL (vCenter, hmail, Orchestrator), hmail, RabbitMQ	Windows 2K8R2, 2 vCPU, 2 GB, 40 GB
vCenter	SSO, WebClient, Inventory Service, vCenter, vRA IaaS	Windows 2K8R2, 2 vCPU, 2 GB, 40 GB
WinvCO	Orchestrator, PowerShell, PowerCLI, PowerGui	Windows 2K8R2, 2 vCPU, 2 GB, 40 GB
AppVCO	Orchestrator appliance	SLES, 2 vCPU, 2 GB, 40 GB
vESXi	Virtual ESXi	ESXi, 2 vCPU, 6 GB, 4 GB
vRA	vRA Appliance	SLES, 2vCPU, 6 GB, 55 GB

The trick is to choose the minimum amount of VMs to power on at the same time.

Who this book is for

This book addresses the novice as well as the advanced VMware enthusiast. No previous know-how about Orchestrator is needed. The structure of this book is layered out so that a novice can start at the beginning and work his way through the chapters building up know-how in Orchestrator. An advanced user with knowledge of Orchestrator can just jump into any recipe. Most recipes are linked to other recipes or to external sources for more in-depth understanding or usage of a given concept.

Example workflows

All workflows, actions, and so on that you can find in this book are also available for download. The example package that contains more than 100 workflows and actions is available for download. Follow these instructions:

1. Navigate to `www.packtpub.com/networking-and-servers/vmware-vrealize-orchestrator-cookbook`.
2. Click on **Code Files** and download the example package.

3. Follow the *Working with packages* recipe in *Chapter 5, Basic Orchestrator Operations*, to upload the example package into your Orchestrator.

All example workflows can be found in the `Orchestrator Cookbook` folder and all actions are in the `com.packtpub.Orchestrator-Cookbook` module.

Conventions

In this book, you will find a number of styles of text that distinguish between different kinds of information. Here are some examples of these styles, and an explanation of their meaning.

Code words in text, database table names, folder names, filenames, file extensions, pathnames, dummy URLs, user input, and Twitter handles are shown as follows: "The AD domain is called `mylab.local`."

A block of code is set as follows:

```
var current = new Date();
return current;
```

When we wish to draw your attention to a particular part of a code block, the relevant lines or items are set in bold:

```
configurationElement.setAttributeWithKey(Key, Value);
```

Any command-line input or output is written as follows:

```
esxcli network firewall ruleset set --ruleset-id snmp --allowed-all true
--enabled true
esxcli network firewall refresh
```

New terms and **important words** are shown in bold. Words that you see on the screen, in menus or dialog boxes for example, appear in the text like this: "Click on **Test Connection** and make sure it works."

Warnings or important notes appear in a box like this.

Tips and tricks appear like this.

Reader feedback

Feedback from our readers is always welcome. Let us know what you think about this book—what you liked or may have disliked. Reader feedback is important for us to develop titles that you really get the most out of.

To send us general feedback, simply send an e-mail to `feedback@packtpub.com`, and mention the book title via the subject of your message.

If there is a topic that you have expertise in and you are interested in either writing or contributing to a book, see our author guide on `www.packtpub.com/authors`.

Customer support

Now that you are the proud owner of a Packt book, we have a number of things to help you to get the most from your purchase.

Downloading the example code

You can download the example code files for all Packt books you have purchased from your account at `http://www.packtpub.com`. If you purchased this book elsewhere, you can visit `http://www.packtpub.com/support` and register to have the files e-mailed directly to you.

Errata

Although we have taken every care to ensure the accuracy of our content, mistakes do happen. If you find a mistake in one of our books—maybe a mistake in the text or the code—we would be grateful if you would report this to us. By doing so, you can save other readers from frustration and help us improve subsequent versions of this book. If you find any errata, please report them by visiting `http://www.packtpub.com/submit-errata`, selecting your book, clicking on the **errata submission form** link, and entering the details of your errata. Once your errata are verified, your submission will be accepted and the errata will be uploaded on our website, or added to any list of existing errata, under the Errata section of that title. Any existing errata can be viewed by selecting your title from `http://www.packtpub.com/support`.

Piracy

Piracy of copyright material on the Internet is an ongoing problem across all media. At Packt, we take the protection of our copyright and licenses very seriously. If you come across any illegal copies of our works, in any form, on the Internet, please provide us with the location address or website name immediately so that we can pursue a remedy.

Please contact us at `copyright@packtpub.com` with a link to the suspected pirated material.

We appreciate your help in protecting our authors, and our ability to bring you valuable content.

Questions

You can contact us at `questions@packtpub.com` if you are having a problem with any aspect of the book, and we will do our best to address it.

1
Installing and Configuring Orchestrator

In this chapter, we explore how to install and configure Orchestrator. We will be looking at the following recipes:

- Getting Orchestrator running in 5 minutes (or less)
- Deploying the Orchestrator appliance
- Installing Orchestrator on Windows
- Two ways to configure Orchestrator
- Important Orchestrator base configurations
- Configuring Orchestrator with external LDAP or Active Directory
- Integrating Orchestrator into SSO and vSphere Web Client
- Configuring an external database

Introduction

vRealize Orchestrator (vRO) is the new name (since October 2014) of vCenter Orchestrator (vCO). In this book, we will refer to vRO/vCO simply as *Orchestrator*.

This chapter is dedicated to the configuration of Orchestrator and discusses how to set the tone for your Orchestrator deployment. Configuring Orchestrator wasn't easy in the past; therefore, not many people really used it. But now, the initial configuration is already done out-of-the-box and people can start using Orchestrator without too much fuss. However, if one plans to use Orchestrator in a production environment, it is important to know how to configure it properly.

There are four different Orchestrator versions. One version is shipped with vCenter Server and the other with vRealize Automation appliance. Then, there is the Windows-based installation and a preinstalled Linux appliance.

Orchestrator and vRealize Automation (vRA)

The vRealize Automation (formerly vCloud Automation Center or vCAC) appliance is shipped with a preinstalled and preconfigured vRO (Orchestrator). Orchestrator installed on vRA is already configured and works the way the normal Orchestrator appliance does.

If you are using the vRA-integrated version, just read all the recipes in this chapter and the next chapter as if you are using the appliance.

You can read more about vRA Orchestrator integration in the introduction to *Chapter 7, Working with VMware Infrastructure*.

Appliance or Windows install?

The question most people are asking these days is what type of Orchestrator should one use for a production environment or which one is recommended.

There isn't really a right answer. The appliance runs on Linux and therefore consumes less CPU and memory and, saves money on a Windows license. However, more people are familiar with Windows than with Linux.

There is another fact that one should be aware of. VMware has already announced that the Windows version update from 5.1.x to 5.5.x will not update the database. This, in my personal opinion, indicates that the Windows version doesn't receive as much attention from VMware as the appliance version. However, the version that is installed along with vCenter is pretty integrated; see the first recipe of this chapter.

A consideration you should be aware of is that, depending on your Windows security settings or other installed applications, such as antivirus, backup agents, or infrastructure discovery agents, your Windows Orchestrator installation might be impaired.

So, what is right for you? My personal preference and that of most of the VMware consultants I know is the appliance; it is easy to use, install, and update. However, keep in mind that Windows works just as well.

Orchestrator and vCenter/vRA on the same server?

Another question that is constantly asked is: Should one install Orchestrator on the same server as vCenter or vRA? As with the issue of appliance or Windows installation, it really depends on the objective of your Orchestrator installation. Installing Orchestrator on a vCenter Server where the Single Sign-On (SSO), the Web Client, Inventory, and vCenter services are already competing for resources makes quite an impact. If the Orchestrator installation is aimed at automating a sizable production environment, sharing Orchestrator resources with vCenter isn't such a great idea. For a small environment, a shared vCenter/Orchestrator VM can be quite a good solution.

The vRA-integrated Orchestrator installation is also fine for smaller environments; however, if you plan to automate a production environment with vRA, it is recommended that you use a separate Orchestrator installation and maybe even an Orchestrator cluster (see *Chapter 2, Optimizing Orchestrator Configuration*).

What it basically comes down to is managing the Java heap sizes of the different services (see the *Tuning Java* recipe in *Chapter 2, Optimizing Orchestrator Configuration*). A correct sizing of all the Java heap sizes (vCenter services as well as Orchestrator) will allow a good coexistence of all services. However, you should consider issues such as manageability as well as the ability to monitor and update all the services.

Getting Orchestrator running in 5 minutes (or less)

In this recipe, we will get Orchestrator up and running using the Orchestrator version that is installed along with vCenter or vRealize Orchestrator.

Getting ready

You either need administrative access to the Windows OS of your existing vCenter Server (5.1 or higher) installation, or you need a functional vRealize Automation installation (see the introduction to *Chapter 7, Working with VMware Infrastructure*, for more information).

How to do it...

This recipe is not the same for vCenter-integrated and vRA-integrated Orchestrator implementations. There is a slight difference.

On your marks, get set, GO!

vCenter-integrated Orchestrator

Follow these steps if you are using the vCenter-integrated Orchestrator.

1. Log in to the Windows OS of your existing vCenter installation.
2. Open the Services—for example, for Win 2008 R2, navigate to **Start** | **Administrative Tools** | **Services**.
3. Find the **VMware vCenter Orchestrator Server** service.

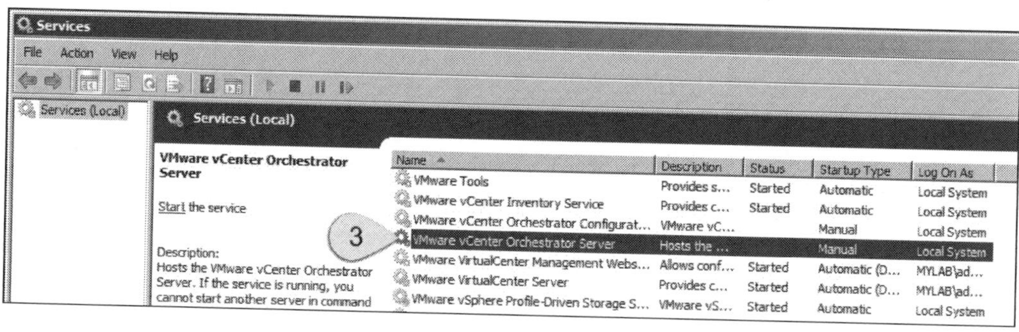

4. Right-click and select **Start**. If the service fails to start, have a look at the *There's more...* section of this recipe. The first start might take a while and Windows might complain about it, but just have patience.
5. When the service has started, use vCenter Orchestrator Client to connect to Orchestrator. You'll find the client by navigating to **Start** | **VMware** | **vCenter Orchestrator Client**.
6. Enter `localhost:8281` as **Host name**, `administrator@vsphere.local` as **User name** with the corresponding password, and click on **Login**.

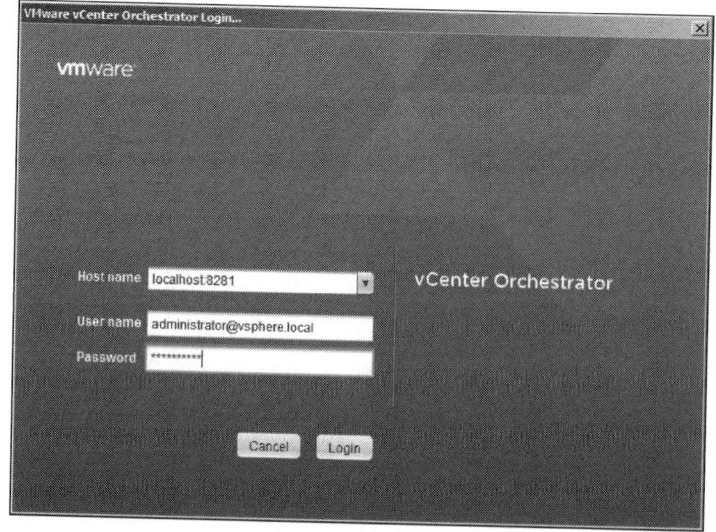

Finished! Orchestrator is up and running.

vRealize Automation-integrated Orchestrator

Follow these steps if you are using the vRA-integrated Orchestrator:

1. Open a web browser and enter the IP or FQDN of the vRA appliance.
2. Click on the **vRealize Orchestrator Client** link.
3. Enter `[IP or FQDN of the vRA appliance]:8281` as **Host name,** `administrator@vsphere.local` as **User name** with the corresponding password, and click on **Login**.

Finished! Orchestrator is up and running.

How it works...

When you install vCenter, you also automatically install Orchestrator; however, what you probably don't know is that the installer also configures Orchestrator to use the vCenter database, registers itself with SSO, and configures the vCenter plugin. Orchestrator is now easily accessible and fully configured to work with vCenter/vRA.

That said, one needs to understand that we have just started another hungry service on vCenter/vRA VM. As already discussed in the introduction, you might want to rethink this.

Looking at how the vCenter-integrated Orchestrator is configured, we find that the whole configuration process is triggered by the `vco.properties` file in the `C:\Program Files\VMware\Infrastructure\Orchestrator` directory. It contains all relevant information, but no passwords.

If you look into Orchestrator's configuration using the Orchestrator Configuration tool (see the *Two ways to configure Orchestrator* recipe in this chapter), you will find the following configurations:

- In the **Network** section, the vCenter and the SSO SSL certificates have been added.
- In the **Authentication** section, SSO is configured. If we log in to the SSO server, we find an existing group called vCOAdministrators and that the administrator (@vsphere.local) is a member of this group. We also find that Orchestrator is registered as an application user.
- In the **Database** section, there is a new and unique database type: vDB. This is a connection to the ODBC drivers you set up for vCenter.
- In the **Licensing** section, Orchestrator has been licensed with the vCenter license key.
- Last but not least, the vCenter plugin is configured with vCenter details.

This all makes the vCenter Orchestrator installation the most easy to use for beginners. Basically, you only have to start the Orchestrator service on vCenter Server and you are ready to go.

There's more...

If you get an error while starting the Orchestrator service, have a quick look at `C:\Program Files\VMware\Infrastructure\Orchestrator\app-server\logs`. There is a file called `server.log`. This is the logfile for the Orchestrator service. The most common problem at this point is that the database cannot be accessed. If this is the case, I would recommend switching the database type to embedded.

See also

To fully integrate Orchestrator into your vCenter, continue with the *Integrating Orchestrator into SSO and vSphere Web Client* recipe in this chapter as well as the recipe *Orchestrator and vSphere Web Client* in *Chapter 5, Basic Orchestrator Operations*.

Deploying the Orchestrator appliance

We will now deploy the Orchestrator appliance based on Linux.

Getting ready

We can deploy the Orchestrator appliance on either a vSphere environment or on VMware Workstation (or Fusion if you are a MAC user).

The Orchestrator appliance needs the following (defaults):

- Two vCPUs at 2 GHz (less is OK, but it will be slower)
- 3 GB memory
- 12 GB disk space
- One IP that is either a fixed IP or via DHCP

How to do it...

In this recipe, we will learn how to download and deploy Orchestrator.

Download

1. Navigate to `http://vmware.com` and select **Downloads**.
2. Enter `Orchestrator appliance` in the search text box and press *Enter*.
3. Select the latest version from the menu.
4. Download the file that ends in `.ova`.

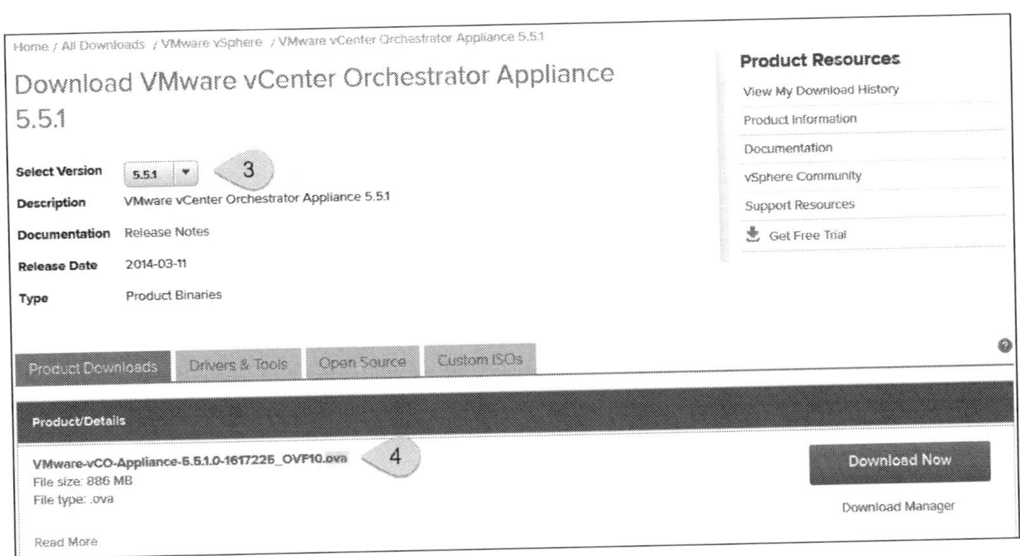

Please note that vCenter Orchestrator (vCO) was renamed vRealize Orchestrator (vRO) in version 6.0.

Deploy

1. Log in to vCenter using WebClient.
2. Right-click on the cluster or ESXi Server and select **Deploy OVF Template...**.
3. The **Deploy OVF Template** wizard starts. Select the OVA file you have downloaded and click on **Next**.
4. Accept the EULA and click on **Next**.
5. Select a name (or accept the default) as well as the vCenter folder for the Orchestrator appliance and click on **Next**.
6. Select the cluster or ESXi Server or a resource pool for the Orchestrator appliance and click on **Next**.
7. Select the datastore you would like to deploy the Orchestrator appliance on and click on **Next**.

8. Select a network for the Orchestrator appliance and click on **Next**.
9. In the **Customize template** section, set a password for the root and the Orchestrator configuration account.
10. Set a hostname for the Orchestrator appliance.
11. If you want to use a fixed IP, expand the **Network Properties** section, enter all IP-related entries, and then click on **Next**. If you want to use DHCP, just click on **Next**.

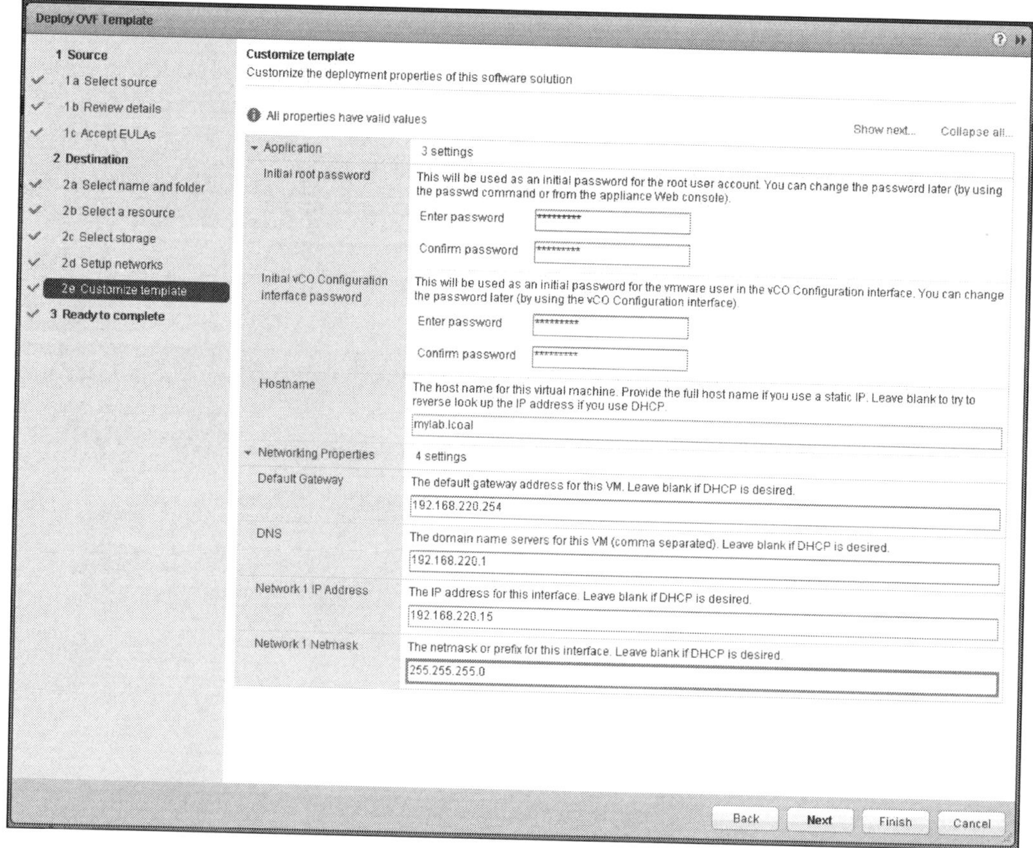

12. Opt to power on the VM after deployment and click on **Finish**.
13. Wait until the VM has finished deploying and is powered on.
14. Open the console of the Orchestrator appliance and wait until the install process has completed and the VM console shows the following screen:

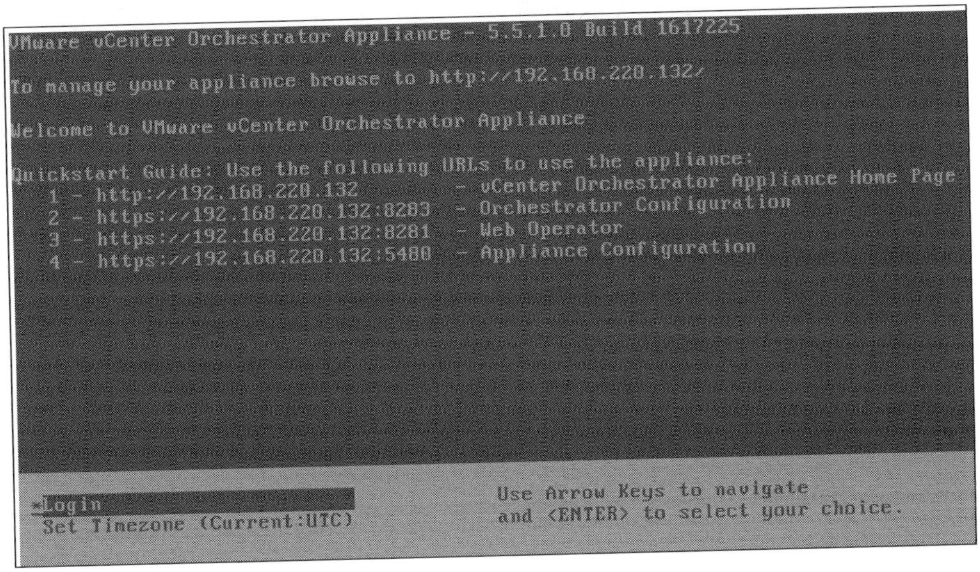

```
VMware vCenter Orchestrator Appliance - 5.5.1.0 Build 1617225

To manage your appliance browse to http://192.168.220.132/

Welcome to VMware vCenter Orchestrator Appliance

Quickstart Guide: Use the following URLs to use the appliance:
   1 - http://192.168.220.132          - vCenter Orchestrator Appliance Home Page
   2 - https://192.168.220.132:8283    - Orchestrator Configuration
   3 - https://192.168.220.132:8281    - Web Operator
   4 - https://192.168.220.132:5480    - Appliance Configuration

 *Login                                  Use Arrow Keys to navigate
  Set Timezone (Current:UTC)             and <ENTER> to select your choice.
```

Let's go...

1. Open a browser and browse to the IP of the Orchestrator appliance (for example, `http://192.168.220.132`).

2. Depending on your environment, you might need to accept the SSL certificate. You are now on the Orchestrator home page with several useful links to all important Orchestrator topics.

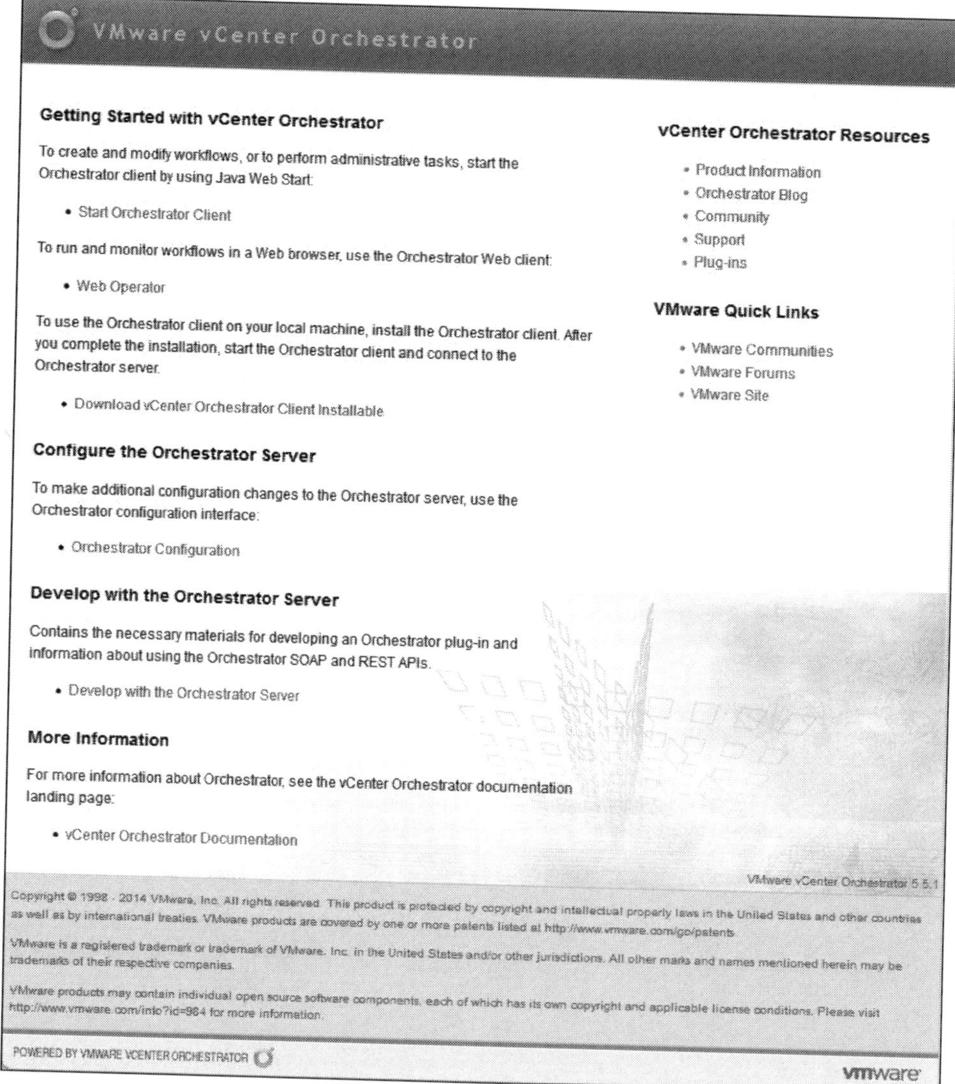

3. To open up the Orchestrator Client, click on **Start Orchestrator Client**.
4. Enter `vcoadmin` as user with the password `vcoadmin`.

How it works...

vCO 5.5.2.1 appliance is a preconfigured Orchestrator installation that uses the following:

- Suse Linux Enterprise Server (SLES) 11 Patch level 2
- PostgreSQL 9.1.9
- OpenLDAP 2.4.26

Everything is ready to run; however, no integration with vCenter or any external service is configured. The Orchestrator appliance comes with a 90-day evaluation license installed.

The LDAP has the following preconfigured entries:

Username	Password	Group membership
`vcoadmin`	`vcoadmin`	`vcoadmins`
`vcouser`	`vcouser`	`vcousers`

Both LDAP and DB are protected to allow only local access to them.

There's more...

If you want to deploy the Orchestrator appliance on VMware Workstation, the process of deploying the Orchestrator appliance differs from the one described in this recipe. Follow these steps instead:

1. Use Windows Explorer to navigate to the downloaded `.ova` file.
2. Double-click on the OVA file. VMware Workstation opens up.
3. Select a name and a path for the new VM and click on **Import**.
4. Accept the EULA and wait until the VM is deployed.
5. You might need to select a different network (for example, Host-Only) depending on your lab environment.

6. Power on the VM and wait until the install pauses at the line indicated in this screenshot:

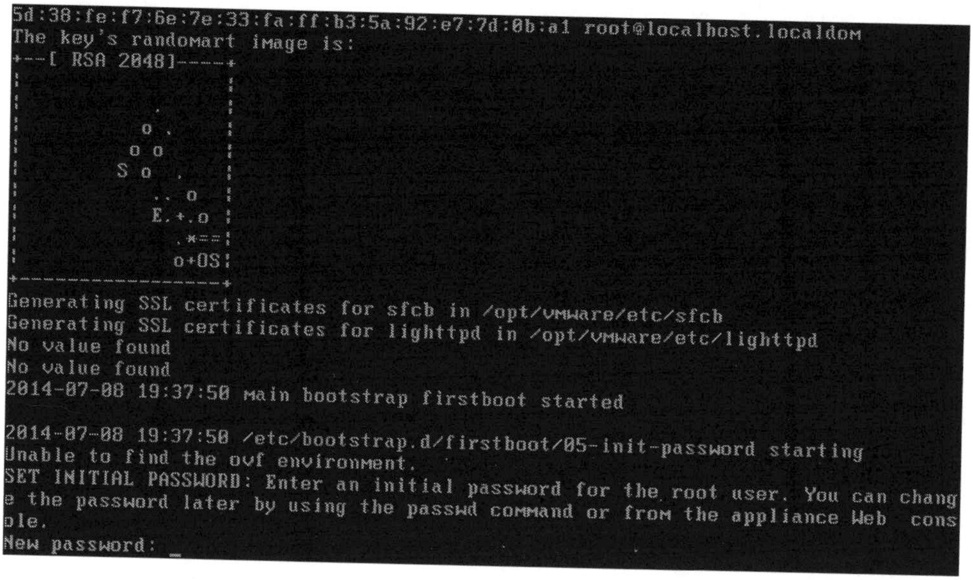

```
5d:38:fe:f7:6e:7e:33:fa:ff:b3:5a:92:e7:7d:0b:a1 root@localhost.localdom
The key's randomart image is:
+--[ RSA 2048]----+
|                 |
|        .        |
|       o .       |
|      o o        |
|     S o .       |
|        . . o    |
|       E.+.o     |
|         .*==    |
|         o+OS    |
+-----------------+
Generating SSL certificates for sfcb in /opt/vmware/etc/sfcb
Generating SSL certificates for lighttpd in /opt/vmware/etc/lighttpd
No value found
No value found
2014-07-08 19:37:50 main bootstrap firstboot started

2014-07-08 19:37:50 /etc/bootstrap.d/firstboot/05-init-password starting
Unable to find the ovf environment.
SET INITIAL PASSWORD: Enter an initial password for the root user. You can chang
e the password later by using the passwd command or from the appliance Web  cons
ole.
New password: _
```

7. Enter and confirm a new password for the root account.
8. Then, enter and confirm a new password for the Orchestrator Configuration tool. The installation will now continue. Wait until it has finished.

   The appliance will start with a DHCP address from Workstation. To set a static IP, you will have to access the admin interface of the appliance.

See also

See the *Tuning the appliance* recipe in *Chapter 2, Optimizing Orchestrator Configuration*.

Installing Orchestrator on Windows

The Windows version of Orchestrator requires slightly more work to set it up.

Getting ready

To get the Windows install working, we need the following:

- The VMware vCenter Server ISO file

- A Windows VM with the following system requirements:
    - 64-bit Windows (for example, Windows 2008 R2)
    - Two vCPUs at 2 GHz (less is OK, but it will be slower)
    - 4 GB memory
    - 2 GB disk space
    - One static IP (DHCP is not recommended)

How to do it...

We assume that you are installing Orchestrator on a freshly installed Windows VM.

Install

1. Insert the ISO image into the VM (for example, mount it via vCenter).
2. Use Explorer to browse to the `[CDROM]:\vCenter-Server\vCO` directory.
3. Execute the install file. The install wizard starts.
4. Skip the introduction by clicking on **Next**.
5. Accept the EULA and click on **Next**.
6. Select the path where you want to install Orchestrator and click on **Next**.
7. Click on **Client - Server** and then on **Next**.

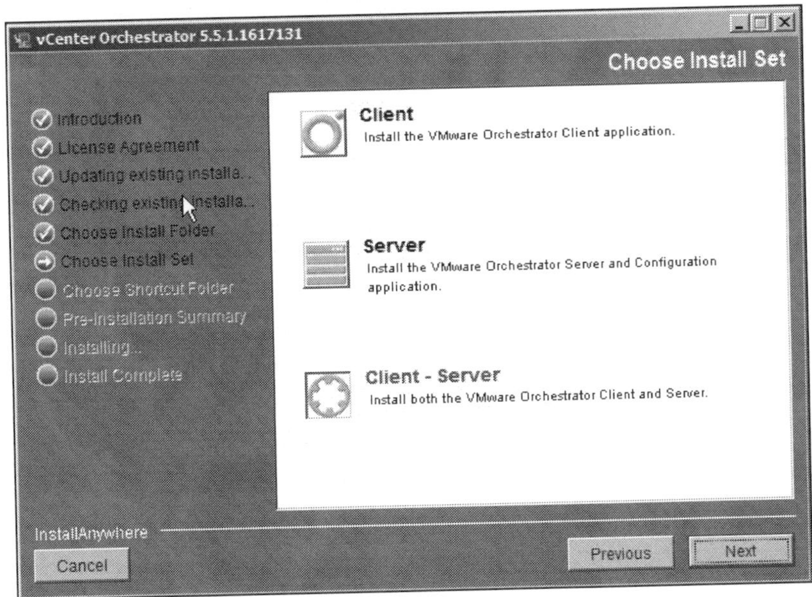

8. Leave the icon selection alone and just click on **Next**.
9. On the **Pre-Installation Summary** page, click on **Install**.
10. Wait till the installation has finished then click on **Done**.

Starting and configuring the Orchestrator service

We now need to make sure that Orchestrator's Windows services are starting and are configured correctly:

1. In Windows, open **Services**, for example, Win 2008 R2, and navigate to **Start | Administrative Tools | Services**.
2. Look for the service named **VMware vCenter Orchestrator Server**. Make sure it has started and is set to **Automatic**.

Setting the **Orchestrator Configuration** service to **Automatic** or starting it now is not really needed; we will start and stop it when required.

Accessing the vCenter Orchestrator home page

To access the vCenter Orchestrator home page, follow these steps:

1. Open a web browser and enter the `https://[ip of the vCO VM]:8281/vco/` URL.
2. To open up the Orchestrator Client, click on **Start Orchestrator Client**.
3. Enter `vcoadmin` as the user with the password `vcoadmin`.

Alternatively, you can access the web page from the VM itself by clicking on **Start | VMware | vCenter Orchestrator Home Page**.

How it works...

The Windows Orchestrator version now also comes with embedded LDAP and database, making the first steps much easier.

The embedded database and LDAP can't be as easily accessed as with the appliance because there isn't really a need to do so. If you want to be serious about Orchestrator, you should use an external database and you will want to use at least your Active Directory (AD), if not SSO, as an authentication source.

The Windows installation also comes with a 90-day evaluation license.

Two ways to configure Orchestrator

In this recipe, we will learn how to access the Orchestrator configuration. There are two ways, both of which work; however, the future is in workflows.

Getting ready

We need an Orchestrator instance up and running, as described in the recipes about installing.

To use the Configuration tool, we just need a web browser; and for the workflow method, we need either a local Java install to start the Java Web Client or an installed Orchestrator Client.

How to do it...

There are two ways to configure Orchestrator; I would encourage you to explore both.

Using the Orchestrator Configuration tool

If you are using the Orchestrator appliance, read the *Accessing the Orchestrator Configuration tool* section of this recipe. If you are using the Windows or vRA-integrated Orchestrator, follow these steps.

Windows or vCenter-integrated Orchestrator

1. In Windows, open **Services**. For example, in Win 2008 R2, navigate to **Start** | **Administrative Tools** | **Services**.
2. Right-click and start the **VMware vCenter Orchestrator Configuration** service.
3. Wait until the service has started successfully.

vRA-integrated Orchestrator

1. Log in to the vRA appliance OS using the root account.
2. Run the following command:

   ```
   service vco-configurator start
   ```

3. Now access the Orchestrator Configuration tool.
4. Wait until the service has started successfully.

Accessing the Orchestrator Configuration tool

1. Open a web browser and enter `https://[ip OR FQDN of Orchestrator]:8283`.
2. In the Orchestrator configuration login screen, enter `vmware` as the username and the password you assigned during the deployment. If you are using the Windows or vRA-integrated installation, the initial password is `vmware`. As soon as you are logged in, you will be requested to change the password.

The Orchestrator configuration page opens as shown in the following screenshot:

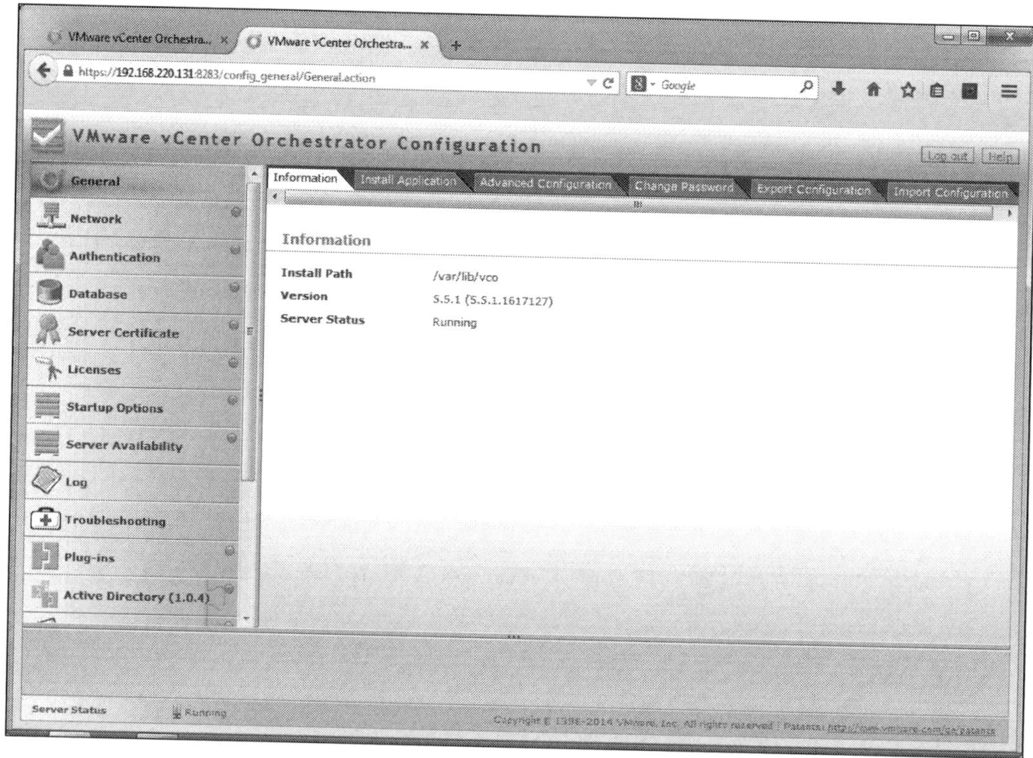

Here are all the sections that can be used to configure Orchestrator.

Using the workflow method

1. Access the Orchestrator Client, open a web browser, and navigate to the Orchestrator home page `http://[ip of the vCO VM]:8281/vco/` and click on **Start Orchestrator Client**.
2. Enter your credentials, which are `vcoadmin` with the password `vcoadmin` (except for the vCenter-installed Orchestrator version where you have to use the user account `administrator@vsphere.local`).

3. You might need to accept the SSL certificate. Click on **Install this Certificate...** to not have this come up again and then click on **Ignore**.
4. Once the Orchestrator Client opens, click on workflows (the blue icon with white in it) and then expand the tree, as seen in the next screenshot.
5. Here, you'll find all the Orchestrator-specific configuration workflow. Start one by right-clicking on it and choosing **Start workflow**.

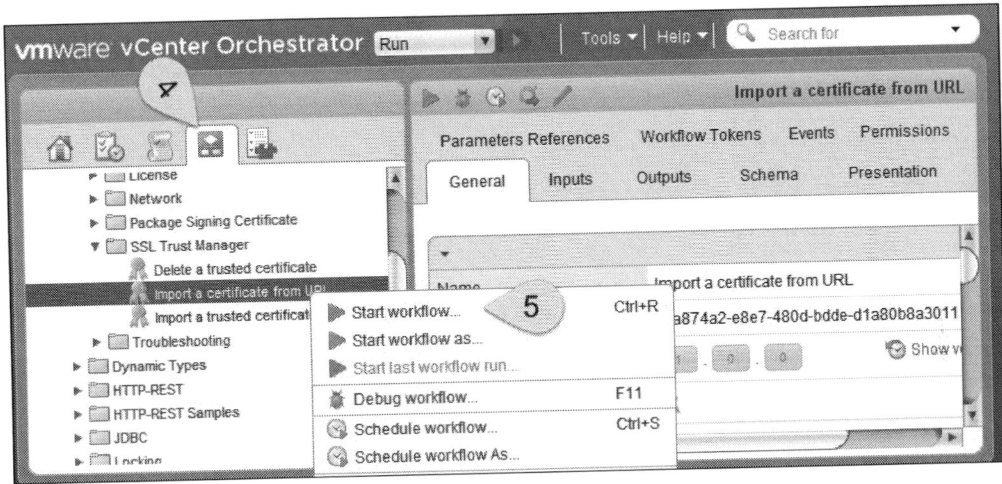

6. After entering the required information and clicking on **Submit**, the workflow will start.
7. A green tick next to the workflow execution will show you that the workflow was executed without an error. A red cross shows that the workflow encountered an error and has stopped. See the *How it works...* section of this recipe.

Base-configuring Orchestrator

Independent of the way you choose to configure Orchestrator, please continue with the recipe *Important Orchestrator base configurations* as the recipes in the rest of this chapter require the use of either method.

How it works...

The Orchestrator Configuration tool is an independent service in Windows as in Linux. The service doesn't require to be switched on all the time; it is more or less a one-off tool to get the initial deployment working.

The Orchestrator Configuration tool was commonly used to configure Orchestrator, and you will find countless websites still quoting it. It is a generally straightforward tool that helps you configure Orchestrator. The trick is to work your way down, starting with the **General** section. Every time you configure an item correctly, the little light next to the section title will switch to green. The light turns red if the item is not configured or is misconfigured. When you log in to Orchestrator for the first time, you will notice that all the lights are green; this is because it uses the preconfigured settings. You can still reconfigure all items to your own specifications.

The future of the Configuration tool

VMware announced that the Configuration tool will be removed in future releases. From then on, the workflow method will be the way to do it. However, currently there is no workflow to import and configure plugins, so this still has to be done using the Orchestrator Configuration tool. The Configuration tool also gives a lot more options for most configuration items than the workflows. In addition, there is also no workflow for exporting or importing the Orchestrator configuration for backup (see the *Backup and recovery* recipe in *Chapter 2, Optimizing Orchestrator Configuration*).

It will be interesting to see how the final version of VMware's vision for configuration pans out.

Working with errors in the workflow method

If the workflow doesn't run successfully, you probably will want to know why and resolve the error. To do so, follow these steps:

1. Click on the failed workflow execution. It has a red icon with a white X in it.
2. Click on **Schema**.
3. Click on **Variables**.
4. The error message is displayed in red.
5. To start the workflow again, just right-click on the failed execution and select **Run Again**.

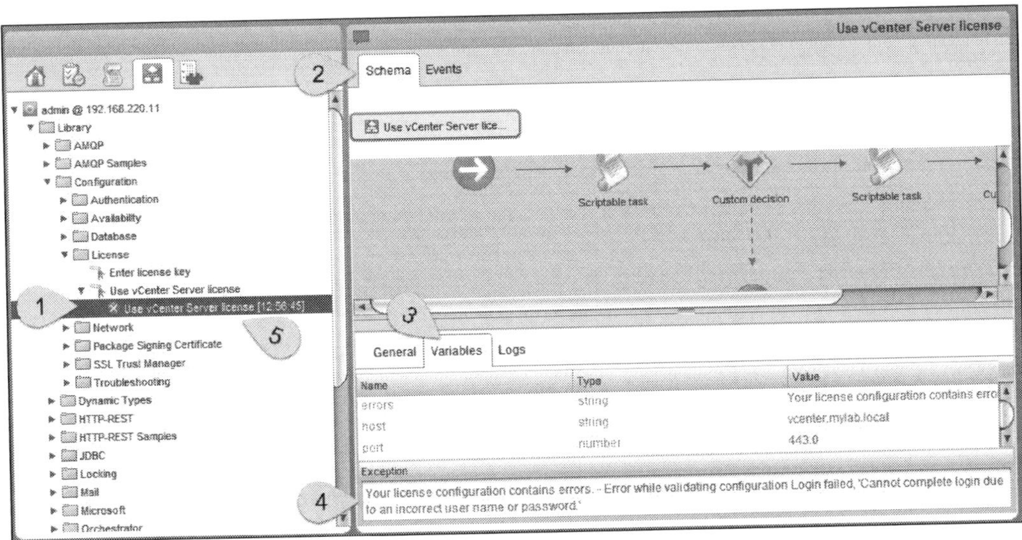

This will start the workflow again; however, it preserves all the information you have entered already into the workflow. No retyping is needed as everything from the last run is still displayed in the forms. The only exceptions are passwords, which is a good thing.

There's more...

There is actually a third way of configuring Orchestrator. Using the REST API of Orchestrator, you can connect to Orchestrator Server and run the configuration workflows. Showcasing this is beyond the scope of this book; however, you can find some instruction in the Orchestrator documentation and also in the *Accessing the Orchestrator API via REST* recipe in *Chapter 6, Advanced Operations*.

Important Orchestrator base configurations

In this recipe, we will configure basic aspects of Orchestrator, such as licensing, network, and SSL certificates. It is highly recommended you work through this recipe before continuing on to add an external LDAP or database.

Getting ready

You need an installed and running Orchestrator. You should also be comfortable with using one of the methods described in the *Two ways to configure Orchestrator* recipe.

How to do it...

These are some basic configurations that have to be done to Orchestrator to make it production-ready. I will describe the use of the Orchestrator Configuration tool as well as the workflow method.

Configuring the network

The network setting configures the interface by which Orchestrator communicates and the default is set to **0.0.0.0**. You can change it to an IPv4 or IPv6 address. The Windows install has already configured the correct setting and only requires a change if you would like to switch to IPv6.

Using the Orchestrator Configuration tool

1. Open the Orchestrator Configuration tool.
2. Click on the **Network** section and then select **Network**.
3. Select the correct IP address and click on **Apply changes**.

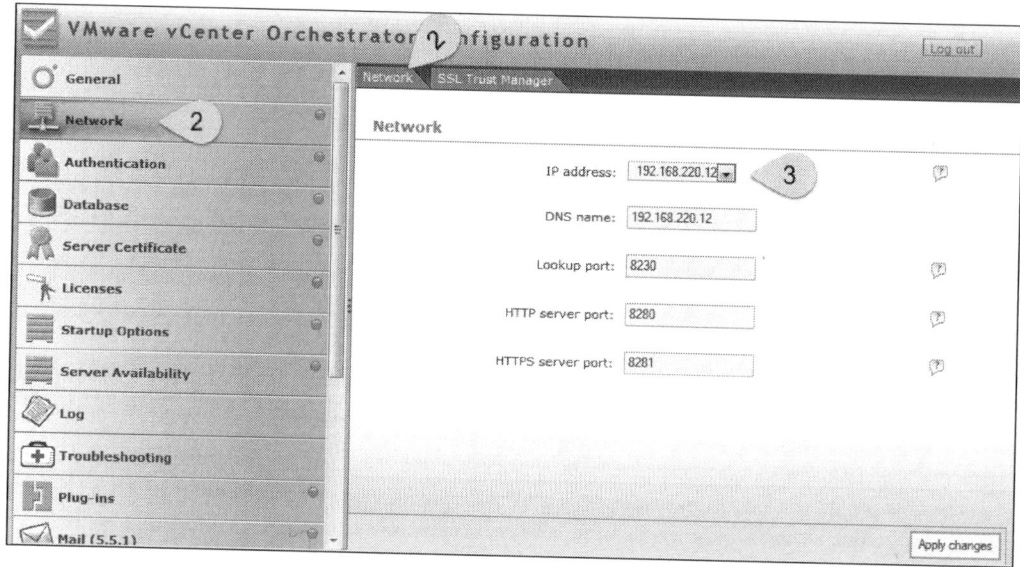

Using the workflow

1. Open the Orchestrator Client.
2. Navigate to **Library** | **Configuration** | **Network**.

3. Right-click on the workflow **Configure the network settings** and select **Start Workflow**.
4. Select the correct IP address and click on **Submit**.
5. Wait until the workflow has successfully finished.

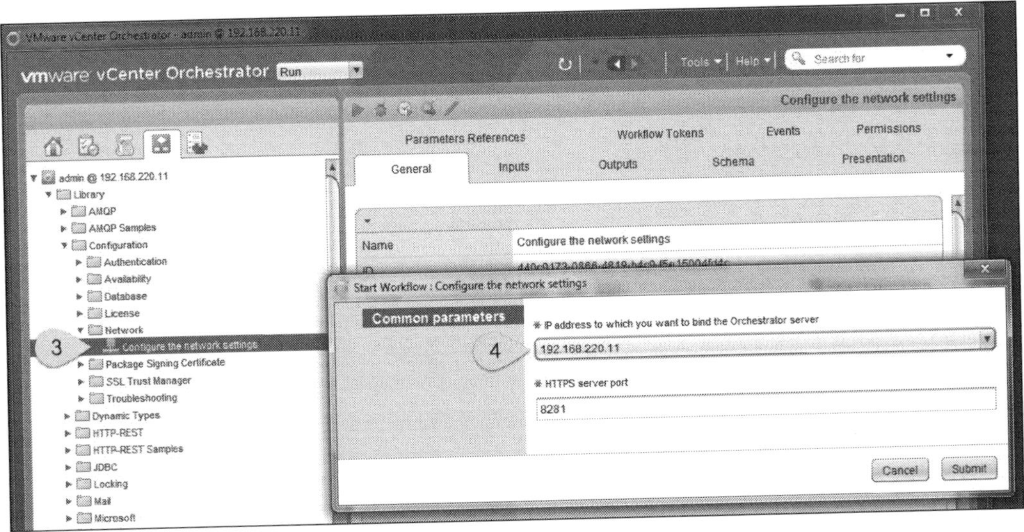

Importing SSL certificates

In order for Orchestrator to connect to any other SSL-based service, the SSL signature of this service has to be added to Orchestrator first. The SSL certificate for the Orchestrator Server itself is discussed in the *Configuring the Orchestrator Service SSL certificate* recipe in *Chapter 2, Optimizing Orchestrator Configuration*.

Using the Orchestrator Configuration tool

1. Open the Orchestrator Configuration tool.
2. Click on the **Network** section and then on **SSL Trust Manager**.
3. Enter the URL of the server that you wish to add and click on **Import**.
4. The SSL certificate will be shown. Click on **Import**.

5. The SSL certificate has been added. You can delete it by clicking on **Delete**.

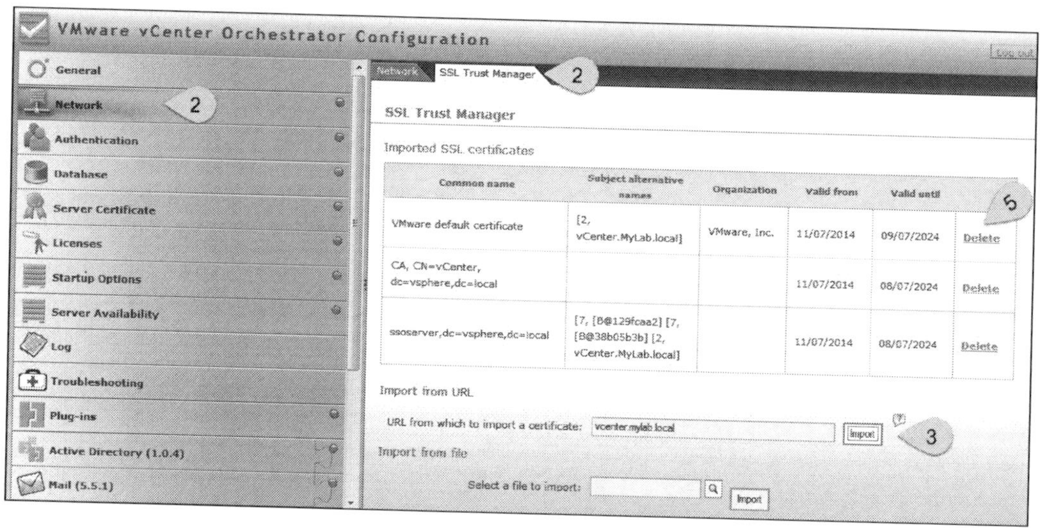

Using the workflow

1. Open the Orchestrator Client.
2. Navigate to **Library** | **Configuration** | **SSL Trust Manager**.
3. Right-click on the **Import a certificate from URL** workflow and select **Start Workflow**.
4. Enter the URL of the server that you wish to add.
5. Select **Yes** to accept the SSL certificate even if there are warnings and click on **Submit**.

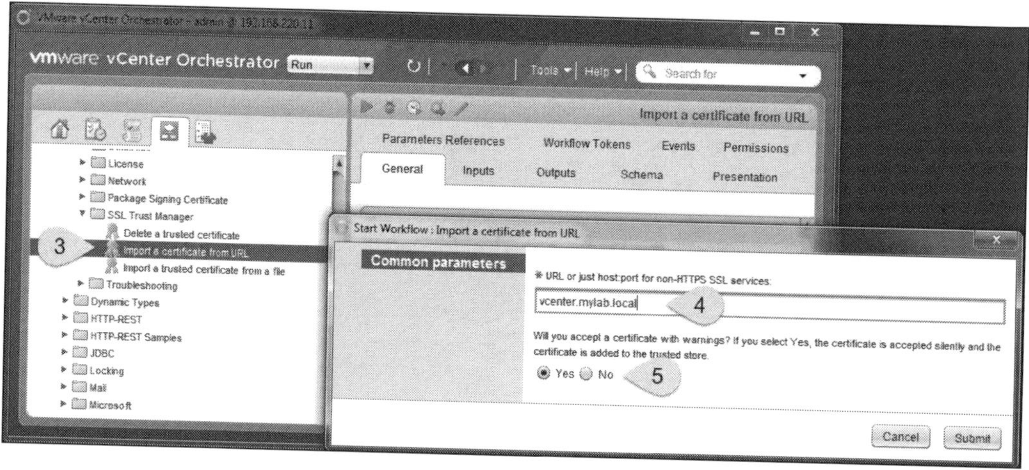

Licensing

Both the Orchestrator Windows version and the appliance come with a 90-day evaluation license. Orchestrator is licensed with vCenter. The vCenter license key is the Orchestrator license key, and no extra purchase is required. However, if you are using the vCenter Essential license, you can only run workflows; you cannot create or edit them.

You can either enter a license key manually or connect to the vCenter Server to acquire the license.

Before you begin, add the vCenter SSL Certificate to Orchestrator.

Using the Orchestrator Configuration tool

1. Open the Orchestrator Configuration tool.
2. Click on the **Licenses** section.
3. Select **Use vCenter Server license**.
4. Enter the FQDN to vCenter.
5. Enter an administrative vCenter username and the corresponding password.
6. Click on **Apply changes**.

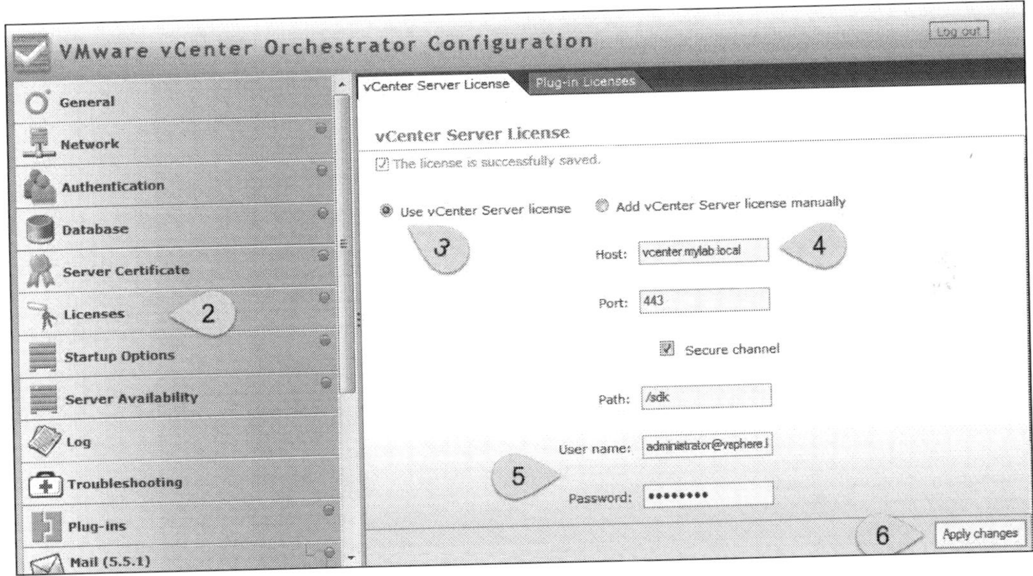

Using the workflow

1. Open Orchestrator Client.
2. Navigate to **Library** | **Configuration** | **Licensing**.
3. Right-click on the workflow **Use vCenter Server license** and select **Start Workflow**.
4. Enter the FQDN to the vCenter host.
5. Enter an administrative vCenter username and the corresponding password.
6. Click on **Submit**.

Wait till the workflow has finished successfully.

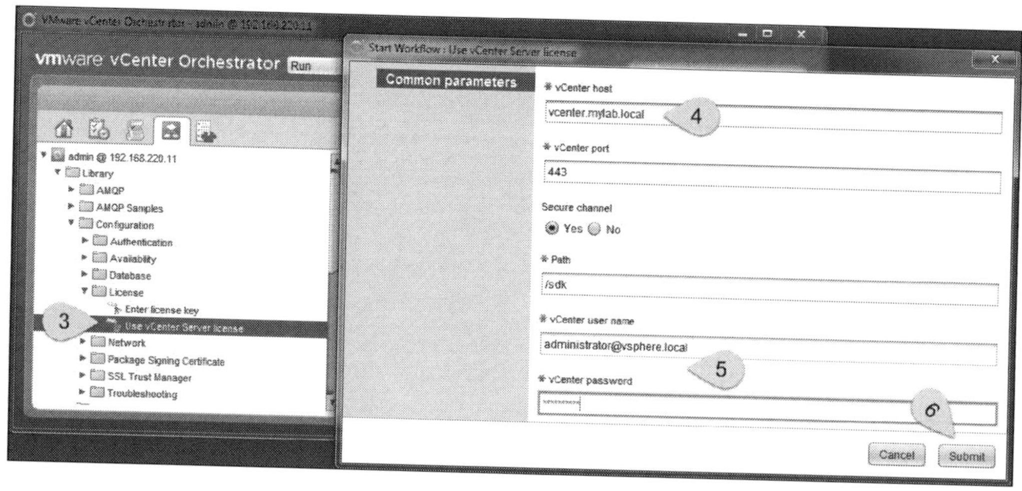

Creating a Server Package Signing certificate

The Server Package Signing certificate is an SSL certificate that is used to encrypt exports from Orchestrator, such as workflows and packages. It makes a lot of sense to at least personalize this with a self-signed certificate but be aware that, once created, it is not so easy to change.

It is not the SSL certificate of Orchestrator Server that is used for communication. The SSL certificate for Orchestrator Server is discussed in the *Configuring the Orchestrator Server SSL certificate* recipe in *Chapter 2, Optimizing Orchestrator Configuration*.

Using the Orchestrator Configuration tool

1. Open the Orchestrator Configuration tool.
2. Click on the **Server Certificate** section.
3. Click on **Create a certificate database and self-signed server certificate**.
4. Enter the required information, and select a country from the drop-down menu, and click on **Create**. Your new certificate will now be shown.

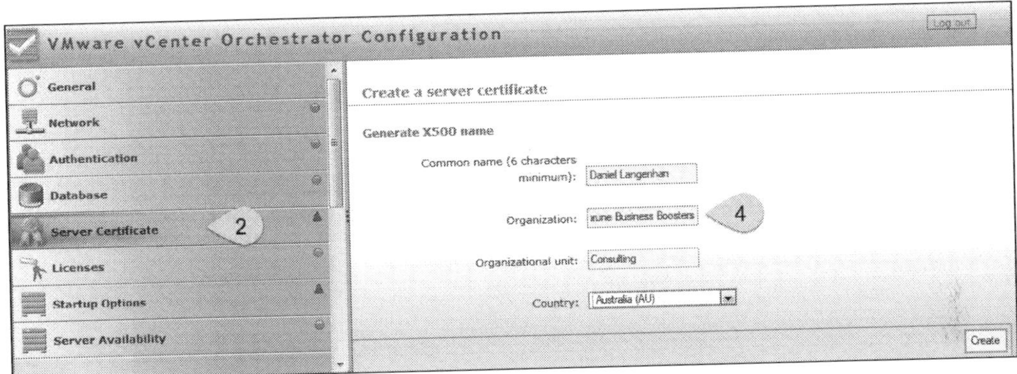

Using the workflow

1. Open Orchestrator Client.
2. Navigate to **Library** | **Configuration** | **Package Signing Certificate**.
3. Right-click on the workflow **Create a self-signed server certificate** and select **Start Workflow**.
4. Enter the relevant information.
5. Choose the two-letter code for your country (search the Web for the SSL certificate's country code) and click on **Submit**.

Wait till the workflow is successfully finished.

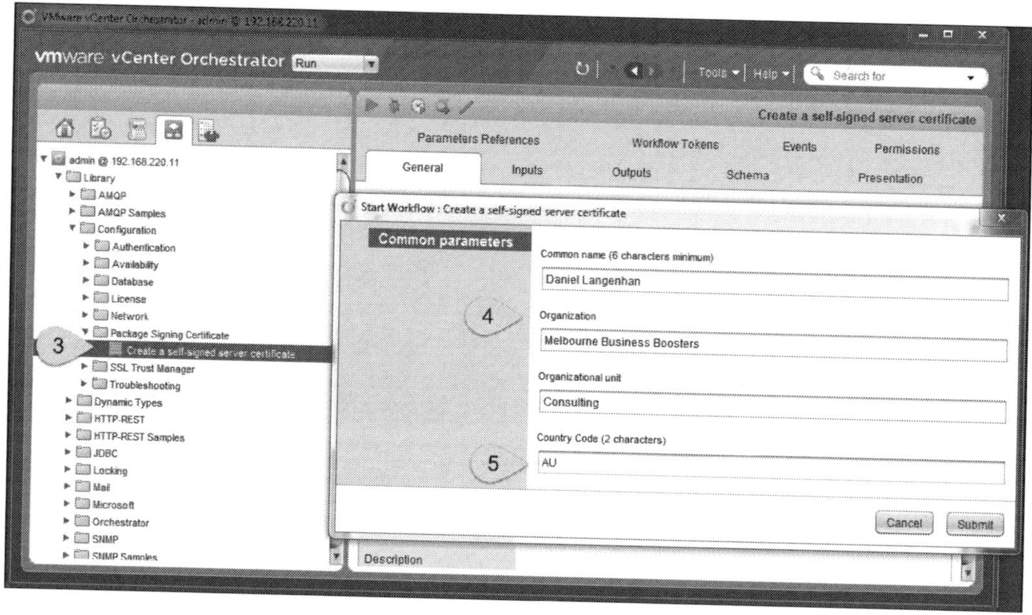

How it works...

You can see that, for the most part, the workflow method requires the same inputs as the Orchestrator Configuration tool; however, you have probably also noticed that there are not as many options in workflows as with the Configuration tool.

The settings we just applied are important and need to be done in order to make Orchestrator production-ready. The network configuration, the package signing, as well as the licensing need to be done only once. Importing an SSL certificate is an action that we will encounter more often. Every time we want to establish a secure connection (SSL) between Orchestrator and another server, we first have to import this server's SSL certificate.

Please note that, in earlier versions of Orchestrator, you had to restart the Orchestrator Configuration tool or the Orchestrator service after importing the SSL certificate; this is no longer the case.

The SSL certificate we configured here is used to sign exports or packages to be used with other Orchestrator installations. We will work with exports and imports in the *Importing and exporting Orchestrator elements* recipe in *Chapter 5, Basic Orchestrator Operations*. In the *Working with packages* recipe of that chapter, you will find some more detailed information about how to manage and use this SSL certificate.

At the time of writing of this book, there is a small bug that appears from time to time with the network configuration. When using the appliance and changing the network setting to anything else but 0.0.0.0, some things, such as the Orchestrator home page, won't work anymore. To fix the problem, check out this VMware community article available at `https://communities.vmware.com/thread/477955`.

See also

Have a look at the *Backup and recovery* recipe in *Chapter 2, Optimizing Orchestrator Configuration*, to learn how to export and import the configuration.

Configuring Orchestrator with an external LDAP or Active Directory

In this recipe, we will configure Orchestrator with an external LDAP or Active Directory service. VMware best practice is to use Orchestrator together with SSO, which is described in the *Integrating Orchestrator into SSO and vSphere Web Client* recipe. This recipe doesn't work with the vRA-integrated Orchestrator.

Getting ready

You need a supported LDAP service configured and running. The following LDAP services are supported in vCO 5.5:

- Windows Server 2008 Active Directory
- Windows Server 2012 Active Directory
- OpenLDAP
- Novell eDirectory Server 8.8.3
- Sun Java System Directory Server 6.3

We also need to create a group and a user in these services, so you should have access to these services.

You should be comfortable with using one of the methods described in the *Two ways to configure Orchestrator* recipe.

If your LDAP (AD) requires SSL (Kerberos), you will need to import the SSL certificate first (see the *Important Orchestrator base configurations* recipe in this chapter.

Changing the authentication might require changing the plugin credentials. For more details, see the *Plugin basics* recipe in *Chapter 2, Optimizing Orchestrator Configuration*.

How to do it...

We will focus on linking Orchestrator to AD. Connecting Orchestrator to LDAP is pretty much the same procedure; for anyone who understands LDAP, this will be a breeze.

AD is basically the same as LDAP but most Windows administrators have problems with the LDAP representation of AD, which is why we focus on AD in this recipe.

We will configure SSO in the *Integrating Orchestrator into SSO and vSphere Web Client* recipe.

Creating an Orchestrator Admin group and user

Before we can add an external LDAP, we need to configure at least one group and one user. To do this, perform the following steps:

1. Log in to your LDAP or AD.
2. Create an Orchestrator Administrator group and an Orchestrator Administrator user.
3. Make the Orchestrator Administrator user a member of the Orchestrator Administrator group.

For this example, I have created a user called `vcoadmin` as well as a group called `vcoadmins` in AD. The AD domain is called `mylab.local`.

LDAP entries are always case-sensitive.

Again, we will show both methods.

Using the Orchestrator Configuration tool

1. Open the Orchestrator Configuration tool.
2. Click on the **Authentication** section.
3. Select **LDAP** as the authentication method.
4. In **LDAP client**, select **Active Directory**.
5. In the **Primary LDAP host** field, enter `mylab.local` as the Active Domain DNS name.

6. The standard port for Microsoft Active Directory LDAP is 389.
7. Enter `dc=mylab,dc=local` as the root for your domain.
8. If you have secured your AD with Kerberos, you need to activate SSL (don't forget to import the SSL certificate first).
9. The username can be entered in both formats: user@Domain or domain\user. The user can be any active user within the AD; however, its best to use Orchestrator Admin.
10. The user and group lookup base is easiest set to the root of your domain, for example, `dc=mylab,dc=local`. However, if your AD or LDAP is large, performance-wise it might be better to choose a different root.
11. The Orchestrator Admin group path can be easily found. Enter the name of the group (case-sensitive) and click on **Search** to the right.

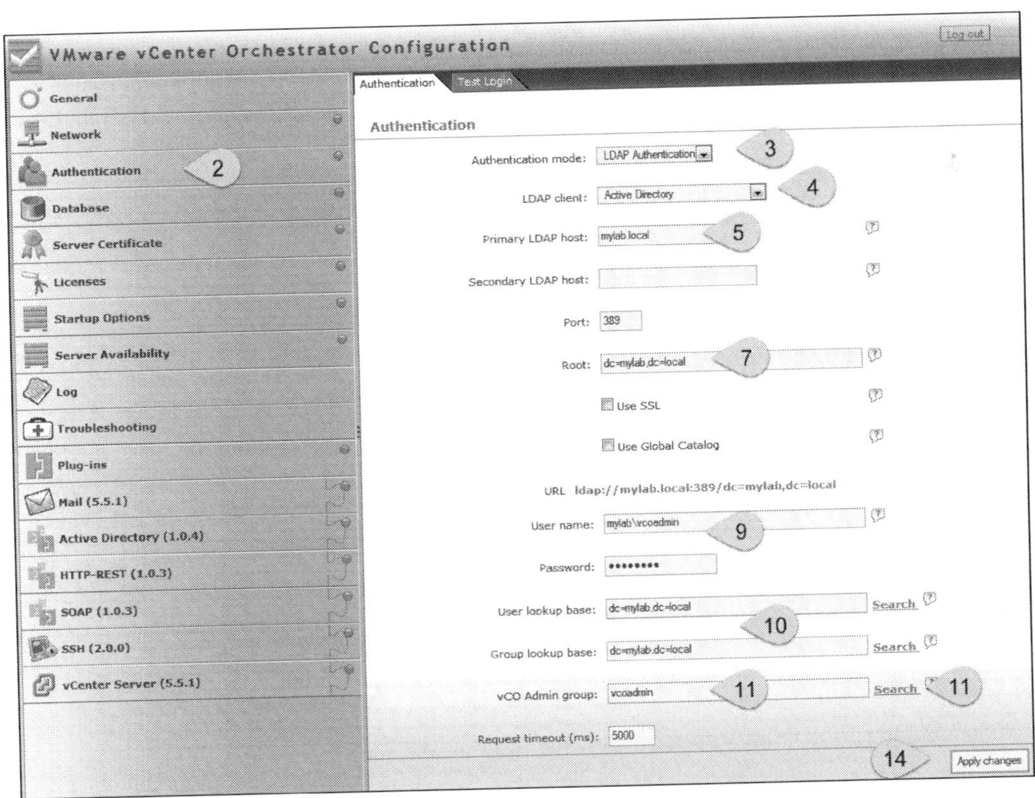

12. If the name has been entered correctly, the path should be shown. Click on the LDAP path. The path is now populated with the correct setting.

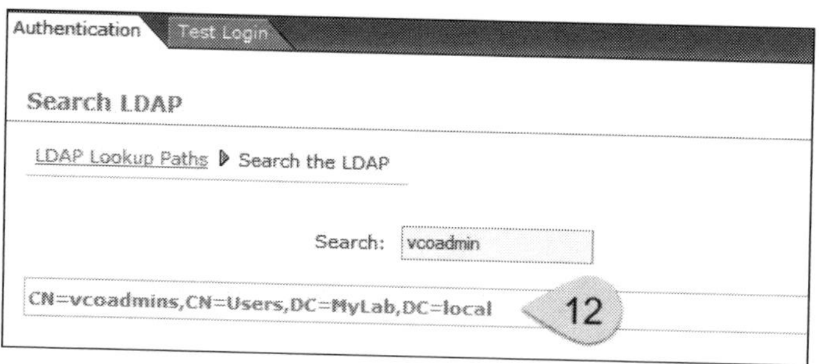

13. The rest of the settings can be left alone for most AD settings.
14. Click on **Apply changes**.
15. At this stage, you should try the test login described in the *There's more...* section of this recipe.
16. Click on **Startup Options** and then restart the Orchestrator Server.
17. Now, try to log in to the Orchestrator Client using the AD user.

Using the workflow

1. Open the Orchestrator Client.
2. Navigate to **Library** | **Configuration** | **Authentication** | **LDAP**.
3. Right-click on the workflow **Configure Active Directory** and select **Start Workflow**.
4. In the primary host, enter `mylab.local` as the Active Domain DNS name.
5. The standard port for AD LDAP is 389.
6. If you secured your AD with Kerberos, you need to activate SSL.
7. Click on **Next**.
8. Enter `dc=mylab,dc=local` as the root for your domain.
9. The username can be entered as user@mylab.local or domain\user. The user can be any active user in the AD; however, its best to use Orchestrator Admin.
10. The user and group lookup base is easiest set to the root of your domain, for example, `dc=mylab,dc=local`. However, if your AD or LDAP is large, it might be performance-wise better to choose a different root.
11. The Orchestrator Admin group needs to be constructed, but there is no automated tool for it. We use the `CN=vcoadmins,CN=Users,DC=MyLab,DC=local` values.
12. Click on **Submit** and wait until the workflow is successfully completed.

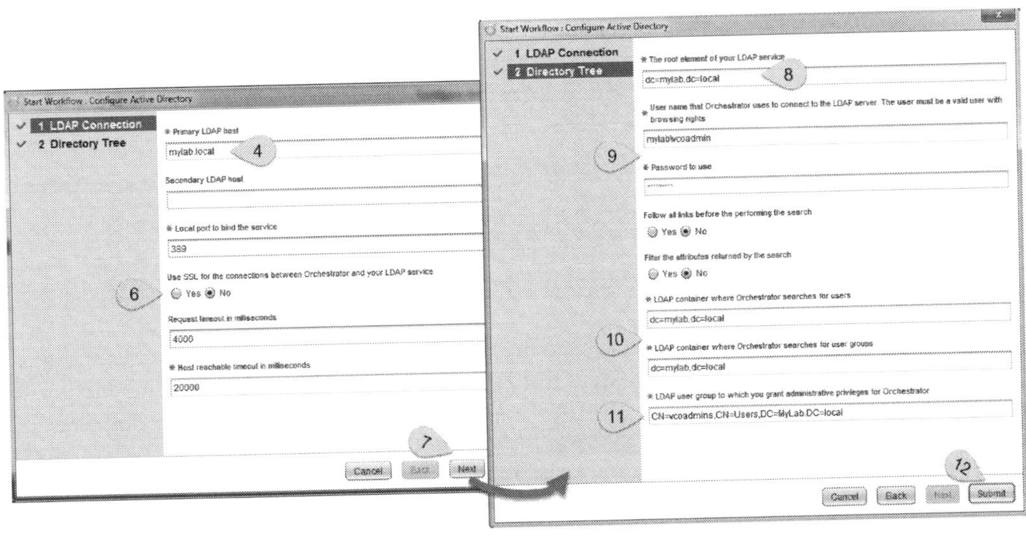

Sadly, there isn't a test to check whether your settings are correct as there is with the Configuration tool. Have a look at the test login described in the *There's more...* section of this recipe.

There is no workflow to restart Orchestrator Server, so you have to restart the Orchestrator Server another way:

- In Windows, use services (*vCenter Orchestrator Server*)
- In Linux, use the services command from the OS or use the Orchestrator Configurator (see the *Tuning the appliance* recipe in *Chapter 2, Optimizing Orchestrator Configuration*)
- Reboot the Orchestrator Server

Now, try to log in to the Orchestrator Client using the AD user.

How it works...

Configuring Orchestrator to work with an external authentication enables AD users to log in to the Orchestrator Client. The alternative would be either having only one user using it or adding users to the embedded LDAP. However, for a production Orchestrator, the embedded LDAP solution is not viable. As SSO is now a highly integrated part of vSphere, using Orchestrator with AD (or LDAP) isn't really such a good solution any longer. SSO can proxy multiple AD and/or LDAP domains and lets you integrate Orchestrator directly into vCenter as well as other corner pieces of VMware software offerings, making SSO integration the better choice for the future.

In the recipe above, we used the domain DNS address as the primary LDAP host rather than an individual AD server. The DNS entry for AD will forward the LDAP query to the next available AD server, which makes it a more reliable choice.

There's more...

There are some things you should be aware of when working with LDAP.

Test login

In order to find out whether everything is working as it should, we need to test it. However, there is no workflow for this, so you have to trust your entries or use the Configuration tool.

1. Using the Orchestrator Configuration tool, click on **Authentication**.
2. Click on the **Test Login** tab.
3. Enter the Orchestrator Admin username and its password and click on **Test Login**.
4. Read the message carefully. It should be green and confirm that you can log in and that the user is part of the Orchestrator Admin group.

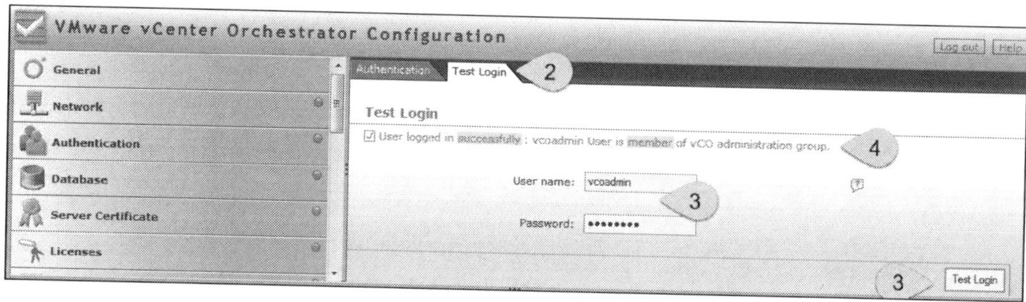

A red message mostly indicates that the user provided isn't in the LDAP or that the password is wrong.

If the message doesn't confirm an Orchestrator Admin group membership, review the membership of the user account.

Common LDAP errors

When you encounter a problem while setting up LDAP, you will get an error code. This table shows the most commonly encountered error codes:

Code	Meaning	What to do
525	User not found	The user for login isn't found; check whether you have written the domain correctly.
52e	Password is incorrect	Change the password in the password field.
530 531	The User is not allowed to log in	Access LDAP or AD and make sure that the user is allowed to log in remotely and from Orchestrator Server.
532	Password expired	Access LDAP or AD and set a new password.
533	Account disabled	Access LDAP or AD and enable the account.
701	Account expired	Access LDAP or AD and create a new account or use a different user.
773	Must reset password	The User has to reset the password on login. Access LDAP or AD to set a new password or use other methods to set a new password.
775	User locked	Access LDAP or AD and unlock the user account.

See also

See the *Integrating Orchestrator into SSO and vSphere Web Client* recipe in this chapter to learn how to configure Orchestrator with VMware SSO.

Integrating Orchestrator into SSO and vSphere Web Client

Integrating Orchestrator into the vCenter Web Client enables vCenter Server users to directly run Orchestrator workflows just by right-clicking vCenter objects. The vRA-integrated Orchestrator is already configured with the SSO that vRA uses.

Getting ready

vCO 5.5 (and higher) requires an SSO server 5.5, as it won't work with an SSO 5.1 server.

We need an up-and-running Orchestrator as well as access to vCenter Web Client.

Make sure that you set the Orchestrator Network configuration (see the *Configuring the network* section in the *Important Orchestrator base configurations* recipe)

You should be comfortable with using one of the methods described in the *Two ways to configure Orchestrator* recipe.

You should have an AD group for your vCOAdministrators with at least one user in it. You can use the precreated SSO group vCOAdministrators@vsphere.local. The account administrator@vsphere.local is a member of this group.

How to do it...

Again both configuration methods are shown. Choose the one you're most comfortable with.

Registering Orchestrator with SSO

If you are using the Orchestrator installation that came with vCenter, you can skip this step.

Using the Orchestrator Configuration tool

1. Open the Orchestrator Configuration tool.
2. Click on the **Network** section and then on **SSL Trust Manager**.
3. Enter `[IP or FQDN of SSO server]:7444` as the URL and click on **Import**.
4. Acknowledge the import by clicking on **Import**.
5. Repeat steps 2 to 4 and register the SSL certificate for vCenter with port 443.
6. Click on the **Authentication** section.
7. Select the authentication mode as **SSO Authentication**.
8. Enter the SSO server FQDN.
9. Enter an SSO administrative user (for example, `administrator@vsphere.local`).
10. Click on **Register Orchestrator**.

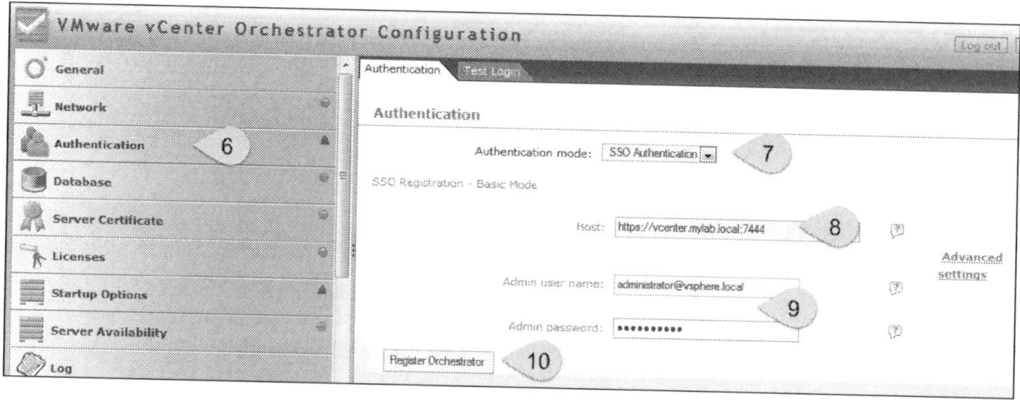

11. This registration registers a new application user in SSO.
12. Select from the drop-down menu the group you would like to use for Orchestrator administrators.
13. Click on **Accept Orchestrator Configuration**.

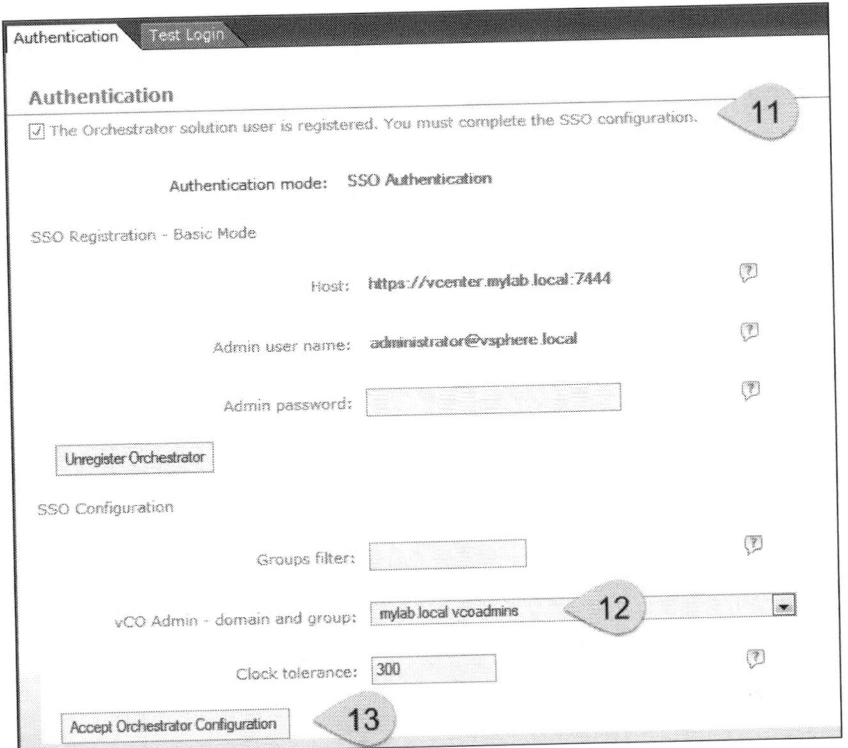

Using the workflow

1. Open the Orchestrator Client.
2. Navigate to **Library** | **Configuration** | **SSL Trust Manager**.
3. Right-click on the **Import a certificate from URL** workflow and select **Start Workflow**.
4. Enter `[IP or FQDN of SSO server]:7444` as the URL.
5. Select **Yes** to accept the SSL Certificate even if there are warnings and click on **Submit**.
6. Wait till the workflow has successfully finished.
7. Navigate to **Library** | **Configuration** | **Authentication** | **SSO**.
8. Right-click on the workflow **Configure SSO** and select **Start Workflow**.

9. Enter `[IP or FQDN of SSO server]:7444` as the URL.
10. Enter an SSO administrative user (for example, `administrator@vsphere.local`).
11. Enter the SSO Admin Group (ignore if it says domain/group). The existing SSO default group is called VCOAdministrators (case-sensitive).
12. Click on **Submit** and wait until the workflow is completed successfully.

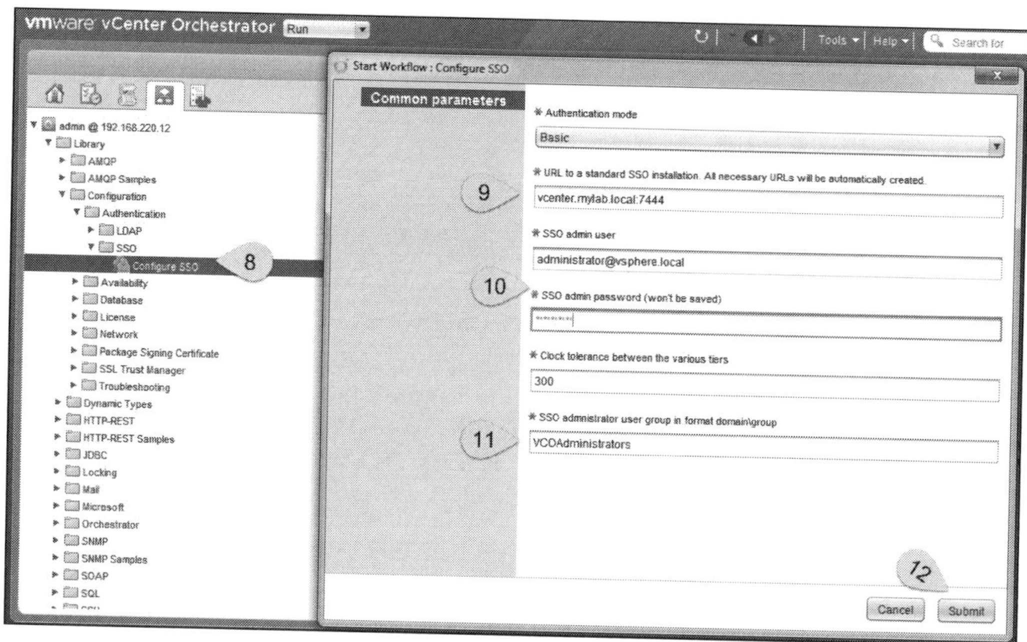

Configuring the vCenter Server plugin

The integration of Orchestrator with vCenter Web Client requires us to also configure the vCenter Server plugin.

Using the Orchestrator Configuration tool

1. Open the Orchestrator Configuration tool.
2. Click on the **vCenter Server** plugin.
3. Click on **New vCenter Server Host**.
4. Enter your vCenter FQDN.
5. If you are using Windows, you can define a domain; the Linux appliance doesn't have this selection. You can leave it empty.

6. Enter a vCenter Server administrative user and click on **Apply changes**.

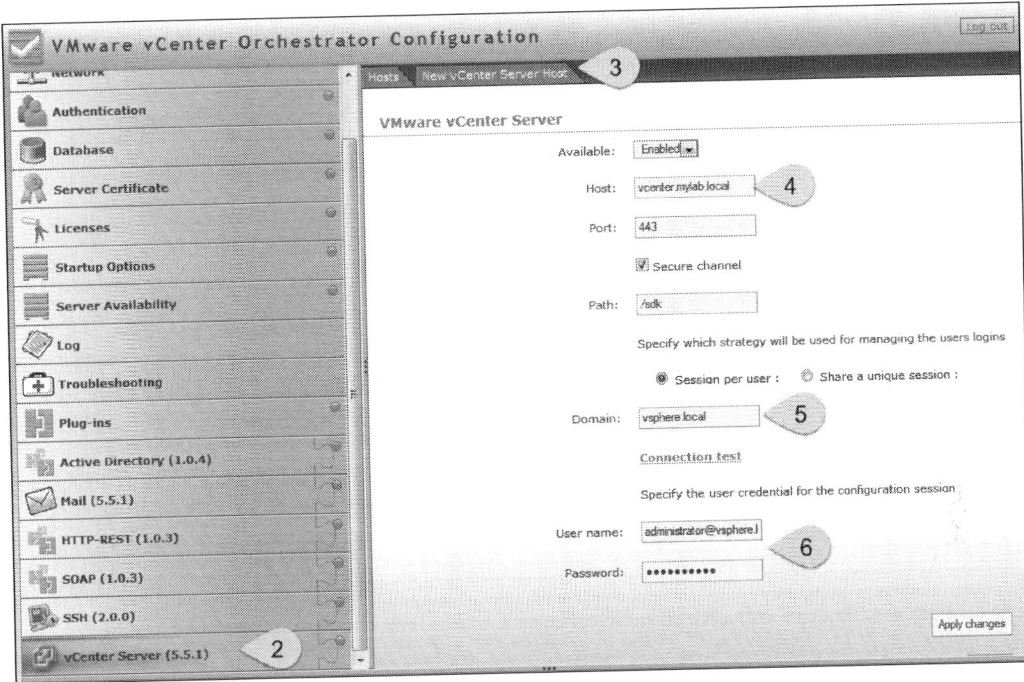

Using the workflow

1. Open Orchestrator Client.
2. Navigate to **Library** | **vCenter** | **Configuration**.
3. Right-click on the **Add a vCenter Server instance** workflow and select **Start Workflow**.
4. Enter your vCenter FQDN.
5. Select that you would like to orchestrate this instance as well and that you would like to accept SSL certificates even if they are self-signed.
6. Click on **Next**.
7. Enter a vCenter Server administrative user and the password.

8. You can define a domain name, or leave it empty. Click on **Submit**.

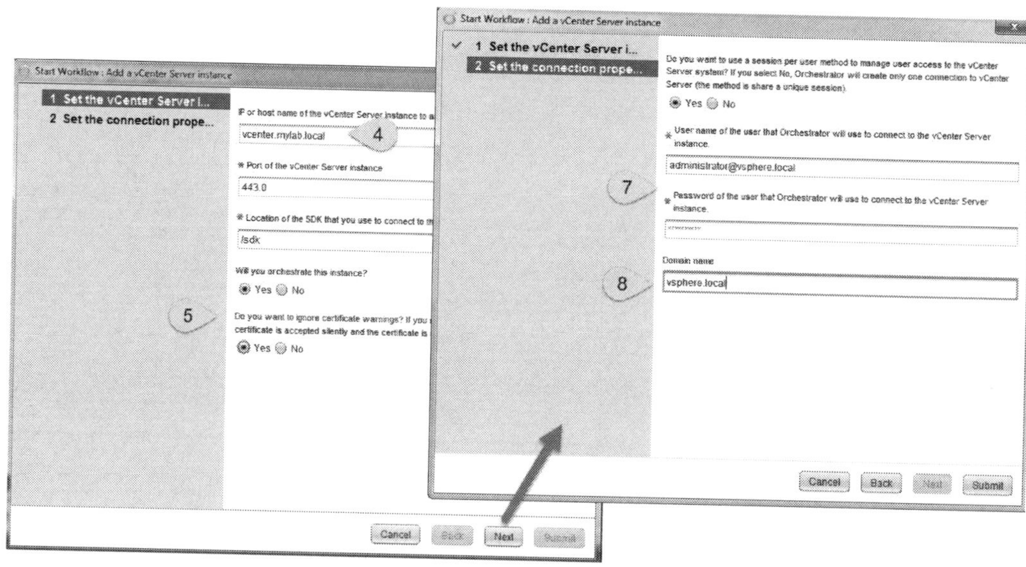

Wait until the workflow is successfully finished.

Configuring the connection between vCenter Server and Orchestrator

In the Web Client only one Orchestrator Server can be paired to each vCenter Server. To configure the pairing, follow these steps:

1. Open vSphere Web Client.
2. Click on vCenter Orchestrator and then on **Manage**.
3. Mark vCenter Server and click on **Edit Configuration**.
4. The server that you have integrated should show up in the **Registered as VC extension** selection. If this is not the case, you can try to enter its FQDN or IP.
5. Click on **Test Connection** and make sure it works. If it doesn't, this indicates that the integration hasn't worked correctly.
6. Click on **OK**.

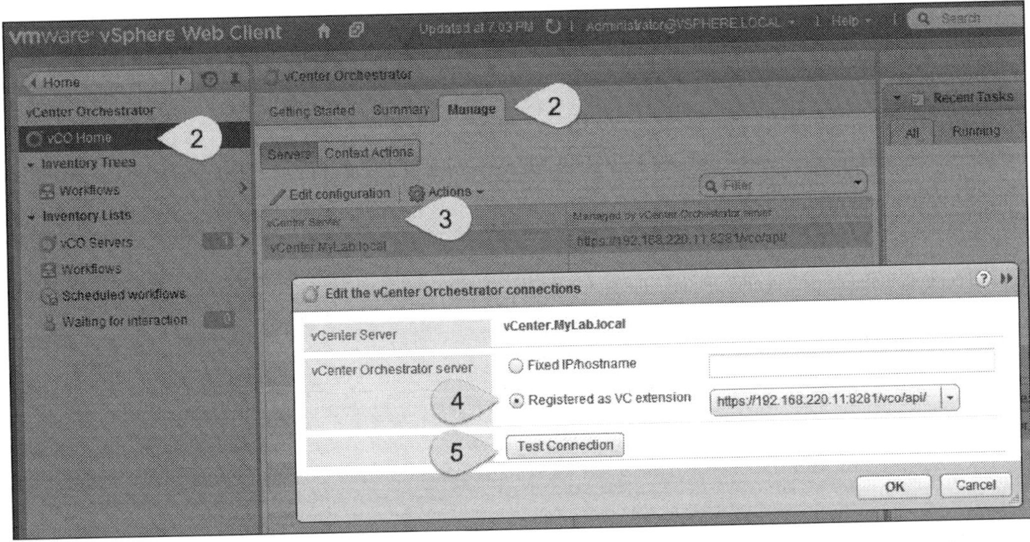

How it works...

Since vCenter Server 5.1, vSphere Web Client is (or better, should be) the main method for accessing vCenter. Orchestrator completely integrates with vSphere Web Client, making it possible for Orchestrator workflows to be executed directly from vSphere Web Client.

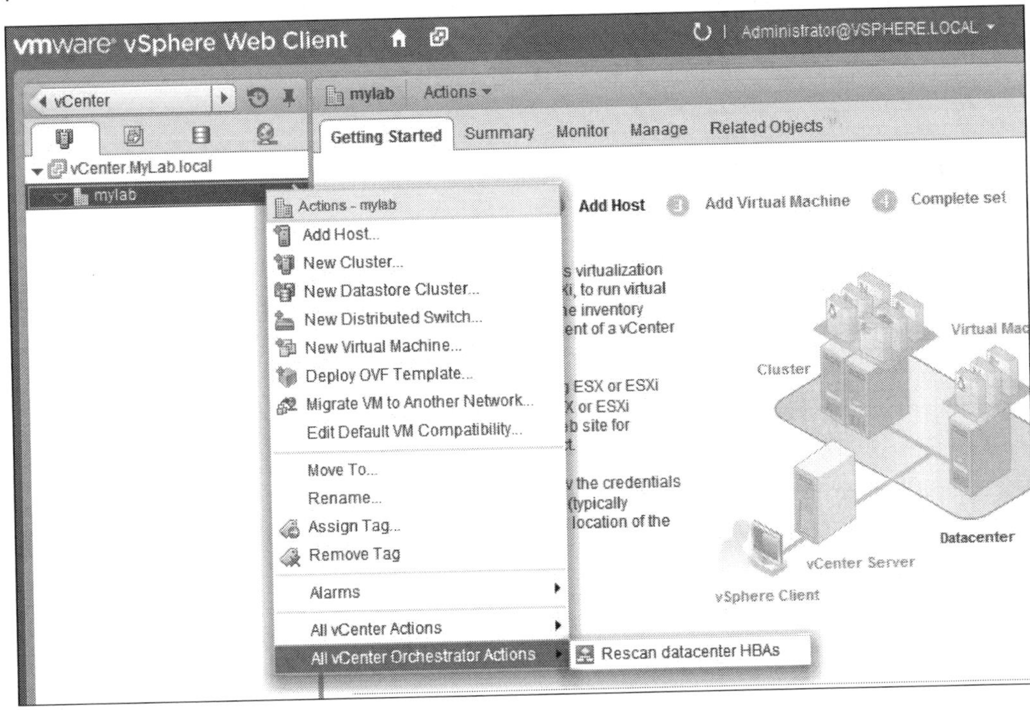

You can configure which workflows can be run from the vSphere Web Client. We will discuss this configuration in detail in the *Orchestrator and vSphere Web Client* recipe in *Chapter 5, Basic Orchestrator Operations*.

Using SSO for Orchestrator login requires that you log in into Orchestrator Client or vSphere Web Client using a user that is a member of the group you defined as vCOAdmins. If you used the VCOAdministrators@vsphere.local group, you can add other SSO and AD groups or users to this group via the SSO group membership configuration.

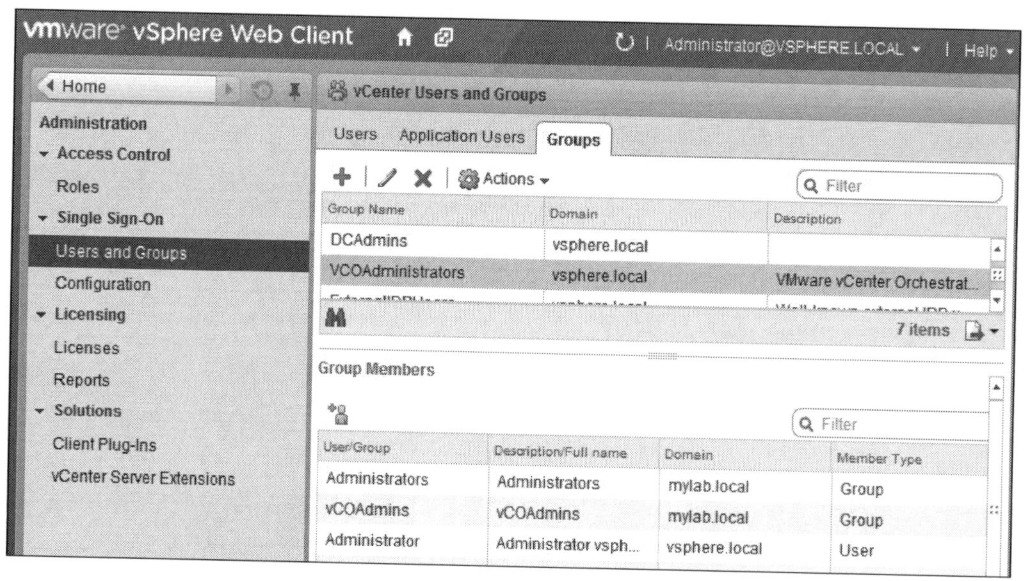

See also

To learn more about Orchestrator user management, see the *User management* recipe in *Chapter 5, Basic Orchestrator Operations*.

To configure Orchestrator workflows in vSphere Web Client, see the *Orchestrator and vSphere Web Client* recipe in *Chapter 5, Basic Orchestrator Operations*.

Configuring an external database

In this recipe, we will attach Orchestrator to an external database. This is a more secure and reliable method than using the embedded database.

Getting ready

We will need a database; the following databases are supported with vCO 5.5.2.1:

- Oracle 11g
- SQL Server 2005
- SQL Server 2008
- SQL Server 2012
- SQL Server Express
- PostgreSQL

You will need to create an empty database for Orchestrator, and you should also create a dedicated user account for Orchestrator to access the database.

You should be comfortable with using one of the methods described in the *Two ways to configure Orchestrator* recipe.

If your Database requires SSL, you will need to import the SSL certificate first; for this, see the *Important Orchestrator base configurations* recipe in this chapter.

When you replace the database, you will have to reconfigure the following items: Licensing and Server Certificate.

How to do it...

Both configuration methods will be shown; choose the one you prefer. In this example, we have added a SQL database to Orchestrator. The other databases are not that much different.

Database information

The following information is needed for each type of database:

Database type	Oracle	SQL Server	PostgreSQL
Login	required	required	required
SSL	optional	optional	optional
Hostname	required	required	required
Port	1521 or custom	1433 or custom	5432 or custom
Database name	-	required	required
Instance	required	optional	-
Domain	-	optional	-
Use NTLMv2	-	optional	-

Using the Orchestrator Configuration tool

1. Open the Orchestrator Configuration tool.
2. Click on the **Database** section.
3. Select the **Database** type. The information on the screen will adapt to your choice.
4. Enter all the relevant information and click on **Apply changes**.
5. An error occurs, which is totally OK. It just means that the database is empty and needs tables.
6. Click on the **Create the database tables** link.
7. Then click on **Apply changes** again.

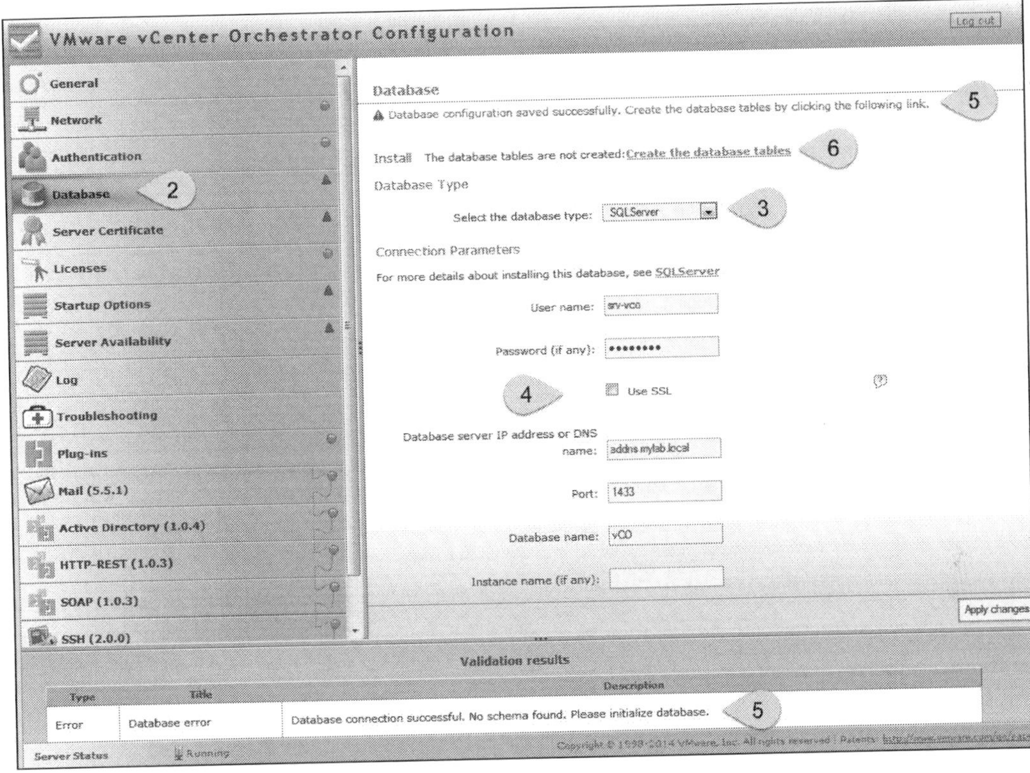

Using the workflow

1. Open the Orchestrator Client.
2. Navigate to **Library** | **Configuration** | **Database**.
3. Right-click on the appropriate workflow for your database and select **Start Workflow**.
4. Enter all the relevant information and click on **Submit**.

5. Wait until the workflow has successfully finished.

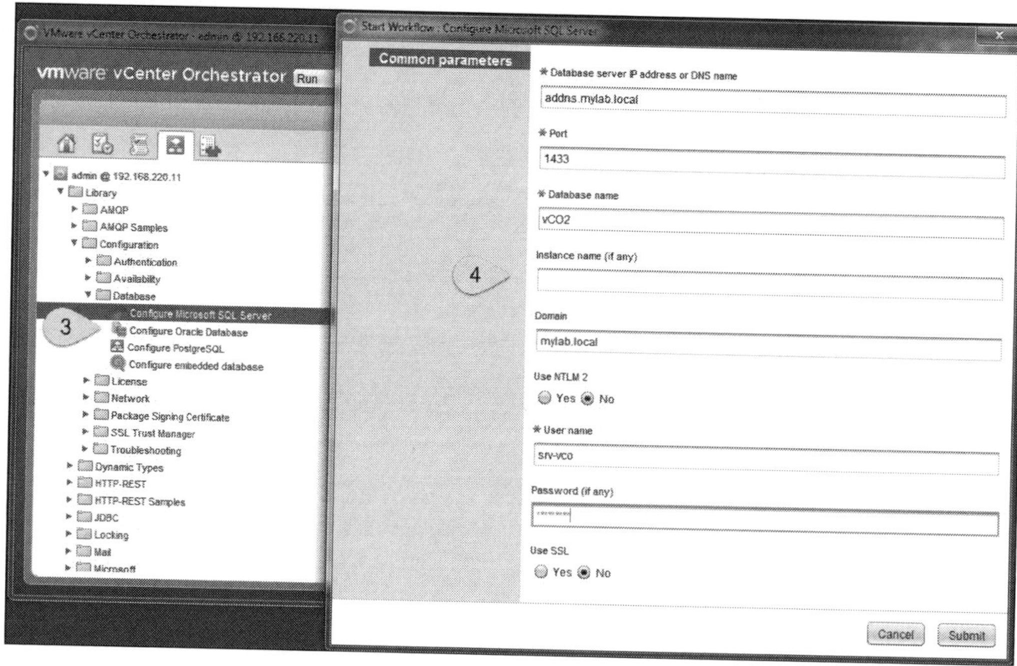

How it works...

The Orchestrator database contains the entire configuration, workflows, workflow runs, events, runtime information, actions, and a lot more. Therefore, it is quite important to consider using an external database. Without an external database, certain Orchestrator features, such as resuming a workflow after an Orchestrator Server crash, will not work or will be impaired.

All Orchestrator versions come with the embedded PostgreSQL database or use the vCenter Server database. A production environment dictates the use of an external database that integrates with the business continuity processes of your company.

In addition to this, the embedded database isn't really sized or optimized for large deployments and doesn't allow the use of Orchestrator Clustering.

Using the vCenter Server database for Orchestrator is not really a very pretty solution either. IT best practices dictate using dedicated resources for production environments. Putting the database on the same VM as Orchestrator is something to think about as it results in a competition for resources between the database and the Java process.

Sizing

Sizing is hard to predict. Each workflow run consumes around 4 KB, and most objects (for example, vCenter Server Object) require around 50 KB each. VMware recommends 1 GB for a production database. The good thing is that Orchestrator regularly runs clean-up jobs to reduce the database content. Also have a look at the *User preferences* recipe in *Chapter 5, Basic Orchestrator Operations*, where we discuss certain properties that influence how much information is kept in the database.

Database roles

For the initial setup (and for updates), you should give the dedicated Orchestrator user the db_owner rights on the Orchestrator database.

For a normal usage scenario the Orchestrator user only requires the db_dataread and db_datawrite rights.

There's more...

Here are some things you might find useful.

Microsoft SQL

Giving the database the settings ALLOW_SNAPSHOT_ISOLATION and READ_COMMITTED_SNAPSHOT will reduce the chance of a deadlock occurring and is also a prerequisite for Orchestrator clusters.

Oracle

The database should have NLS_CHARACTER_SET = AL32UTF8 set before you start allowing Orchestrator to build its tables.

To avoid an ORA-01450 error, it is important that you have the database block size configured in accordance with your database index.

2

Optimizing Orchestrator Configuration

In this chapter, we will explore how to optimize the Orchestrator installation and look at the following recipes:

- Plugin basics
- Tuning the appliance
- Tuning Java
- Backup and recovery
- Creating an Orchestrator cluster
- Configuring the Orchestrator Service SSL certificate
- Configuring e-mail
- Redirecting the Orchestrator Syslog to an external Syslog server
- Configuring the Kerberos authentication
- Configuring access to the local filesystem
- Updating Orchestrator

Introduction

Before we get into the recipes themselves, here is some background on how to configure service accounts and the information needed for firewall configuration.

Service accounts

As in all production environments, you should consider using dedicated service accounts for connections between different services. For Orchestrator, there are several connections that we should have a look at. The connections between Orchestrator and SMTP, LDAP, and the Orchestrator database should be facilitated with a normal AD service account. The connection between Orchestrator and SSO uses the registered SSO application user.

The connection between Orchestrator and vCenter depends on how you would like to handle the role and rights management between them. You can either use one administrative connection between Orchestrator and vCenter, or choose to limit access by the role and rights of the logged-in Orchestrator user. We will discuss some more details of this in the *Plugin basics* recipe in this chapter.

The connection between clients (desktops and application servers) and Orchestrator is regulated by membership of the Orchestrator Administration group and by nonadministrative users in Orchestrator. We will discuss how to add nonadministrative users to Orchestrator in the *User management* recipe in *Chapter 5, Basic Orchestrator Operations*.

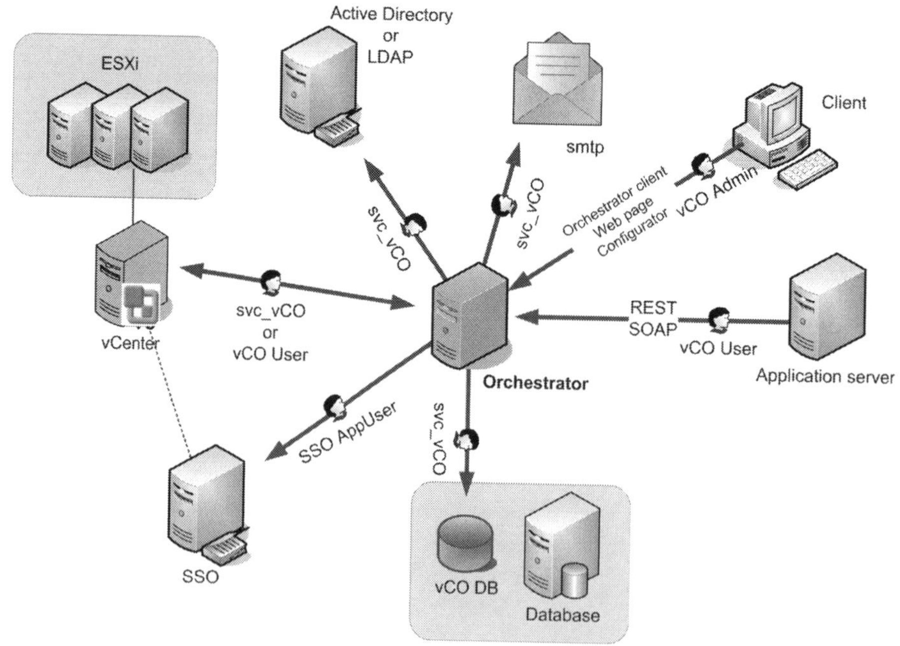

Ports and firewalls

The following standard ports are used by Orchestrator for communication:

Port	Source	Target	Use
TCP 8280	Web browser Orchestrator Web Client	Orchestrator	Orchestrator Web Client; redirects to 8281
TCP 8230, 8286, 8287	Orchestrator Client	Orchestrator	Orchestrator Client connection to Orchestrator
TCP 8281	Web browser	Orchestrator	Orchestrator home page
TCP 8283	Web browser	Orchestrator	Configuration tool
TCP 389 TCP 636	Orchestrator	LDAP LDAPS	LDAP connection
TCP 7444	Orchestrator	SSO	SSO connection
TCP 1433	Orchestrator	SQL	MS SQL connection
TCP 5432	Orchestrator	PostgreSQL	PostgreSQL connection
TCP 1521	Orchestrator	Oracle	Oracle connection
TCP 443	Orchestrator	vCenter	vCenter plugin

Ports for further connections are discussed in the various recipes that feature them.

Plugin basics

In this recipe, we will learn how to install and configure plugins for Orchestrator. We will only deal with the installation and base configuration of plugins in general and not any programing-related configurations. Programming-related configurations are discussed in *Chapter 4, Working with Plugins*.

Getting ready

We need an Orchestrator server installed and running.

You should be comfortable using the Orchestrator Configuration tool described in the *Two ways to configure Orchestrator* recipe in *Chapter 1, Installing and Configuring Orchestrator*, as there is currently no workflow-driven method.

How to do it...

This recipe is made up of four different parts: obtaining, authenticating, installing, and configuring plugins.

Obtaining plugins

You get plugins from these three main pages:

- Go to `www.vmware.com`, navigate to your downloads for vSphere (or vRealize Automation) version, then click on **Drivers & Tools**, and then look for the vCenter Orchestrator plugins
- VMware Solution Exchange can be found at `https://solutionexchange.vmware.com/store`
- An overview of all plugins can be found at `http://www.vcoteam.info/links/plug-ins.html`

There are many different plugins, such as VMware based plugins for vRealize Automation (vRA) or vCloud Director (vCD), as well as plugins from EMC, Netapp, CISCO UCS, Infoblox, and F5.

When you download a plugin, you download it as a `.vmoapp` file (sometimes it is zipped).

General plugin authentication

You need to provide the user credentials of a user who is a member of the Orchestrator Administrator group in order to install new plugins. This might especially be the case if you change authentication types. To do this, perform these steps:

1. Open the Orchestrator Configuration tool.
2. Click on the **Plug-ins** section.
3. Enter a user account and password of an Orchestrator administrator and click on **Apply Changes**.

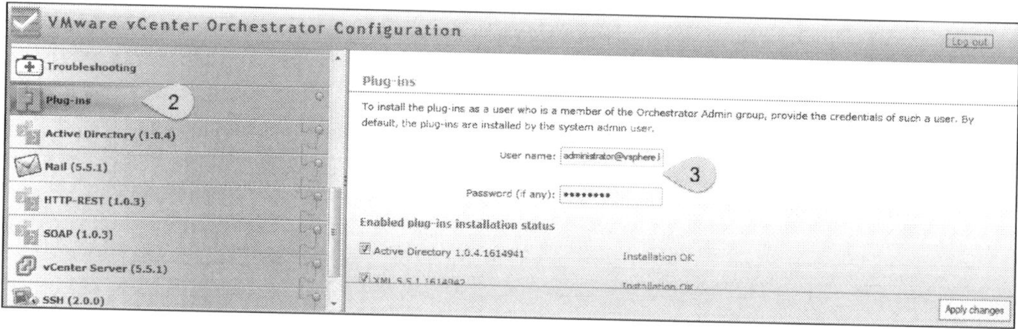

Installing plugins

1. Open the Orchestrator Configuration tool.
2. Click on the **Plug-ins** section.
3. Click on the magnifying glass icon, select the plugin you would like to install, and then click on **Upload and Install**. You might need to accept the EULA of the plugin.

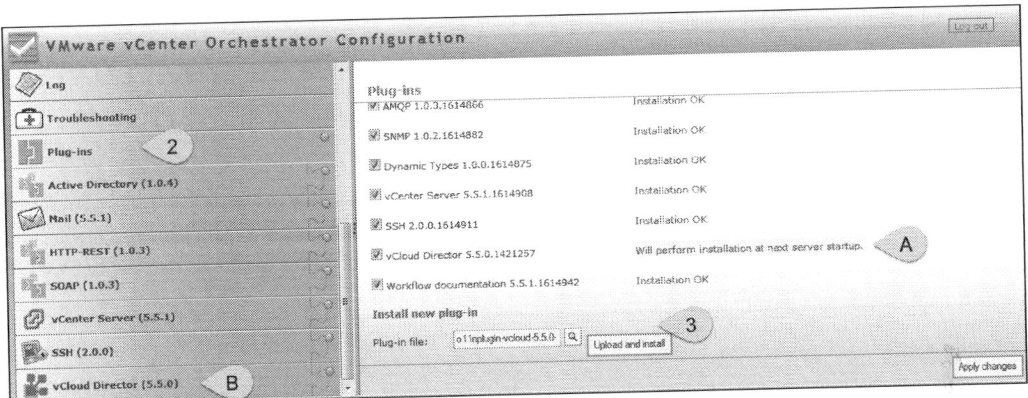

Once the upload is complete, a restart of the Orchestrator service is required to complete the installation. This is indicated as **A** in the preceding screenshot. Also, notice (shown as **B**) that some plugins install new sections in the Orchestrator Configuration tool that require further configuration.

Configuring plugins

Some plugins, such as the vCenter and vCloud Director plugin may require additional configuration. For vCenter, see the *Integrating Orchestrator into SSO and vSphere Web Client* recipe in *Chapter 1, Installing and Configuring Orchestrator*. The configuration for **vCloud Director** (now rebranded as vCloudAir) is more or less the same as described in that recipe, the only difference is that it asks which vCD Organization it should connect to. If you want to automate vCloud deployment, you need to decide whether you want to automate the complete vCD or just one organization. If you want to automate vCD completely, the **System** (capital S) organization is the right one; otherwise, you connect it to your organization name.

How it works...

Orchestrator becomes more exciting with additional plugins, such as plugins from VMware and other vendors. The current version of vRO (5.5.2.1) comes with quite a few plugins already installed, such as:

vCenter Orchestrator vCenter Plug-In 5.5.2.1	vCenter Orchestrator Mail Plug-In 5.5.1
vCenter Orchestrator SQL Plug-In 1.1.1	vCenter Orchestrator SSH Plug-In 2.0.0
vCenter Orchestrator SOAP Plug-In 1.0.3	vCenter Orchestrator HTTP-REST Plug-In 1.0.3
vCenter Orchestrator Plug-In for Microsoft Active Directory 1.0.5	vCenter Orchestrator AMQP Plug-In 1.0.3
vCenter Orchestrator SNMP Plug-In 1.0.2	vCenter Orchestrator PowerShell Plug-In 1.0.4
vCenter Orchestrator Multi-Node Plug-In 5.5.2.1	vCenter Orchestrator Dynamic Types 1.0.0

These make it possible to use Orchestrator in a variety of possibilities. For instance, connecting to Microsoft System Center Virtual Machine Manger (SCVMM) is possible via SOAP, or connecting to Red Hat Satellite can be done using SSH or by orchestrating your Cisco UCS hardware.

Last but not least, you can create your own plugins. There is an Orchestrator plugin SDK guide that is dedicated to the creation of plugins.

We will discuss how to use most of the aforementioned plugins in *Chapter 4, Working with Plugins*.

There's more...

There are some things that are worth mentioning about plugins.

Shared session versus session per user

Some plugins (such as vCenter Server or vCloud Director) allow you to decide whether you want to share a unique session or have a session for each user. Using a shared session requires you to define one user account that Orchestrator then uses to facilitate all tasks between Orchestrator and the plugin target. This is mostly used when using automation solutions, where an external service calls Orchestrator to execute a workflow. This user should be a dedicated user for this service, so the logs have better readability.

Using a session per user means that users will be authenticated with their credentials and use their permissions in the form of actions against the plugin target. This is mostly used when integrating, for example, vCenter Server into the vSphere Web Client to make sure those users only run workflows with their credentials and only in their permission context. In addition to this, a lot of plugins *do not* support passing SSO credentials to the user session. For example, see the *Working with PowerShell* recipe in *Chapter 4, Working with Plugins*.

Another huge difference is that a shared session shares the same connection session, where one connection session is opened per user. This can lead to problems when too many users try to use Orchestrator.

Have a look at the *Changing credentials* recipe in *Chapter 3, Visual Programming*, for more ideas on how to use a different user account in a workflow.

Resetting the plugins

Sometimes, it happens (especially when changing authentication methods) that one logs into Orchestrator and there are no more than a few entries in the library. All the plugins have disappeared. Here is how to remedy this:

1. Open the Orchestrator Configuration tool.
2. Click on the **Troubleshooting** section.
3. Click on the **Reset current version** link next to **Reinstall the plug-ins when the server starts**.
4. Restart the Orchestrator Server.

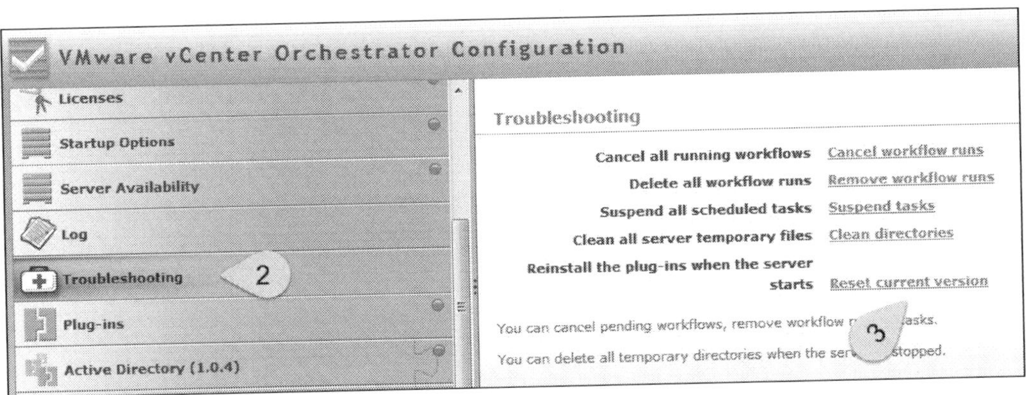

If this doesn't solve the problem, check whether the authentication user for the plugins (the **Plug-ins** section) is set correctly; the user must be an Orchestrator administrative user.

There is also a workflow for this called **Reinstall the plug-ins when the server starts**, however, with no plugins showing up in the Orchestrator Client, the workflow can't be accessed, except when using the API.

See also

In *Chapter 4, Working with Plugins,* we will be working with the most important plugins.

Tuning the appliance

In this recipe, we will learn how to tune Orchestrator appliance. This includes changing, IP settings as well as switching off unused services to get more performance out of the appliance.

Getting ready

We need a configured and running Orchestrator appliance as well as a web browser and an SSH tool (such as putty).

How to do it...

There is a lot that could be done to tune the Orchestrator appliance.

Open the Orchestrator appliance admin area

1. Open up a web browser and enter `https://[vCO IP or FQDN]:5480`.
2. The typical VMware appliance console opens up. Depending on your environment, you might have to accept the SSL certificate.
3. Enter `root` as the user name and the password you set during deployment.

Change the IP and hostname

The IP and hostname should normally be assigned when the appliance is deployed; however some aftercare has to be performed when using DHCP or VMware Workstation.

1. Open the Orchestrator Admin area.
2. Click on **Network** and select **Address**.
3. Change all settings as required.

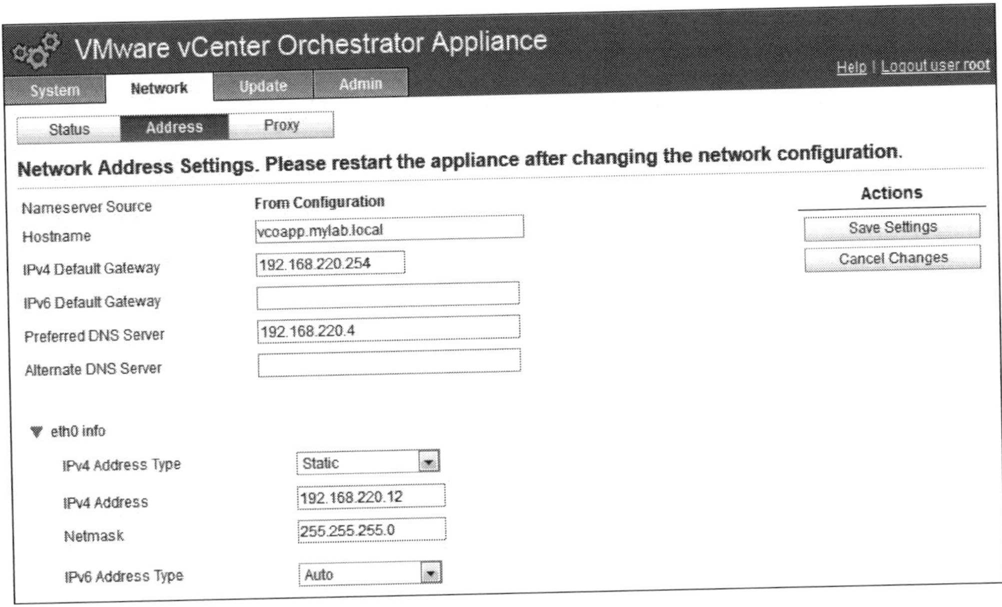

4. Click on **Save Settings**.
5. Reconnect the browser to the new IP.

Setting the time (NTP)

This is especially important when using encrypted services such as Kerberos and Orchestrator clusters.

1. Open the Orchestrator Admin area.
2. Click on **System** and then on **Time Zone**.
3. Set the correct time zone and click on **Save settings**.
4. Click on **Admin** and then select **Time Settings**.
5. Set **Time Sync. Mode** to **Use Time Server**.

6. Enter NTP servers in **Time Server** fields and click on **Save Settings**.

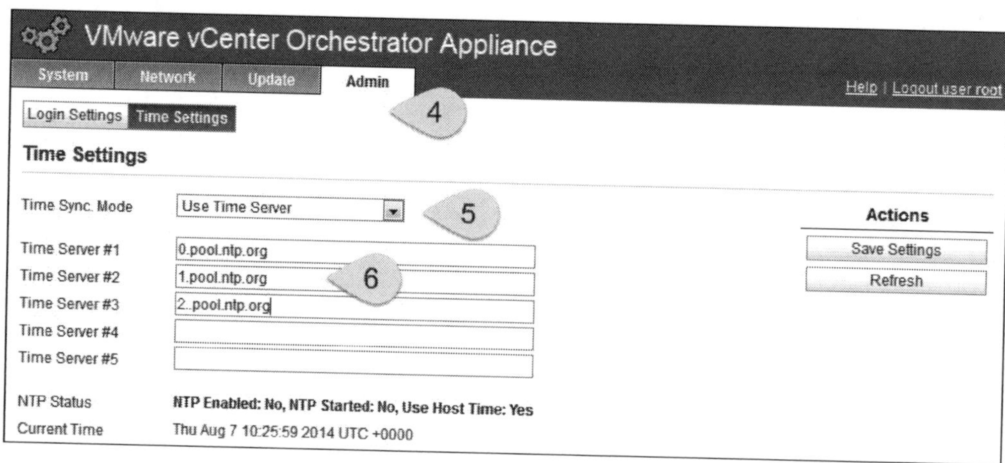

It is very important to have the same time settings in Orchestrator Server and Orchestrator Client. If the drift between the Orchestrator Server and Orchestrator Client is too high, some updates, such as the workflow system logs, might not get updated properly.

Turning SSH access to Orchestrator on and off

SSH access to the Orchestrator appliance is by default switched on. If your environment requires stricter security policies, here is how you can switch SSH off:

1. Open the Orchestrator Admin area.
2. Click on **Admin** and then select **Login Settings**.
3. Click on **Toggle SSH settings**.
4. You can see the current status of SSH here:

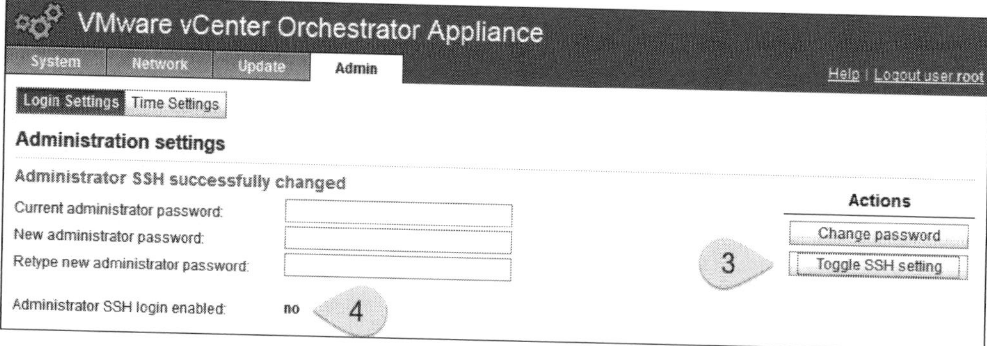

Using SSH to connect to the Orchestrator appliance operation system

1. Use an SSH client (for example, putty) to connect to your Orchestrator appliance.
2. Accept the SSL certificate.
3. Use the root user and the password you defined during deployment to log in.

The appliance uses a standard SUSE Linux (SLES).

Switching off unneeded services

If you are using external LDAP and database, you might as well switch off the database and LDAP services to gain more resources for Orchestrator. If you switch a service off, the service will not start on the next reboot.

1. Using SSH, log in to your Orchestrator appliance.
2. To see the status of a service, type `chkconfig [Linux service name]`.
3. To switch off a service, type `chkconfig [Linux service name] off`.
4. To switch the service back on, type `chkconfig [Linux service name] on`.
5. To stop, start or restart the service immediately, use the `service [Linux service name] {start|stop|restart}` command.

Here is the list of all Linux service names that are relevant for Orchestrator appliance:

Service	Linux service name
Orchestrator Server	vco-server
Orchestrator Configurator Tool	vco-configurator
Embedded Database	postgresql
Embedded LDAP	ldap

Root account expires

By default, the root account expires after 365 days; to change this setting, follow these steps:

1. Using SSH, log in to your Orchestrator appliance as root.
2. Use the command `passwd -x 99999 root`.

Your root password will now never expire, as 99999 (some 273 years) is the highest value that can be entered.

How it works...

The Orchestrator appliance comes with a fully-working Linux operating system and therefore is highly adaptable to your needs.

If you are into Linux, you also can use the `yast` command or edit the config files. Please note that the SLES licensing used for the appliance might not cover additional YAST packages. Also, installing additional software on the Orchestrator appliance might not be supported by VMware.

The appliance's `iptables` firewall is not configured and the YAST component for it is not installed. So, if you want to configure the firewalls, you have to use the `iptables` commands.

There's more...

There is quite a bit more that can be done in case one is using the Orchestrator appliance, especially for small labs.

Accessing the local LDAP

You can access the local LDAP and add users or groups. However, you need to know how to work with LDAP. For this, have a look at `https://www.suse.com/documentation/sled11/book_security/data/sec_ldap_yast_client.html`. As this goes beyond the scope of this book, I will only give you the most important LDAP information. Please also note that the embedded LDAP is configured for use with the local host only.

The following diagram shows how the Orchestrator appliance LDAP server is configured:

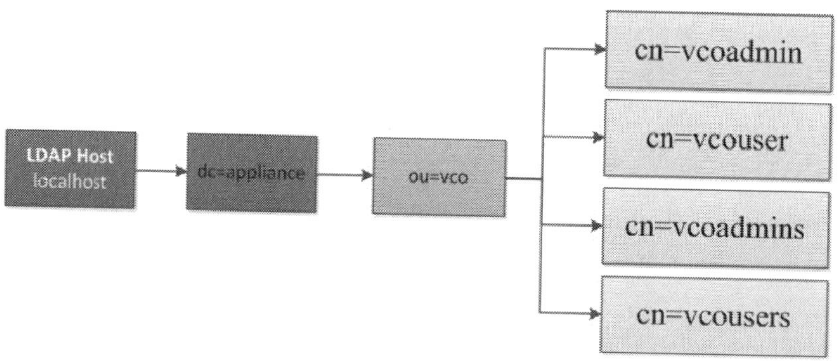

Accessing the local database

The postgreSQL DB that Orchestrator runs on is configured to not interact with the network; only the local system can use it.

To access the local DB (for example, for backups), you need the following information:

Database name	vmware
User	vmware
Password	vmware

To make the PostgreSQL database accessible from the outside, follow these steps (please note that this is not recommended and not supported, as these steps will make the database extremely vulnerable to outside influences.):

1. Log in to your Orchestrator Appliance as root.
2. Edit the `/var/lib/pgsql/data/postgresql.conf` file.
3. Uncomment the lines `listen_addresses = 'localhost'` and `port = 5432`.
4. Change the line `listen_addresses = 'localhost'` to `listen_addresses = '*'`.
5. Next, edit the `/var/lib/pgsql/data/pg_hba.conf` file and add the following line:

   ```
   host  all  all  192.168.220.0/24 trust
   ```

   You need to change the IP range.

6. Restart the appliance.

See also

See the *Configuring access to the local filesystem* recipe in this chapter.

Tuning Java

This recipe shows how to increase the Java heap size so that Orchestrator performs better by making better use of the allocated memory resources.

Getting ready

First of all, we need more virtual memory allocated to the VM on which Orchestrator is running.

Then, we need to be able to log in to the operation system, that is, log in to Windows (RDP) or Linux (SSH).

How to do it...

Depending on the version of Orchestrator you have, you need to follow one set of instructions or the other.

Windows

1. Log in to the Windows operating system of your Orchestrator.
2. Stop the **vCenter Orchestrator Server** service.
3. Open explorer and navigate to `C:\Program Files\VMware\Orchestrator\app-server\bin`.
4. Make a copy of the `wrapper.conf` file as a backup.
5. Open the `wrapper.conf` file using Notepad.
6. Find the `wrapper.java.maxmemory=2048` line.
7. The heap size is given in MB; change the setting to an appropriate setting and save the file.
8. Start the **vCenter Orchestrator Server** service.

Linux

This how-to is for vCO 5.5 and higher, for versions 5.1 and lower please see `kb.vmware.com/kb/2007423`.

1. Log in to the Linux operating system of your Orchestrator.
2. Stop the Orchestrator service with `service vco-server stop`.
3. Make a backup of the file with `cp /usr/lib/vco/app-server/bin/setenv.sh /usr/lib/vco/app-server/bin/setenv.sh.bak`.
4. Type `vi /usr/lib/vco/app-server/bin/setenv.sh`.
5. The `vi` command opens up and displays the content of the file.
6. Move the cursor to the line that starts with `MEM_OPTS="-Xmx2048m`.
7. Press *I* and remove `2048`. Enter your desired heap size in MB.
8. Press *Esc* and then type `:qw` to exit and save. If you want to exit `vi` without saving, enter `:q!` instead.
9. Start the Orchestrator service with `service vco-server start`.

How it works...

By default, the Java heap size is set to 2 GB. Both the Linux and Windows services are Java processes. Before going ahead and increasing the Java heap size, it's probably a good idea to check how much resources the Java process actually takes.

In Windows, this is done (if you have no special tools available) by starting the **Windows Task Manager** and looking for the `java.exe` process. In Linux, use the `top` command and look for the Java process. There might be more than one Java process; this can be the Orchestrator Configuration tool or other Java processes such as vCenter. Without some Windows tools such as Process Explorer or Linux command-line knowledge it's rather hard and out of scope for this book to explore in detail.

After changing the heap size and restarting the services, it's a good idea to monitor the behavior of the Java process by checking on how often the Java garbage collection is running. See `http://www.cubrid.org/blog/dev-platform/how-to-monitor-java-garbage-collection/` for more details on this.

You need to balance the amount of memory that you give to the Orchestrator Java process with the rest of the memory usage of the system. This is especially important if you are running Orchestrator together with the vCenter server or vRealize Automation. You can easily end up with programs competing for memory, which will slow the whole system down.

If you are increasing the virtual memory assigned to the VM, you will also need to increase the Java heap size, as it doesn't automatically adjust itself.

Backup and recovery

In this recipe, we look into backing up and restoring the Orchestrator configuration. To back up and restore single packages or workflows, please see the *Importing and exporting Orchestrator elements* and *Working with packages* recipes in *Chapter 5, Basic Orchestrator Operations*.

Getting ready

We need an installed and running Orchestrator server.

You should be comfortable with using the Orchestrator Configuration tool described in the *Two ways to configure Orchestrator* recipe in *Chapter 1, Installing and Configuring Orchestrator*, as there is currently no Workflow-driven method.

How to do it...

A backup (or restore) of the Orchestrator configuration is easy to make using the Orchestrator Configuration tool.

Backup

1. Open the Orchestrator Configuration tool.
2. Click on the **General** section.
3. Select **Export Configuration**.
4. You can choose a password to protect the exported values.
5. Click on **Export**.
6. If you are using the Windows installation, the backup file will be stored in `C:\Program Files\VMware\Orchestrator\vmo_config_[ DateTime].vmoconfig`.
7. If you are using the Appliance, the backup file can be found in `/var/lib/vco/vmo_config_[DateTime].vmoconfig`.

Restore

Assuming that your Orchestrator installation died and you would like to recover or move from one method of Orchestrator to the other (for example, from a Windows-installed version to appliance), here is how to restore the configuration on a freshly installed/deployed Orchestrator.

1. Open the Orchestrator Configuration tool.
2. Stop Orchestrator Service.
3. Click on the **General** Section.
4. Select **Import Configuration**.
5. If you used a password for your backup export, enter it here.
6. Click on the magnifying glass icon and select the `.vmoconfig` file to restore and click on **Import**.

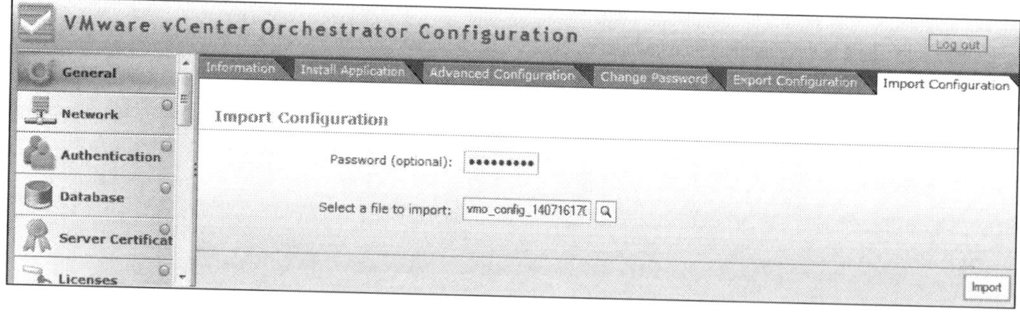

7. Wait until the import has finished. You might need to re-enter some passwords as well as the licensing information.
8. Start Orchestrator Service.

How it works...

The Configuration tool helps quite a bit with preserving the configurations you entered; however, it's not perfect. The best protection against loss is solid documentation, where you write down the Orchestrator configurations, as well as why an item is configured the way it is.

More or less every setting gets saved in the export; however, two things will not be saved, the Orchestrator (vCenter Server side) licensing information as well as credentials.

Database

Using an external database for Orchestrator has the immense advantage that this database can be backed up using the already-existing methods of your business. The Orchestrator database contains most parts of the configuration, but more importantly, it contains all workflows and workflow executions. Having a regular database backup is important.

If one restores the database, it's important to *stop* the Orchestrator Server first.

See also

The *Working with packages* recipe in *Chapter 5, Basic Orchestrator Operations*, on how to back up elements in Orchestrator.

Creating an Orchestrator cluster

In this recipe, we explore how to create clustered Orchestrator servers. Clustered Orchestrator servers guarantee high availability and load balancing to protect production installations, such as vRealize Automation.

Getting ready

We need two Orchestrator installations. One should be fully configured and the other should be a completely new installation. We will call the configured one the first Orchestrator server, and the new one will be called the second Orchestrator server.

We also need access to the Orchestrator database that is configured with the first Orchestrator server.

How to do it...

This recipe is divided into different sections. The database section and the first server section only have to be performed once, but the last sections might need to be repeated for different servers.

Configuring the database

We have to configure the database to prepare it for multiple servers writing into it.

SQL Server

Using SQL Server, we need to set the following two settings on the Orchestrator database. In this example, the Orchestrator database is called vcoDB:

```
ALTER DATABASE vcoDB SET READ_COMMITTED_SNAPSHOT ON
ALTER DATABASE vcoDB SET ALLOW_SNAPSHOT_ISOLATION ON
```

Oracle server

There's nothing to do as Oracle is set up correctly out of the box.

Configuring the first Orchestrator server

For this recipe, we assume that the first Orchestrator server is configured, which means that it is connected to an external authentication service such as SSO, as well as being connected to an external database. See *Chapter 1, Installing and Configuring Orchestrator*, for help on these topics. To start building a cluster, follow these steps:

1. Log in to the Orchestrator Configurator of the first Orchestrator server (see the *Two ways to configure Orchestrator* recipe in *Chapter 1, Installing and Configuring Orchestrator*).
2. Click on the **Startup Options** sections and stop the Orchestrator service.
3. Click on the **Server Availability** section.
4. Select **Cluster mode**.
5. Set the **Number of active notes nodes** to `2`.
6. Click on **Apply changes**.

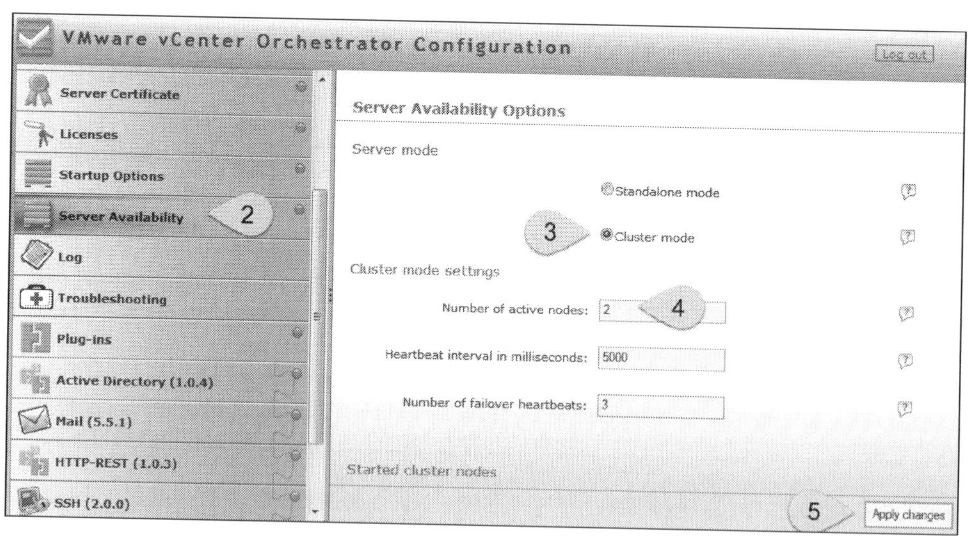

7. Export the Orchestrator Server configuration as shown in the *Backup and recovery* recipe in this chapter.
8. DO NOT start the Orchestrator server yet.

Configuring the second Orchestrator server

1. Log in to the Configurator on the second Orchestrator server.
2. Make sure that the Orchestrator service is stopped.
3. Install all the same plugins you have in the first Orchestrator server.
4. Import the Orchestrator configuration from the first server as shown in the *Backup and recovery* recipe in this chapter, but don't start the Orchestrator Server service yet.
5. Make sure all plugins are configured in the same way.
6. Change the network setting in **Network | Network | IP Address** to reflect the new IP of the server. See the *Important Orchestrator base configurations* recipe in *Chapter 1, Installing and Configuring Orchestrator*.
7. Make sure that the clocks on both Orchestrator servers are synced to the same time and both servers are in the same time zone. See the *Important Orchestrator base configurations* recipe in *Chapter 1, Installing and Configuring Orchestrator*.
8. Make sure that all the Orchestrator objects (workflows, actions, and so on) are synced between the servers; see the *Synchronize Orchestrator elements between Orchestrator servers* recipe in *Chapter 5, Basic Orchestrator Operations*.

Now that you have configured an additional node for the cluster, it is time to start the cluster.

Starting the cluster

1. Log in to the first Orchestrator Server and start the Orchestrator service.
2. Click on the **Server Availability** section and wait until the first Orchestrator service shows **RUNNING**.
3. Log in to the second Orchestrator Server and start the Orchestrator service.
4. Click on the **Server Availability** section.

5. After a while (have patience, this could take a few minutes), you should see the second Orchestrator server showing **RUNNING**. The cluster is now active.

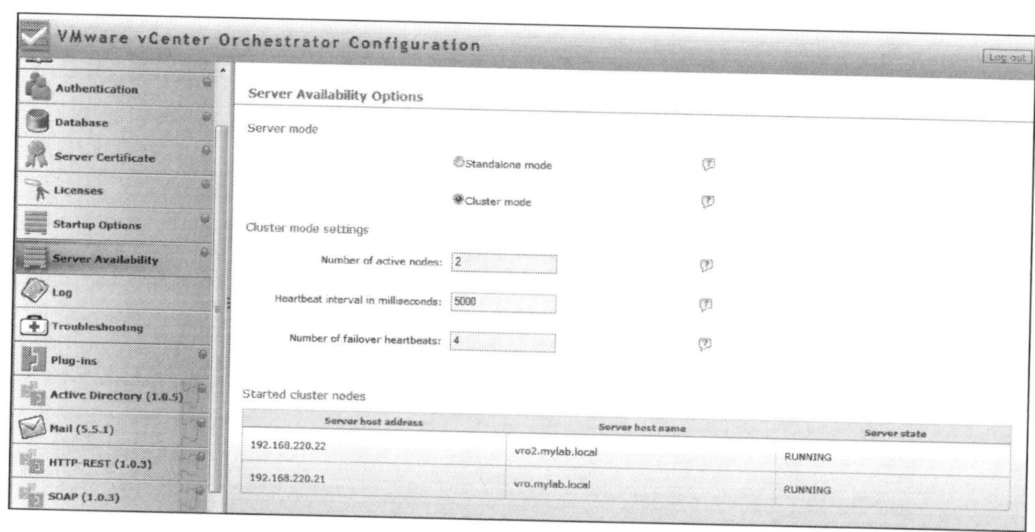

How it works...

The first question one asks is why someone would create a cluster of Orchestrator servers. The answer is pretty easy—Orchestrator can be used as a production tool, such as for VM provisioning or together with vRealize Automation. This makes an Orchestrator cluster a very good idea.

The Orchestrator cluster provides not only high availability, but also load balancing.

The clustering is a zero-touch configuration, which means that the Orchestrator cluster is managing itself. The maximum amount of active nodes you defined in the configuration dictates how many nodes are switched from *standby* to *running*. For example, you define the amount of active nodes as two; however, you configured three Orchestrator installations in this cluster and powered them all on. This would result in two nodes being active and one being in standby mode. If you now proceed to power off one of the active nodes, the standby node will become active. You can test this using this recipe and setting **Number of active nodes** to `1`.

There are certain drawbacks you should be aware of. It is not recommended to use the Orchestrator Client to connect to the nodes running in a cluster. This is done on purpose to make sure that changes to workflows can't occur. You can still use the API or the multinode plugin access and use a workflow you have created. However, do not change any items such as workflows, actions and so on.

To use the Orchestrator multinode plugin, see the *Managing remote Orchestrator* recipe in *Chapter 6, Advanced Operations*. To use the REST API, see the *Accessing the Orchestrator API via REST* recipe in *Chapter 6, Advanced Operations*.

There is also a workflow that can configure the Orchestrator Cluster, and it is located under **Library** | **Configuration** | **Availability**; however, as stated before, if you have configured an Orchestrator cluster, you shouldn't access workflows via the Orchestrator Client, you can use the multinode plugin.

Making changes to the cluster

If you have to make changes to the cluster, such as updating or changing a workflow or an action, follow these steps:

1. Shut down all Orchestrator services in the cluster, except one.
2. Make the changes.
3. Start all the other Orchestrator services in the cluster one after another.

If you want to make configuration changes to the cluster, you need to import/export the configuration again.

There's more...

After creating a cluster, we need to talk about load balancing. Please note that a step-by-step discussion about configuring a load balancer is out of the scope for this book. However, here are the things you need to know:

- Use a HTTPS based load balancer
- The health check is best done on `https://[vCO server ip]:8280/vco`
- Load balance the whole IP, or if needed, check the port table in the introduction
- SSL offload is preferable to SSL pass-though, especially when working with vRealize Automation

The VMware KB (`kb.vmware.com/kb/2058674`) provides a step-by-step example of how to set up Orchestrator with an Nginx load balancer.

See also

The *Synchronize Orchestrator elements between Orchestrator servers* recipe in *Chapter 5, Basic Orchestrator Operations* and the *Managing remote Orchestrator* recipe in *Chapter 6, Advanced Operations*.

Configuring the Orchestrator Service SSL certificate

In this recipe, we will have a closer look at the SSL certificate of the Orchestrator Server.

Getting ready

You need a running Orchestrator server.

If you are intending to use an SSL certificate signed by a **Certificate Authority** (**CA**), you need to be able to sign a certificate request. You also need the CA root certificate so that you can import it into the Orchestrator SSL store.

How to do it...

We will split the recipe into multiple parts. The SSL certificate store, as well as Keytool, are both present in the appliance and the Windows installations.

SSL store	`C:\Program Files\VMware\Orchestrator\jre\lib\security\jssecacerts` `/etc/vco/app-server/security/jssecacerts`
Keytool	`C:\Program Files\VMware\Orchestrator\jre\bin\keytool.exe` `/usr/java/jre-vmware/bin/keytool`

In the following parts, you need to substitute the correct paths (and commands) depending on the Orchestrator version you are using.

Back up and remove the default certificates

First of all, we need to back up the default certificate that comes with Orchestrator:

1. In Windows, open a command prompt with administrative rights or log in to the Orchestrator appliance as the root.
2. Make a copy of the existing SSL store.
3. Remove the existing default certificate with the following command:

```
keytool -keystore [SSLstore] -delete -alias dunes -storepass
dunesdunes
```

Create a self-signed certificate

To generate a self-signed certificate, use the following steps:

1. Stop the Orchestrator service. The following command will start the creation of the self-signed certificate:

   ```
   keytool -keystore [SSLstore] -storepass dunesdunes -genkey
   -alias dunes -keypass dunesdunes -validity 3650
   ```

2. As the first and last names, you have to enter the FQDN of the server name.
3. Fill in the rest of the required information.
4. Start the Orchestrator service.

You now have replaced the existing SSL certificate with a self-signed certificate.

Using a CA-signed certificate

To use a CA-signed certificate, follow these steps:

1. Stop the Orchestrator Service.
2. Generate a new certificate-signing request (CSR) with this command:

   ```
   keytool -keystore [SSLstore] -storepass dunesdunes -alias dunes
   -certreq -keypass dunesdunes -file [file name].csr
   ```

3. Have the certificate request signed by your CA. Make sure that it is in DER encoding.
4. Import the CA's root certificate into the keystore:

   ```
   keytool -keystore [SSLstore] -import -storepass dunesdunes -alias
   root -file [root file certificate]
   ```

5. Import the CA-signed certificate into the keystore:

   ```
   keytool -keystore [SSLstore] -import -storepass dunesdunes
   -keypass dunesdunes -alias dunes -file [file name].crt
   ```

6. Start the Orchestrator Service.

Your CA-signed certificate is now imported into Orchestrator.

How it works...

Orchestrator uses an Apache web server that is installed along with Orchestrator. The SSL certificate is stored within the Java environment of the Orchestrator installation. The SSL certificate we discuss here is the certificate that Orchestrator uses to communicate with other instances such as the Orchestrator Client or other programs. The SSL certificates that were imported in the *Important Orchestrator base configurations* recipe in *Chapter 1, Installing and Configuring Orchestrator*, are the SSL certificates that Orchestrator knows of from other services.

The SSL certificates that are used with Orchestrator use the DER encoding, and any request and signed certificate has to be in the same encoding. To convert to DER encoding, you can use the `openssl` command as well as other online available tools.

Default, self-signed, or CA-signed?

The question now is which certificate should we use, the default SSL certificate, a self-signed certificate, or a CA-signed certificate?

The main difference between the default and the self-signed certificates is that the self-signed certificate is issued with the correct FQDN of the Orchestrator Server and therefore more secure than the default certificate.

A CA-signed certificate is the most secure method, as it is automatically accepted by all hosts that trust the CA.

What is this "Dunes" business in Orchestrator?

Looking at the code, you probably wonder about the alias `dunes` and the password `dunesdunes`. The answer is pretty simple. In 2007, VMware acquired the Swiss-based company Dunes. You will find quite a lot of Dunes references in vCenter Orchestrator, especially in error messages and in the API, as Orchestrator was invented by Dunes.

See also

The *Working with packages* recipe in *Chapter 5, Basic Orchestrator Operations*.

Configuring e-mail

In this recipe, we will configure a default e-mail server that can be used with Orchestrator.

Getting ready

As always, we need a working Orchestrator installation. We also need an e-mail server (SMTP) as well as an e-mail account we can use with it.

How to do it...

To start configuring a default e-mail server, perform the following steps:

1. Log in to Orchestrator Configurator of Orchestrator Server.
2. Click on the **Mail** section.

3. Tick **Define default values**; the screen will now show the configuration items.
4. Fill in the required information and click on **Apply Changes**.

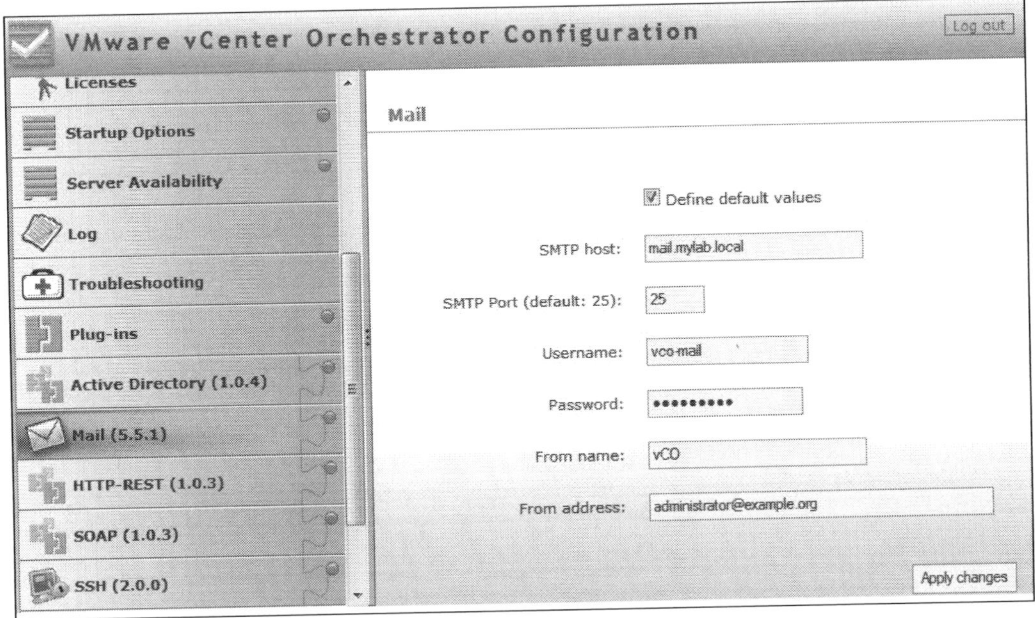

How it works...

Mail is an extremely important tool in Orchestrator. You can use an e-mail to send not only notifications to users but also interaction requests; you can also use Orchestrator workflows to check an e-mail server and wait for a specific e-mail to arrive.

The e-mail workflows and actions that are implemented in Orchestrator can use either the default settings that we have just configured or custom settings, however with the custom setting you will then need to configure the e-mail settings for each use.

See also

See the *Working with mails* recipe in *Chapter 4, Working with Plugins*.

Redirecting Orchestrator Syslog to an external Syslog server

In this recipe, we will configure the Orchestrator Server to send all logs to a centralized Syslog server. This is especially important when using Orchestrator clusters.

Getting ready

You need a Syslog server as a target. In this example, we will use the VMware Syslog server that can be installed from the vCenter Server installation media (ISO image).

We also need access to the local OS (either Windows or Orchestrator appliance).

How to do it...

This recipe splits off into installing and using the vSphere Syslog server and the redirection of the Orchestrator Syslog.

Install VMware vSphere Syslog Collector

You can use any Syslog server, however, if you don't have one already, the one supplied by VMware isn't that bad.

1. Insert the vSphere installation media DVD.
2. Click on **VMware vSphere Syslog Collector**.
3. Follow the installation and choose the path to store the Syslog data.

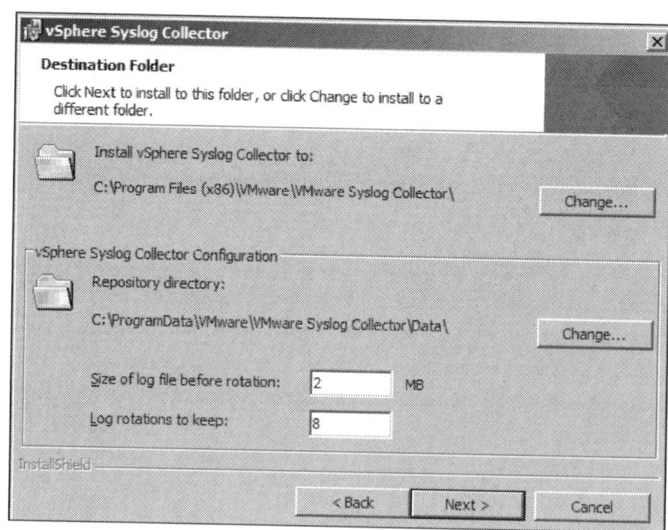

4. Choose the **VMware vCenter Server Installation** option if you want the Syslog server to be integrated in the vSphereClient.
5. Finish the installation.
6. Make sure that the port UDP/TCP 514 is opened (firewall).

Working with VMware vSphere Syslog Collector

1. The data files for Syslog are stored by default in `ProgramData\VMware\VMware Syslog Collector\Data\[ip or hostname of Server]\syslog.log`, or the path you choose during installation.
2. Open the `syslog.log` file.
3. If you like to watch the Syslog file, you can use the PowerShell command: `Get-Content [filename]-Wait`.

Redirecting Orchestrator for Syslog

1. Log in to the operating system of your Orchestrator installation as an administrative user.
2. Depending on the operating system you are using, here are the paths to the configuration file:

Operation system	Path
Windows	`C:\Program Files\VMware\Orchestrator\app-server\conf\`
Appliance	`/etc/vco/app-server/`

3. Make a backup of the file called `log4j.xml`.
4. Open the `log4j.xml` file (using WordPad or vi).
5. There are two sections you need to change. The first is the Syslog entry. Scroll down until you see the following:

```
<!-- ================================ -->
<!-- Append messages to the syslogd -->
   <!-- ================================ -->
   <!--
    <appender name="SYSLOG" class="org.apache.log4j.net.
SyslogAppender">
         <param name="Threshold" value="INFO"/>
         <param name="Facility" value="<<FACILITY>>"/>
         <param name="SyslogHost" value="<<HOST>>"/>
         <param name="FacilityPrinting" value="true"/>
         <layout class="org.apache.log4j.PatternLayout">
```

```
            <param name="ConversionPattern" value="vCO: prio:%-5p
thread:%t token:%X{token} wf:%X{workflowName} wfid:%X{workflow}
user: %X{username} cat:%c{1} msg:%m%n"/>
        </layout>
    </appender>
    -->
```

You need to delete the `<!--` section before `<appender name="SYSLOG"` and `-->` after `</appender>`. It is a comment and if not deleted, the instructions between the start and end tags will be ignored.

You need to replace `<<FACILITY>>` with `USER` and `<<HOST>>` with the FQDN or the IP of your Syslog host.

6. The second section we have to edit is further down and looks like this:

```
<root>
        <priority value="INFO" />
        <appender-ref ref="CONSOLE" />
        <appender-ref ref="FILE" />
<!--
<appender-ref ref="SYSLOG" />
-->
<!--
<appender-ref ref="EVENT_LOG" />
        -->
    </root>
```

Here, we have to delete the comment tags (`<!--` and `-->`) before and after `<appender-ref ref="SYSLOG" />`.

7. Save the changes.
8. If you are using Windows, make sure that the Windows server allows UDP Port 514. The Linux appliance is already properly configured.

No restart of the Orchestrator server is needed.

How it works...

Redirecting Syslog files to a central logging facility can be a quite a useful thing. Not only does the Orchestrator Syslog contain the normal Orchestrator Syslog entries, but also information on who ran which workflow when. See the *Working with logs* recipe in *Chapter 3, Visual Programming*, for more information.

Make sure that you keep a copy of the `log4j.xml` file so that in the case of a restore or an update of the Orchestrator appliance, you still have the correct settings.

Log roll

The file also contains the logroll instructions; the respective settings are `MaxFileSize` and `MaxBackupIndex`.

There's more...

Other Syslog Servers you could use instead of the VMware ones are:

- `http://www.kiwisyslog.com/`
- `http://www.splunk.com`
- `http://www.balabit.com/network-security/syslog-ng`

All Linux servers come with a Syslog service installed and can be used as well. However, in general they do not have a comfortable web or GUI frontend.

See also

The *Working with logs* recipe in *Chapter 3, Visual Programming*.

All Orchestrator logfiles can be found at `kb.vmware.com/kb/1010956`.

Configuring the Kerberos authentication

This recipe shows how to configure the Kerberos authentication with Orchestrator. Even if you are using the Windows version, this still has to be done, as Kerberos needs to be configured for Java that runs Orchestrator. The Kerberos configuration is only needed for special plugins, such as PowerShell.

Getting ready

We just need administrative access to the Orchestrator operating system. You need to make sure that the clocks are in sync between Orchestrator and the KDC. See the *Tuning the appliance* recipe in this chapter. The domain in this example is called `mylab.local` and the AD server (KDC) is called `addns.mylab.local`.

How to do it...

1. Log in to the Orchestrator operation system with administrator privileges.
2. Edit the `krb5.conf` file. You might have to create this file.

Operating system	Path
Windows	`C:\Program Files\Common Files\VMware\VMware vCenter Server - Java Components\lib\security\krb5.conf`
Appliance	`/usr/java/jre-vmware/lib/security/krb5.conf`

3. Add the following lines to the file. In the following example, replace `mylab.local` with your domain settings. Make sure that you use the same case as in the example:

```
[libdefaults]
default_realm = MYLAB.LOCAL
udp_preferences_limit = 1
[realms]
MYLAB.LOCAL = {
kdc = addns.mylab.local
default_domain = mylab.local
}
[domain_realms]
.mylab.local=MYLAB.LOCAL
mylab.local=MYLAB.LOCAL
```

4. Save the file and then restart the Orchestrator service.

How it works...

Kerberos is an authentication protocol that uses tickets that allow systems to securely talk to each other.

Let's see how Kerberos works with a simple example. A client (Orchestrator) wants to communicate with a server (Windows host) securely. The client will communicate with a **Key Distribution Center** (**KDC**), in Windows this is your AD controller to be authenticated as a valid user to have access to this system. The KDC issues a ticket and this again is used to contact the server to gain access.

Configuration of the `krb5.conf` file is needed for Orchestrator in any version, as the connecting service is really the Java process and not the operation system underneath.

Since Windows 2000, Microsoft uses Kerberos as its main method for authentication. It is a secure method that uses encrypted communication and therefore the best choice for any production environment.

See also

In the recipes in *Chapter 4, Working with Plugins*, we will be able to use Kerberos authentication. This recipe is especially important for the *Working with PowerShell* recipe.

Configuring access to the local filesystem

Here, you will learn how to set permission for Orchestrator to access its local filesystem and make an external filesystem accessible to Orchestrator.

Getting ready

We need administrative access to the operation system of Orchestrator.

How to do it...

There are two ways to give Orchestrator access to its local filesystem.

Fast and easy

1. Connect to the operation system where Orchestrator is installed with administrative rights.
2. In Windows, create the `C:\orchestrator\` directory. With the appliance, you can simply use the existing folder `/var/run/vco`.

Orchestrator has full access to the directories mentioned in step 2 and can read and write from them.

Configuring access

1. Connect to the operation system where Orchestrator is installed with administrative rights.
2. Make sure that the directory you would like to use with Orchestrator is accessible for the Orchestrator user.

Operating system	User
Windows	User that installed Orchestrator
Appliance	User: vco Group: vco

3. Browse to the following directory:

Operating system	**User**
Windows	`C:\Program Files\VMware\Orchestrator\app-server\conf`
Appliance	`/etc/vco/app-server/`

4. Edit the `js-io-rights.conf` file.
5. To give Orchestrator access to a directory, simply add the directory path and the rights such as `+rwx` (see the *How it works...* section of this recipe).
6. Save and close the file.
7. Restart the Orchestrator Service.

How it works...

Access for Orchestrator to its local filesystem is needed for quite some things such as using SCP and uploading and downloading files. The access for Orchestrator is regulated by the entries in the `js-io-rights.conf` file. The following shows the default settings (Version 5.5.x) of the config file:

Windows	**Appliance**
-rwx C:/ +rwx C:/orchestrator/ # relative to user.dir which is %orchestrator_install_dir%\app-server\bin +rx ../../app-server/logs/ +rx ../../configuration/logs/ +rx ../bin/ -rwx ../../app-server/conf/security/ +rx ../../app-server/conf/ +rx ../../apps/ +r ../../version.txt	-rwx / +rwx /var/run/vco/ -rwx /etc/vco/app-server/security/ +rx /etc/vco/ +rx /var/log/vco/

As you can see, the Windows installation has full access preconfigured for the `c:/orchestrator/` directory.

Please note that Orchestrator uses the forward slash (/) for Windows, except when using shares.

The available rights for Orchestrator are as follows:

Allow	Deny	Read	Write	Access
+	-	r	w	x

The x operator means that Orchestrator has the right to access the directory, for example to list the content or to execute a file.

There's more...

You can use the file writer to write to a shared directory. This follows the same principle as the normal file writing. The only thing is that the methods differ between Orchestrator OS versions.

Orchestrator appliance (Linux)

1. Create a new directory and make sure it has the correct permissions.
2. Make sure Orchestrator has rights to access this directory.
3. Mount the Windows directory `mount -t cifs //host/share /orchestrator/share/ -o username=user,password=password`.
4. Access the `/orchestrator/share/` directory as you have learned.

Windows

1. Make sure that you can access the network share.
2. Add the network share to the `js-io-rights.conf` file as:

   ```
   +rwx \\hostname\share
   ```

3. Access the share via Orchestrator in the `\\\\hostname\\share\\file` form. This is due to the fact that we need to escape the backslashes, and so for each backward slash, you have to use two backward slashes.

See also

See the *Working with SSH* and *File operations* recipes in *Chapter 4, Working with Plugins*.

Updating Orchestrator

This recipe focuses on updating the Windows as well as the Appliance version of Orchestrator.

Getting ready

We need an old, installed, and running version of Orchestrator as well as a newer version. As of writing of this book, the newest generally available version is vRealize Orchestrator, which is version 5.5.2.1, and we will update the existing 5.5.1 to this version.

For the Windows installation, you will need to download the new VMware vCenter Server ISO file which you can find under the vSphere Suite downloads.

For Appliance, you need to download the `updaterepo.iso` file which you can find in the directory of the Orchestrator appliance in the vSphere suite downloads. Alternatively, you can also use the online repository for downloads.

The vRealize-integrated Orchestrator is updated with the vRealize Automation update.

How to do it...

We will split this recipe into two parts: the Windows and Appliance updates.

Windows update

1. Create a snapshot of the Windows VM so that if something goes wrong, you can return to a working version. It is also a good idea to export all the workflows and packages that you have created and/or back up the *external* Orchestrator database.
2. Using vCenter, connect the downloaded ISO file to the Orchestrator VM.
3. Log in to the Windows OS with administrator rights and browse to the `[CDROM]:\vCenter-Server\vCO` directory.
4. Execute the installation file and wait until the install wizard starts.
5. After accepting the EULA, you are asked if you would like to update.

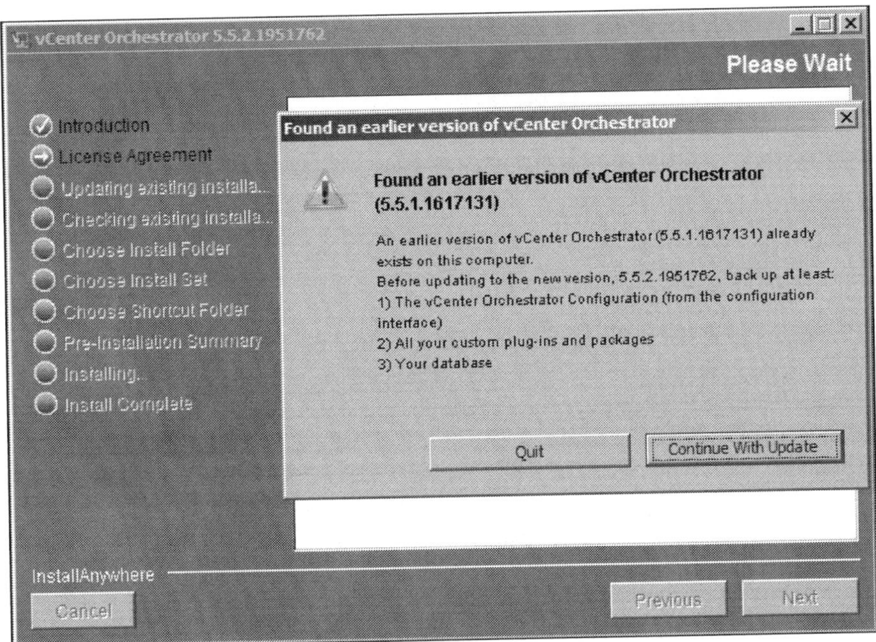

6. Continue to click on **Next** until the update starts. Wait until the update has finished.

The update has finished and Orchestrator can be used directly without further steps.

Appliance update

1. Create a snapshot of the appliance so that if something goes wrong, you can return to a working version. It is also a good idea to export all the workflows and packages that you have created and/or back up the *external* Orchestrator database.
2. Using vCenter, connect the downloaded ISO file to Appliance.
3. Using a browser, connect to `https://[IP or FQDN of the Appliance]:5480` and log in with the user root.
4. Click on **Update** and then on **Settings**. Choose **Use CDROM Updates** and then **Save Settings**. If you have an Internet connection from Appliance; you can also choose to use **Use Default Repository**.

5. Click on **Status** and then on **Check Updates**. After a moment, you will see the following screenshot:

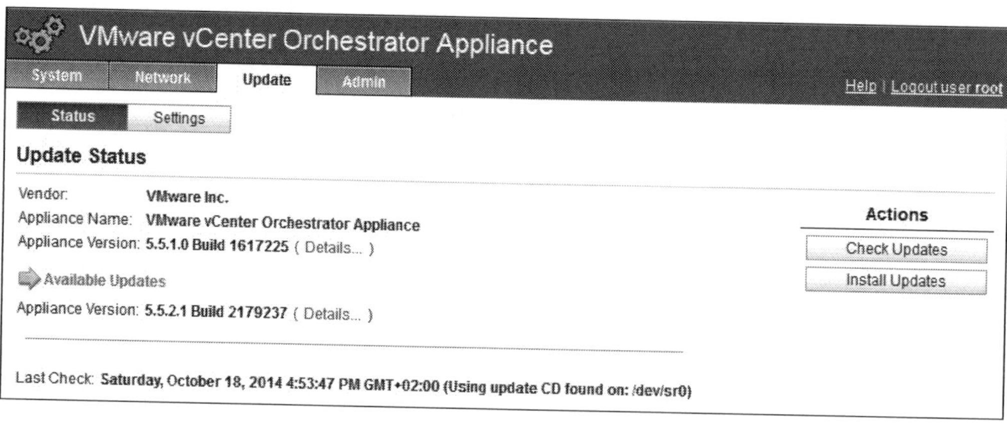

6. If this is the version you want to upgrade to, click on **Install Updates**.
7. Accept the EULA and confirm that you want to update.
8. The update process can take a while, so be patient.
9. When the update is completed, you will need to reboot the appliance.

How it works...

Updating is quite an important process when working with Orchestrator and should be done on a regular basis. This update is not the only update we discussed in this recipe but it is also the update of the installed plugins.

Before you update Orchestrator, you should make sure you have backed up all important items. This not only includes the workflows, and actions, among others, but also all the changes you might have made to Orchestrator's config files, such as local file permissions.

Another important thing to do is to always have a look at the release notes of any new version, to understand what has changed and whether there are any changes to the update process.

After you have updated Orchestrator, you should make sure that all the workflows as well as all the config file changes still exist.

3

Visual Programming

This chapter will introduce you to working with the visual programming feature of Orchestrator. We will look at the following recipes:

- Workflow basics
- Version control
- Working with logs
- Error handling in workflows
- Resuming failed workflows
- Using the workflow debugging function
- Working with decisions
- Working with loops
- Working with presentations
- Working with configurations
- Working with actions
- Linking actions in presentations
- Waiting tasks
- Sending and waiting for custom events
- Using asynchronous workflows
- Working with user interactions
- Changing credentials

Introduction

Orchestrator is a visual programming tool; in this chapter, we will focus on the visual programming of Orchestrator. In addition to this, you will also find some introductions for JavaScript.

How this chapter works

If you are new to Orchestrator, or even programming, then just follow the recipes one after the other, as they are built one after the other, otherwise just pick and choose as you like.

In most recipes, we will use an example in order to explain the functions, aims, and gains of the recipe. The recipes in this chapter don't require vCenter or anything else, so if you want, you can just use the base Orchestrator appliance and start working from there. In addition to the visual programming, we will introduce the JavaScript equivalents in each recipe, if there are any, to make this chapter more interesting to advanced readers. If you are new to Orchestrator or JavaScript, you can simply ignore them for the time being and return to them later.

The example package

Every workflow shown in this chapter is also available in the example package present in the code bundle for download. In the *See also* section of each recipe, we will state the name of the workflows that are available for each recipe.

Please see the preface of this book for download and installation instructions.

JavaScript (the very basics)

The following is a very short and quick reference for JavaScript. It is aimed at people who already know a programming language and just need to adapt to the syntax of JavaScript.

If you already know any programming language, the transition is quite easy. I will point out some basic Java stuff in each recipe, as it is needed.

To learn JavaScript, you can have a look at `http://www.w3schools.com/js/`.

Here is a list that shows the very basic things one needs to know about JavaScript:

- Every line ends with a semicolon (`;`)
- Single-line comments are done with `//`
- Multi-line comments begin with `/*` and end with `*/`
- Everything in JavaScript is case sensitive

- Variables are just text (for example, `myTest5`) and must start with a letter
- Math operations are performed using symbols such as `+`, `-`, `*`, and `/`
- Strings are combined using the `+` operator, for example, `"a" + "b"` or `stringVaribale + " text to append"`
- JavaScript is not Java; make sure you always search for JavaScript in the web
- Have a look at `http://javascript.crockford.com/code.html` to understand how JavaScript should be formatted

Working with the Orchestrator Client

The Orchestrator Client is a Java-based client that can be launched via the Orchestrator home page or can be locally installed.

The Orchestrator Client is an integrated development environment to create and operate workflows; see *Chapter 1, Installing and Configuring Orchestrator* for instructions on how to access it.

The icons for this chapter

The Orchestrator Client has three modes: **Run**, **Design** and **Administer**. The setting can be changed by selecting the value from the top drop-down menu. We will use the Orchestrator Client in this chapter in the **Design** mode, as it shows all the items we will be working with in this chapter. All other modes and sections are explained in the *Introduction* section of *Chapter 5, Basic Orchestrator Operations*. The following screenshot shows all the icons that we will be using in this chapter, with a little description of what they are called:

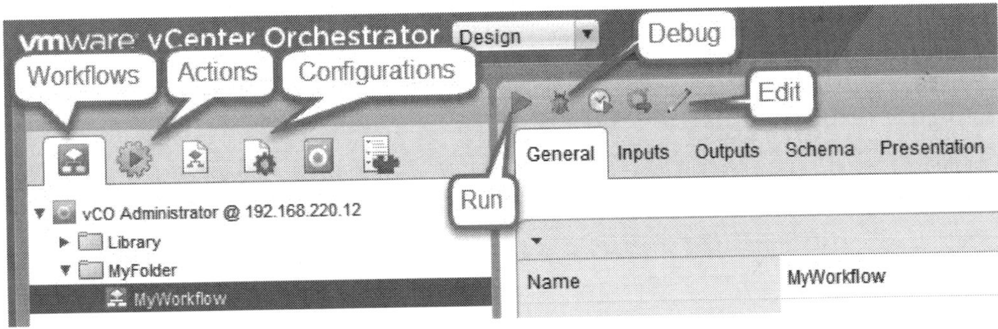

Working with the schema

Any Orchestrator workflow programming is done in the **schema**; each element in the schema is connected by either a blue (normal), green (true), or dotted red (error/false) line between a start point and an endpoint. You can have more than one endpoint, but only one start point.

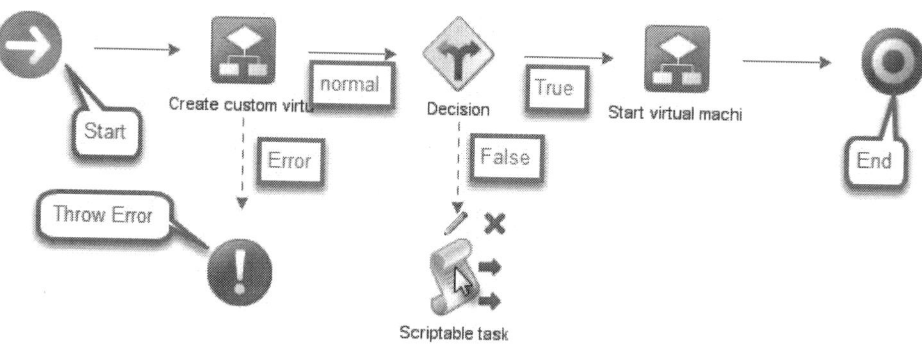

Dropping an element on a line will insert it into the flow. You can delete elements or lines by right-clicking on them and selecting **Delete** (you can also use the *Delete* key).

To create a new line, hover the mouse above an element (see **Scriptable task** in the previous figure) and then drag one of the arrows to the destination element.

You can rename any element by just double-clicking on it and entering a new name.

Gotcha

One of the things you need to know is that when Orchestrator asks you for something (for example, workflows) you might end up with an empty window like the following:

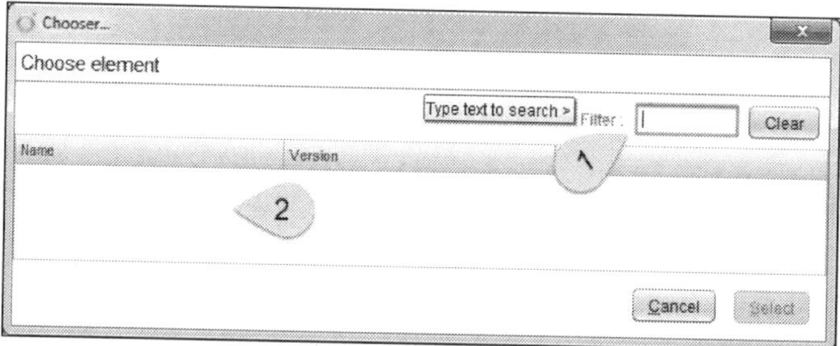

You need to enter something into **Filter** (**1**) and then press *Enter* (or just press *Enter*). The area below (**2**) will then fill up with the available options you can choose from.

Working with variables

Each workflow can have **variables** in three different areas. Variables are called attributes or parameters depending on where they are.

In JavaScript, the naming convention for variables is to start with lowercase and use uppercase when a new word starts, for example, `myFirstAttribute`, `currentVM`, and so on.

Variables in the general section

A variable in the general section is called an **attribute**. An attribute is accessible throughout the whole workflow, but not outside it. An attribute can have an initial value at the start of a workflow but it can also be changed at any stage.

Attributes are mostly used for two things: as a constant (defined once and not changing) or as a way to exchange a value between two workflow elements. You can lock an attribute (see the following screenshot) to make sure that the initial value can't be changed.

You can move an attribute to become an input or output parameter if you have created it in the wrong spot. Just right-click on the variable and choose the **Move as...** option.

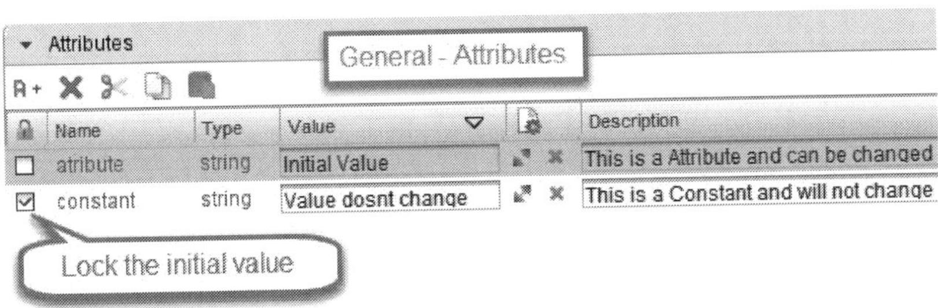

Variables in the input section

A variable in the input section is called an **in-parameter**. The content of an input variable is defined at runtime and entered by the user. Input variables cannot be changed during workflow execution directly, as you cannot assign an in-parameter as output of a workflow element. You can move an input parameter to become an attribute.

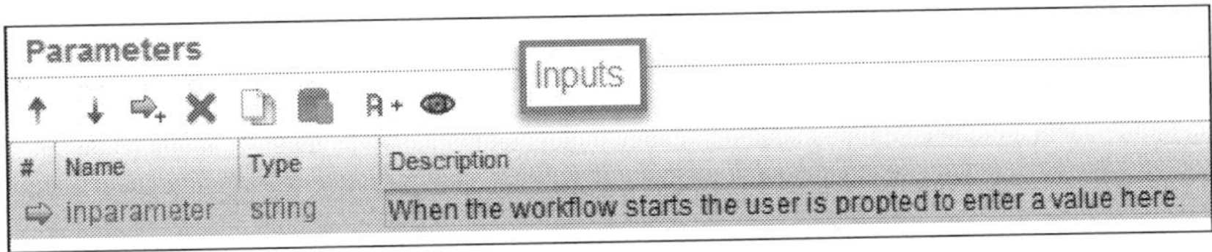

Variables in the output section

A variable in the output section is called an **out-parameter**. The content of an output variable can be defined within the workflow and is available to other elements when the workflow has finished. You can move an output parameter to become an attribute.

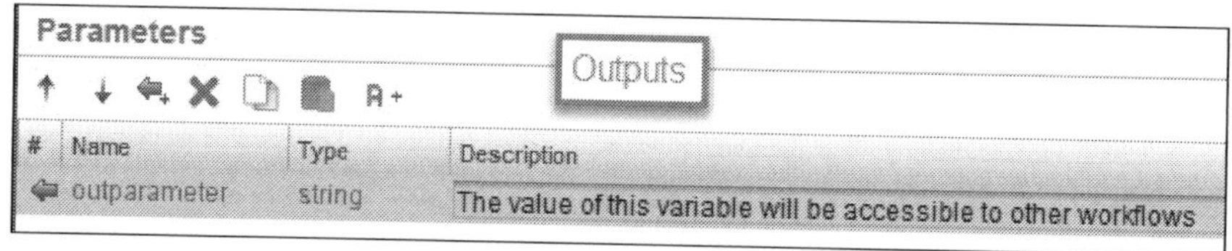

Variable types

There are many variable types that are already implemented in Orchestrator out of the box, but the basic variable types are as follows:

Variable type	Description
any	This can contain any content. It is used to carry variables to other elements that are not defined in the Orchestrator GUI, such as XML. Please note that this type should only be used if nothing else will do, as it has been known to mishandle some content, such as complex variables.
boolean	This has only two values, either True or False. However, Orchestrator uses Yes and No in the GUI.
credential	This contains a username and password. The password is encrypted.
date	This is used to store date or time in the JavaScript format.
number	This contains only numbers, which can be integers or real numbers. Everything is stored as floats in Orchestrator.
secure string	When entering values, *s will be shown instead of characters. The value is plain text and visible to the workflow developer but encrypted when the workflow runtime information is stored in the database.
encrypted string	This is like secure string , but the value is always encrypted.
string	This can contain any characters.
NULL	This is not really a type, but defining a variable as NULL means that anything that is put into it will be discarded.

In addition to the base types, each plugin will install its own type. These types are identified by their prefixes. For example, types that come with the vCenter plugin have the **VC:** prefix and types from the SSH plugin have the **SSH:** prefix.

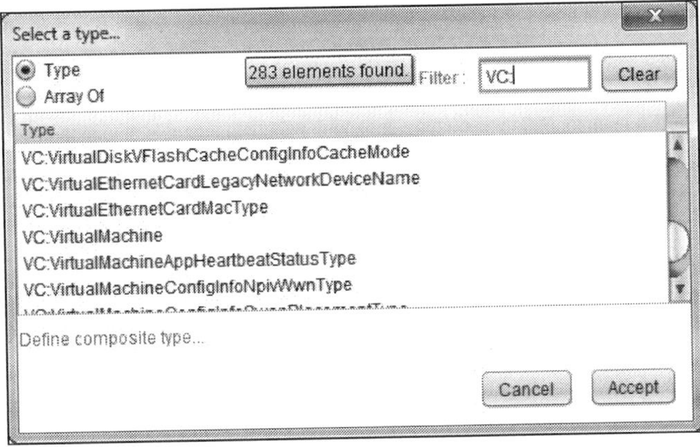

In JavaScript, you define variables using the `var` statement:

```
var variable name = new variable_type;
```

For example, `var myString = new String();`

Building arrays

Any variable type can be made into an **array**. An array is a container that holds multiple values of the same variable type. For example, an array of the variable type String can contain the values "Mum", "Dad", "Sister", and "Brother" whereas an array of VC: VirtualMachine will contain multiple VMs.

When defining a new variable, you can make it an array by simply clicking on **Array Of** (**1**) and then selecting the variable type (**2**). You can change an existing variable to an array (or the other way around), but any content in it will be lost.

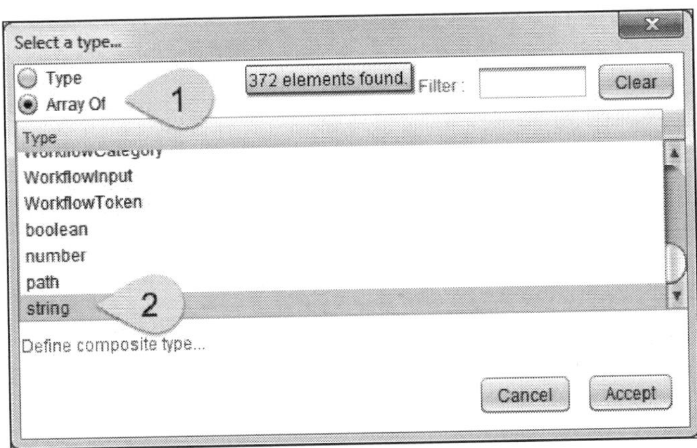

If you have an array as an in-parameter or an attribute, you can fill the array with content. The array entry window has quite a lot of functions:

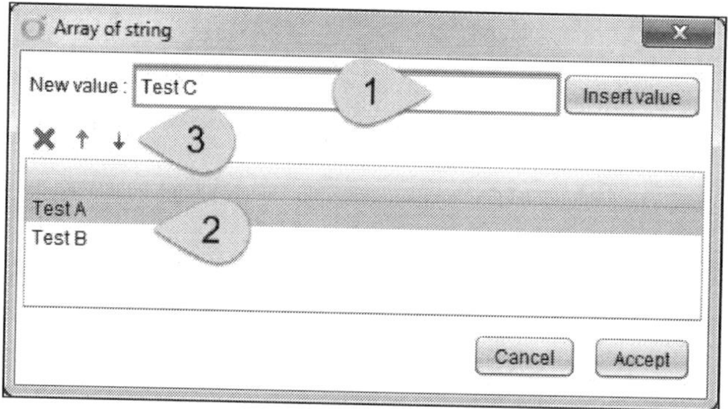

Enter a value in **1**. If this is a more complex type, such as a VM, then you will see an **Insert Value** link in the **New Value** field. After choosing or entering a value, click on **Insert value** to add it to the array.

The area marked as **2** shows the current content of the array, as well as the order these array elements are in. With the function buttons in **3**, you can sort the array elements as well as delete array elements. Do not forget to click on **Accept**, otherwise all entries or changes are lost.

In JavaScript, you define and set an array by defining its content:

```
var family = new Array("Mum", "Dad", "Sister", "Brother");
```

An array can also be defined in the following manner:

```
var family=["Mum", "Dad", "Sister", "Brother"];
```

Alternatively, if you want to initialize an empty array:

```
var family = new Array();
```

You typically access the content of an array via JavaScript. To access an array, you use square brackets `[ ]` and write in it the number of the elements you would like to access. Please note that the content count of an array starts from 0 (zero). For example, `family[2]` will return `"Sister"`.

To add a value to an existing array, use the push function `family.push("Aunt")`.

Workflow basics

In this recipe, we will work through the process of creating a workflow. We will see how to add and use variables as well as run a workflow.

Getting ready

We just need a working Orchestrator, and you will need the rights to create new workflows and run them. We will work with the Orchestrator Client.

How to do it...

We will break up the recipe into several sections.

Creating a new workflow

1. Open the Orchestrator Client and switch to the workflows.
2. If you haven't made a new folder yet, right-click on the root of the tree and select **Add Folder**.
3. Give the folder a name and click on **OK**.
4. Right-click on the new folder and select **New workflow**.
5. Give the workflow a name. The workflow will open in the edit mode.

Adding an attribute

1. Click on **General** and then scroll down to **Attributes**.
2. Click on A+. A new variable will be put under **Attributes** and named **att0**.
3. Click on **att0** and give the variable a new name, such as `text`.
4. Click on **String** under the **Type** column to change the variable type, but for this example, we leave it as **String**.
5. In the **Value** column, fill in some text, such as `Test`. Give it a description. A description isn't needed, but it's a best practice to document what this variable is used for.

Adding an input parameter

1. Click on **Inputs** and then on ➡+ .
2. Add an input parameter named `input` by following the same procedure as in *Adding an attribute*.

Note that you cannot define a value here, as it is defined during runtime.

Add an output parameter

1. Click on **Outputs** and then on ⬅+ .
2. Add an output parameter named `output` by following the same procedure as in *Adding an attribute*.

Note that you cannot define a value here, as it is defined during the workflow execution.

Adding a scripting element

A scripting element allows us to use JavaScript in it and manipulate the variables we have defined earlier.

1. Click on **Schema**.
2. Drag **Scriptable task** between the start and end symbols.
3. Hover the mouse on the scriptable task and then select the edit icon (the pencil icon).
4. Click on **In** and then the bind icon (see the following screenshot).
5. All in-parameters and attributes are displayed. Select the **input** variable as well as the **text** attribute you have created earlier.

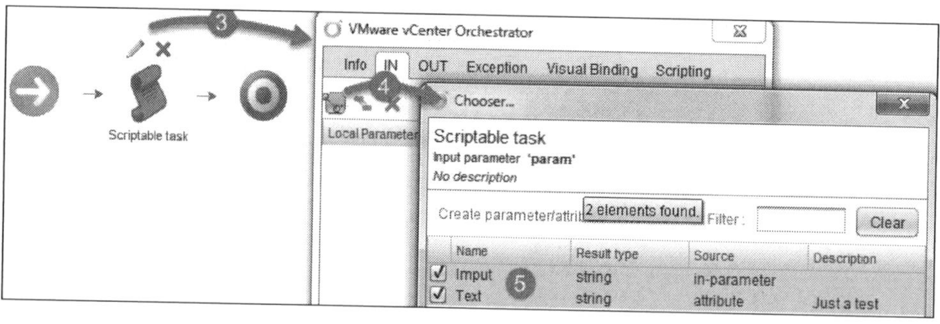

6. Click on **OK** and then **OUT**.

7. Follow the same method as the previous one to bind the output parameter **output** to the script element.
8. Click on **Scripting**. You will now see all the variables you have assigned to the scriptable task.
9. By clicking on a variable, you can insert it into the script. Make the following script:

```
output=input+text;
```

10. Click on **Close** to close the scriptable task.
11. Click on **Save and Close**.
12. You are asked whether you would like to increase the version history. Click on **Increase version**. See the *Version control* recipe in this chapter for more information.
13. Run the workflow by clicking on the **RUN** icon (the play button).
14. Enter a text for the input variable and click on **Submit**.
15. Check the result of the workflow by clicking on the workflow execution and then on **Variables**, as seen in the following screenshot:

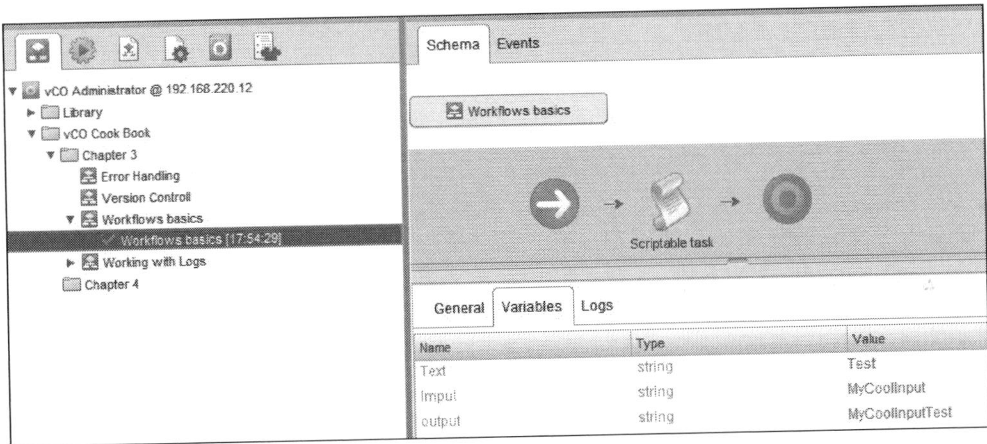

How it works...

In this recipe, we have introduced some very basic working methods that are essential for this chapter and the next chapter. Let's just discuss some more details we have glossed over.

Exiting a workflow

There are four buttons on the bottom of the edit workflow screen:

Button	Description
Cancel	Before exiting the edit mode, Orchestrator will display the **Save and Close** or **Close anyway** options. **Close anyway** will exit the workflow without saving any changes.
Revert	This reverts the workflow to the state when it was opened for edit. Be careful that it doesn't ask you whether you are sure.
Save	This saves changes to the workflow without exiting.
Save and Close	This will save all changes to the workflow and exit the edit mode.

Validation

When you are exiting the edit mode, Orchestrator will **validate** the workflow. This means that Orchestrator checks whether all the variables are assigned, they are not used, and a script contains errors. It also checks whether elements, such as other workflows, actions, configuration items, and so on exist. You can run the validation at any stage by just clicking on **Validate** in the schema.

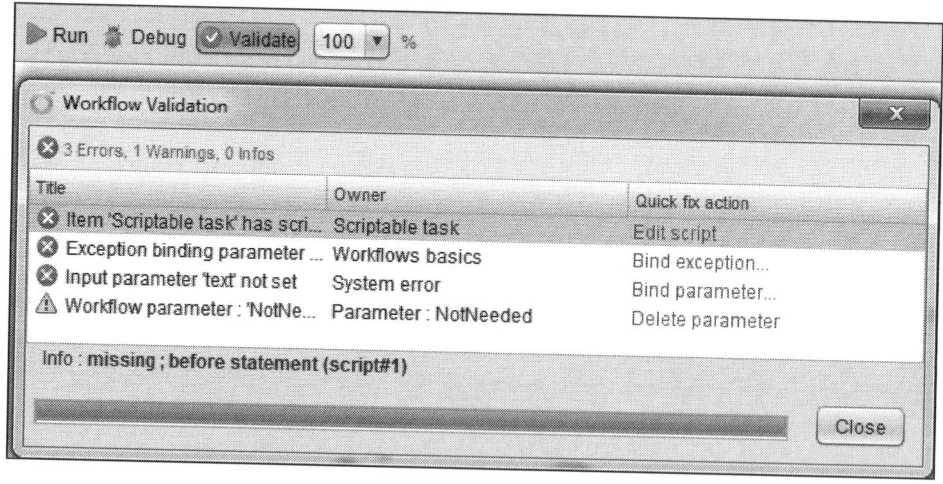

In the validation window, you will see each error or warning message (**Title**) and next to it, the element (**Owner**) that is the source of the problem; the **Quick fix action** link can be used to access the element and remedy the problem. You should always check the warning/error before using a quick fix action. For example, the quick fix action for an attribute that is not used in a workflow is **Delete parameter**, but maybe you have just forgotten to bind it as an input or output of one of the workflow elements, so first check before using the quick fix action. A typical example here is an attribute that is used for presentation purposes only.

Warnings can be ignored, whereas errors will result in workflows not being able to start. However, it's always best to resolve all issues.

Assigning a workflow variable

When you add an existing workflow, action, or workflow element to your schema, you will need to bind its input and output variables to your variables.

1. In a workflow, hover the mouse over an element and then click on **Edit** (the pencil icon).
2. Select **IN** and click on **not set** for any one of the variables.
3. You now can either select an already-existing variable, or create a new one by clicking on **Create parameter/attribute in workflow**.
4. You can choose whether you want to create an input (or output) parameter or an attribute. If you define an attribute, you can also assign it a value directly.

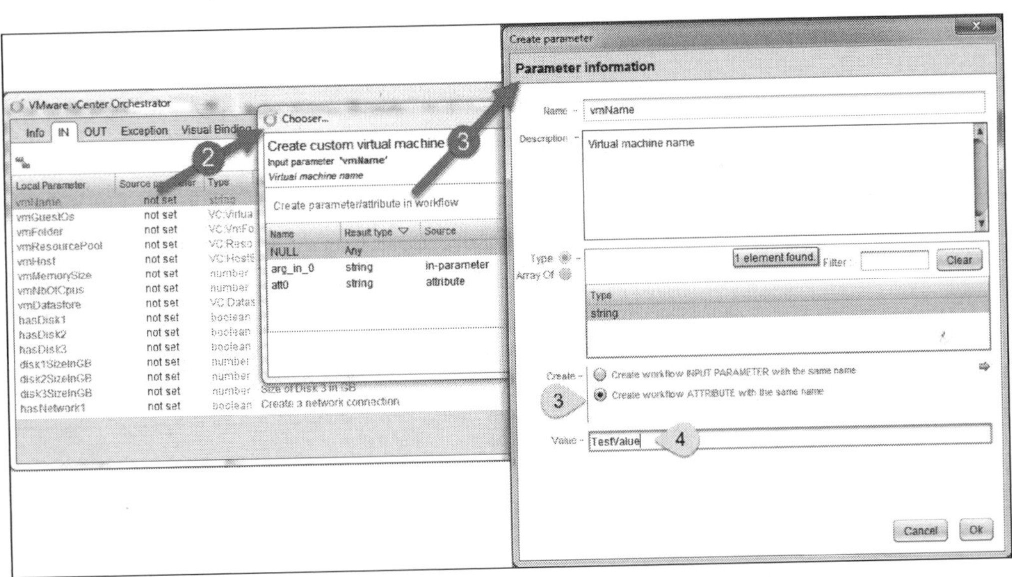

Re-run a workflow

You can rerun a workflow by either:

- Right-clicking on the workflow and selecting **Start last workflow run**
- Right-clicking on a workflow execution and selecting **Run again**

Also, you can run a workflow with other credentials by choosing **Start workflow as**.

See also

The example workflow 3.01 in the *Workflow basics* recipe.

We will discuss linking in the *Working with configurations* recipe.

Version control

In this recipe, we will look at how to use the Orchestrator version control and use it to control your software development.

Getting ready

A working Orchestrator is required, and you will need the rights to create new workflows and run them. We will work with the Orchestrator Client.

We need an existing workflow which we can play around with. In this recipe, we will use the workflow we have created in the *Workflow basics* recipe (3.01 in the example package).

How to do it...

1. Make a duplicate of the workflow we have created in the *Workflow basics* recipe.
2. Click on **General** and have a look at the current version (see the following screenshot).
3. Open the workflow for editing by right-clicking on it and selecting **Edit**.
4. Drag a system log element from the log section into the schema.
5. Edit the system log and bind the text in-parameter to an existing string variable as we have discussed in the *Workflow basics* recipe.
6. Click on **Save and Close** and then select **Increase version**.
7. The version counter in the General section should now been increased.
8. Click on **Show version history** to see an overview of all existing versions.

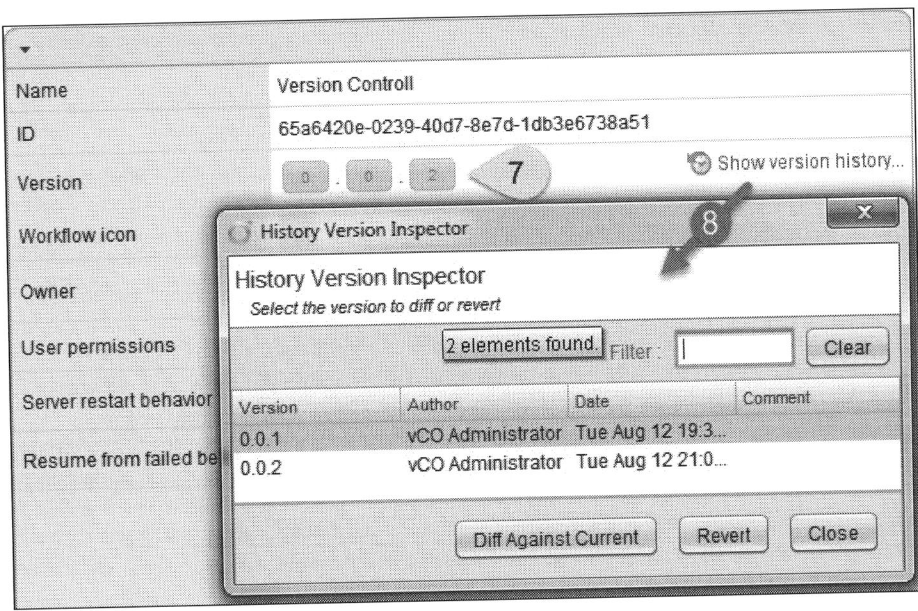

Showing differences between versions

You use this function to compare the differences between versions of a workflow.

1. On the workflow **General** tab, click on **Show version history**.
2. Select the version you would like to compare the present one against and click on **Diff Against Current**.
3. A window will pop up and show both versions next to each other. Resize the window as required.
4. When you are finished, click on **Close**.

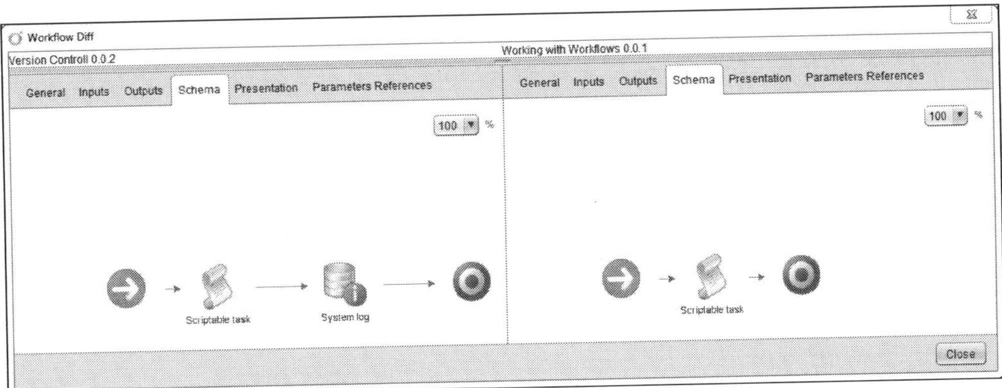

Reverting to an older version

1. Click on **Show version history**.
2. Select the version you'd like to revert to and click on **Revert**.

Your workflow is now of an earlier version, but the newer version is still available. You can also *revert* to a newer version if you wish.

How it works...

Version control is a very important tool in software development. It not only helps you keep track of your code development, but also helps you in other ways. For instance, when you import a workflow or a package, you can directly see whether the import is newer or older than the existing one. The other thing is that you can check versions against each other as well as revert to different versions. You can use the revert function to make duplicates of older versions.

You can manually increase the version by clicking on the version numbers directly (number 7 in the previous screenshot). It's always a good idea to write an update into the version log. Such an update should include what you have changed.

Version control is also available for Orchestrator objects such as workflows, actions, resources, configurations, policy templates and WebViews.

See also

The example workflow 3.02 Version Control.

Working with logs

In this recipe, we will look into how logging works in Orchestrator. You will learn how to create log entries and where they are stored.

Getting ready

We just need a working Orchestrator, and you will need the rights to create new workflows and run them. We will work with the Orchestrator client.

Additionally, we need administrative (root) access to the Orchestrator's operating system.

How to do it...

1. Create a new workflow.

2. Drag all log elements from the **Log** section into the workflow and arrange them as shown here:

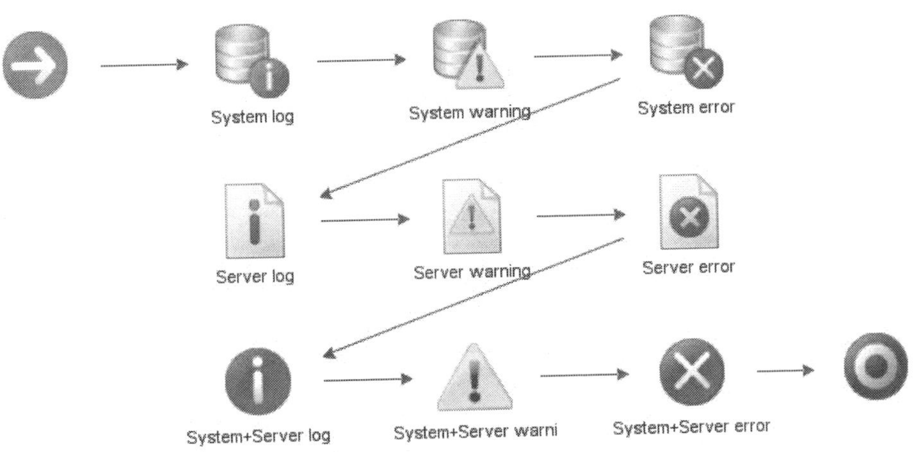

3. Create the following variables:

Name	Type	Section	Binds with
`logText`	String	IN	Transports error text
`logObject`	String	IN	Transports object text

4. Bind each log element with the required in-parameter.
5. Save and exit the workflow.
6. Run the workflow and enter two different phrases such as **LogText** and **LogObject**.
7. Check the result of the workflow by clicking on **Logs** as seen in the following screenshot. Also check the **Events** tab of the workflow.

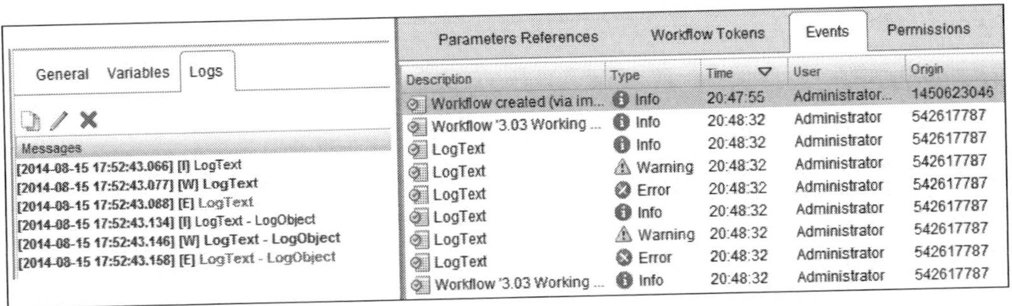

8. Check the log files of the server by logging into the OS of the Orchestrator Server and reading in the following log file:

Operating system	Path
Windows	`C:\Program Files\VMware\Orchestrator\app-server\logs\ scripting.txt` `C:\Program Files\VMware\Orchestrator\app-server\logs\ server.txt`
Appliance	`/var/log/vco/app-server/scripting.log` `/var/log/vco/app-server/server.log`

You should see the following entries:

Scripting	**2014-08-15 15:52:43.134+0000 INFO {vcoadmin:40285c8c47d921bb0147da5ef52f0041} [SCRIPTING_LOG] [3.03 Working with Logs (8/15/14 15:52:42)] LogText - LogObject**
Server	**2014-08-15 15:52:43.134+0000 [WorkflowExecutorPool-Thread-4] INFO {vcoadmin:3.03 Working with Logs:11975820-a84f-4037-9f06-0185e9f3c4d7:40285c8c47d921bb0147da5ef52f0041} [SCRIPTING_LOG] [Working with Logs (8/15/14 15:52:42)] LogText - LogObject**

Looking at the server logfiles, you'll see the additional information of what workflow (**3.03 Working with Logs**) was executed and also the Orchestrator user (**vcoadmin**) who executed it.

How it works...

Logs are an important tool for programmers as well as for system administrators. Log files help programmers understand where a program went wrong or show them the values of variables during runtime. For system administrators, log files help them keep track of who ran what workflow when.

In the logs that are generated by the execution of a workflow, you can copy the content (the copy icon), insert a `***` line (the pencil icon), or delete the whole log (the red X icon).

The main difference between server and system logs is that server logs are stored in the Orchestrator database and system logs are stored in the system's log files. The server log files get rolled as specified in the `log4j.xml` file, as shown in the *Redirecting the Orchestrator Syslog to an external Syslog server* recipe in *Chapter 2, Optimizing Orchestrator Configuration*. Server logs are stored with the workflow execution until purged depending on user settings (see the *User preferences* recipe in *Chapter 5, Basic Orchestrator Operations*). Server logs are persistent as they are stored in log files on the Orchestrator Server.

A log event can have four categories:

Syslog value	Debug	Info	Warn	Error
Workflow element	-	Log	Warning	Error
Logs	[D]	[I]	[W]	[E]
JavaScript	System.debug (text)	System.log (text)	System.warn (text)	System.error (text)
	Server.debug (text, object)	Server.log (text, object)	Server.warn (text, object)	Server.error (text, object)

Each of the four categories can be chosen at will. Any information that would be critical to troubleshoot a workflow several hours/days after it's run should be logged using the server.

Sending excessive logs to the server will dramatically increase the size of the Orchestrator database and slow down the orchestration engine performance, so it must be used wisely.

In JavaScript, using logs is quite a good way to fix bugs. A typical thing to do is to write out variables that exist only inside a script element, for example, `System.log("Mark")`, `System.log("Log: "+variable)`.

See also

The example workflow 3.03 Working with Logs.

The *Redirecting the Orchestrator Syslog to an external Syslog server* recipe in *Chapter 2, Optimizing Orchestrator Configuration*.

Error handling in workflows

This recipe is dedicated to show how to handle errors in workflows. We will learn how to catch errors and redirect them.

Getting ready

We just need a working Orchestrator, and you will need the rights to create new workflows and run them. We will work with the Orchestrator Client.

How to do it...

1. Create a new workflow. We will reuse this workflow in the *Resuming failed workflows* recipe in this chapter.
2. Add the following variables:

Name	Type	Section	Use
number	Number	IN	Used to create an intentional error

3. Assemble the workflow (as seen in the following screenshot) by dragging a scriptable task into the workflow and then a **Throw exception** element from the generic section *onto* the scriptable task. Add the two log elements to the workflow by just dropping them onto the lines.

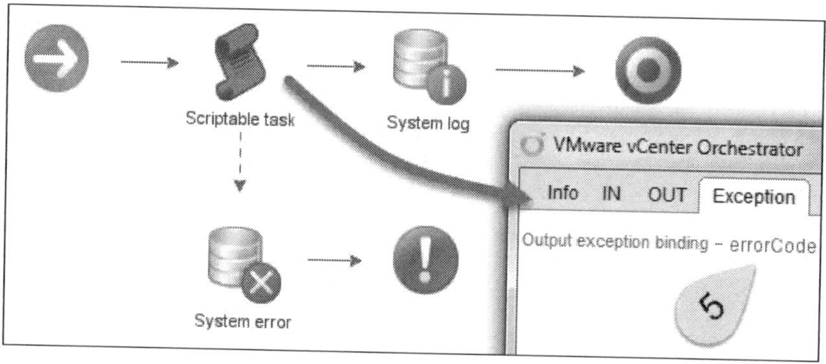

4. Bind the in-parameter to the scriptable task and add the following script that will throw an error when the value `5` is entered:

```
if (Number==5) {
    throw "Intentional Error";
}
```

5. In the scriptable task, click on **Exception**. You will find that Orchestrator has automatically created a new workflow attribute called **errorCode** of the `String` type and bound it to the **Output exception**.
6. Use the log elements to indicate in the logs which path has been taken. You can do this by removing the in-parameter `Text` in the Log element. In the scripting part of the Log element, replace the variable `Text` with something such as `"Normal Path"` and `"Error Path"`.
7. Save and close the workflow.
8. Run the workflow. If you enter `5`, the workflow will exit with an error. Check the workflow logs.

How it works...

Error handling is defined as a reaction to an error (an **exception**) when it occurs.

In automation, there are generally two types of handling errors, pushthrough and rollback. What this means is that you can either decide that you push on and try to resolve the error in the code, or that you roll back any change that you made to the system. It mostly depends on the task you are performing and exceptions you have.

In our little example, we intentionally created an error using the JavaScript command `throw`, as errors normally only occur when one doesn't need or want them.

Each Orchestrator element has an **Exception** section in which you can define an attribute of the type `String`, which will carry the error message that occurred in this element. In addition to this, each Orchestrator element has a blue line (normal execution) and red dashed line (exception).

We connected the red (exception) line to the **Throw exception** element to stop the further execution of the workflow, but we used a log element in between. Have a closer look at the workflow. You will notice that there is a red line from the scriptable task to the error log, but there is a blue line between it and the **Throw exception** element. What this means is that if an error occurs in the scripting, we fork the program into a new path. Instead of stopping the workflow in a "failed" state, we could have used other programing elements to resolve the error.

For example, if you have a workflow that creates a VM and the workflow fails with the error "not enough space", you can then use Orchestrator to attach an additional datastore and then rerun the created VM workflow.

There's more...

Lets have a look at how to ignore errors as well as what is new in vRO 6.0.

Ignore errors

It is also possible to ignore errors in a workflow. To do so, you just drag the red line to the same element that the blue line already points to. The result is a red and blue dashed line. This basically means that the workflow continues with or without an error to the next element. If you don't need the error message that will be generated, bind the exception to **Null**.

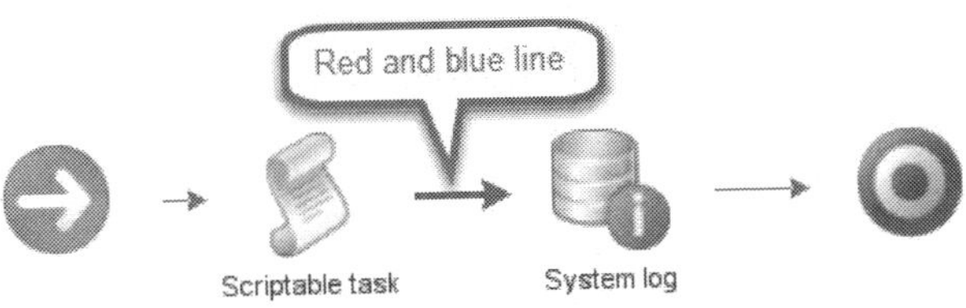

A typical example for this configuration is deleting a VM. If you want to delete a VM, it has to be stopped. The workflow, **Power off virtual machine and wait** will give an error if the VM is already switched off. To solve this, you can connect the blue and the red path of the **Power Off** workflow to the **Delete VM** workflow. This will make sure that a VM is powered off, and if not, then the error will just be ignored.

New in vRO 6.0 – default error handler

There is a new workflow element in vRA 6.0 that catches error, the default error handler. To use it drag the element onto the surface of the schema (not onto another element or a line).

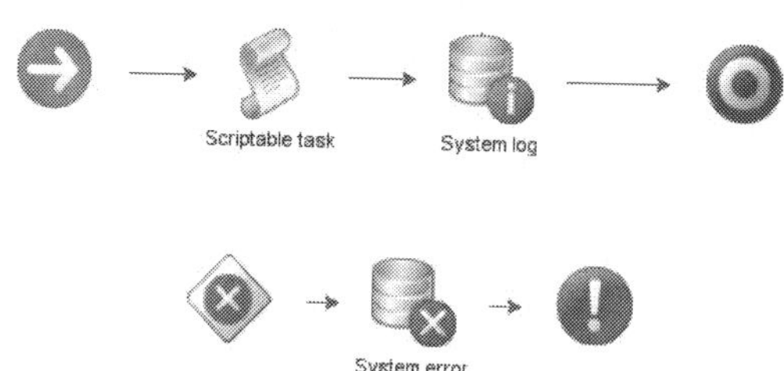

The default error element will catch all errors that are not handled by any other error handling process.

See also

The example workflows:

- 3.04.1 Error Handling
- 3.04.2 Ignore Errors
- 3.04.3 Default Error handler

Resuming failed workflows

This recipe looks at the ability to resume a failed workflow, which has been introduced in version 5.5. It allows you to resume a workflow when an error has occurred.

Getting ready

We just need a working Orchestrator, and you will need the rights to create new workflows and run them. We will work with the Orchestrator Client.

To make it easier, we reuse the workflow we created in the *Error handling in workflows* recipe in this chapter (3.04.1 in the example package). If you don't have it, please create it as described or use the example package that is supplied with this book.

How to do it...

1. Create a new workflow.
2. Drag **Workflow element** onto the schema and select the workflow we created in the *Error handling in workflows* recipe in this chapter.
3. Assign the in-parameter of the **Error Handling** workflow to the in-parameter of the workflow you have added in step 2.
4. Drop an additional **System log** instance before the workflow element and have it write something, such as `Beginning` into the log.
5. Drop a **Throw exception** element directly onto the workflow from step 2.
6. Click on **General** in the main workflow and then select **Enable** for **Resume from failed behavior**.

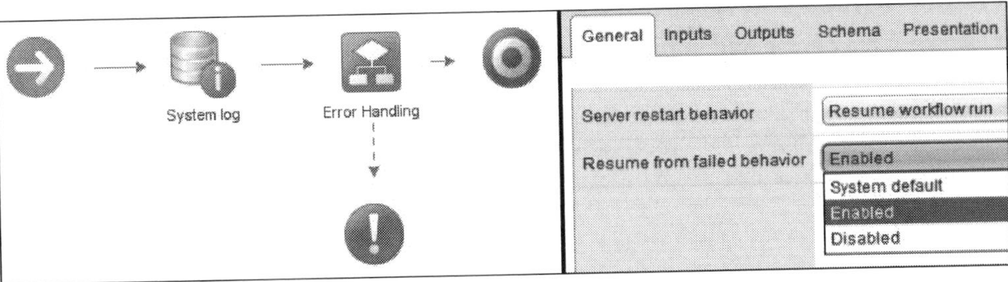

7. Click on **Save and Close**.
8. Run the workflow and enter `5` (this will result in an error). A window will now pop up and ask whether you would like to **Cancel** or **Resume** the workflow.

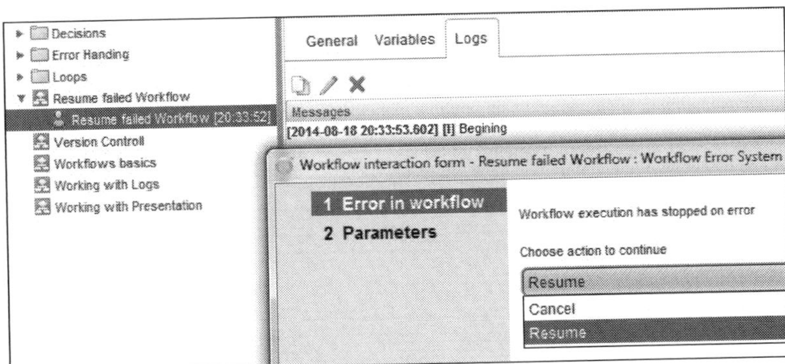

9. Choose **Resume**. You can now change *all* the variables of the workflow. Enter `2` and click on **Submit**.
10. The script now runs through as if nothing has happened. Check the logs.

Notice that the first log message `Beginning` and the log message from the **Error Handling** workflow was only written once, so the resume process would just rerun the scriptable task and not the whole workflow from the beginning.

How it works...

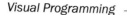

The ability to resume a workflow has been added to vCO 5.5 and is quite a powerful tool. Instead of rerunning failed workflows again, and in some cases roll back the previous operations, you are now able to resume at the same element the error occurred in.

Please note that in our little example we used a workflow inside a workflow, and the workflow that failed didn't have the resume action assigned to it. What this means is that you don't have to assign the resume action to all workflows, but just to the main one that calls all the others. Also, you see that only the failed element gets to be rerun, which in our case is the scriptable task inside the **Error Handling** workflow, not the whole workflow of error handling.

For example, you have a workflow that creates a VM, adds a virtual disk, and powers it on. If the workflow fails because you are out of disk space on the datastore, you would have to rerun the workflow again. This is especially true if some other application triggers the workflow via the Orchestrator API. Now, you can simply add the required disk space to the datastore and resume the workflow, or just use a different datastore.

However, you need to understand that you can only change variables or rerun the same failed element. If the error can't be remedied by a change of the variable content or by rerunning later, the resume function will not help you.

In addition to this, rerunning some failed elements can have very undesirable results. For example, if you add two items to a database using one scriptable task, the insertion of the second fails. You resume the workflow and the result is that you added the first item twice. So be careful.

The secret to the resume feature lies in the way that Orchestrator works. When a workflow is executed, Orchestrator writes checkpoints in its database before each step in the workflow is executed. These checkpoints consist of all variable values. This is why when you resume a workflow, you are presented with all the variables that exist in the workflow.

There's more...

The resume function is by default switched off system-wide. You can switch it on system-wide using the following steps:

1. You have to change the `vmo.properties` file that is located in the following locations:

Windows	`C:\Program Files\VMware\Orchestrator\app-server\conf`
Appliance	`/etc/vco/app-server/`

2. Set `com.vmware.vco.engine.execute.resume-from-failed=true`.
3. Additionally, you can define a timeout in seconds with `com.vmware.vco.engine.execute.resume-from-failed.timeout-sec`.

If you consider using the resume function, it is a good idea to define the timeout. The timeout defines how long a workflow waits in resume mode before failing. This feature can be used to make sure that workflows don't stay in resume mode indefinitely and that a human interaction can take place in a certain time frame.

I personally would caution switching on the resume feature system-wide, because as mentioned, not every workflow can or should be recoverable. Instead of switching on the resume feature system-wide, consider writing a good error response and making a general decision if you want to roll back or push forward.

See also

The workflow in 3.05 Resume failed Workflow.

Using the workflow debugging function

This recipe showcases how to use the debug feature to find and resolve errors in a workflow. The debug function was introduced in version 5.5.

Getting ready

We just need a working Orchestrator, and you will need the rights to create new workflows and run them. We will work with the Orchestrator Client.

We need a new workflow, and to make things easier we reuse some old workflows, such as the ones from the *Workflow basics* and *Error handling in workflows* recipes (3.01 and 3.04.1 in the example package).

How to do it...

1. Create a new workflow and add the workflows from the *Workflow basics* and *Error handling in workflows* recipes (as shown in the following screenshot).
2. Bind all variables as required.
3. Right-click on the first element of your workflow and select **Toggle breakpoint**. A blue ball appears on the left next to the element.
4. You can debug a workflow either while still in edit mode or when you exit it. Choose one and click on **Debug** (the bug icon) to start the debug process.
5. The debug process starts the workflow and will stop the execution on the first breakpoint. It will not execute the step the breakpoint is located on, but stops before it. Please note that you have access to all variables and logs during the debug process.

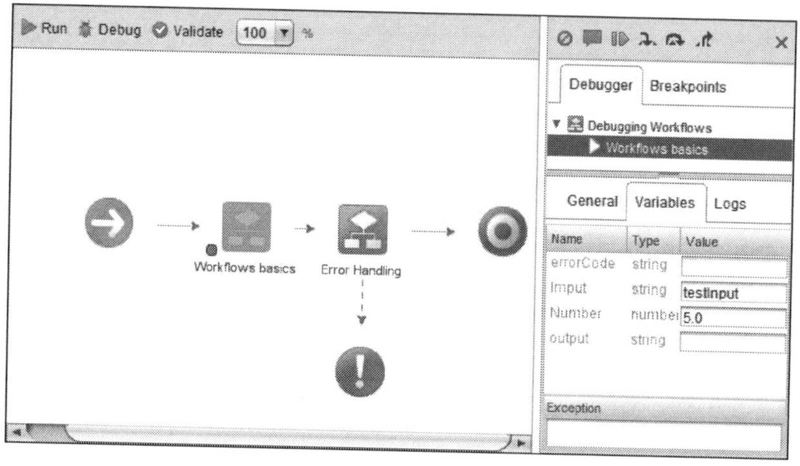

6. While debugging a workflow, you have the choices such as **Cancel**, **Answer**, **Resume** (*F8*), **Step into** (*F5*), **Step over** (*F6*) and **Step return** (*F7*). You can use the icons or the function keys to perform the said processing. See the *How it works...* section for more details.
7. Use **Step into** to work through the workflow.

How it works...

The debugging feature was introduced in vCO 5.5. Before this feature existed, debugging Orchestrator was quite a bit more complicated and mostly involved using logs to write checkpoints and display variable content. With the debugging feature, things are now fairly easy. The debugging feature ties in with the checkpoints that Orchestrator uses when it executes a workflow. Orchestrator writes all variable content to its database before it executes one step. These checkpoint variables are displayed in the debug process.

You can set multiple **breakpoints** in each script and advance to them directly using **Resume** (*F8*).

The following table shows all the actions you can take during debugging:

Cancel	This stops the workflow execution.
Answer	This answers an interaction that the workflow has issued.
Resume	This resumes the workflow until the next breakpoint.
Step into	This steps into an element and starts debugging inside the element. This can also be used to go to the next element.
Step over	This will step over an element. The debugging will not enter the element.
Step return	This steps out of an element. The debugging will continue with the main element.

There's more...

When you use complex variables such as arrays or objects (for example, a VM), then the content can be rather vast and won't be displayed in the **Values** section. In this case, have a closer look at the **Variables** screen. You will notice a small **i** icon before the variable value. Clicking on it will show you the content of the variable in a separate window. However, this doesn't work for all variable types. Properties and complex variables such as PowerShell output will not show up.

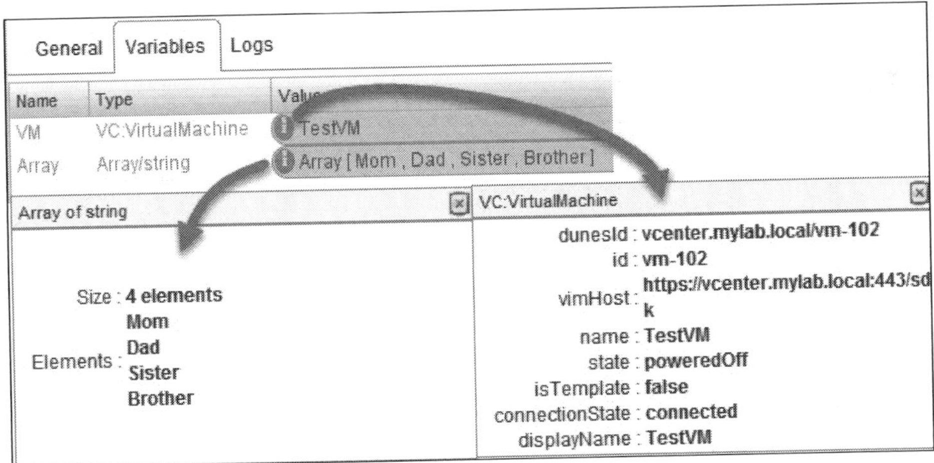

See also

The example workflow in 3.06 Debugging Workflows.

Working with decisions

In this workflow, we will see how decisions can be implemented with Orchestrator. You will learn how to create basic and custom decisions.

Getting ready

We just need a working Orchestrator, and you will need the rights to create new workflows and run them. We will work with the Orchestrator Client.

We need a new workflow where we can add a decision. You also should know how to work with logs.

For the Decision Activity element, we will be reusing the workflow we created in the *Workflow basics* recipe in this chapter (3.01 in the example package).

How to do it...

There are three decisions that can be used in Orchestrator; we will discuss each in the following sections.

Basic decision

The basic decision lets you check a single variable against a condition. A condition is always something that is either true or false. For example, the condition 5 > 3 is true, whereas the condition "Team" contains "i" is false.

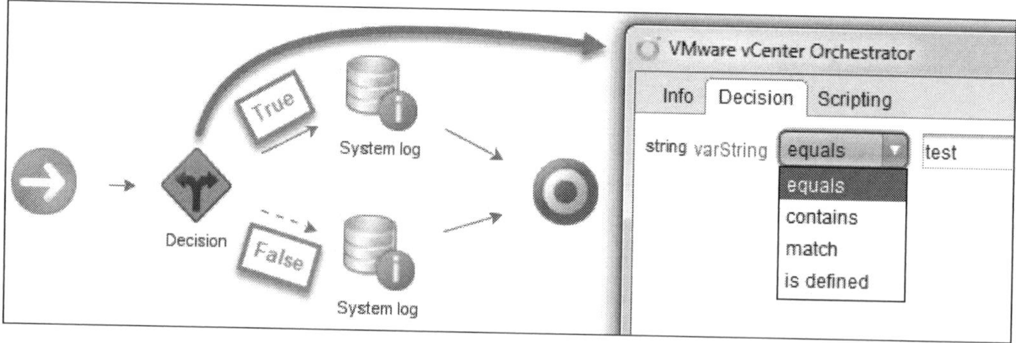

1. Create a new workflow and define an in-parameter of the `String` type.
2. Assemble the structure as seen in the previous figure. You will need to rearrange the lines of the workflow as shown in the introduction of this chapter.
3. Have the **System log** element write something like **True** (green line) or **False** (red dashed line) into the logs.

4. Edit the **Decision** element and click on **Decision**.
5. Choose a condition and set a value as seen in the previous figure. When done, click on **Ok**.
6. Save and run the workflow.

What happens is that the workflow will check whether the value entered fulfills the condition you have specified and then will fork to either the true or false path.

Try this out for several other variable types. Each variable type has other conditions with it. For example, the type `VC:VirtualMachine` has not only the name of a VM, but also its state (power).

Custom decisions

A custom decision enables you to check single variable or multiple variables against complex conditions using the JavaScript code.

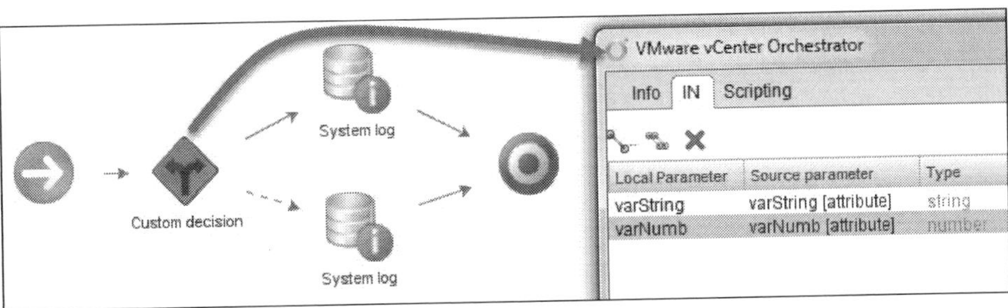

1. Create a new workflow (or reuse the last one) and define two in-parameters.

Name	Type	Section	Use
`varString`	String	IN	This contains a word
`varNumber`	Number	IN	This contains the length of the word

2. Assemble the structure as seen in the previous figure.
3. Have the **System log** element write something like true (green line) or false (red dashed line) into the logs.
4. Edit the **Custom decision** element and bind both in-parameter to **IN**.
5. Click on **Scripting** and enter the following script (see also the *How it works...* section of this recipe).

```
if (varString.length == varNumber)  {
    return true;
} else {
    return false;
}
```

6. Save and run the workflow.

When the workflow executes **Customer Decision**, it will compare the entered string's length with the entered number and then will fork to either the true or false path.

Please note that you have to use the JavaScript command `return` with either `true` or `false` to make this decision element work.

Decision activity

A decision activity lets you check the output of a workflow against a basic condition.

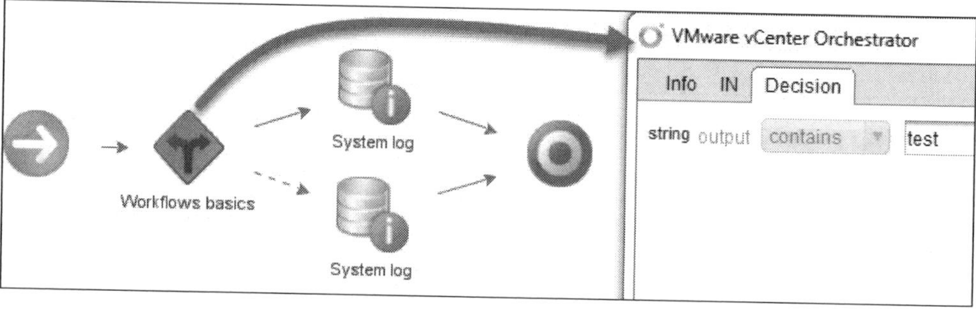

1. Create a new workflow (or reuse the last one) and define an in-parameter of the type `String`.
2. Assemble the structure as seen in previous figure. When you add the **Decision activity** element, you will be asked what workflow you want to use with it. For simplicity, we will reuse the workflow from the *Workflow basics* recipe in this chapter.
3. Click on **IN**. You will now see all the in-parameters of the workflow you selected. Bind the workflow input to the in-parameter you defined in step 1.
4. Click on **Decision**, choose one of the output variables of the workflow you selected, and then choose a basic condition you would like to test the output against. Click on **OK** when finished.
5. Have the **System log** element write something like true (green line) or false (red dashed line) into the logs.
6. Save and run the workflow.

When you run the workflow, the in-parameter you defined will be forwarded to the basic workflow and then the output of the workflow will be checked against the condition you have defined.

How it works...

Decisions are a commonly-used tool in programming. Each of the three decision types lets you fork your workflow into different areas.

The **basic decision** is on itself easy to use and powerful, as it doesn't require you to use any JavaScript. The previous example showed you which conditions are possible for the type `String`, but each variable type comes with its own pool of conditions.

The **custom decision** is useful if your decision depends on things that the basic decision doesn't cover or more than one variable is needed to make a decision. It requires you to use JavaScript, but you also gain a lot more agility.

The **decision activity** checks one output of a workflow against a basic condition. It is commonly used to check whether a workflow produced a certain result. The decision activity can be substituted by the following schema:

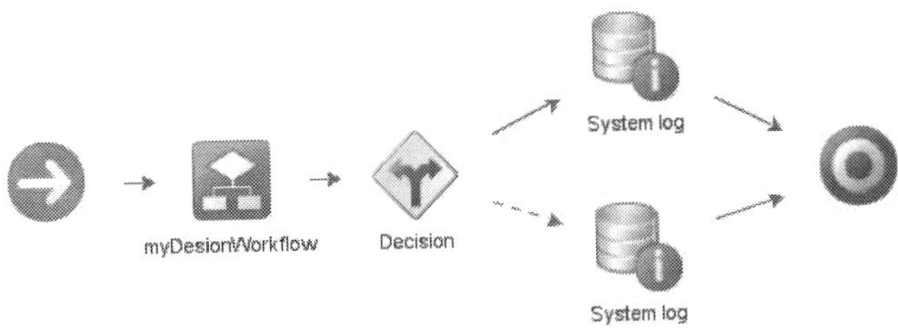

The major difference is that you won't have to use an attribute to "park" the output of the workflow and then use this attribute in the basic decision. However, a decision activity is good only for a single variable and a basic condition. If you need a more complex condition or multiple variables, you would need to build the preceding schema and use a custom decision element.

JavaScript – if and else

As we already saw in the *Custom decision* section, the JavaScript code for an `if` statement isn't that difficult. It is made up of operators and the `If-cause` itself. The form looks like this:

<table>
<tr><th>Statement</th><th>Example</th></tr>
<tr><td><pre>if (condition) {
    code block
} else if (condition) {
    code block
} else {
    code block
}</pre></td><td><pre>if (varString == "test") {
    return true;
} else {
    return false;
}</pre></td></tr>
</table>

The condition is made up of a statement that is either true or false. This statement is built using operators. The operators that JavaScript knows are the following:

and	or	not	Equal	Not equal	Smaller	Bigger
`&&`	`||`	`!`	`==`	`!=`	`< <=`	`>= >`

As an example, if you want to know whether the number that is stored in the variable `A` is bigger than 5, the conditional statement will be `(A > 5)`.If you want to know whether the string stored in the variable `Text` equals "Hello", the statement will be `(Text == "Hello")`.

You can glue conditions together with the `&&` (and) and || (or) operators as well as normal breaks `( )`. For example, if `A` is bigger than 5 and `Text` is "Hello", the conditional statement will look like this: `((A>5) && (Text == "Hello"))`.

There's more...

In this section, we go a bit deeper and show how a `case` or `switch` statement is built with the Orchestrator schema and JavaScript.

Switch case in the schema

Sometimes, you might like to check a variable for multiple conditions and fork to different parts. A typical example is you check a `String` variable that contains the OS type against Red Hat, SUSE, Windows 2008, or Windows 2012 and then fork to different parts of the script, as shown in the following example:

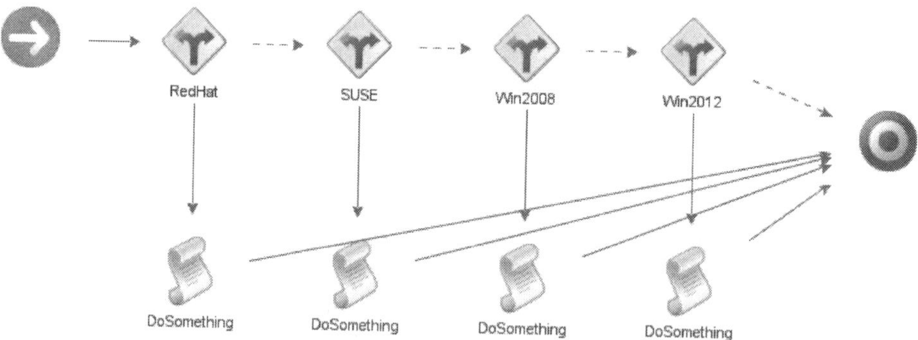

The following steps will help you generate a `switch` statement as seen in the preceding figure:

1. Create multiple decisions that are linked through the false path. The true path is connected to the different option paths.
2. Then, connect the options back to the main path.

It is easier to just use a scripting element and with the JavaScript command `switch` (see the following section) and then output the values you need, but sometimes a structure like this is needed. A typical example is that you want to fork to different parts depending on the VM operating system. You need different provisioning workflows for Linux as compared to Windows or other OSes. This function helps you create these structures. For an example, see the Orchestrator library workflow **Clone virtual machine from properties**.

New in vRO 6.0 – Switch element

A new feature was introduced in vRO 6.0, the Switch element. This element introduces multiple choices. Just drag a blue arrow from the Switch element to the case element and then enter a basic condition.

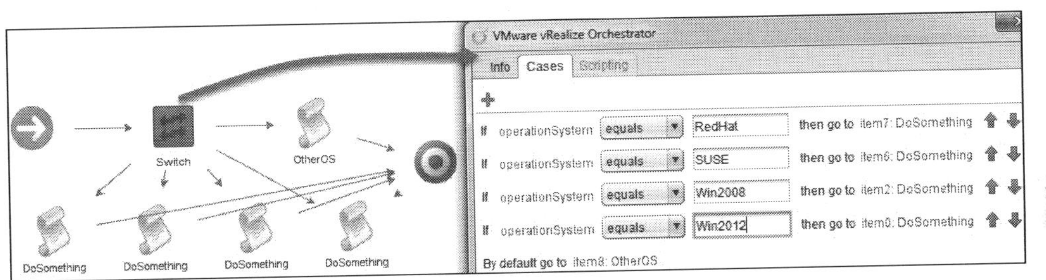

JavaScript – switch

The `switch` statement in JavaScript looks like this:

Statement	Example

`Switch (expression) {`
`    case condition:`
`        code block`
`        break;`
`    default:`
`        default code block`
`}`
	`Switch (GuestOS) {`
	`    case "RedHat":`
	`        SCSI="LSi Logic";`
	`        break;`
	`    case "Win2008":`
	`        SCSI="Paravirtual";`
	`        break;`
	`    default:`
	`        throw "Unknown OS";`
	`}`

In `expression`, you fill in the variable you would like to check, and in the `case condition:` part, you fill in the condition you want to check against. Please note that you can only check the equals (==) condition with the switch statement. The `default:` part is used if all other tests fail.

See also

Example workflows:

- 3.07.1 Basic Decision
- 3.07.2 Custom decision
- 3.07.3 Decision activity
- 3.07.4 Case

Working with loops

Here, we will explore how to create loops with Orchestrator. You will learn how to build loops and use them.

Getting ready

We just need a working Orchestrator, and you will need the rights to create new workflows and run them. We will work with the Orchestrator Client.

You need to understand how decisions are used in Orchestrator, as it was explained in the *Working with decisions* recipe.

For the **For Each** element, we will be reusing the workflow we created in the *Workflow basics* recipe in this chapter (3.01 in the example package).

How to do it...

There are several types of loops one can create, however they can all be reduced to the following two basic types of loops.

The decision loop

This basic kind of loop runs until a certain condition is met. We will build a so-called `for` loop in this example. A discussion about the different types of decision loops (for, do-`while`, and `while-do`) can be found in the *How it works...* section of this recipe.

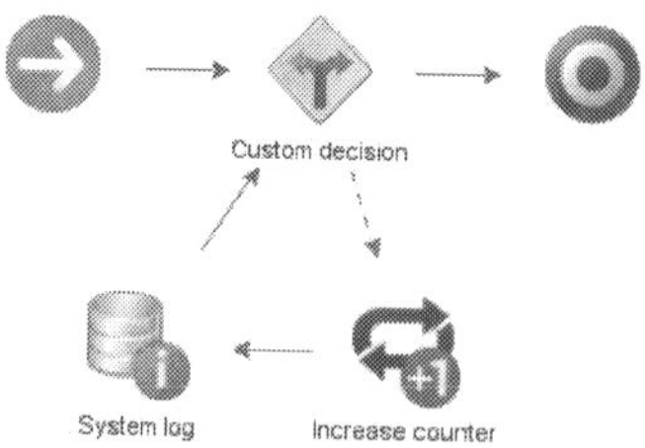

1. Create a new workflow and build the preceding schema.
2. Add the following variables:

Name	Type	Section	Use
number	Number	IN	This is used to stop the loop
counter	Number	Attribute	This has the value 0 and counts the loop iterations

3. Assign the **counter** attribute the initial value 0.
4. Bind the **counter** attribute to the **IN** and **OUT** sections of the **Increase counter** element.
5. Bind the text in-parameter of **System log** to the counter. This will write the current count into the logs.
6. In the **Custom decision** element, bind the counter and the in-parameter to the **IN** section.
7. In the **Scripting** section, enter the following script:

```
if (number == counter) {
    return true;
} else {
    return false;
}
```

8. Save and run the workflow.
9. The workflow will run as many times as the value entered.

What happens is that the decision will check whether the attribute counter is equal to the value entered, and if it is not, the loop will run and increase the counter by one.

The For each loop

A `For each` loop will repeat one workflow with different inputs. As input, you must select an array.

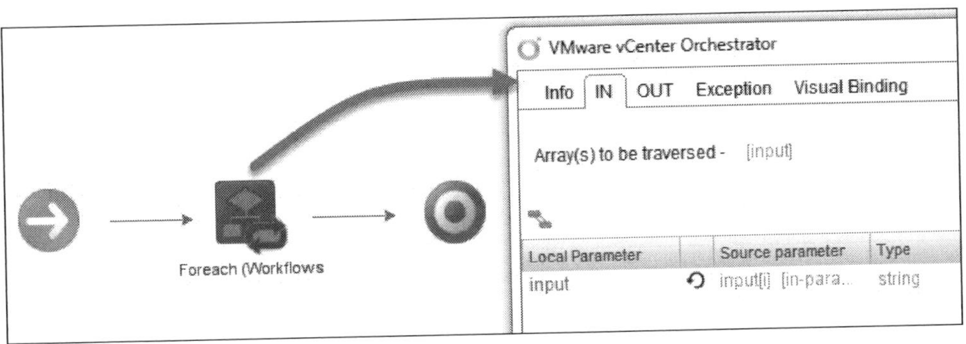

1. Create a new workflow and create the following variables:

Name	Type	Section	Use
input	Array of String	IN	This is an array of input variables
output	Array of String	OUT	This is an array of output variables

2. Drag the `Foreach` element onto the schema. You will be asked what workflow you want to use with it. For simplicity, we will reuse the workflow from the *Workflow basics* recipe in this chapter.
3. Open the `Foreach` element in the **IN** section. You will see that the input is already bound. If in another workflow, you want to choose another iterator, click on **Array(s) to be traversed** and choose another array and bind the variable.
4. Bind the output variable.
5. Save and run the workflow.

When the workflow runs, you will be prompted to enter values into an array. The basic workflow will run for each element you have entered into the array. The result of each run will be stored in the array.

Have a look at the *There's more...* section about how to deal with exceptions in the `Foreach` element.

How it works...

Loops are a very common tool in programming. They enable programs to go through repetitions. The two basic types we have introduced are different in the way they work. Decision loops use a condition to terminate, whereas the `For each` loop terminates when all elements of the input have been processed.

An example of a decision loop is a loop that checks for e-mails with a certain subject every minute. The loop in this example is actually a combination of a `do-while` loop and a `for` loop at the same time. The double loop is done to make sure the loop doesn't run forever. After 10 runs, the loop will terminate.

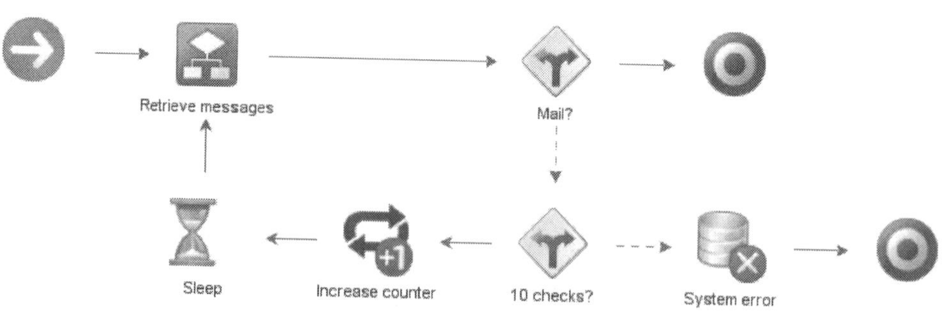

The classic example for a `For each` loop is the renaming of multiple VMs. You would define in one array the VMs you want to rename and in the other the new names.

Types of decision loops

There are three types of decision loops:

`for`	A counting variable is used to count the number of runs. The loop terminates when the count has reached a predefined value.
`do-while`	An action is performed, and after that, the result of the action is checked against a condition. As in the previous e-mail example, we check whether the e-mail has arrived. This loop will run at least once.
`while-do`	This is the same as the do-while loop, except the check is performed before any action is taken. If the check is true, the loop will not be run.

Foreach and arrays

The `Foreach` element needs arrays for input and for output. However, if you create a normal (non-array) variable in **General** or **Input**, you can add it as an input parameter for the `Foreach` element, meaning that this would be a static value for all runs of the `Foreach` element. Please note that you still need at least *one* array as input.

An example for this discussion is the creation of 10 VMs that all have the same attributes except their name. You would use a `Foreach` loop on the Create VM workflow and the VM name would be an array, and all the others would be normal attributes.

If you want to add an attribute array to a `Foreach` element, then you need to follow these steps:

1. Add the arrays to **Array(s) to be traversed**.
2. Your arrays are now selectable when setting them.

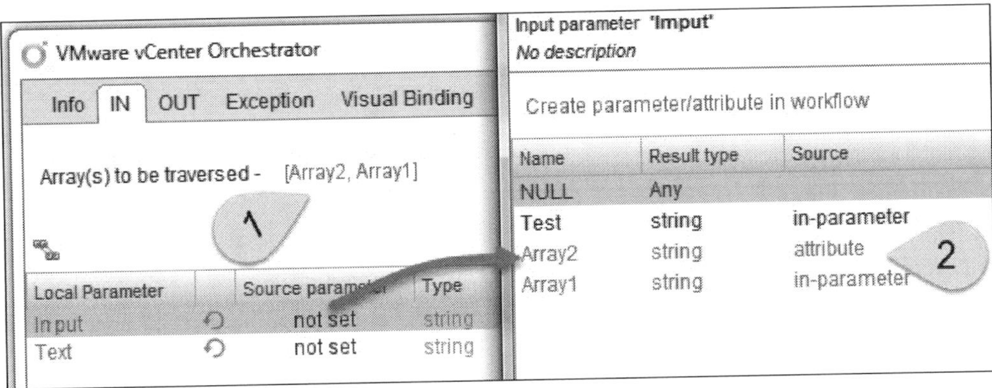

JavaScript

JavaScript has the following loops:

	Statement	Example

`for`	`for (start,`
	`  condition,`
	`  increase) {`
	`    code block;`
	`}`
		`for (i = 0; i < 5; i++) {`
		`    System.log(i);`
		`}`

`while`	`while (condition) {`
	`    code block;`
	`}`
	
	`do {`
	`    code block;`
	`}`
	`while (condition);`
		`Var i = 0;`
		`while (i < 10) {`
		`    System.log(i);`
		`    i++;`
		`}`

`for each`	`for each (variable in array) {`
	`    code block;`
	`}`
		`for each (day in week) {`
		`    System.log(day);`
		`}`

This is straightforward. `condition` is like any other condition we explained in the *Working with decisions* recipe in this chapter. `code block` is any JavaScript code you would like to implement. The only thing that might need a bit of explanation is `for each`. The `(variable in array)` part defines a new `variable` that is filled each time with a new element from the `array`. For example, if we have an array that contains the days of the week, each time the loop is run, the `day` variable will be filled with another day.

There's more...

When handing exceptions with the `For each` loop, there are some extras you might find useful. Just adding the output exception will stop the `For each` loop as soon as an error occurs. If you activate **Catch any exception and continue with the next iteration**, the `For each` loop will not stop, but will continue. Additionally, you can add code that will be executed each time an exception happens in the loop. You have access to all the in-parameters of the `For each` loop, but also the `$index` variable, which contains the current iteration of the loop.

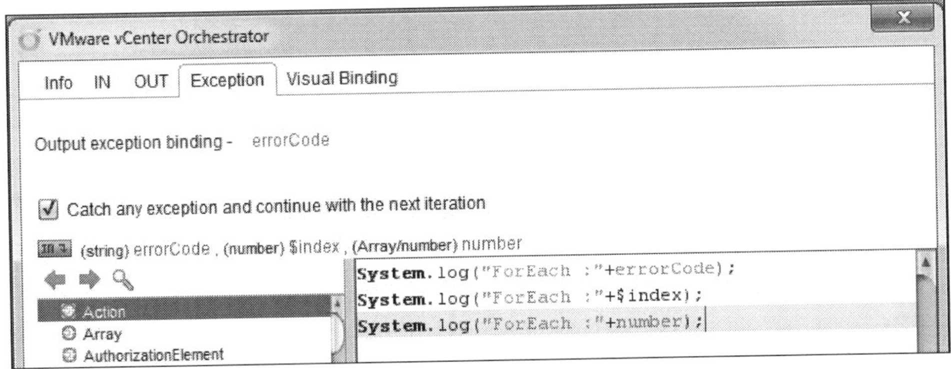

See also

The example workflows:

- 3.08.1 Decision-Loop
- 3.08.2 ForEach-Loop
- 3.08.3 DoWhile-Loop
- 3.08.4 ForEach-Exceptions

Working with presentations

In this recipe, you will learn how to configure the input window (the presentation) and make it more user friendly. You will learn how to link values, hide inputs on conditions, as well as use predefined answers.

Getting ready

We just need a working Orchestrator, and you will need the rights to create new workflows and run them. We will work with the Orchestrator Client.

How to do it...

We will split this recipe into several sections. We will only create a presentation, not a "working" workflow.

Preparation

This preparation is just so that we can see some results.

1. Create a new workflow following variables:

Name	Type	Section	Use
number	Number	IN	This is used for presentation
string	String	IN	This is used for presentation
boolYesNo	Boolean	IN	This is used for presentation
input	Array of Strings	IN	This is used for presentation
text	String	IN	This is used for presentation
selection	Array of String	Attribute	This fills this array with string in the order: first, second, third,...
length	Number	Attribute	This sets the value to 8

2. Create a log task and assign all the variables to it. This is just so that the validation of the workflow will work.

Description

1. Switch to **Presentation** and click on the first variable you see.
2. Click on **General** and enter some text into **Description**.

Each element in the presentation has a **General** tab with a **Description** field. In this tab, you can enter text that will be displayed when the workflow runs. Each in-parameter automatically gets the name of the respective in-parameter in **Description**. You can, and probably should, change this to a bit more meaningful description.

The description is interpreted as HTML but not all tags work; however, `<br>`, `<u>`, `<b>`, `<i>`, `<l>` and `<a href>` work quite well.

There is a way to include the content of a simple variable in **Description** of a variable. Just add the variable in the `${variableName}` form.

In-parameter properties

You can add to each in-parameter a list of different properties to change the presentation. We cannot discuss all the properties in this recipe, just the basic ones (see also the *Linking actions in presentations* recipe in this chapter).

1. Click on **Presentation** and onto one of the in-parameters.
2. Click on **Properties** and then on **Add property** (the blue triangle icon).

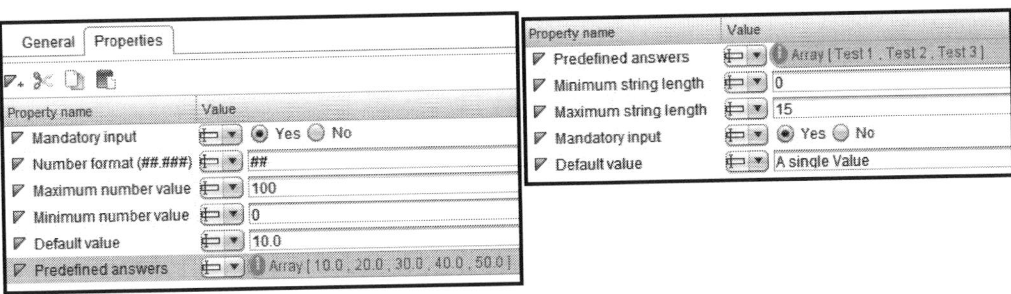

3. You can now add various properties that can differ for each variable. Go and try them out.

Default value	This is a value that is displayed when the input window is displayed.
Predefined answers	This is a list of elements that you can select from. A drop-down list will be displayed.
Minimum	This is the minimum length/value. You will receive an error message if you exceed the maximum.
Maximum	This is the maximum length/value. You will receive an error message if you are under the minimum.
Mandatory input	The user has to enter a value before the workflow can be started. An error will be displayed if this variable is empty (NULL).
Number format	This defines a format in which numbers are displayed.
Matching regular expression	This uses a regular expression to check the content. An error is displayed if the content isn't part of the regular expression.
Multi-lines text input	This displays a larger text window instead of one line, where more text can be entered.

4. Make some settings and run the workflow to see the results. I really recommend that you play with the properties shown in the preceding table. Have a look at the example workflow 3.09 Working with Presentation.

Steps and groups

Steps and groups let you sort inputs by themes, such as one page for general parameters and one for advanced inputs.

1. In **Presentation**, click on the root element presentation.
2. Click on **Create new Step** (the paper icon).
3. A new step is added to the end of the presentation tree. Give it a new name by double-clicking on the step, typing a new name into the textbox, and pressing *Enter*.

4. Now, click on the Boolean value and hold and drag it under the new step. Move at least three more variables underneath this step.
5. Create a second step and drag all the rest of the variables underneath it.
6. Now, we add a group. Click on the first step you created and then on **Create Display Group** (the yellow bar icon).
7. A new group has been added; you can rename the group as required and press *Enter*.
8. Now, drag variables under the group.
9. Create another group and drag some other variables underneath it.
10. Run the workflow. I would also recommend some playtime with this feature.

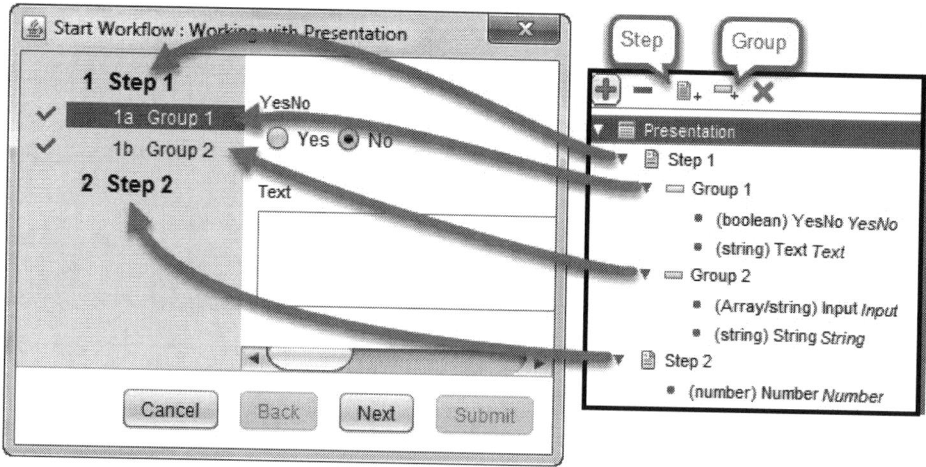

Hide input values

To make the input window even more user-friendly, it's sometimes better to hide some inputs, steps, or groups if they are not used. For example, a step that contains advanced parameters can be hidden.

1. In **Presentation**, make sure that the Boolean in-parameter is the first one in the presentation tree.
2. Add the **Default value** property to it and set it to `True`.
3. Click on the second step you created and add the **Hide parameter input** property.
4. Click on the pencil icon on the right of the hide property. A pop up will appear; select the Boolean variable and click on **Accept**. Note that the variable is now shown in the `#[variableName]` format. You can also enter directly the value as `True` or `False`.

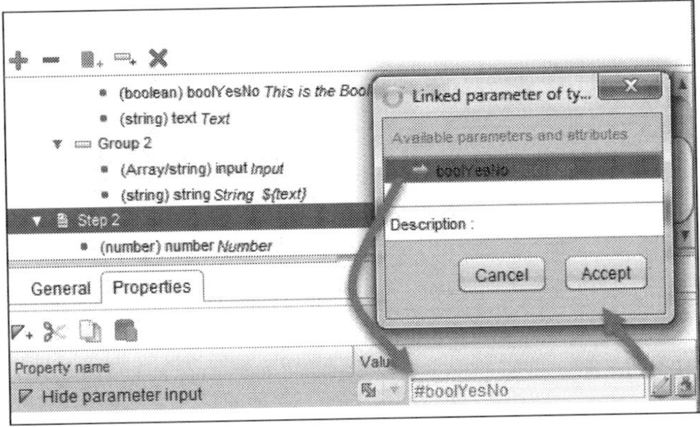

5. Repeat these steps to link a hide property to a group and to an in-parameter variable.
6. Run the workflow. Change the Boolean value to `false` and watch the results. All elements that have the hide-property will respond to the value change in the Boolean value.

Basic linking

We actually have already used linking in the instruction to hide inputs, now we will dive a bit deeper. Linking can help you create drop-down boxes or define default values.

1. Click on **Presentation** and then select one of the string in-parameters.
2. If you have not already done so, assign it the **Maximum string length** property.
3. Now, click on the drop-down menu in front of **Value** and select the yellow arrows (**dynamic binding**). The box icon represents the **static binding**.
4. You will see that the **Value** field changes. Click on the pencil icon (Help editing OGNL), and in the pop-up window, you will see all the variables (attributes and in-parameters) that can be used in this field. Select the **number** attribute and click on **Accept**.
5. Select a string in-parameter in **Presentation**, assign it the **Predefined answers** property, and link it to the array of strings attributes.
6. Run the workflow and test out the results.

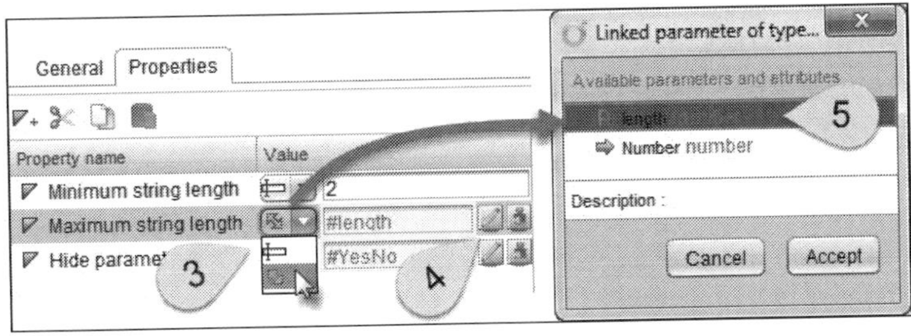

How it works...

The presentation section of a workflow allows us to change the general layout of the input window that a user encounters when he starts the workflow. With the different properties that can be defined, it is easy to create a presentation that helps the user interact with the workflow and make sure that he enters the correct (or expected) values. This can dramatically reduce the amount of errors a user is able to cause by making incorrect entries. A typical example of this is to provide the user with a list of predefined answers they can choose from, making sure that only the correct values are entered.

We haven't discussed all the properties that are available. The *Linking actions in presentations* recipe in this chapter will showcase some others in more depth.

In the previous example, we linked several properties to different variables. If you have a look at the value field, you will notice that Orchestrator will use the # symbol to mark a variable. In the example workflow, we used a Boolean named `boolYesNo` that shows up in the hide-property as `#boolYesNo`. The entries that we can make in these value fields follow **OGNL** (**Object-Graph Navigation Language**). We will have a closer look at OGNL in the *Linking actions in presentations* recipe in this chapter.

Plugin-specific properties

Certain plugin objects (such as the vCenter plugin) come with additional properties that can be extremely useful. We will now have a look at the most commonly-used properties that come with the base plugins.

select value as

The `select value as` property has three choices: **Tree**, **List**, and **Dropdown**. This property makes it easier to manage what the input of an object looks like.

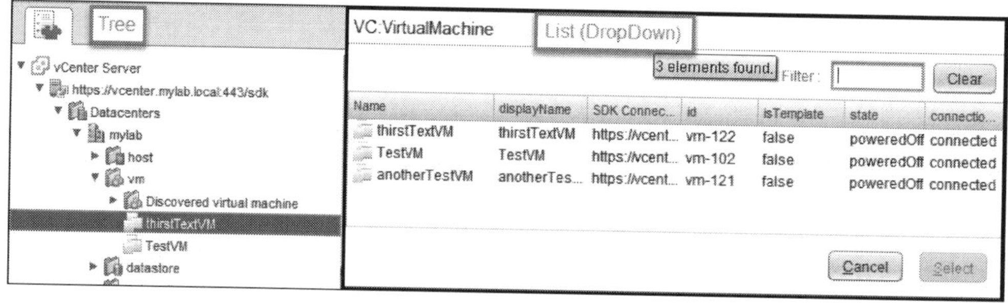

Show in inventory

The `show in inventory` property is quite a powerful property. When you start a workflow from vSphere Web Client, the object you started the workflow on will be passed to the workflow as an in-parameter. We discuss this in more detail in the *Orchestrator and the vSphere Web Client* recipe in *Chapter 5, Basic Orchestrator Operations*.

This property also makes the workflow accessible from the Orchestrator inventory. This means that you can right-click on an object in the inventory and then select a workflow to be executed on to it.

Specify a root object to be shown in the chooser

This setting lets you define a certain start point for your searches. For example, if you choose an ESXi cluster as the root element, then a user can only select objects under this cluster. To use the root element, you need to link an action or a variable to this property. The following is an example:

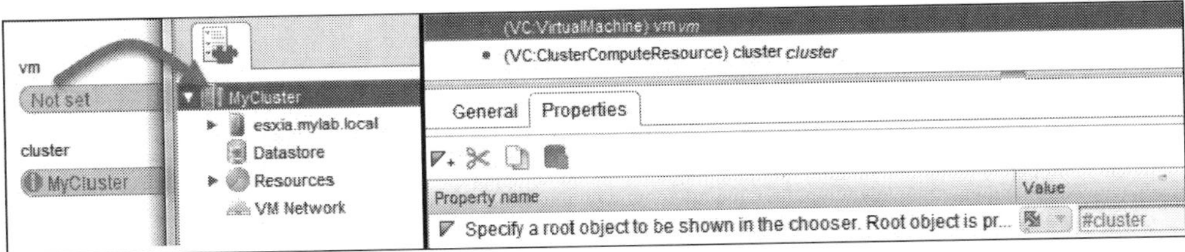

Authorized only

Adding this property to an in-parameter will make sure that only an authorized user can access this in-parameter.

There's more...

When trying to hide things, there are two more methods you can use. First, there is the **Show parameter input** property. Linking this property to a Boolean will make sure that an element is visible when true.

The second thing is that you can use the JavaScript operator `NOT` to change the behavior of the hide-property. The `NOT` operator in JavaScript is the **!** symbol. Just put `!` before the variable, for example, `#boolYesNo` will become `!#boolYesNo`. This will mean that an element will be hidden when the Boolean `#boolYesNo` is `false` instead of `true`.

See also

Learn regular expressions at the following links:

- `http://regexone.com/`
- `http://regex.learncodethehardway.org/book/`

The example workflow 3.09 Working with Presentations.

The *Integrating Orchestrator workflows in vRA* recipe in *Chapter 7, Working with VMware Infrastructure*.

Working with configurations

In this recipe, we will see how configurations can improve our design. Configurations are like global variables that are centrally defined and can be used by all workflows.

Getting ready

We just need a working Orchestrator, and you will need the rights to create new workflows and run them. We will work with the Orchestrator Client.

We just need to be able to create a new workflow and a new configuration.

To make things easier, we will reuse the workflow from *Working with presentations* (3.09 in the example package).

How to do it...

We will split the recipe in two sections, the creation and the usage of a configuration.

Creating a configuration

1. Using the Orchestrator Client, click on **Configurations** (the white paper with a gear icon).
2. Right-click on the top element and create a new folder. Give the folder a name. It's always a good idea to use new folders.
3. Right-click on the new folder and select **New element**. Give the new element a name. The new configuration opens up in the edit mode. Click on **Attributes**.
4. Now, we can create new variables as we used to in a normal workflow. Create the following variables:

Name	Type	Value(s)	Use
`selectionList`	Array of String	First, Second, Third	This represents a selection list
`passwordLength`	Number	8	This limits the amount of letters that can be entered

5. Click on **Save and Close**.

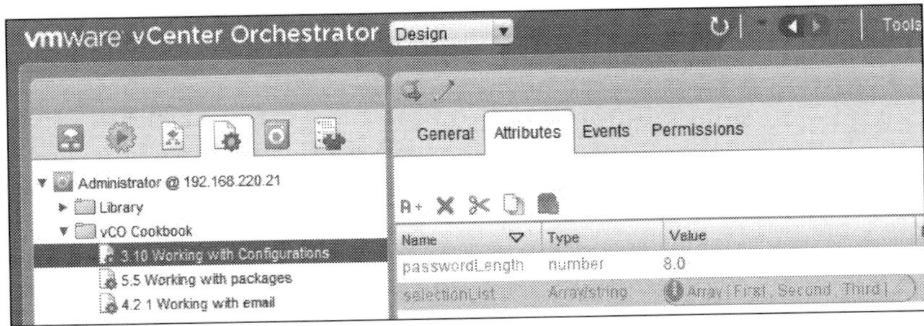

Using a configuration in a workflow

We will now make use of the variables we created in the configuration.

1. Using the Orchestrator Client, either make a duplicate of the workflow from *Working with Presentations* or edit it.
2. Click on the **selection** attribute and click on the two blue arrows right next to value (see the following screenshot).
3. In the window that pops up, you will find all the configurations that Orchestrator knows; click on the one you created.
4. You now see all the variables that you have defined in this configuration; please note that only the ones that match the current type are black and selectable, all others are grayed out.
5. Select the array of strings and click on **Select**. See how the value of the attribute has changed and now it points to the configuration.
6. Link the **length** attribute to the configuration element of the same name.

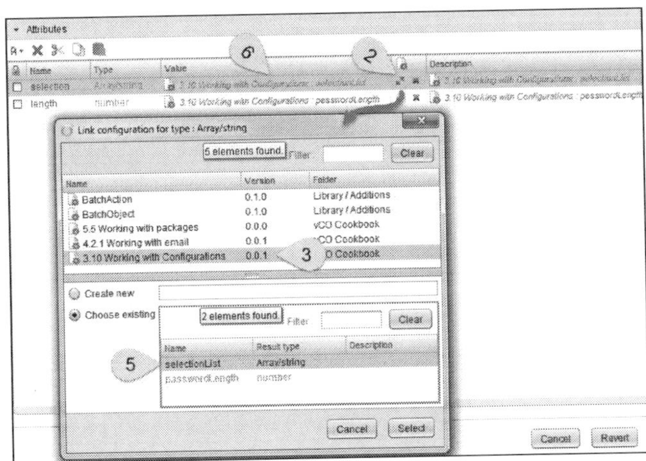

7. You are now able to use the values from the configuration inside the workflow. Give it a go.

How it works...

A configuration is what programmers would call a global variable. A global variable is a centrally stored variable that is accessible to all workflows. Configurations are commonly used to define global objects, for example, the FQDN and credentials of a mail server or general password policies.

Let's look at a typical example for the usage of configurations. You have a Dev environment and a Prod environment. In each environment, you have different vCenters, mail servers, and so on. You develop your workflows in Dev and then use them in Prod. Using configurations, you can point the workflow to different configurations that are stored in Dev or Prod Orchestrator.

Another example is to reduce the number of input a workflow requires by pushing the variables to configurations. We will explore this in the recipes in *Chapter 7, Working with VMware Infrastructure*. Last but not least, you can use configuration to share the same variables between different workflows, such as mail server configurations.

To integrate a configuration into a workflow you have to link an attribute to the configuration variable. The variables have to be of the same type. After you integrated the configuration attribute into the workflow, you can use it to not only pass information along (such as credentials or common server names) but also link presentation properties (such as predefined values to reduce the possible selections). We will explore this in the *An approval process for VM provisioning* recipe in *Chapter 7, Working with VMware Infrastructure*.

You also can create new attributes in a configuration from a workflow. You probably noticed the **Create New** selection in the **Link Configuration** window.

Please note that a configuration also has a history like the workflows do; see the *Version control* recipe in this chapter for more information.

There's more...

You can use JavaScript to read and write configuration values. The scripting classes are as follows:

- `ConfigurationElement`
- `ConfigurationElementCategory`
- `Attribute`

To read a configuration, you can use this:

```
Attrib=configurationElement.getAttributeWithKey(Key);
```

Here, `Key` is a string, which contains the name of the attribute. The return value is of the type attribute.

To set a configuration attribute, use this:

```
configurationElement.setAttributeWithKey(Key, Value);
```

Here, `Key` is a string that contains the name of the attribute and `Value` is the value you would like to set.

See also

The example workflows:

- 3.10.1 Working with configurations
- 3.10.2 Read and write configurations

Example configuration 3.10.1 Working with configurations.

The *An approval process for VM provisioning* recipe in *Chapter 7, Working with VMware Infrastructure*.

Working with actions

In this recipe, we will take a look at actions and their differences to workflows as well as their creation and usage.

Getting ready

We just need a working Orchestrator and you will need the rights to create new workflows and actions as well as the right to run workflows. We will work with the Orchestrator Client.

JavaScript arrays will be used; so, you should read the introduction to this chapter.

How to do it...

We split this recipe into two sections, the creation and the implementation of an action.

Creating a new action

1. In the Orchestrator Client, click on **Actions** (the gray gear icon).
2. Right-click on the top level (the orange icon) and select **New module**.
3. Give the module a name that is based on either your URL or the type of work you intent to do with it. For example, I chose `com.packtpub.Orchestrator-Cookbook`.
4. Right-click on the module you created and select **Add-action**.

5. The name should be descriptive and tell a user directly what it does. For this example, I chose the name **getElementFromArray**.
6. Click on **Add Parameter** (the yellow right arrow icon) and add the following variables.

Name	Type	Values
`number`	`Number`	This is the number of array elements that should be returned
`array`	`Array`	This is the array that contains all elements

7. Now, click on **void** directly to the right of **Return type** and select `String`.
8. In the scripting field, enter the following code:

```
return array[number];
```

9. Click on **Save and Close**.

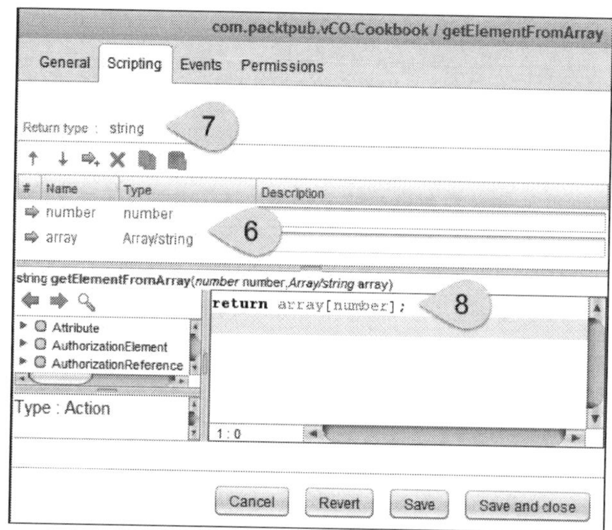

You created your first action.

Implementing an action into a workflow

1. Using the Orchestrator Client, create a new workflow.
2. Drag **Action element** (out of **Generic**) onto the schema. In the **Choose Action Dialog** field, enter the beginning of the name of the action you have just created. As you type, you will see the list of objects to choose from decreases. Alternatively, you can also use the **All Actions** section and browse through the existing actions.
3. Add the **getElementFromArray** action to the schema.

4. Create and assign the following variables to the action:

Name	type	Variable type
`number`	`IN`	This is a number
`array`	`Attribute`	This is an array of String values such as Mon, Tue, Wed, Thu, Fri, Sat, Sun
`output`	`Out`	This is a String value

5. Click on **Save and Close** to save and close the workflow and run the workflow.

When you now enter a number during workflow execution, the output will be one of the days of the week.

How it works...

Actions are what programmers would call functions. There are multiple differences between a workflow and an action; the main difference is that an action can only return *one* variable whereas a workflow can return multiple variables. Another is that actions are pure JavaScript-based and do not contain any visual programming. Actions can still call other actions; however, you will need the JavaScript command `System.getModule([Module]).[Action]([in-parameter])` to call them. As you can see, an action is called using its module name while a workflow is called (for example, via the API) using its ID. This is a rather important difference, as renaming an action is hard because its name, and maybe the module name, must be changed everywhere.

In an action, in-parameters are defined the same way as in a workflow; however, the return type is a bit different. The return code is always one variable and its value is assigned using the JavaScript `return` command. If you don't want or need any return code, define the return code as `void`.

Binding an action into a workflow can be done just as you would integrate any workflow—by dragging the **Action element** onto the schema. When binding the out-parameter of an action, you will notice that the name that is displayed in the action element is ActionResult. Your attribute or out-parameter that is bound to the return value of the Action element should be named something more meaningful.

Another thing that is important for good programming is the name of the action and the module you place it in. Browse through the existing action modules to explore how other programmers have done it.

A good recommendation is to start the name with a verb, such as get, set, create, delete, and so forth. Then, describe what the action is doing. A good way to make the name more readable is to capitalize each word (except the first). Examples of good naming are startVM, removeAllSnapshots, and getAllVMsOfVApps. If you need more information on this, check the JavaScript style guide at `http://javascript.crockford.com/code.html`.

Exploring the existing action library, you will find a lot of useful actions that are precreated and can be used in your own workflows.

See also

Example workflow 3.11 Working with actions and the getElementFromArray action.

Linking actions in presentations

This recipe will show how to further improve and automate the presentation in workflows by linking actions into the presentation. This is done to present to the user only a specific list of options derived on runtime.

Getting ready

We will create a new workflow and reuse the action we created in the *Working with actions* recipe in this chapter (see the `com.packtpub.vCO-Cookbook` module in the example pack).

You should be familiar with the topics we introduced in the *Working with presentations* recipe in this chapter.

How to do it...

1. Using the Orchestrator Client, create a new workflow.
2. Create the following variables:

Name	Type	Section	Use
string	String	IN	This is a placeholder for the linked action
number	Number	IN	This is used to select a value from an array
Array	Array of String	Attribute	This can take values such as Mon, Tue, Wed, Thu, Fri, Sat, Sun

3. Create a log element and bind all variables so that the workflow validation will succeed.
4. Click on **Presentation** and then select the string in-parameter.
5. Add the **Data binding** property to the string in-parameter.
6. On the **Data binding** property, click on **Link action** (the purple puzzle piece icon).
7. In the pop-up window, in the filter, enter the name of the action you want to use. We will use `getElementFromArray`.

8. Click on the action; underneath it, you will see the in-parameters that this action requires. You might also notice that each in-parameter can take either a **Static** value (the white rectangle icon) or an OGNL-linked parameter (the yellow arrow icon).
9. Bind the number and the array in-parameter to the action and click on **Apply**.

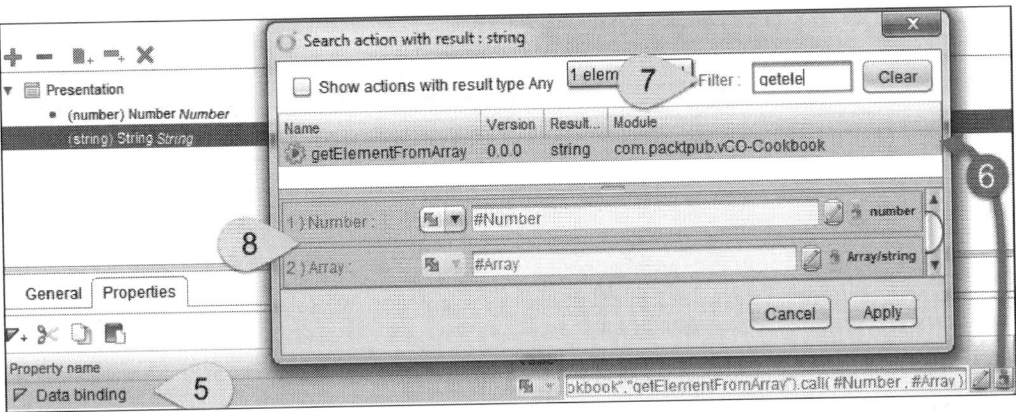

10. Save and run the workflow.
11. Enter a value between 0 and 6 into the **Number** field and see how the value of the string fields changes.

How it works...

Basically, Orchestrator uses OGNL to create the interaction with an action. OGNL is used most commonly with the Apache webserver to enhance presentations; however, VMware has deprecated the full use of OGNL in Orchestrator from version 4.1 onwards; the only remains are the variables and the ability to call actions. Variables are identified with a leading # symbol and the action call is `GetAction([Module],[Action]).call([in-parameters])`. You can use action linking for a lot of things. A typical example is that you use an action such as getAllVMsOfVApps to display a list of **Predefined list of elements** for a user to select a VM from.

The in-parameter property **Data binding** makes sure that values in the presentation are updated as soon as the value that it is bound to changes. If you use other properties, such as **Default value**, the value might not be updated instantaneously in the presentation.

There are a couple of predefined OGNL variables that Orchestrator recognizes and can become useful:

`#__username`	This is the username of the user that started the workflow
`#__userdisplayname`	This is the full name of the user (if available) that started the workflow.
`#__serverurl`	This is either the IP or the name of the Orchestrator Server on which the workflow was started
`#__datetime`	This shows the current date and time
`#__date`	This shows the date current date at midnight
`#__timezone`	This shows the time zone configured in the Orchestrator Server that started the workflow

In addition to linking variables, you can also directly insert values using `#`. For example, instead of referencing a Boolean in **Hide parameter input**, you can also just add the value directly. Just enter the value as `true` or `false`.

See also

Example workflow 3.12 Linking actions in presentations.

Waiting tasks

This is a recipe that will make you wait for it...

Getting ready

We need a new workflow and time!

How to do it...

There are two different kinds of wait tasks—tasks that wait for a duration and tasks that wait for a specific date and time until they proceed.

Creating help task

We need to create an action to help us track time. It will just log the current date and time.

1. Create a new action and call it `getNow`. There is no need to define any in- or out-parameter.

2. In the script section, place the following script:

```
var current = new Date();
System.log(current);
```

Using the Sleep task

1. Create a new workflow.
2. Drag a **Sleep** task onto the schema and create the **SleepTime** in-parameter as input for the workflow.
3. Add the **getNow** action we have just created before and after the Sleep task.
4. When running the workflow, check the log. You will notice how the workflow will wait for the allocated seconds.

Waiting for a date

1. Create a new workflow.
2. Drag a **Wait until date** task onto the schema and create the **waitDate** in-parameter as input for the workflow.
3. Add the **getNow** action we have just created before and after the **Wait until date** task.
4. When running the workflow, check out the log. You will notice how the workflow will wait until the allocated date and time.

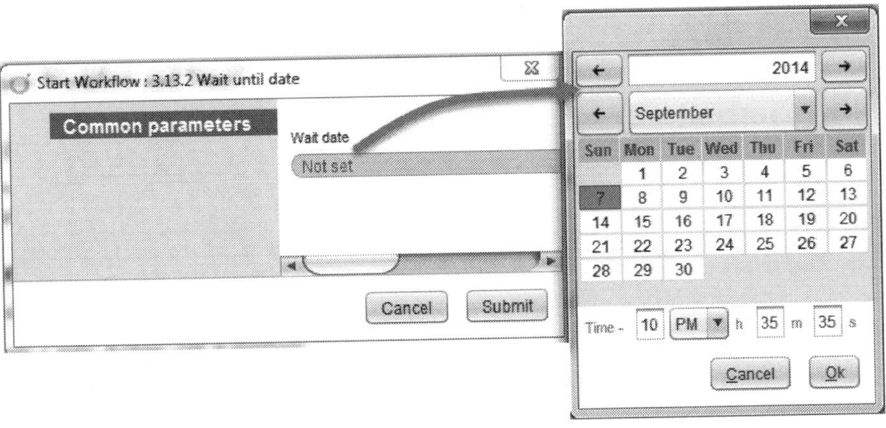

How it works...

A wait task will pause the workflow execution for a certain amount of time. The main difference between a **Sleep** task and a **Wait Until** task is the amount of system resources that are used for waiting.

The **Sleep** tasks will just wait; however, it will still require memory and one thread per sleep task. The **Wait until** task is more specific in how it saves system resources. When the **Wait Until task** starts, the workflow is saved to the Orchestrator database and is woken up again on the specified date and time. Orchestrator uses a single thread to deal with the all the workflows that are set to wait until a certain date/time. This preserves quite a bit of resources.

This leads us directly to the most important usage for wait tasks, long-running workflows. If a workflow is running for a long time, such as polling for new e-mails or waiting for a user interaction, a wait task can reduce the amount of system resources consumed during the wait period.

There are actually two waits for date tasks, one in **Generic** called **Waiting timer** and the other in **Basic** called **Wait until date**. Both are essentially the same.

There's more...

Let's have a look at how wait tasks work in JavaScript.

JavaScript – wait

The JavaScript commands for waiting are `System.sleep([milliseconds])` and `System.waitUntil([Date],[Number of milliseconds])`.

Please note that the `sleep` command is working with milliseconds, whereas the **Sleep** schema element is working with seconds.

The `waituntil` command has two inputs: the date and the number of milliseconds. The milliseconds define the delay time between two checks too see whether a certain date has been reached. Also, the command returns a Boolean value that is true when the wait has finished.

All JavaScript wait tasks will not save any system resources as the schema tasks do.

JavaScript – working with dates

Just a few words on working with the **Date** type in JavaScript. Working with date is easy if you understand how it works. Basically, date counts the milliseconds since January 1, 1970 (in 1970, UNIX was released). If you want to read or set the time, its best to use the methods that are encapsulated with the type.

	Values	Read	Write
Day in the week	0-6	`getDay`	`setDay`
Day of the month	1-31	`getDate`	`setDate`
Number of month	0-11	`getMonth`	`setMonth`
Year	For digit year for example, 1970	`getFullYear`	`setFullYear`
Milliseconds since 01.01.1970		`getTime`	`setTime`
Seconds	0-59	`getSeconds`	`SetSeconds`
Minutes	0-59	`getMinutes`	`setMinutes`
Hours	0-23	`getHours`	`setHours`

It is also important to know that if you set a workflow attribute of the `Date` type, it is null (it doesn't contain the current time or the time you started the workflow); however, if you set a date as a workflow in-parameter, you will automatically see the current date and time when you try to define it.

To initialize a `Date` attribute, you can bind it to an action to do it for you. Create an action with an out-parameter of the `Date` type and the following script:

```
var current = new Date();
return current;
```

This action will set an existing attribute to the current time when the action is invoked. See also the example workflow 3.13.3 Working with date attributes and example action setNow.

See also

The example workflows:

- 3.13.1 Sleep task
- 3.13.2 Wait until date
- 3.13.3 Working with dates attributes

Example actions: getNow and setNow

Sending and waiting for custom events

This recipe will showcase how to send interactions between workflows. This is mostly used together with asynchronous workflows, which we will explain in the *Using asynchronous workflows* recipe in this chapter.

Getting ready

We need to be able to create two workflows.

We will reuse the action getNow that we created in the *Waiting tasks* recipe in this chapter (see the `com.packtpub.Orchestrator-Cookbook` module in the example pack).

How to do it...

This recipe requires us to create two workflows and then use them together.

Receiving a custom event

First, we create the receiving part:

1. Create a new workflow using the setup shown in the following figure:

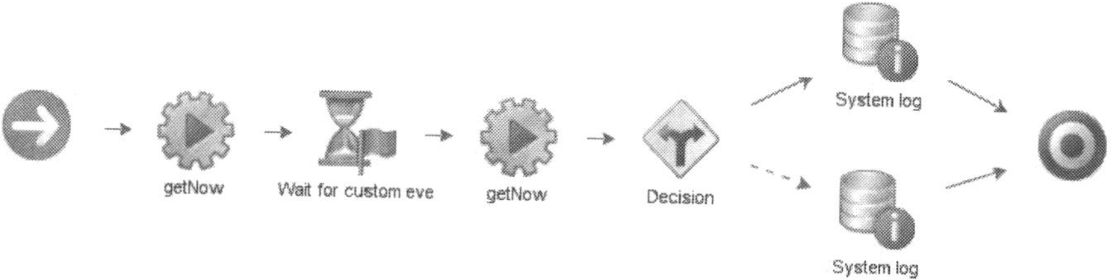

2. Create the following variables:

Name	Type	Section	Use
`isExternalEvent`	Number	Attribute Value: false	This is a setting to indicate where Orchestrator has to listen to for the Event.
`eventName`	String	IN	This is a string that contains the event identifier.
`endDate`	Date	IN	The date/time until Orchestrator should listen for the event.
`success`	Boolean	Attribute	This returns a value from the wait element. True indicates that the event was received.

3. Bind the all variables to the **Wait for customer event** task; only `success` will be bound to the output.
4. Bind the **Decision** task to the `success` attribute.
5. Add some meaningful text to the System log tasks, such as `Success` and `Failure`.
6. Save and close, but don't run this workflow yet. Proceed to the next section.

Sending a custom event

We now create the workflow that sends the custom event.

1. Create a new workflow with the following variable:

Name	Type	Section	Use
eventName	String	IN	This is a string that contains the event identifier

2. Just drag a **Send Custom event** task onto the schema and bind the **eventName** in-parameter to it.
3. Save and close the workflow. Don't run this workflow yet. Proceed to the next section.

Trying it out

As we now created all the moving parts, let's give it a spin:

1. Start the Receive workflow and enter an event name such as `getthis` as well as a date/time that is in the future (10 minutes or so).
2. Now, start the Send workflow and enter the same event name you entered in the Receive workflow. Watch the result and the logs.

Start both workflows again but this time, let the time expire and watch the result.

How it works...

Custom events are Orchestrator internal events that help exchange states between workflows. A typical example is that you have a workflow that needs to wait for another workflow to finish. Another example is that a workflow should not proceed before a certain event has taken place. In the *Using asynchronous workflows* recipe in this chapter, we will have a closer look at how this works. Another possibility is to use an event as a crude approval mechanism.

There's more...

Notice that the Receive custom event has an attribute called `isExternalEvent`, which is a Boolean; however, if you take a look under the cover (opening the scripting part of the **Wait for custom event** element), you will find that it is translated into a string with the `external` or `internal` value. The event we used in the previous example is an internal event. External events mean that Orchestrator is listening for an external source. For example, you can send someone a URL via an e-mail; when they click on it, it will trigger a workflow to continue.

An external event is an event that is triggered from outside Orchestrator. Let's build an example:

1. Duplicate **Receive Custom Event** and change the `isExternalEvent` attribute to `True`.
2. Create a new workflow and drag a scriptable task onto the schema.
3. Create the following variables:

Name	**Type**	**Section**	**Use**
`eventName`	String	IN	This is the name of the custom event
`externalURL`	String	Out	This contains the URL of the external event as a String

4. Bind the variables to the scriptable task.
5. In the scripting part of the scriptable task, enter the following script:

```
var myURL = new URL();
//get the custom event URL
myURL=System.customEventUrl(eventName, false);
//convert the URL type into a string
externalURL=myURL.url;
```

6. Save and close the workflow.
7. Run the new receive workflow you have created and allocate enough wait time (30 minutes).
8. Run the send external workflow you just created. The output will be an URL in the string format.
9. Copy and paste the URL into a browser.
10. Watch how the external event you just pasted triggers the receive workflow.

The custom event URL creates an URL that always looks like `http://[server IP]:8280/vmware-vmo-webcontrol/SendCustomEvent?EventName=[event name]`.

You don't have to use the command all the time; instead, you can directly post the URL to Orchestrator using the previous template. Try! Please note that there is *zero* security and anyone can post events to an Orchestrator Server. The only security you can get is using HTTPS instead of HTTP, but this would only encrypt the information sent. To use HTTPS, just replace with the following:

```
//get the custom event URL with HTTPS
myURL=System.customEventUrl(eventName, true);
```

Otherwise, you can simply use `https://[server IP]:8280/vmware-vmo-webcontrol/SendCustomEvent?EventName=[event name]`.

We will use this function in the *An approval process for VM provisioning* recipe in *Chapter 7, Working with VMware Infrastructure*.

See also

The example workflows:

- 3.14.1 Receiving custom event
- 3.14.2 Sending custom event
- 3.14.3 Generate External Event
- 3.14.4 Receive External Event

The *An approval process for VM provisioning* recipe in *Chapter 7, Working with VMware Infrastructure*.

Using asynchronous workflows

A workflow executes its elements along its path one after another. Using asynchronous workflow execution, we can change this behavior and actually execute workflows in parallel.

Getting ready

We will need to build a new workflow.

For the first example, we will reuse the sleep workflow as well as the `getNow` action we created in the *Waiting tasks* recipe in this chapter. (3.13.1 and the `com.packtpub.Orchestrator-Cookbook` module in the example pack).

How to do it...

We will see two examples to demonstrate the asynchronous feature.

The first example

Here are some basics:

1. Create a new workflow and create the following variables:

Name	Type	Section	Use
`sleepTime`	`Number`	`IN`	It defines the time the workflow should sleep
`wfToken`	`WorkflowToken`	`Attribute`	The workflow token of the asynchronous workflow

2. Drag an **Asynchronous workflow** task into the schema.
3. When prompted, enter the name of the sleep workflow we created in the *Waiting tasks* recipe in this chapter (3.13.1 in the example package).
4. Now, edit the **Asynchronous workflow** tasks. The in-parameter is the one from the sleep workflow. Bind it to the `sleepTime` in-parameter.
5. The out-parameter is a `workflowToken`. Bind it to the `wfToken` attribute.
6. Drag one `getNow` action on each side of the **Asynchronous workflow** tasks.
7. Save the workflow and run it.

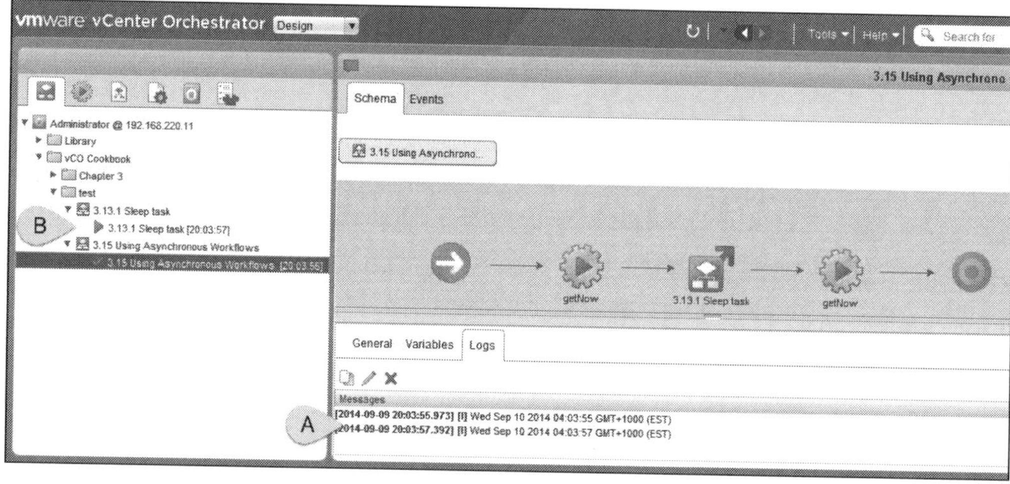

Have a look at the execution. The workflow that started the sleep workflow asynchronously has finished (**A** in previous screenshot) but the sleep workflow is still running (**B**). Also, please note that the sleep workflow doesn't write its logs into the main workflow.

The second example

This example shows how to combine asynchronous workflows with custom events.

1. Duplicate the sleep workflow we created in the *Waiting tasks* recipe in this chapter (3.13.1 in the example package).
2. Edit the workflow and add the following variable:

Name	Type	Section	Use
`eventName`	String	IN	This transports the custom event name

3. Add **Send custom event** after the **Sleep** task and bind the `eventName` in-parameter to it.

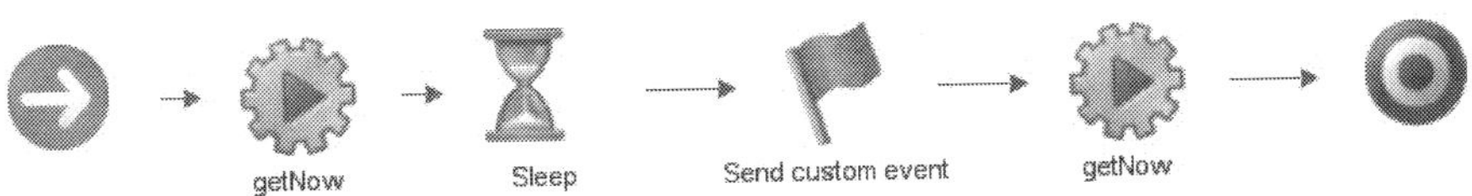

4. Save and exit the workflow. Don't run it now.
5. Create a new workflow with the following variables:

Name	Type	Section	Use
`sleepTime`	`Number`	`IN`	Time the asynchronous workflow for when it should sleep
`eventName`	`String`	`IN`	This is a string that contains an event name
`endDate`	`Date`	`IN`	This is the date/time until the workflow should wait
`success`	`Boolean`	`attribute`	This is the return value from the wait for a custom event
`wfToken`	`WorkflowToken`	`attribute`	This is the return value from an asynchronous task

6. Drag an **Asynchronous workflow** task onto the schema.
7. When prompted, enter the name of the workflow you have just created (3.15.2 in the example package).
8. Add a **wait for custom event** element to the schema as well as some `getNow` actions (see the following figure).
9. Bind the variables to the **Asynchronous** task and the **Wait for custom event** element.
10. Save and run the workflow. Watch the execution.

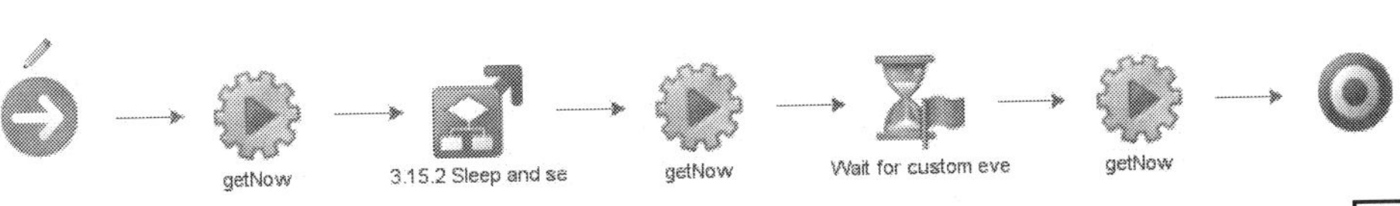

You will see that the main workflow will wait until it has received the custom events, which indicate that the asynchronous workflow has finished.

How it works...

Normally, a workflow executes one element after the other in a serial approach. From time to time, this can mean that your main program has to wait for some other tasks to finish before continuing. Using asynchronous execution, we can make workflows execute in parallel. A typical example is that you clone a VM (which can take a few minutes), and while it clones, you can create a new PortGroup that you can later attach to the cloned VM. To do this, create a new workflow that runs the create VM workflow asynchronously and sends a custom event when it is finished. In the meantime, the main workflow creates the PortGroup and then waits for the custom event to signal that the VM is ready. After the custom event has arrived, you can then map the PortGroup to the VM.

There's more...

The workflow **token** that the asynchronous workflow element generates is quite handy too. Each workflow has a unique token and you can access it via JavaScript or the API (see the *Accessing the Orchestrator API via REST* recipe in *Chapter 6, Advanced Operations*). When you look at a workflow run (the items underneath a workflow), you see nothing else but the Orchestrator Client accessing the data stored in the workflow token.

Each workflow token has simple properties, and they are as follows:

`wfToken.startDate`	This is the date and time the workflow was started.
`wfToken.endDate`	This is the date and time the workflow was finished. `Null` means that it is still running.
`wfToken.state`	This is the state the workflow is in. The different states are `waiting`, `failed`, `completed`, `cancelled`, and `running`.
`wfToken.name`	This is the name of the workflow.
`wfToken.exception`	This is the error message a workflow generated and is `Null` if no error occurs.
`wfToken.getAttributes()`	This helps get all the attributes of the workflow; it returns a JavaScript property.
`wfToken.getInputParameters()`	This helps get all the in-parameters of the workflow; it returns a JavaScript property.
`wfToken.getOutputParameters()`	This helps get all the out-parameters of the workflow; the return is a JavaScript property.

You might notice that you could use the workflow token status instead of a custom event to check whether an asynchronously started workflow has finished.

Let's look at an example. You start an asynchronous workflow and check with a custom decision on the status of the `wfToken.state =="completed"` workflow and create a loop with a sleep task around it.

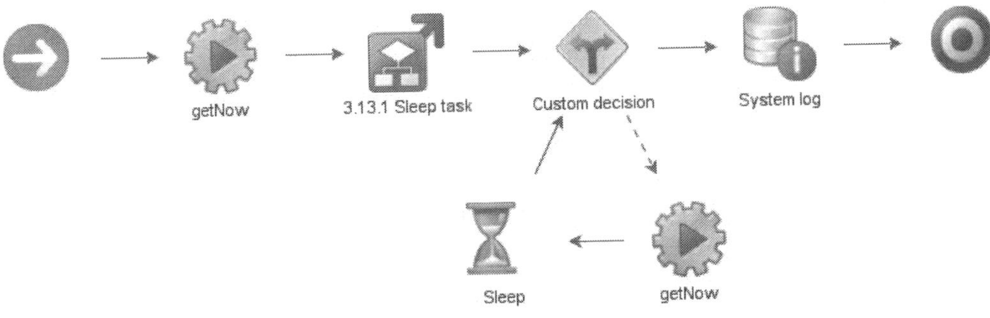

See also

Example workflows:

- 3.15.1 Using Asynchronous Workflows
- 3.15.2 Sleep and send event
- 3.15.3 wait for Asynchronous Workflows to finish
- 3.15.4 Wait for Workflow Token

Working with user interactions

This recipe will teach us how to create user interactions. User interactions are additional input that can be asked of users during the workflow execution.

Getting ready

We need to be able to create a new workflow.

For this recipe, you will need to have more than one AD/LDAP/SSO group configured to access Orchestrator. Remember that you can use the Orchestrator internal LDAP to test this. To facilitate this, please follow the *User management* recipe in *Chapter 5, Basic Orchestrator Operations*.

For the example in the *There's more...* section, we will also showcase the interaction with the vSphere Web Client.

How to do it...

We will split this recipe into two parts, the creation of the interaction workflow and the test run that will show how to answer the interaction.

Creating the workflow

1. Create a new workflow with the following variables:

Name	Type	Section	Use
`group`	`LdapGroup`	`Attribute`	This contains the group that is enabled to answer the interaction
`userString`	`String`	`Attribute`	This is defined when the user answers the interaction
`errorCode`	`String`	`Attribute`	This contains the error code
`date`	`Date`	`IN`	This is the date until the customer interactions waits for answers
`inString`	`String`	`IN`	This is a String value that is defined when the workflow starts

2. Define for the `group` attribute an LDAP group that should be allowed to answer the interaction (if you don't have an LDAP/AD/SSO, you can use **vcousers** from the local Orchestrator LDAP).
3. Drag a **User interaction** element onto the schema and edit it.
4. The **User interaction** element looks different from the elements you encountered before. The **Attributes** tab contains the `security.group` and `timeout.date` attributes. The `security.group` attribute defines which users are allowed to answer this user interaction. Bind this attribute to the `group` attribute. The `timeout.date` attribute defines when this user interaction expires. Bind the `date` in-parameter to it.

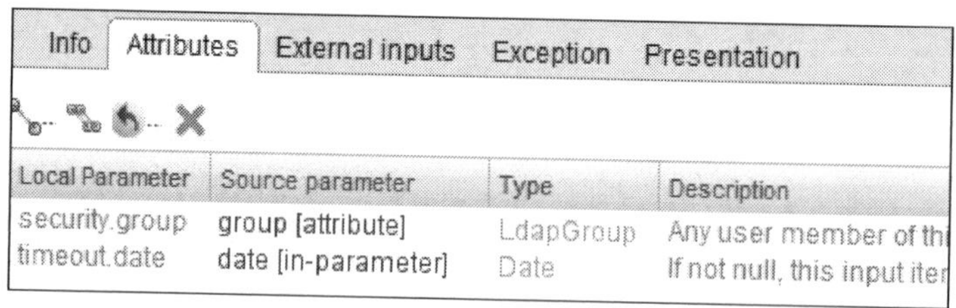

5. The **External inputs** tab defines what variables the user interaction asks for. You can add workflow attributes or out-parameters here. For our example, we just add the `userString` attribute.

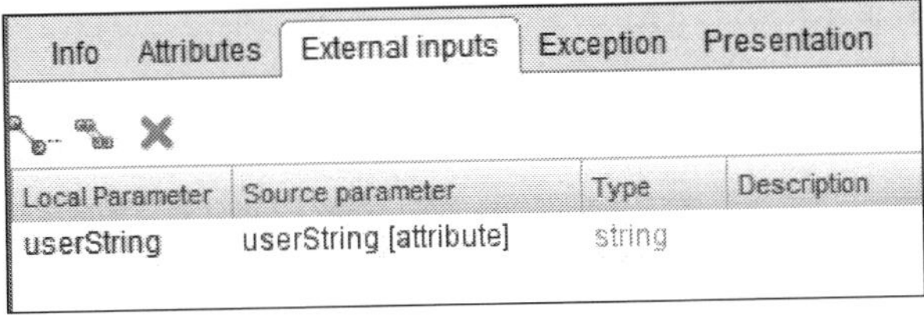

6. The **Presentation** tab works the same way as the normal workflow presentation (see the *Working with presentations* recipe in this chapter).

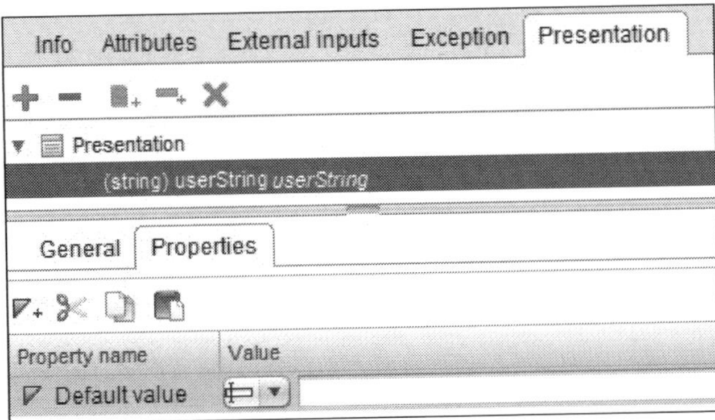

7. We will be building the following structure in the next steps:

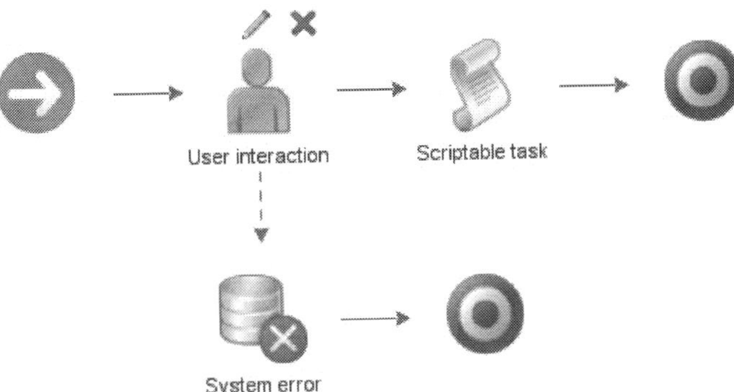

8. Drag the **System error** element onto the **User Interaction** element and make sure that the bindings are correct (see the *Error handling in workflows* recipe).
9. To make sure that something happens after the interaction, add **Scriptable task** to the schema (see the previous screenshot) and bind the `inString` and `userString` variables as an in-parameter to it. Also, bind the `outString` out-parameter as an out-parameter. In the scripting section, add `outString=inString+UserString`.

10. We now need to make sure that the group that should answer the interaction actually is able to access the workflow. In the **Permission** tab of the workflow, add the group you defined as the security group in step 4. The user group needs the **Execute** permission. Check the *User management* recipe in *Chapter 5, Basic Orchestrator Operations*.
11. Save and close the workflow.

Answering the user interaction

1. Run the workflow you have just created.
2. First, you are presented with the normal input request from the workflow. Enter an expiration date (maybe 15 minutes from now) and some text.
3. If you are an Orchestrator Admin, you will now be presented with the user interaction input. If this is the case, click on **Cancel**.
4. Have a look at the workflow, you will notice that it is still running and is now waiting for a user input. Log in to a second Orchestrator Client as a member of the group you defined as the security group in step 10 of the previous section.
5. Select the **Run** mode of the Orchestrator Client and click on the **Waiting for Input** tab. Here, you find all the workflows that are currently waiting for input.

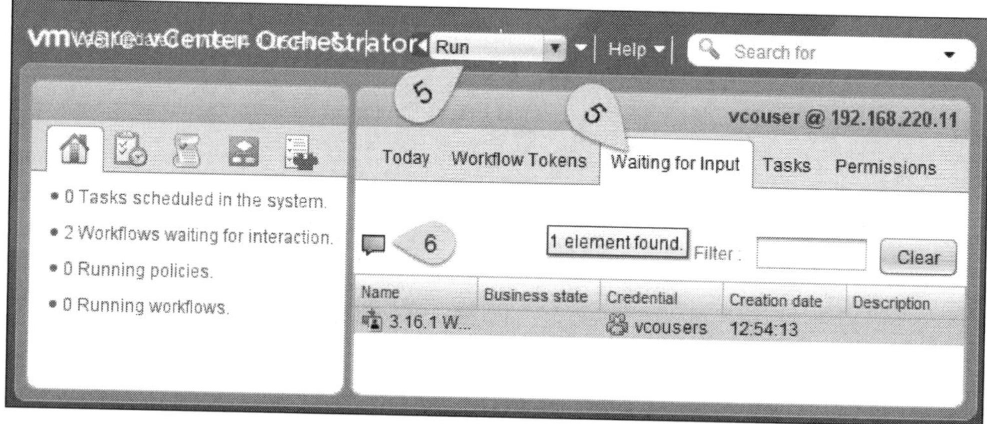

6. Click on the workflow and then on **Answer a user interaction** (the speech bubble icon).
7. The input for the user interaction will now pop up. Enter a value for `userString` and click on **Submit**.
8. Wait till the workflow has finished and then change back to the Orchestrator Client with the administrator login.
9. Take a look at the finished workflow execution.

How it works...

User interactions are created so that a workflow can get additional input when it is already running. You can define variables (**External inputs**) as input that a user should use, and you can format the input as you have already learned in the *Working with presentations* recipe in this chapter.

The important thing is that you can define a security group that is the recipient of this user request. This makes it possible that one group of Orchestrator users (for example, VM requesters) can start a workflow and have the workflow wait until a different group (VM approvers) has answered the user interaction.

The expiry date is also useful as it lets you define when a user action was not answered in a certain timeframe. If a user interaction was not answered, the **User interaction** element will generate an error with the **Timeout on signal** message. This makes it possible to create a follow-up action, for example, send an e-mail to the VM requester that his request has failed.

A workflow that is in the state of **Waiting** keeps this state, even if the Orchestrator Server is powered off, as this information is stored in the Orchestrator database.

A common practice is to put the security group that is used into a configuration (see the *Working with configurations* recipe in this chapter).

There's more...

To use the Web Client to answer a user interaction, follow these steps:

1. Login to vSphere Web Client as a member of the group you defined as the security group in step 4 in this recipe (or as an Orchestrator Admin).
2. Click on **vCenter Orchestrator** and then on **Waiting for interaction**. (You might need to wait a moment for Web Client to load the information.)
3. You will see all currently waiting workflows. Mark the workflow and select **Answer the workflow run** (the blue person icon). A pop-up window will show you the user interaction.

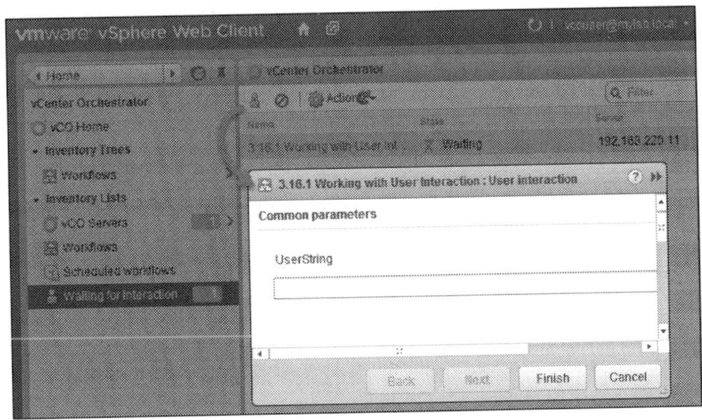

Answering using vRealize Automation

When you start a workflow using **vRealize Automation** (**vRA**) and this workflow contains a user interaction element, the user can answer by navigating to **Inbox** | **Manual User Action**.

See also

The example workflow 3.16.1 Working with user interaction.

Changing credentials

This recipe will show you how to use the **Change credential** element to change the user who is currently executing the workflow.

Getting ready

We need to create a new workflow.

For this recipe, you will need to have more than one AD/LDAP group configured to have access to Orchestrator. Remember that you can use the Orchestrator internal LDAP to test this. To facilitate this, please follow the *User management* recipe in *Chapter 5, Basic Orchestrator Operations*.

How to do it...

1. Create a new workflow with the following variable:

Name	Type	Section	Use
`newCredential`	`Credential`	`IN`	The user name and password of the new user

2. Drag a **Change credential** element onto the schema.
3. Bind the `newCredential` in-parameter to the **Change credential** element.
4. Now, drag one **System log** element before and one after the **Change credential** element.
5. Edit the **System log** elements. Remove the text input and change the log to `workflow.runningUserName`. This will log the username that is currently running the workflow.
6. Save and run the workflow.

7. When asked, enter new credentials (for example, vcouser). When the workflow is finished, have a look at the logs. You should see that the name of user who executed the workflow has changed (see the following figure):

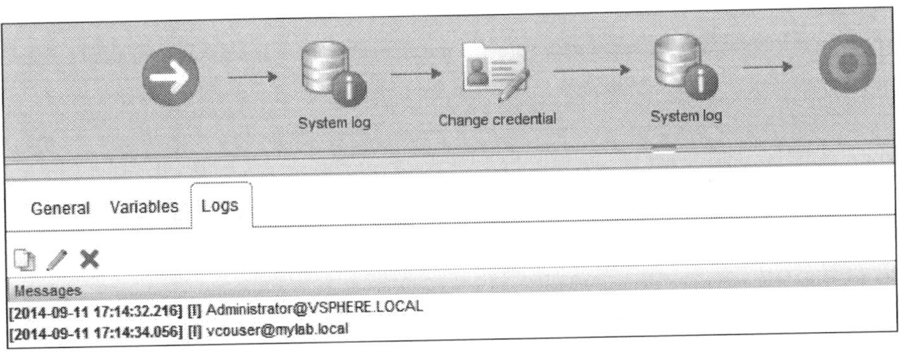

How it works...

The usage is simple; you define the user who executes the workflow from the **Change Credential** element onward.

A typical usage is that you have a workflow that is started by a user who has no rights to create a VM on vCenter. So, what you need to do is switch credentials before the VM is created and switch them back for the rest of the workflow. Best practice (please note that this is only true when you use the vCenter plugin with session per user) for this is to put the elevated credentials that are used into a configuration (see the *Working with configurations* recipe in this chapter).

See also

The example workflow 3.17 Changing credentials.

4

Working with Plugins

This chapter focuses on using Orchestrator plugins. We will be delving into the following plugins that are now shipped with the current Orchestrator version:

- Working with the API
- Working with mails
- File operations
- Working with SSH
- Working with XML
- Working with SQL
- Working with PowerShell
- Working with SOAP
- Working with REST
- Working with Active Directory
- Working with SNMP
- Working with AMQP

The vCenter and vRealize Automation (vCAC) plugin will be discussed in detail in *Chapter 7, Working with VMware Infrastructure*.

Introduction

This chapter centers on working with different plugins. We will explore how each plugin can help with achieving better automation and integration. For that, we need to have a closer look at the API itself. What we mean by API here is the internal workings of Orchestrator.

This chapter enables you to integrate all the aforementioned plugins into vRealize Automation. See the *Integrating Orchestrator workflows in vRA* recipe in *Chapter 7, Working with VMware Infrastructure*.

We discussed how to install plugins in the *Plugin basics* recipe in *Chapter 2, Optimizing Orchestrator Configuration*; however, the plugins we will discuss here are the basic ones that are shipped with Orchestrator (Version 5.5.x or higher). Each plugin adds its own variables, classes, objects, and so on to Orchestrator. We will discuss the API and how to search and work with it in the *Working with the API* recipe in this chapter.

How this chapter works

Like *Chapter 3, Visual Programming*, this chapter's recipes will showcase how to utilize the plugin and enable you to generate your own solutions using them. We will be working a lot with JavaScript code in this chapter; therefore, the following knowhow will be needed before we can attack this chapter:

- The introduction to *Chapter 3, Visual Programming*
- The *Working with decisions* recipe in *Chapter 3, Visual Programming*
- The *Working with loops* recipe in *Chapter 3, Visual Programming*

In each recipe, wherever you find a script, you will also find comments in it. The comments will explain what the next line of code is doing. In the *How it works...* section of each recipe, you will find more in-depth explanations.

Please note that you can also download the example package with all the workflows of this chapter. See the *Preface* of this book for download instructions.

Advanced JavaScript

Throughout *Chapter 3, Visual Programming*, we introduced JavaScript; now let's expand on that.

The try, catch, and finally functions

When writing any code, you want to make sure that when the code produces an error, you are still able to execute some critical operations, such as closing an open connection. For this purpose, most programming languages use `try`, `catch`, and `finally`. The `try`, `catch`, and `finally` functions work as follows.

The whole main code will go into the `try` section. The `catch` section contains all the error-handling code and will only be used if an error has occurred in the `try` section. The `ex` variable in the `catch` statement contains the error message that is passed from the `try` section into the `catch` section. The `finally` section will always execute and should contain the critical clean-up operations, such as closing open connections.

```
try  {
    //Main code;
}
catch( ex )  {
    // error handling
    throw ex;
} finally {
    //Final Part
}
```

A typical example is when you open a connection to a database and make sure that if an error occurs, the open connection to the database can be closed properly. Open connections can cause servers to perform slower, rendering them more vulnerable to intrusion or even corrupt data. You would open the connection in the `try` section and write the close function in the `finally` section.

The function command

The `function` command enables us to repeat a program code. A function needs to be defined before it is used, which means that it is placed at the beginning of a program. If `try`, `catch`, and `finally` are used, you place the function before the `try` command. A function is similar to the way an action works. We discussed actions in the *Working with actions* recipe in *Chapter 3, Visual Programming*.

The following code shows you how the `function` command is used. The `function` command creates a new function with the `functionName` name. The `parameter1` and `parameter2` parameters take their values from the function call. They are local and not accessible outside the function:

```
function functionName (parameter1, parameter2) {
    // program example
    parameter3 = parameter1 + parameter2
    return parameter3
}
```

The function would be executed (called) in the following way:

```
result = functionName(2,3);
```

The call will put value `2` into `parameter1` and value `3` into `parameter2` of the `functionName` function. The `result` variable will contain the return value of the function.

In the *Working with XML* recipe in this chapter, we have a helpful example on how to use the function command to simplify a program.

Variable type – Properties

The `Properties` variable type can be extremely useful to transport complex content. A **property** can be seen as a hash table, which means that you can assign multiple pairs of keys with their values. The following script shows you how to create a property and add the `myKey` key with the `Key Value` value to it:

```
var myProp = new Properties();
myProp.put("myKey","Key Value");
```

Note that even if you define a property in Orchestrator (attributes or out-parameters), you still need to initialize it (the first line of the preceding script) before you can fill it.

An example would be the following:

```
var family = new Properties();
family.put("Father","James");
family.put("Mother","Mary");
```

You can get all the keys in an existing property by using `myProp.keys`, which will return an array of strings. This is especially useful if you are using a `for-each` loop such as `for each (key in myProp.keys)`. To read a single value of a key, you use `value=myProp.get(key)`.

An array of properties can be even more useful, as JavaScript doesn't really do multidimensional arrays. An array of properties is more or less a two-dimensional array. To create an array of properties, use the following steps:

```
var myArray = new Array();
var myProp = new Properties() ;
myProp.put("myKey","Key Value") ;
myArray.push(myProp);
```

An example of an array of properties would be:

```
Var mails = new Array();
var mail = new Properties() ;
mail.put("subject","Test Email 1") ;
mails.push(mail);
var mail = new Properties() ;
mail.put("subject","Test Email 2") ;
mails.push(mail);
```

We will use properties in the *Working with mails* recipe in this chapter.

Working with the API

To be efficient in programming using Orchestrator plugins, one needs to know how to work with the Orchestrator API. In this recipe, we showcase how to access and get information from the Orchestrator API.

Getting ready

We only need the Orchestrator Client with rights to edit a workflow.

How to do it...

We will split this recipe into several sections.

Searching for items in the API

The first step is to have a look at the API. To access the API, follow these steps:

1. Open the Orchestrator Client.
2. Navigate to **Tools** | **API Explorer**.

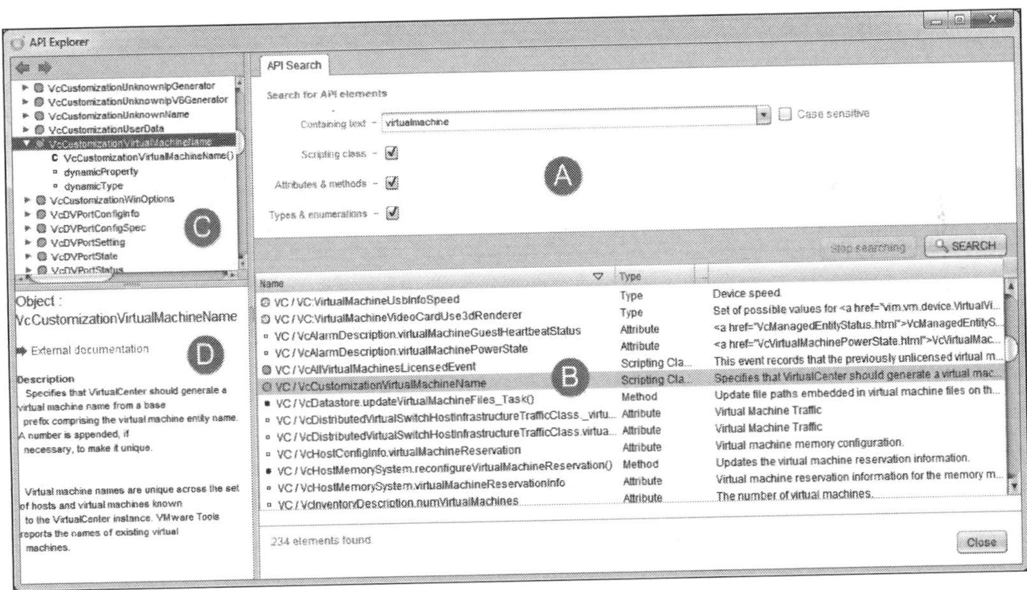

The API Explorer opens, and you have four sections as marked in the preceding screenshot:

- **A (search)**: Here, you can enter a search word such as `virtualmachine` as well as select what kind of results you are after.

- **B** (**search results**): This section shows you the result of the search: the name, the type (refer to the *How it works...* section of this recipe), and a short description.
- **C** (**API tree**): Double-clicking on a search result in section B will browse the selected result and open the API tree on that element.
- **D** (**detail**): Clicking on an item in section C will show a more detailed description of the item in the API.

Programming help from the API

This part will showcase how the Orchestrator API can help us program. In this showcase, we will begin to write a program similar to the one that we will create in the *Working with mails* recipe later in this chapter. Please note that this is only a showcase and won't result in a working program:

1. Create a new workflow.
2. Add a scriptable task to the schema.
3. Edit the element and click on **Scripting**.
4. On the right-hand side, you can see the API tree and explore it by browsing it. Try it!
5. Click on **Search** (the magnifying glass icon) and enter `mailclient` in the pop-up search window.
6. Click on **SEARCH**, mark the only result, and then click on **Go to selection**. This will display the `MailClient` object in the API tree.

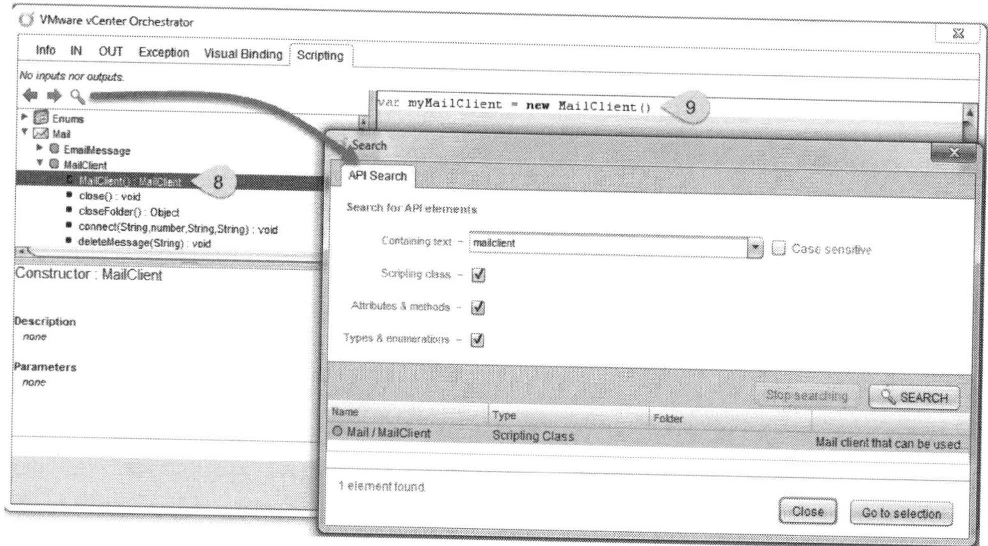

7. Close the search window.
8. Right-click on the constructor (the C Symbol) **MailClient()** and select **Copy**. If there is no dedicated constructor, you can always copy the object (the green circle) directly.

9. In the script area, right-click again and select **Paste** to auto-create a new constructor for the `MailClient` object. See the preceding screenshot. This will create an instance of the `MailClient` type and assign it to the `myMailClient` variable.
10. In the API tree, scroll down to and click on **connect() method**. In the detail area underneath, you will see details for this command, such as what inputs are needed and of what type. The method needs a host, a port, a username, and a password.
11. Now, copy-and-paste the **connect()** method as you did in step 8 and 9 into a new line in the scripting area. Orchestrator automatically fills in some parts and the new line will look like this:
    ```
    connect(?String_host , ?number_port , ?String_username ,
    ?String_password)
    ```
12. To make this line work, we will need to put an object before it; in this case, it's the `MailClient` object we created in step 9. Just add `myMailClient` before **connect** with a period between them. This will enact the method `connect` on the `MailClient` instance. The result will look like this:
    ```
    myMailClient.connect(?String_host , ?number_port , ?String_
    username , ?String_password)
    ```
13. The next step is to substitute each of the placeholders (the `?names`) with either Orchestrator variables or values. Replace the first placeholder `?String_host` with a mail host address, such as `mail.mylab.local`.
14. As we want to showcase the API a bit more, we will get the value for the `?number_port` placeholder a bit differently. Insert a new line above the connect line.
15. Use the API search to search for `getDefaultPort`. You will see that it is an action in the module called `com.vmware.libary.mail` and needs an input of type String (a protocol name). Its return value is a number (the port). If you like, take a look at the action itself and its script. This will help you understand how it works and what input it requires.
16. Now, copy-and-paste the action from the API tree to the scripting area, as done previously. You will see that additional code is created and looks like this:
    ```
    System.getModule("com.vmware.library.mail").
    getDefaultPort(protocol)
    ```
17. We want the output of the action to be put into a local variable, so insert `var port =` before `System.getModule`.
18. Now, we need to tell the action what protocol we want, so replace `protocol` with `"imap"`. This will save the default port for IMAP into the variable `port`.
19. Next, replace the `?number_port` placeholder in the connect line with the `port` variable.
20. Last but not least, let's add an Orchestrator variable to the connect line. In the scriptable task, create an in-parameter of a type string called `userName`.
21. Replace the `?String_username` placeholder with `userName`. Notice the color change of `userName` when it matches the in-parameter.

At this stage, we leave the showcase, as we have explored the interesting parts. Your little script should look something like this:

```
var myMailClient = new MailClient();
var port = System.getModule("com.vmware.library.mail").
getDefaultPort("imap");
myMailClient.connect("192.168.220.4" , port , userName, ?String_
password);
```

The full working script can be found in the *Working with mails* recipe in this chapter.

How it works...

The Orchestrator API contains all types, methods, attributes, objects, and so on that can be used for programming. All the content comes from Orchestrator or its plugins and gives the Orchestrator programmer a wide range of tools to use.

As you can see in the preceding showcase, the items in the API are color-coded; the following table shows you all the item colors along with a short description of their meaning.

Icon	**Name**	**Usage**
Grey bullet	Type	Types are complex variables.
Purple bullet	Function set	A set of functions that centers on certain topics, for instance, the `System` function set that contains the `.log` and `.warn` methods.
Blue bullet	Primitive	A primitive is a basic variable type. These are array, function, number, object, SecureString, String, Boolean, and char. String and array contain methods.
Green bullet	Object	Objects contain attributes, constructors, and methods.
Grey and blue gear	Module	Modules contain actions. We worked with actions and modules in the *Working with actions* recipe in *Chapter 3, Visual Programming*.
Color icons	SDKModule	SDKModule is part of the plugins and contains types and objects.
C shaped icon	Constructor	A constructor creates a new entity of a given type. Sometimes, there is no constructor; in this case, you can try to copy-and-paste the parent object.
Empty square	Attribute	An attribute is a property of an object; it can be either read-only or read-write.
Filled square	Method	The function (action) that is implemented with the object and acts on the object.

See also

In the *Working with the vCenter API (to change a VM's HA settings)* recipe in *Chapter 7, Working with VMware Infrastructure*, we will explore the vCenter API integration in Orchestrator.

Working with mails

In this recipe, we will learn how to interact with e-mails and discuss configuring, sending, and receiving e-mails with Orchestrator. We will discuss both mail objects that the API currently has.

Getting ready

Unsurprisingly, we need a mail server. If you don't have one handy, you can use hmailServer for Windows; refer to the *There's more...* section of this recipe to learn how to install and configure this free, open source mail server.

For this recipe, we will use IMAP and SMTP to connect to the mail server. In the *How it works...* section, we also take a quick look at POP3 and SSL. We will also need two e-mail addresses. In our example, we will use `vcotest@mylab.local` and `vcotest2@mylab.local`.

There are two API Objects that can be used when working with mails: the `MailClient` object and the `EmailMessage` object. We will use `EmailMessage` to send messages and `MailClient` to receive mails.

How to do it...

We will break this recipe down into configuration and sending and receiving mail.

Configuring the mail connection

You can define the e-mail setting for Orchestrator globally in the Orchestrator configurator, as shown in the *Configuring e-mail* recipe in *Chapter 2, Optimizing Orchestrator Configuration*. The global settings are automatically stored as part of the `EmailMessage` object (sent mails); however, they are not accessible to the `MailClient` object (received mails). Typically, the hostname, username, and password are the same for sending and receiving mails; therefore, we need to find a method to make these settings available to both. There are two such methods:

- The global settings you configured are stored in the `EmailMessage` object in the following attributes:

  ```
  var message = new EmailMessage();
  message.smtpHost
  message.smtpPort
  message.username
  message.password
  ```

```
message.fromName
message.fromAddress
```

You can simply pass these attributes into the `MailClient.connect` method.

- A better alternative would be to store all the necessary mail configuration information in a configuration, as shown in the *Working with configurations* recipe in *Chapter 3, Visual Programming*. Follow these steps to prepare the information you need to interact with a mail server:

  1. Create a new configuration.
  2. Create the following items:

Variable name	**Type**	**Description**
`mailHost`	String	The IP or FQDN of the mail server
`mailUser`	String	The username that is needed to access the e-mail account (it's the e-mail in the case of hmail)
`mailPass`	SecureString	The password for the user account
`smtpPort`	Number	The TCP Port that should be used (the default port is TCP 25)
`SmtpFromName`	String	A string that identifies the sender—for example, the full name of the user
`smtpFromMail`	String	The e-mail address of the sender
`receiveProtocol`	String	The protocol used: either POP3 or IMAP

You can now use this configuration in workflows, as shown in the *Working with configurations* recipe in *Chapter 3, Visual Programming*.

Sending e-mails

To send e-mails, there is a readymade workflow that we can use by navigating to **Library** | **Mail** | **Send notification**; However, we will create a new one to understand the code and the API a bit better:

1. Create a new workflow and create the following variables:

Variable name		**Type**	**Description**
`mailTo`	IN	String	The e-mail address the e-mail should go to
`mailCC`	IN	String	The e-mail address that should be sent to CC (carbon copy)
`mailBCC`	IN	String	The e-mail address that should be sent to BCC (blind carbon copy)—the BCC e-mail address is not disclosed to other e-mail recipients

Variable name		Type	Description
`mailSubject`	IN	String	The subject of the e-mail
`mailContent`	IN	String	The text content you want to send
`mailHost`	Attribute	String	The link with the corresponding configuration attribute
`mailUser`	Attribute	String	The link with the corresponding configuration attribute
`mailPass`	Attribute	SecureString	The link with the corresponding configuration attribute
`smtpPort`	Attribute	Number	The link with the corresponding configuration attribute
`smtpFromName`	Attribute	String	The link with the corresponding configuration attribute
`smtpFromMail`	Attribute	String	The link with the corresponding configuration attribute

2. Add a scriptable task to the schema and enter the following code:

```
//Create a message object
    var message = new EmailMessage();
// set connections parameters
    message.smtpHost = mailHost;
    message.smtpPort = smtpPort;
    message.username = mailUser;
    message.password = mailPass;
    message.fromName = smtpFromName;
    message.fromAddress = smtpFromMail;
//Set email specific information
    message.toAddress = mailTo;
    message.ccAddress = mailCC;
    message.bccAddress = mailBCC;
// the subject of the message
    message.subject = mailSubject;
// the mail content, message type and the character set
    message.addMimePart(mailContent,"text/html;
      charset=UTF-8");
// send the message
    message.sendMessage();
```

3. Save and run the workflow.

You can now use this workflow to send e-mails.

Receiving e-mails

There are already two workflows to receive e-mail by navigating to **Library | Mail**; they are called **Retrieve messages** and **Retrieve messages (via MailClient)**. The problem with them is that they don't have any output that we can use and therefore, they are quite useless to anyone who wants to use e-mails to check for content. In this example, we will use the more powerful `MailClient` object to create a workflow that receives mails and outputs the important parts of an e-mail.

1. Create a new workflow and define the following variables; link them to the configuration from the first part as required:

Variable name		Type	Description
`mailHost`	Attribute	String	Link with the configuration
`receiveProtocol`	Attribute	String	Link with the configuration
`mailUsername`	Attribute	String	Link with the configuration
`mailPassword`	Attribute	SecureString	Link with the configuration
`deleteMail`	IN	Boolean	Should the messages be deleted?
`outMail`	OUT	Array of properties	The output array for messages

2. Add a scriptable task and bind all the variables to it.
3. Enter the following script:

```
// initialize array
var outMail = new Array ();
// initialize Property
var mail = new Properties();
//mail constructor
var myMailClient = new MailClient();
//get the default port for the protocol
var mailPort=System.getModule("com.vmware.library.mail").
getDefaultPort(receiveProtocol)
myMailClient.setProtocol(receiveProtocol);
// connect to mail server
myMailClient.connect( mailHost, mailPort, mailUsername,
mailPassword);
//open the inbox
myMailClient.openFolder("Inbox");
// get messages
var messages = myMailClient.getMessages();
//if there are any messages loop thought them
if ( messages != null && messages.length > 0 ) {
    for (i = 0; i < messages.length; i++) {
```

```
//get the mail details and write them into a property
        var mail = new Properties();
        mail.put("from",messages[i].from);
        mail.put("date",messages[i].getSentDate());
        mail.put("subject",messages[i].subject);
        mail.put("content",messages[i].getContent());
        // push Properties into array.
        outMail.push(mail);
        //delete messages if this was chosen
        if (deleteMail) {
            messages[i].delete();
        }
    }
} else {
    System.warn( "No messages found" );
}
// Close mail connection
myMailClient.closeFolder();
myMailClient.close();
```

4. Save and run the workflow.

This workflow will output one array, with these property keys: `from`, `date`, `subject`, and `content`. Refer to the introduction to this chapter to learn how to access the output of this workflow.

Check out the *Working with XML* recipe in this chapter to change the output of this workflow to XML.

How it works...

E-mail can quickly become a really important addition to Orchestrator. Just think about the possibilities of sending e-mail to users after a task has been successfully finished (or not) or for sending a report of some sort.

In Orchestrator, the `Mail.EmailMessage` object is responsible for sending e-mails; to receive or work with e-mails, there are actually three objects: `Mail.MailClient`, `Net.POP3Client`, and `Net.IMAPClient`.

`Mail.MailClient` is the more powerful of the objects to read e-mails, as it comes with a lot of types and methods centered around e-mails that can be useful, such as extracting attachments or using different e-mail folders. The other two objects are more rudimentary and more directed at either POP3 or IMAP. For more information, I would suggest that you check out the API and look for the available attributes and methods that they contain.

The receive workflow that we have created in the recipe isn't very sophisticated, but it lets you build a workflow that extracts all e-mails so that you can check for specific content. Take a look at the example workflow 3.8.3 DoWhile loop to see how it can be used.

Working with attachments

Sending an attachment is more or less easy; we will showcase it by uploading the attachment as an Orchestrator resource. We will cover how to work with resources in the *Working with resources* recipe in *Chapter 6, Advanced Operations*. Basically, you send attachments as a JavaScript Object Notation (JSON). To facilitate this, follow these steps:

1. You will need to add the following variable to the send the workflow:

Name	Type	Section	Use
attachment	`ResourceElement`	IN	Contains the Orchestrator resource for the attachment

2. Add the following code to the send script:

```
var myMimeAttachment = new MimeAttachment();
myMimeAttachment.name = "Picture";
myMimeAttachment.content = attachment;
message.addMimePart(myMimeAttachment, "application/json;
charset=UTF-8");
```

In order to fetch an attachment from an e-mail, we need to have a much closer look at how the `MailClient` object works. Each e-mail can have multiple content parts, such as attachments and text. To check whether a message contains more than one part, use the `MailClient.isContentMultiPart()` method; it returns either true or false. To get all the parts, use this:

```
var multiPartContent = message.getMultiPartContent();
```

This will return an array (`multiPartContent`). Now we need to look into each of the parts by looping through them. We get a single part by using this:

```
var bodyPart = multiPartContent.getBodyPart(counter);
```

To know whether the body part is an attachment, check `bodyPart.isAttachment()`. To fetch the attachment, use this:

```
var attachment = bodyPart.getAsMimeAttachment();
```

You now have the attachment as a JSON type and can process it further. Refer to the *Working with resources* recipe in *Chapter 6, Advanced Operations*.

To get the mime type of the attachment, use `attachment.mimeType`; to get the name, use `attachment.name`.

There's more...

A fast and pretty easy way to configure the e-mail server is the open source hmail server that you can download from `www.hmailserver.com`.

Creating a non-relaying local-only mail server is pretty straightforward. I will not waste too much page space, so there are no screenshots. The following steps let you create a mail server and e-mail addresses that are configured for SMTP, POP3, and IMAP:

1. In Windows, download hmail and start the installer.
2. Make sure that SMTP (TCP 25), POP3 (TCP 110), and IMAP (TCP 143) can pass through the Windows firewall.
3. Select a folder where you would like to place the program binaries (this is not the place where the e-mails will end up; hmail needs less than 15 MB disk space).
4. Install **Server** and **Administrator tools**.
5. You can now choose to use an external DB (MSSQL, MySQL, or PostgreSQL) or the Microsoft SQL Server Compact Edition (2 MB installation size) that is shipped with hmail (use the compact edition for the lab).
6. You are now asked whether you would like to create a shortcut (recommended for lab).
7. Set a password for the admin access of hmail.
8. After the installation is finished, run **Administrator tools**.
9. Connect to the localhost mailserver and enter the admin password from step 7.
10. After the administrator console is open, click on **Domains** and then click on **Add**.
11. In the **Domain** field under **General**, enter your domain name and click on **Save**.
12. Your domain is now created. Click on your domain, then click on **Accounts**, and then click on **Add**.
13. To create an e-mail address, just fill in the name of the account by navigating to **General** | **Address** and give it a password. Adjust **Maximum size (MB)** to 10 MB (we will just use some text mails). Finally, click on **Save**.

That's it. Now you can play with this recipe.

See also

The example workflows are:

- 4.02.1 SendMail
- 4.02.2 getMail
- 4.02.3 getMail(XML)
- 4.02.4 SendAttachment

File operations

In this recipe, we will explore how Orchestrator can interact with the filesystem of its operating system. We will also take a look at how to access a network share and execute local files.

Getting ready

Orchestrator needs to be able to access a directory on the local filesystem. To configure this access and set the access rights, take a look at the *Configuring access to the local filesystem* recipe in *Chapter 2, Optimizing Orchestrator Configuration*.

In addition to this, you should have administrative (root) access to Orchestrator's operating system.

In my example, I have granted full access (`rwx`) to the `/orchestrator` directory.

How to do it...

We have a bit of ground to cover, so let's start!

Writing a file

This part showcases how to write into a file with and without a line feed as well as how to append to an existing file:

1. Create a new workflow and create the following variables:

Name	Type	Section	Use
`fileName`	String	IN	The name of the file, including its path
`fileContent`	Sting	IN	Some random content

2. Add a scriptable task to the schema and enter the following script:

```
//FileWriter constructor
var myFileWriter = new FileWriter(fileName);
//open the file for writing
myFileWriter.open();
//Empties existing file. Without it we append
myFileWriter.clean();
//write a line into the file
myFileWriter.writeLine(fileContent);
//write without line feed
myFileWriter.write(fileContent);
myFileWriter.write(" -:- ");
```

```
myFileWriter.write(fileContent);
//write line feed
myFileWriter.write("\n");
//Close the file
myFileWriter.close();
```

3. Run the workflow and check the result; you should have a file that contains something like this:

```
Test
Test -:- Test
```

If the `clean` method is not used when opening an existing file, it will be opened for appending. Try it!

Reading a file

This part showcases how to read a file fully as well as line-by-line.

1. Create a new workflow and create the following variables:

Name	Type	Section	Use
`fileName`	String	IN	The name of the file, including its path

2. Add a scriptable task to the schema and enter the following script:

```
//File reader constructor
var myFileReader = new FileReader(fileName);
// check if the file actually exists
if (myFileReader.exists){
//Open the file
    myFileReader.open();
//read everything
    System.log(myFileReader.readAll());
// Close the file (undocumented in API).
    myFileReader.close();
    System.log("----------------------");
//read line by line until the file is empty
    myFileReader.open();
    do{
        temp=myFileReader.readLine();
        System.log(temp);
    } while(temp!=null);
    myFileReader.close();
}
```

3. Run the workflow and check the logs.

Getting information on files

This section showcases how to access information about a directory or file:

1. Create a new workflow and create the following variables:

Name	Type	Section	Use
fileOrDirectory	String	IN	The name of the file, including its path

2. Add a scriptable task to the schema and enter the following script:

```
//File constructor
var myFile = new File(fileOrDirectory);
//Does the file or directory exist?
if (myFile.exists){
//is it a directory?
    if (myFile.isDir) {
        System.log("This is a directory. It Contains:");
//list the content of the directory
        System.log(myFile.list());
    } else {
//read file properties
        System.log("This is a File");
        System.log("Path: "+myFile.path);
        System.log("Directory: "+myFile.directory);
        System.log("FileName: "+myFile.name);
        System.log("FileExtention: "+myFile.extension);
        System.log("Readable: "+myFile.canRead());
        System.log("Writeable: "+myFile.canWrite());
    }
}
```

3. Run the workflow once with a directory and then with a file. Check the logs.

Creating, renaming, and deleting a file or directory

We now showcase how to create an empty file, rename it, and then delete it:

1. Create a new workflow and create the following variables:

Name	Type	Section	Use
directory	String	IN	The name of the file, including its path

2. Add a scriptable task to the schema and enter the following script:

```
//File Constructor
var myDir = new File(directory);
//is it a Directory
```

```
    if (myDir.isDir){
        //create a new File Constructor
        var newFile = new File(Directory+"/TempFile");
        //create an empty file
        newFile.createFile();
        //Show directory
        System.log(myDir.list());
        //Rename the file
        newFile.renameTo(Directory+"/RenamedFile")
        //Show directory
        System.log(myDir.list());
        // new constructor as the file name has changed
        var renamedFile = new File(Directory+"/RenamedFile");
        //Delete the File
    renamedFile.deleteFile();
    //Show directory
        System.log(myDir.list());
    }
```

3. Run the workflow and supply a directory. A file will be created, renamed, and deleted.

If you want to create a directory, use the `createDirectory` method. To rename and delete a directory, the `renameTo` and `deleteFile` methods are used, just as we have seen earlier with a file.

How it works...

As you can see, file operations are quite easy and straightforward. They come in handy if you want to save or load XML or CSV content or anything else, for that matter.

If you want to use a file to write logs, there is a special scripting class called `LogFileWriter`. However, it is not much different from the `FileWriter` class.

Directory dividers are different in Linux and Windows. Where Windows uses a backslash (\), Linux uses a forward-slash (/). However, when we deal with file paths in Orchestrator, we use only the forward-slash.

Executing scripts

You can execute scripts from the local OS using Orchestrator. To do that, Orchestrator needs access (x) to the folder where the script is located and the Orchestrator user needs to be able to read and execute (rx) it. Here is an example script:

```
//prepare command
var command = new Command("c:/Orchestrator/script.bat");
//execute the command
```

```
command.execute(true);
//get the return code
var returnCode = command.result;
//get the output of the command
var returnOutput = command.output;
```

There's more...

You can use the file writer to write to a shared directory. In this example, we will use an SMB share. This follows the same principle as the normal file writing. The only thing is that the methods differ between Orchestrator OS versions. Check out the *Configuring access to the local filesystem* recipe in *Chapter 2, Optimizing Orchestrator Configuration*.

See also

The example workflows are:

- 4.03.1 Write a File
- 4.03.2 Read a File
- 4.03.3 Getting File information
- 4.03.4 Creating, renaming, and deleting

Working with SSH

This recipe centers on using the SSH plugin. With this plugin, you are able to connect to a Linux- or Solaris-based system, run programs, or transfer files.

Getting ready

We need to be able to create a new workflow. We also need a Linux or Solaris system that we can access via SSH (for example, as root). If you don't have any Linux system handy, you can use the Orchestrator appliance itself.

For the SCP example, you need to allow Orchestrator access to its local filesystem. Refer to the *Configuring access to the local filesystem* recipe in *Chapter 2, Optimizing Orchestrator Configuration*.

How to do it...

We split this recipe into three parts: SSH access, SSL key access, and SCP usage.

Using SSH

You will find a very good, while rather chatty (logs) SSH workflow in **Library | SSH | Run SSH command**. However, we will create a new short version to showcase SSH:

1. Create a new workflow and create the following variables:

Name	Type	Place	Usage
`host`	String	IN	The IP or FQDN of the host we want to connect to
`user`	String	IN	The username to connect to the host
`password`	SecureString	IN	The password of the user to connect to the host
`command`	String	IN	The command we want to run on the host
`output`	String	OUT	The result of the command we run
`exitcode`	Number	OUT	The exit code. 0 = OK
`error`	String	OUT	The error message encountered.

2. Add a scriptable task to the schema and enter the following script:

```
// Open a new SSH session with password
var mySSHSession = new SSHSession(host , user);
mySSHSession.connectWithPassword(password);
//execute the SSH command
mySSHSession.executeCommand(command , true);
// prepare output
output=mySSHSession.output;
exitcode=mySSHSession.exitCode;
error=mySSHSession.error;
//disconnect the SSH session
mySSHSession.disconnect();
```

3. Save and close the workflow.

   When running this workflow, you will have to supply a command string. The string can be a single command or a string of commands that the Linux system can utilize. A command you can try is `date`.

Using SSL key authentication

In the previous example, we used password authentication to log in to the Linux host system. We can use SSL keys to allow automatic login without using a password, which is the method commonly used for automation purposes.

To enable SSL authentication, first we need an SSL key, and we need to store it in the target Linux system. We will use the existing workflows to accomplish this:

1. Start the workflow by navigating to **Library | SSH | Generate key pair**.
2. Use the default setting and don't enter a password. Basically, just click on **Submit**.
3. After the workflow has finished, a new SSL key pair with the **vco_key** name is generated in the following directory:

Windows	`C:\Program Files\VMware\Orchestrator\app-server\conf\`
Appliance	`/etc/vco/app-server/`

4. Next, we need to register the SSL key on the host with the user we will use for the connection. To do this, we will use the existing workflow by navigating to **Library | SSH | Register vCO public key on host**.
5. Start the workflow, enter the hostname of the target server as well as the credentials of the user, and click on **Submit**.
6. The SSL pairing is now done. Let's try it out. Create a duplicate (or change the original) of the workflow you have created in the first section of this recipe.
7. Exchange the `mySSHSession.connectWithPassword(Password);` line with `mySSHSession.connectWithIdentity("../conf/vco_key" , "");`. The shorter path works as Orchestrator's working directory is the `app-server` directory.
8. Remove the password in-parameter from the workflow.
9. Run the workflow. You won't need a password any longer.

Using SCP

SCP stands for Secure CoPy and allows you to transfer files using an SSH encryption tunnel. However, before we can copy anything from or to the Orchestrator Server, we need to have a directory that Orchestrator has access to (see the *Configuring access to the local filesystem* recipe in *Chapter 2, Optimizing Orchestrator Configuration*.

1. Make a copy of one of the SSH workflows: either the password or the SSL one.
2. Remove the command in-parameter and add the following in-parameter:

Name	**Type**	**Place**	**Usage**
`filename`	String	IN	The name of the file
`localDir`	String	IN	The directory on the Orchestrator Server
`remoteDir`	String	IN	The directory on the remote host

3. Exchange the `mySSHSession.executeCommand(Command , true);` line with one of the following, depending on whether you want to send or receive a file:

Upload	`mySSHSession.putFile(localDir+file , remoteDir);`
Download	`mySSHSession.getFile(remoteDir+file , localDir);`

4. Save and run the workflow.

How it works...

Using SSH together with Orchestrator generates a very powerful team. You can use SSH to access an existing Linux system, configure it, or to connect to a Linux-based management system, such as a Red Hat Satellite server.

SCP can be used in conjunction with Orchestrator resources to upload and download files or to transfer any other files between Orchestrator and a target system. Please note that you can also transfer files from one remote system to another using Orchestrator as a temporary storage between transfers.

A very savvy hack is to use SSH/SCP to configure and tune new Orchestrator installations.

Key pairing

The actual key registry is done with the `registerVSOonHost` action. The action will use SCP to transfer the SSL public keys to the host and then add its content to the `~/.ssh/authorized_keys` file.

You can also take a look at the API and check what else is available in the SSH objects.

See also

- Refer to the *Configuring access to the local filesystem* recipe in *Chapter 2, Optimizing Orchestrator Configuration*
- Refer to the *File operations* recipe in this chapter

The example workflows are:

- 4.04.1 SSH (short with password)
- 4.04.2 SSH (short with SSL Key)
- 4.04.3 SCPput
- 4.04.4 SCPget

Working with XML

In this recipe, we explore how to use the XML plugin to create and phrase XML structures with Orchestrator. XML is a good way to exchange complex information between systems.

Getting ready

We don't need anything special; however, we need to understand the basics of XML. Take a look at `http://www.w3schools.com/xml/`.

You should be familiar with the JavaScript concept of functions (see the introduction to this chapter).

How to do it...

This recipe is split into two parts; first, we create an XML document and then phrase an XML document.

Creating an XML document

This is the rather more complex part. However, we will go through it slowly:

We will create a simple XML document that looks like this:

```
<?xml version="1.0" encoding="UTF-8">
<MailMessages>
  <Mail>
    <From>test@test.net</From>
    <Subject>Test message</Subject>
    <Content Date="10/12/12">This is a test message
      </Content>
  </Mail>
</MailMessages>
```

1. Create a new workflow and create the following variables:

Name	Type	Where	Usage
`from`	String	IN	The sender of the e-mail
`subject`	String	IN	The subject of the e-mail
`date`	String	IN	The date of the e-mail
`content`	String	IN	The content of the e-mail
`XMLout`	String	OUT	The XML output in a one-line string

2. Drag a scriptable task into the schema and enter the following script:

```
//create empty XML document
var document = XMLManager.newDocument();
// add a root element
var mailMessages = document.createElement("MailMessages");
//add the root element to the document
document.appendChild(mailMessages) ;
//Create new node
var mail = document.createElement("Mail");
//add new node under the root element
mailMessages.appendChild(mail) ;
//add a Child node under the mail node
var nodeFrom = document.createElement("From");
mail.appendChild(nodeFrom);
//set a text value for the From node
var txtFrom = document.createTextNode(from);
nodeFrom.appendChild(txtFrom);
//add another node with a value to the mail node
var nodeSubject = document.createElement("Subject");
mail.appendChild(nodeSubject);
var txtSubject = document.createTextNode(subject);
nodeSubject.appendChild(txtSubject);
//add content node
var nodeContent = document.createElement("Content");
mail.appendChild(nodeContent);
var txtContent = document.createTextNode(content);
nodeContent.appendChild(txtContent);
//Add an attribute to the Content node
nodeContent.setAttribute("Date",date);
//Output the XML Document as string
XMLout=XMLManager.getDocumentContent(document)
```

3. Save and run this workflow. Copy-and-paste the output into Notepad and check the XML structure you created.
4. We now improve the program by using the JavaScript `function` command. Use the following script:

```
function
createNode(doc,rootNode,NodeName,NodeText,attribName,attribValue)
{
    var newNode = doc.createElement(NodeName);
    rootNode.appendChild(newNode);
// if there is no NodeText don't add anything
    if (NodeText!= null){
```

```
            var newTxt = doc.createTextNode(NodeText);
            newNode.appendChild(newTxt);
        }
    // if there is an attribute defined add it
        if (attribName!= null){
            newNode.setAttribute(attribName,attribValue);
        }
    // return the new created node
        return newNode;
    }

    //create empty XML document
    var document = XMLManager.newDocument();

    mailMessages = createNode(document,document,"MailMessages");
    mail = createNode(document,mailMessages,"Mail");
    createNode(document,mail,"From",from);
    createNode(document,mail,"Subject",subject);
    createNode(document,mail,"Content",content,"Date",date);

    //Output the XML Document as string
    XMLout=XMLManager.getDocumentContent(document);
```

You can see how using the function command reduces the amount of lines and makes the code more reusable. Alternatively, you can also create an action and put the function content into it.

If you like, you can now go and integrate XML into the workflow that you built in the *Receiving e-mails* section of the *Working with mails* recipe to format the e-mail output.

Parsing XML structures

Taking the XML string we created, we now focus on how to parse the XML structure:

1. Create a new workflow and drag a scriptable task into it.
2. Create the `XMLin` in-parameter of type String.
3. In the scriptable task, enter the following script:

```
//convert the string into an XML document
var document = XMLManager.fromString(XMLin);
// get all Child elements of the document (type: XMLNodeList)
var docNodelist = document.getChildNodes();
//as we know from the XML structure there is only mailmessages
var mailmessage = docNodelist.item(0);
//now we get all child elements from mailmessages
var maillist = mailmessage.getChildNodes();
```

```
//lets see how many child elements there are
var mails = maillist.length;
//lets walk though each mail (type: XMLNode)
for (i = 0; i < mails; i++) {
    mail = maillist.item(i);
//get the child elements of each mail
    var mailchilds = mail.getChildNodes();
//walk through the mail Childs
    for (j = 0; j < mailchilds.length; j++) {
//get one child
        var child = mailchilds.item(j);
//get child name
        var childName = child.nodeName;
//get child content (type: XMLElement)
        var childText = child.textContent;
//output
        System.log (childName+" : "+childText);
//lets get the childs attributes (type: XMLNamedNodeMap)
        var ChildAttribs=child.getAttributes();
//walk though all attributes
        for (k = 0; k < ChildAttribs.length; k++) {
//get one attribute (type: XMLNode)
            var ChildAttrib = ChildAttribs.item(k);
//get Attribute name
            var ChildAttribName = ChildAttrib.nodeName;
//get Attribute value
            var ChildAttribValue = ChildAttrib.nodeValue;
//output
            System.log("Attribute : "+ChildAttribName+" :
"+ChildAttribValue);
        }
    }
}
```

4. Run the workflow. Paste the XML string that was created earlier into the in-parameter, and watch the logs for the output.

Instead of walking through the XML tree, we can take some shortcuts; take a look at the *How it works...* section of this recipe.

How it works...

XML is a very nice way to exchange complex information. As you can see, forming an XML isn't that hard, especially when using a function or action. Parsing an XML is quite straightforward too; the example we used is very detailed, but it will work for any simple XML. It can be made easier by using some of these XML methods:

- `nodeList = Node.getElementsByTagName(tag)`: This method can be used to create a node list of all nodes that have the same node name
- `attributeValue = Node.getAttribute(attributeName)`: This is an undocumented method that is quite useful, as you can directly access the value of the attribute by supplying the attribute's name
- `XMLDoc = XMLManager.loadDocument(file, validate); XMLManager.saveDocument(XMLDoc,file)`: Using these methods, you can load and save XML documents onto the local Orchestrator filesystem

There's more...

In addition to the XML plugin that we looked at in this recipe, Orchestrator also supports the JavaScript built-in XML (E4X). Please note that most browsers no longer support E4X and therefore it is doubtful how long its shelf life in JavaScript will be.

Here is a short introduction to E4X XML:

- Define a new XML doc:
  ```
  var doc = new XML(XMLin);
  ```
- Output the amount of children:
  ```
  doc.Mail.length()
  ```
- Output all `From` tags:
  ```
  doc.Mail.From
  doc..From
  ```
- Output only the `From` tag from the first child:
  ```
  doc.Mail[1].From
  ```
- Get the `Date` attribute from the `From` tag:
  ```
  doc.Mail[1].Content.@Date
  ```
- Output the `Mail` record for the `From` tag that has the `Username` text in it:
  ```
  doc.Mail.(From=='Username')
  ```
- Change the text of the tag:
  ```
  doc.Mail[1].Subject = "Test";
  ```
- Change the attribute of the tag:
  ```
  doc.Mail[1].Content.@Date = "04.09.14";
  ```
- Loop throughout the children of the element:
  ```
  for each (mail in doc)
  ```

See also

To learn more about E4X, take a look at:

- `http://wso2.com/project/mashup/0.2/docs/e4xquickstart.html`
- `http://www.xml.com/pub/a/2007/11/28/introducing-e4x.html`

The example workflows are:

- 4.05.1 CreateXML
- 4.05.2 CreateXML(Function)
- 4.05.3 phraseXML(General)

Working with SQL

This recipe focuses on the interaction between Orchestrator and a SQL database. You will learn how to send SQL queries as well as commands to a database.

Getting ready

Obviously, we need a database. This database can be PostgreSQL, MS SQL, Oracle, or MySQL. For testing, you can use the PostgreSQL database that is implemented in the appliance (refer to the *Tuning the appliance* recipe in *Chapter 2, Optimizing Orchestrator Configuration*). Also, take a look at the *There's more* section of this recipe.

We will use a Microsoft SQL 2008 R2 database in this example; however, the steps are the same for all databases. The database we will be using is called `vcoapp`.

You will need an existing database and a user who is able to create/drop tables as well as insert/delete information—for example, the DBO role.

How to do it...

This recipe has multiple parts that will cover all aspects of working with a database.

Creating a JDBC connection URL

To connect to a SQL database, Orchestrator uses Java Data Base Connector (JDBC). Therefore, first, we need to create a JDBC URL.

1. Log in to the Orchestrator Client and start the workflow by navigating to **Library** | **JDBC** | **JDBC URL generator**.
2. Select the type of database you would like to connect to.

3. Enter the database's IP or FQDN, the database name, as well as the authentication details.
4. For a Microsoft SQL server, you may need to provide additional information, such as the SQL instance and the DB's domain name.

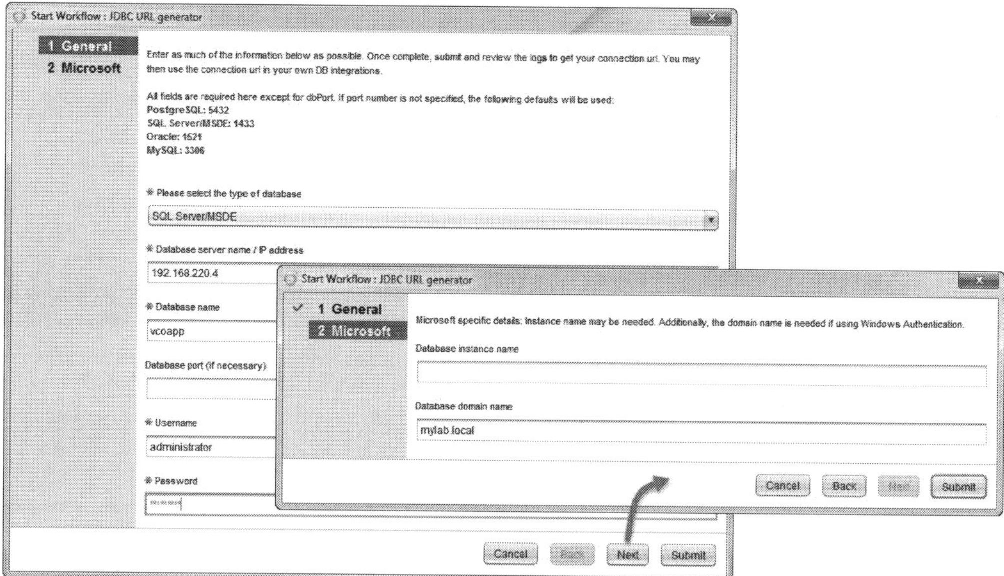

5. After the workflow has finished successfully, it's easy to copy the connection string from the logs. The string for my SQL server looks like the following:

```
jdbc:jtds:sqlserver://192.168.220.4:1433/vcoapp;domain=mylab.local
```

This workflow not only creates the URL, it also tests it, which is quite handy. Keep the URL, as we will need it for all the other parts of the recipe. A good idea is to store the URL in a configuration.

Connecting to and disconnecting from a database using JDBC

We are now going to open and close the JDBC connection to a database:

1. Create a new workflow and the following variables:

Name	Type	Place	Usage
`jdbcURL`	String	Attribute	The JDBC URL from the first part of this recipe
`user`	String	Attribute	The username for the DB connection
`password`	SecureString	Attribute	The password the for DB connection

2. Search for or browse the SDK Module **SQL**. This module contains all the methods we will use in this recipe.
3. Drag a scriptable task onto the schema and enter the following script:

```
// constructors for JDBC DB and connection
var myDB = new JDBCConnection();
var myConnect;
// connect to DB
myConnect = myDB.getConnection(jdbcURL, user , password);

//further scripting

// if the connection is open, close it.
if (myConnect) {
    // disconnect from DB
    myConnect.close();
}
```

Executing a SQL statement using JDBC

Next, we pass a SQL statement to the SQL server to be executed. Note that this executes a SQL statement; we will address SQL queries in the next section of this recipe. The difference is that queries return values, whereas the execution of a SQL statement is either successful or unsuccessful:

1. Duplicate (or add to) the workflow from the first part of this recipe.
2. Create the following variables and bind them to the scriptable task:

Name	Type	Place	Usage
`sqlStatement`	String	IN	The string with the complete SQL command.
`result`	Number	OUT	The result of the SQL command. 0 = OK.

3. Enter the following script after `//further scripting`:

```
// Open SQL statement
var mySQL = myConnect.createStatement();
// Open SQL results
var result = mySQL.executeUpdate(sqlStatement);
//close SQL statement
mySQL.close();
```

4. Run the workflow. The following SQL statement will create a table called `testtbl` that contains the `ID`, `LastName`, and `FirstName` columns:

```
CREATE TABLE testtbl (ID int, LastName varchar(255),FirstName
varchar(255));
```

5. Run the workflow again and use the following statement. It will create an entry in the table:

```
INSERT INTO testtbl VALUES (1,'Langenhan','Daniel');
```

In the *How it works...* section of this recipe, we will discuss the difference between the `createStatement` and `prepareStatement` methods.

SQL queries using JDBC

In this part, we will look at how to deal with the results from a query. We will create a **CSV** of the results of the query:

1. Duplicate the workflow from the first part of this recipe.
2. Create the following variables and bind them to the scriptable task:

Name	Type	Place	Usage
`sqlQuery`	String	IN	The string with the SQL query
`output`	String	OUT	The Output in a CSV format

3. Enter the following script after `//further scripting`:

```
// constructors for JDBC DB and connection
var myDB = new JDBCConnection();
var myConnect;
// connect to DB
myConnect = myDB.getConnection(jdbcURL, user , password);
//initialize output
output="";
//open SQL statement
var mySQL  = myConnect.createStatement();
// open query
var results = mySQL.executeQuery(sqlQuery);
// get number of columns in a table from results metadata
var resultMetaDate = results.getMetaData();
var colCount = resultMetaDate.getColumnCount();
//walk thought all rows
while ( results.next() )  {
    //Walk thought all columns
    for (i = 1; i < colCount+1; i++) {
        // Past row together
        output = output+","+results.getStringAt(i);
    }
    //new line after end of row
    output = output+"\n";
}
```

```
// close query
results.close();
// close SQL statement
mySQL.close();
// if the connection is open, close it.
if (myConnect) {
    // disconnect from DB
    myConnect.close();
}
```

4. Try the workflow with a SQL query such as `select * from testtbl`.

Also, take a closer look at the `ResultSet` and `ResultSetMetaData` objects for more possibilities to deal with the output of a SQL query.

How it works...

Orchestrator's ability to use an external database and queries and execute statements on them makes it possible for Orchestrator not only to integrate with other systems, but also to store and process data. A typical system that Orchestrator will integrate with is a Configuration Management Data Base (CMDB).

The difference between the prepare and create statements

Looking into the methods of the `Connection` object, we find the `createStatement()` method that we used earlier as well as the `prepareStatement()` method. The difference between these is that you can use variables in the `prepareStatement` method; these are defined during runtime, whereas in `createStatement`, we can use only fixed queries. Let's work through an example. We want to delete an entry from the database. The SQL delete statement is the following:

```
DELETE FROM testtbl where (FirstName = "Daniel" and LastName =
"Langenhan")
```

If we wanted to delete something else, we would have to rewrite the whole statement every time. Using `prepareStatement` we don't have to do that. We use the following SQL statement:

```
DELETE FROM testtbl where (FirstName = ? and LastName = ?)
```

To make this work, we have to not only change the code of the script, but also add two new in-parameters (`lastName` and `firstName`). The new code looks like this:

```
var stat = mySQL.prepareStatement( sqlStatement );
// exchange the first ? for the content from the in-parameters
stat.setString( 1, firstName );
// exchange the second ? for the content from the in-parameters
stat.setString( 2, lastName );
```

```
//run the altered statement
var result = stat.executeUpdate();
//close the statement
stat.close ;
```

Basically, we just substituted `?` with the values of in-parameters while the workflow is running.

There's more...

There is quite a lot more—much more than the scope of this book allows—so we'll just take a quick look at the highlights.

The SQL object

The SQL object contains a lot more types, methods, and so on. Basically, there are two methods to deal with databases in Orchestrator. In this recipe, we have focused on the JDBC connector objects. The second method allows us to use a DB and its tables within the inventory of Orchestrator. All the objects that relate to this start with SQL and are under the SQL SDK module.

The best way to explore their functionality is by working though the workflow examples that are stored in **SQL** under **Library**.

Creating a new database in the appliance's PostgreSQL

The appliance comes with a preinstalled PostgreSQL database that can (but should not) be used. The appliance is configured to allow local access, so you just need to create a new database. To do this, follows these steps:

1. Log in to the appliance with the root.
2. Run the following commands one after another:

   ```
   su postgres
   psql
   CREATE USER testuser with PASSWORD 'testpass';
   CREATE DATABASE testdb;
   GRANT ALL PRIVILEGES on DATABASE testdb to testuser;
   \q
   exit
   ```

This will create a database called `testdb` and give `testuser` all rights using the password `testpass`.

See also

You can learn more about SQL at `http://www.w3schools.com/sql/default.asp`.

The example workflows are:

- 4.06.1 Connecting to a DB
- 4.06.2 Execute SQL statement
- 4.06.3 Execute SQL statement (with prepareStatement)
- 4.06.4 Query DB

Working with PowerShell

In this recipe, we will enable Orchestrator to execute PowerShell scripts on a Windows host and deal with the results.

Getting ready

If your Orchestrator version is below 5.5.2.1, you need to download the Orchestrator PowerShell plugin (at the time of writing, the version of this plugin is 1.0.4). Install the plugin as described in the *Plugin basics* recipe in *Chapter 2, Optimizing Orchestrator Configuration*.

The next thing we need is a Windows host where the PowerShell scripts are stored and can be executed from. This can be any Windows host; however, a Windows 2008 R2 (or better) server contains all the programs required to allow Orchestrator to connect to the Windows host.

Note that only plugin Version 1.04 (or newer) can use PowerShell v4 (Windows 2012).

There are two ways to configure the Windows host: one is using OpenSSH and the other is using WinRM. We will be using Windows Remote Management (WinRM), which is already installed and integrated into Windows.

Installing the VMware PowerCLI add-on to PowerShell on the Windows host is optional.

How to do it...

This recipe is split into preparation, adding the host, executing a PowerShell script, and generating a workflow.

Preparing the Windows host with WinRM

Even if the Windows host is the one on which Orchestrator is installed, you will still need to follow this setup. This is due to the fact that the Orchestrator Java environment is executing the PowerShell connection. In this part, we will configure WinRM with basic authentication, HTTP, and unencrypted transfer. To configure WinRM for HTTPS, please refer to the PowerShell plugin documentation:

1. Log in to the Windows OS with administrator rights.
2. Create a local user who is part of the local administrator group.
3. Start a Windows command line with elevated rights.
4. Run the following command to configure the listener:

   ```
   winrm quickconfig
   ```

5. Enable basic authentication and unencrypted transfer for the service by running the following commands:

   ```
   winrm set winrm/config/service/auth @{Basic="true"}
   winrm set winrm/config/service @{AllowUnencrypted="true"}
   ```

6. Last but not least, we need to increase the package size that can be received:

   ```
   winrm set winrm/config/winrs @{MaxMemoryPerShellMB="2048"}
   ```

7. Make sure that TCP 5985 is accessible from Orchestrator to the PowerShell host.

This is a fast and easy configuration that leaves security wanting; however, it enables you to connect Orchestrator to a PowerShell host and run PowerShell scripts without facing any obstacles. If this connection works, you might like to shift to the more secure Kerberos connections (discussed later).

Adding a PowerShell host

Now that have we configured the Windows host, we need to connect Orchestrator to the Windows host. As this is a one-off operation, we will use the existing workflow to do this:

1. Start the workflow by navigating to **Library | PowerShell | Configuration | Add a PowerShell host**.
2. Enter a name for the connection to the PowerShell host. We will use this name later to establish connections to this host. Also, add the FQDN of the Windows host.
3. Choose **WinRM**, **HTTP** as the transport protocol and **Basic** for the authentication.
4. If your Orchestrator is configured for SSO, you have to choose **Shared Session**. Otherwise, you are welcome to use **Session per User**. If you choose **Shared Session**, you will need to provide a username and password.
5. Click on **Submit** and wait until the workflow is completed successfully. If that is not the case, check out the WinRM configuration.

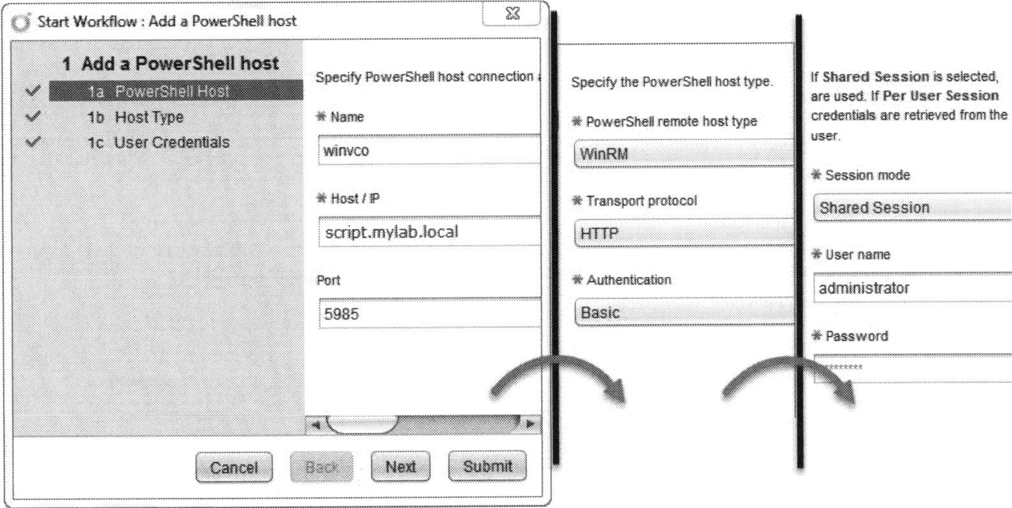

6. In the Orchestrator Client, click on **Inventory** (the paper symbol with a blue puzzle piece) and explore the tree under **PowerShell**. You will find all available PowerShell SnapIns as well as their Cmdlets.

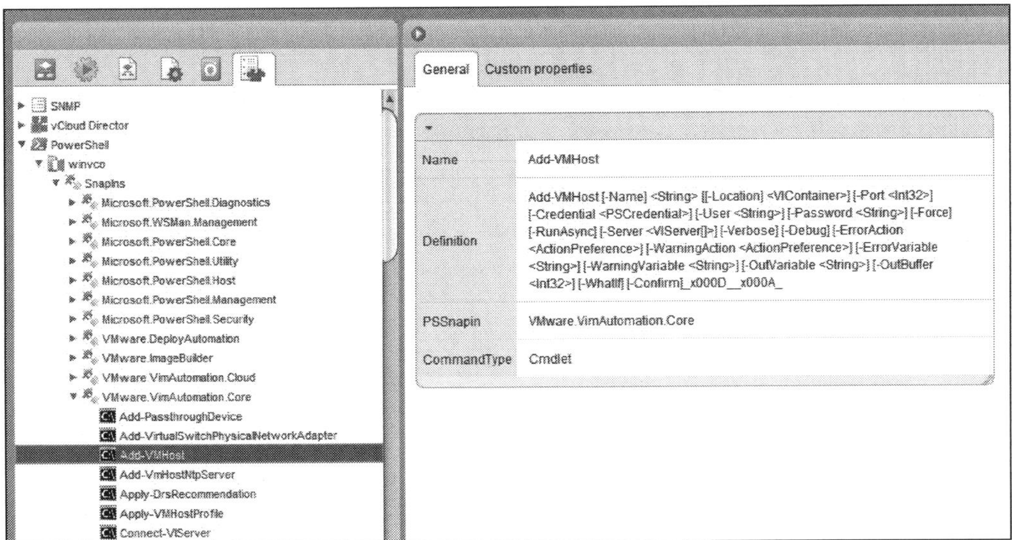

Using Kerberos authentication

In this section, we are configuring Orchestrator to connect to the PowerShell host using Kerberos authentication:

1. In the Windows host, make sure Kerberos is enabled:

   ```
   winrm set winrm/config/service/auth @{Kerberos="true"}
   ```

2. The AD user that should be used needs to be part of the `Administrator` group.
3. Use the *Configuring the Kerberos authentication* recipe in *Chapter 2, Optimizing Orchestrator Configuration*, to configure Orchestrator to use Kerberos authentication (even if you are using the Windows version).
4. Rerun the **Add a PowerShell host** workflow but, this time, use Kerberos as the authentication type.

This should work in most cases; however, Windows can be a bit tricky. If you experience problems, take a look at Spas Kaloferov's awesome article (see the *See also* section of this recipe).

Executing a script

Now that we have added a PowerShell host, we can run a script. There are two workflows that can be used for this by navigating to **Library** | **PowerShell**; they are discussed in upcoming sections.

Calling a script that is stored on the PowerShell host

For this to work, you need a PowerShell script on the PowerShell host—best one that requires some arguments, such as `get-PSDrive -Name C`:

1. Start the workflow by navigating to **Library** | **PowerShell** | **Invoke an external script**.
2. Select the PowerShell host that you added to Orchestrator.
3. Enter the complete path to the script.
4. In **Arguments**, enter all the arguments that you want to transfer like this:

   ```
   -Argument1 value1 -Argument2 value2
   ```

5. Click on **Submit** and wait until the script is executed.
6. Take a look at the logs to see the results.

Sending a script to be executed to the PowerShell host

1. Start the workflow by navigating to **Library** | **PowerShell** | **Invoke a PowerShell script**.
2. Select the PowerShell host that you added to Orchestrator.
3. For the script, enter `Get-PSDrive -Name C`:.
4. Click on **Submit** and wait until the script is executed.
5. Take a look at the logs to see the results.

Generating an action and workflow from a script

The PowerShell plugin brings with it the ability to automatically create an action and a workflow from a PowerShell script. This allows you to integrate PowerShell permanently into your automation:

1. Start the workflow by navigating to **Library** | **PowerShell** | **Generate** | **Generate an Action from a PowerShell script**.
2. Enter the script you would like to run in the script. Replace all argument values with the `{#ParamName#}` placeholder. Here an example:

Original	`Get-PSDrive -Name C:`
Enter	`Get-PSDrive -Name {#DriveName#}`

3. Select a name for the action you would like to create as well as the module where you want to create it.
4. Choose whether you would like to create a workflow and also choose the folder you would like to create it in.
5. Click on **Submit** and wait until the process has finished.
6. Check out the created workflow, called **Invoke Script [Action Name]**.

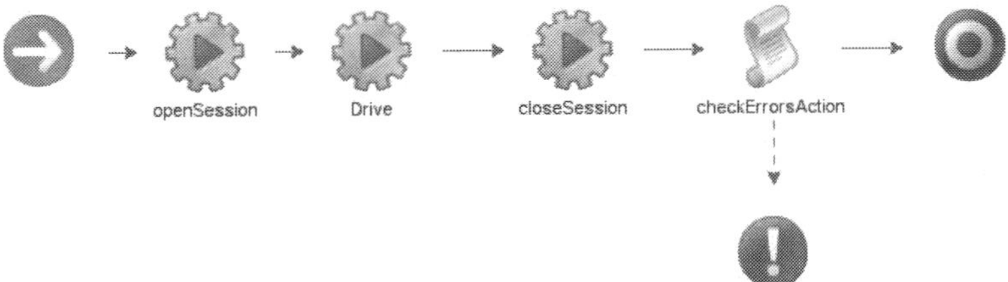

7. See how `{#Parameter#}` has been changed into an in-parameter in the action you created.

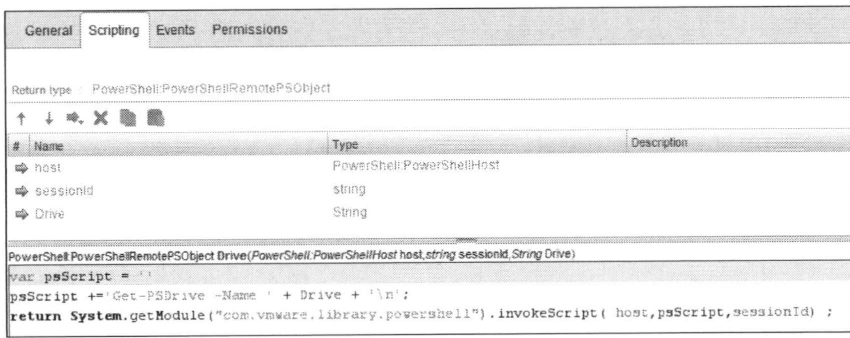

8. Run the new workflow and take a look at the logs.

How it works...

Adding PowerShell to Orchestrator will give you a far greater perspective on what Orchestrator can be used for. In the last few years, PowerShell has become a broadly used tool to write automation scripts. Microsoft uses PowerShell for a lot of management functions, such as System Center Configuration Manager (SCCM), System Center Virtual Machine Manager (SCVMM), and System Center Operations Manager (SCOM).

Using PowerShell with Orchestrator, we are basically able to execute PowerShell scripts with a right-click in the vSphere Web Client and even transport VMware objects to PowerShell scripts.

Workflow TLC

A workflow or action that has been generated by Orchestrator will require some TLC (tender loving care), for instance, changing a password entry from String to SecureString, reworking the naming structure, rearranging the variables in the workflow call, and so on.

Another typical and vital task is escaping variables. What this means is that if you run a command that requires entering a string that contains special characters such as spaces, the variable has to be encapsulated with " or '. However, we need to escape additional ' or use ". In the following example, we will show you both methods:

Original	`psScript +='Get-PSDrive -Name ' + DriveName + '\n';` Output: `Get-PSDrive -Name c:`
Using "	`psScript +='Get-PSDrive -Name "' + DriveName + '" \n';` Output: `Get-PSDrive -Name "c:"`
Escaping '	`psScript +='Get-PSDrive -Name \'' + DriveName + '\' \n';` Output: `Get-PSDrive -Name 'c:'`

The difference between `"` and `'` is that PowerShell will look inside `"  "` for `$` and assumes that what follows is a variable, whereas it will take all content between the `'` as it is.

Entry	"Test $date"	'Test $date'
Output	Test 12.01.12	Test $date

Basic versus Kerberos authentication

In this recipe, we used the basic connection to connect Orchestrator to the PowerShell host. As mentioned, this is the easiest way to build the connection and therefore, it is good for a beginner. As a professional, you want to use Kerberos as the authentication; however, you should first try to connect via the basic method, to make sure that you don't have any Firewall or other basic connection problems before going for the secure connect.

One of the differences between basic and Kerberos authentication is that basic authentication can only use local users whereas Kerberos uses AD users. Secondly, Kerberos uses encryption when communicating, whereas basic doesn't. This is quite a difference, especially in a business environment where local users should really not be used and encryption is a must.

As already mentioned, if you use Orchestrator with SSO, you can *only* use **Shared Session**, as Orchestrator is not able to forward the session. You can use **Session per User** only with an LDAP-connected Orchestrator.

PowerShell output to XML

To convert the PowerShell output into XML, run the following lines:

```
psXML = PowerShellOutput.getXml();
```

The XML output of PowerShell can be quite messy. The first thing that one needs to realize is that the PowerShell XML output adds a massive amount of spaces between tags. To clean this up, run the following regular expression:

```
xmlClean = psXML.replace(/>\s+</g, "><");
```

The following is an example of the `Get-Culture` PowerShell command. You can clearly see how the diminished command-line output (the blue PowerShell window) looks in PowerShell XML.

```
<?xml version="1.0"?>
- <Objs xmlns="http://schemas.microsoft.com/powershell/2004/04" Version="1.1.0.1">
  - <Obj RefId="0">
    - <TN RefId="0">
        <T>System.Globalization.CultureInfo</T>
        <T>System.Object</T>
      </TN>
      <ToString>en-AU</ToString>
    - <Props>
        <I32 N="LCID">3081</I32>
        <S N="Name">en-AU</S>
        <S N="DisplayName">English (Australia)</S>
        <S N="IetfLanguageTag">en-AU</S>
        <S N="ThreeLetterISOLanguageName">eng</S>
        <S N="ThreeLetterWindowsLanguageName">ENA</S>
        <S N="TwoLetterISOLanguageName">en</S>
      </Props>
    </Obj>
</Objs>
```

```
PS C:\Users\Daniel> Get-Culture

LCID             Name             DisplayName
----             ----             -----------
3081             en-AU            English (Australia)
```

As you can see, PowerShell creates tag names along with the variable names (`Obj`=Object, `S`=String, and `I32`=32-bit Integer) and sets the name of the output as an attribute with the `N` key. It's not easy to phrase these constructs, however doable.

See also

- Learn PowerShell:

  `http://technet.microsoft.com/en-us/scriptcenter/powershell.aspx`

- Learn PowerCLI:

  `https://www.packtpub.com/virtualization-and-cloud/learning-powercli`

- Refer to the *Working with XML* recipe in this chapter to learn more about phasing XML with Orchestrator.
- Connecting Orchestrator to PowerShell using Kerberos:

  `http://blogs.vmware.com/orchestrator/2012/06/vco-powershell-plugin-how-to-set-up-and-use-kerberos-authentication.html`

  `http://kaloferov.com/blog/adding-vco-powershell-host-with-account-other-than-the-default-domain-administrator-account/`

The example workflows are:

- 4.07.1 Invoke Script psExample and the action psExample in module `com.packtpub.Orchestrator-Cookbook`
- 4.07.2 Cleanup PS XML

Working with SOAP

This recipe focuses on the interaction between Orchestrator and a SOAP-based server. We will learn how to add a SOAP host to Orchestrator and execute SOAP operations.

Getting ready

We need a host that can present SOAP operations for Orchestrator to use. If you don't have a SOAP host that you can access, you can use Orchestrator itself. Orchestrator has a SOAP as well as a REST interface.

The SOAP interface of Orchestrator is scheduled to disappear but at the time of writing this, we can still use it.

To add a SOAP-based service to the Orchestrator host, we need its WSDL address; for Orchestrator, this is `https://[IP or FQDN Orchestrator]:8281/vco/vmware-vmo-webcontrol/webservice?WSDL`.

How to do it...

Again, this recipe is split into different parts.

Adding a new SOAP client

Before we can execute any SOAP operations, we need to add the SOAP interface of a host to Orchestrator:

1. Open the Orchestrator Client and switch to the **Design** mode.
2. Make sure that you have imported the SSL Certificate of the SOAP host (refer to the *Important Orchestrator base configurations* recipe in *Chapter 1, Installing and Configuring Orchestrator*).
3. Start the workflow by navigating to **Library** | **SOAP** | **Configuration** | **Add a SOAP host**.
4. Choose the name you want to save this SOAP host under.
5. Enter the WSDL address, click on **Next**, and then click on **Next** again, as we don't need a proxy to reach the SOAP host.
6. Choose **Digest** for **Authentication type** and click on **Next**.
7. For the **Session** mode, choose **Per User Session**. Click on **Submit** to finalize.

Now we have access to all SOAP operations that are exposed:

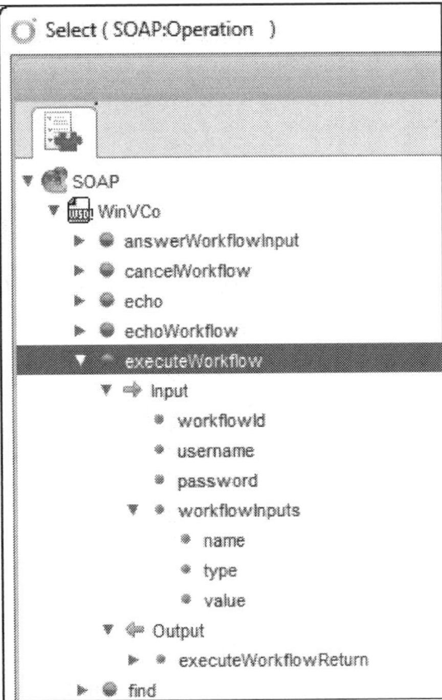

Generating a new SOAP workflow

To invoke a SOAP operation, we will create a new workflow:

1. Open the Orchestrator Client and run the workflow by navigating to **Library | SOAP | Generate a new workflow from a SOAP operation**.
2. Click on **Operation** and select a workflow (**getAllWorkflows** with Orchestrator). Click on **Next**.
3. Choose a name for the new workflow as well as a folder where the new workflow should be located.
4. As the format, you can just use the default.
5. After clicking on **Submit**, a new workflow will be created in the folder you specified. The in-parameters and out-parameters for the workflow are aligned to the inputs and outputs of the SOAP operation.
6. You can now run this workflow. The workflow will invoke the SOAP operation on the SOAP host. The return values will be returned in properties.

How it works...

SOAP (Simple Object Access Protocol) is a common way to access automation or scripting services via a network. A SOAP service advertises what scripts can be run on the SOAP host and what variables are needed to run it on its WSDL interface.

We used the Digest authentication, which provides an encrypted authentication. The other authentication types are basic (no encryption) and NTLM. NTLM (NT LAN Manager) provides encryption using the Window Security Support Provider (SSPI) framework. If you want to use NTLM, the SOAP host you're connecting to must be able to understand and use it (this is not the case with Orchestrator). Additionally, you also need to provide additional information in the configuration workflow. You need to specify the NTLM domain and, additionally, maybe a NTLM workstation.

If your Orchestrator is SSO-configured, we have to use shared sessions, as we already discussed in the *Working with PowerShell* recipe.

A typical SOAP-Orchestrator integration is with Microsoft SCOM or SCVMM.

Most generated workflows require a bit of aftercare. A typical example is that a password is handled as a String not a SecureString. Refer to the *How it works...* section in the *Working with PowerShell* recipe.

See also

Example workflow 4.08.1 Invoke getAllWorkflows from vCO

Working with REST

This recipe showcases how to interact with REST hosts. We will learn how to connect to REST Clients and how to create workflows for further usage.

Getting ready

We will need a REST-capable host. As every REST host handles things a little differently, we will use the REST interface of Orchestrator itself, as well as that of vCloud Director (vCD), to showcase the functionality. I'm aware that these are not the best examples; however, these are examples that are more or less easily accessible to readers and will show some of the difficulties that have to be overcome. I have also collected some other Orchestrator-REST integration examples in the *See also* section of this recipe.

If you are new to REST, I would like to point you to the *Accessing the Orchestrator API via REST* recipe in *Chapter 6, Advanced Operations*, as well as *Accessing REST with Firefox* from my book *VMware vCloud Director Cookbook*. The chapter is free to access at this URL: `https://www.packtpub.com/virtualization-and-cloud/vmware-vcloud-director-cookbook` (start at page 56)

Both recipes show you how to access Orchestrator and the vCloud Director REST interface using Firefox and showcase quite nicely how REST works.

How to do it...

This recipe is divided into connecting, gathering information, sending information, as well as creating workflows.

Connecting to a REST host

The first thing we have to do is add the REST host to Orchestrator:

1. Start the workflow by navigating to **Library** | **HTTP-REST** | **Configuration** | **Add a REST host**.
2. Enter a name under which you want to save this connection.
3. Enter **REST URL** for this host.

Orchestrator	`https://[IP or FQDN Orchestrator]:8281/vco/api/`
vCloud Director	`https://[IP or FQDN vCD]/api/`

4. The default timeouts are OK; click on **Next**.
5. Choose whether you require a proxy (mostly not needed).

6. Choose an authentication method (refer to the *How it works...* section) if you're unsure whether basic authentication will work with all clients; however, it isn't safe for production use.
7. If your Orchestrator is connected to SSO, you can only use **Shared Session**, if your Orchestrator is using AD/LDAP, you can use **Per User Session**.

We will discuss the different security options later.

You have now added the REST host to Orchestrator; however, it isn't that easy, after all.

Whereas the Orchestrator REST interface sends authentication with each request, vCloud Director actually uses a separate login URL, `https://[IP or FQDN vCD]/api/sessions`, to authenticate once only. Some other REST interfaces do the same. To adjust to this behavior, you can use the workflow by navigating to **Library** | **HTTP-REST Samples** | **Set vCloud Director Authentication to a REST host**.

Using GET

We will now demonstrate a GET request to a REST host. GET gets information from a REST host:

1. Start the workflow by navigating to **Library** | **HTTP-REST** | **Configuration** | **Add a REST operation**.
2. Select the REST host to which you want to add the operation.
3. Give the operation a name for the inventory.
4. Add the template URL. The template URL is the URL that you will use the method (in our example here, GET) on. Use the following examples.

Orchestrator	about/	Displays the build numbers and version of Orchestrator
vCloud Director	org/	Displays all available organizations

5. Submit the workflow and wait until it has finished.
6. Start the workflow by navigating to **Library** | **HTTP-REST** | **Invoke a REST operation**.
7. Select the REST operation from the inventory and submit it.

You will see that the GET on Orchestrator will result in a string that contains a JSON object, whereas the vCD one will show an error. The error is best seen in the log files and will tell you this: **The request has invalid accept header**. This is due to the fact that vCD requires an **Accept** header to process return messages. Depending on the REST host, this is quite an important thing; therefore, let's dive into the code behind a request.

The code for a request is pretty simple:

```
//create the request
var request = RESThost.createRequest("GET", "/org", null);
//execute the request
var response = request.execute();
//write the result into a string (JSON object style)
stringOUT = response.contentAsString;
```

What vCD needs is a header that accepts `application/*+xml;version=5.5`. Change the code as follows:

```
//create the request
var request = RESThost.createRequest("GET", "/org", null);
// Add a header to the request
request.setHeader("Accept","application/*+xml;version=5.5");
//execute the request
var response = request.execute();
//write the result into a string (JSON object style)
stringOUT = response.contentAsString;
```

Using POST

While GET gets information, POST will post information to the REST host. We will only use Orchestrator, as the vCD one is a bit more complicated and requires additional input. If you are interested, check out the free chapter mentioned in the *Getting ready* section:

1. Start the workflow by navigating to **Library** | **HTTP-REST** | **Configuration** | **Add a REST operation**.
2. Select the REST host to which you want to add the operation.
3. Give the operation a name for the inventory.
4. Add this as the template URL: `workflows/{id}/executions/`; the `{id}` part will be replaced later at execution.
5. Select **POST** and enter `application/xml` as the content type.
6. Submit the workflow.

Before we can execute the workflow, we need to get the ID of the workflow. In this example, we will use the example workflow 3.01 Workflow basics. Using the Orchestrator Client, browse the workflow and copy its ID from the **General** tab (for example, e8222d1a-4aed-4626-9885-9e0f4bbeab61):

1. Start the workflow by navigating to **Library** | **HTTP-REST** | **Invoke a REST operation**.
2. Select the REST operation from the inventory.
3. Enter the ID of the workflow under parameter 1.

4. Under the content enter the following:

```
<execution-context xmlns="http://www.vmware.com/vco">
    <parameters>
        <parameter type="string" name="input" scope="local">
            <string>Entry String</string>
        </parameter>
    </parameters>
</execution-context>
```

5. Submit the workflow and use the Orchestrator Client to see the result.

The POST request requires you to enter additional information. The content is in the String form; however, it contains XML. The return code should be a 202 status code, which means that the request was accepted.

Creating a workflow from a REST operation

To create a workflow out of a REST operation, follow these steps:

1. Start the workflow by navigating to **Library** | **HTTP-REST** | **Generate a new workflow from a REST operation**.
2. Select the REST operation; if you are using a POST, you will also see the content type you entered.
3. Give the new workflow a name and select a folder for it.

When running the workflow, you will be required to enter the same variables that you entered when using the **Invoke a REST operation** workflow.

How it works...

REST stands for **Representational State Transfer** and is the way that most applications nowadays use as an interface. Even Orchestrator itself switches from a SOAP interface to a REST interface.

Authentications

Orchestrator can use the following authentication methods out-of-the-box.

None	Doesn't use any authentication at all.
OAuth	A token-based authentication. For the difference between v1 and v2, see `https://blog.apigee.com/detail/oauth_differences`.
Basic	Basic authentication, no encryption, and clear text passwords.
Digest	Provides a basic encrypted authentication.

NTLM	NTLM (NT LAN Manager) provides encryption using the Window Security Support Provider (SSPI) framework.
Kerberos	Encrypted authentication using tickets. Also see the *Configuring the Kerberos authentication* recipe in *Chapter 2, Optimizing Orchestrator Configuration*.

Working with the results of a REST request

Let's take a look at the results of a request. The results are part of the `RESTResponse` object. The two important attributes of this object for most users are `contentAsString` and `statusCode`. The `statusCode` attribute contains the status code of the request. You can view the basic response codes at `https://[IP or FQDN Orchestrator]:8281/vco/api/docs/rest.html`.

The `contentAsString` attribute returns a string that represents the XML returned. You can use the information in the *Working with XML* recipe in this chapter to phrase the return code. E4X XML is probably the easiest way to do this. Some REST interfaces, such as Orchestrator, can also be configured to use JSON instead of XML.

There's more...

Taking a look at the code behind the mentioned workflows, we find that authentications are created by the `RESTAuthenticationManager` object using the `createAuthentication()` method. This method requires the authentication type (Basic, OAuth 1.0, and so on) as well as the authentication parameters (`authParams`). The `authParams` variable can have different content depending on the REST host and login method used. Take a look at this example:

OAuth 1.0	`var authParams = [consumerKey, consumerSecret, accessToken, accessTokenSecret];`
OAuth 2.0	`var authParams = [oauth2Token];`
Basic	`var authParams = [sessionMode, authUserName, authPassword];`
vCD	`var authParams = [sessionMode, username, password, organization, loginUrl];`

So, if you have trouble connecting to your REST host, you can simply alter authParams to the specifications of your REST host.

See also

- Orchestrator and VEEAM backup:

  `http://www.vcoportal.de/2014/02/automating-veeam-with-vco-and-the-restful-api/`

- Orchestrator and Nutanix PrismAPI:

  `http://philthevirtualizer.com/2014/03/03/connecting-to-the-nutanix-prismapi-with-vcenter-orchestrator/`

- Orchestrator and Avamar:

  `http://velemental.com/2014/07/18/accessing-avamar-rest-api-from-the-vco-rest-plugin/`

- Orchestrator and vCNS (vShield):

  `https://v-reality.info/2013/04/provisioning-vds-vxlan-virtual-wires-using-vcenter-orchestrator/`

- Orchestrator and NSX:

  `http://virtuallygone.wordpress.com/2014/03/27/automating-firewall-rule-creation-in-nsx-with-vco-and-vcac-part-one-rest-host-configuration-in-vco/`

The example workflows are:

- 4.09.1 vCD Test
- 4.09.2 Invoke Run Workflow: POST workflows/{id}/executions/

Working with Active Directory

In this recipe, we will look at how Orchestrator uses the Active Directory plugin.

Getting ready

We need an AD server for this recipe as well as access to the AD server OS itself.

How to do it...

We split this recipe into multiple parts.

Preparing AD for SSL

You can add AD to Orchestrator without using SSL; however, you will not be able to create users, change passwords, or use any other more secure options. If you decide not to use SSL, skip this step.

First, we will install Active Directory Certificate Services.

Microsoft does not recommend that you run a CA server on a domain controller; however, for a lab, it is totally okay.

To activate SSL for AD, follow these steps:

1. Log in to the Windows server that will host the CA. In my case, this is my domain controller: `ADDNS.mylab.local` with domain administrator rights.
2. Add the **Active Directory Certificate Services** server role.
3. Just click on **Next** and accept all the default settings. In the following screenshot, you'll find all the settings I used (the default ones for my domain):

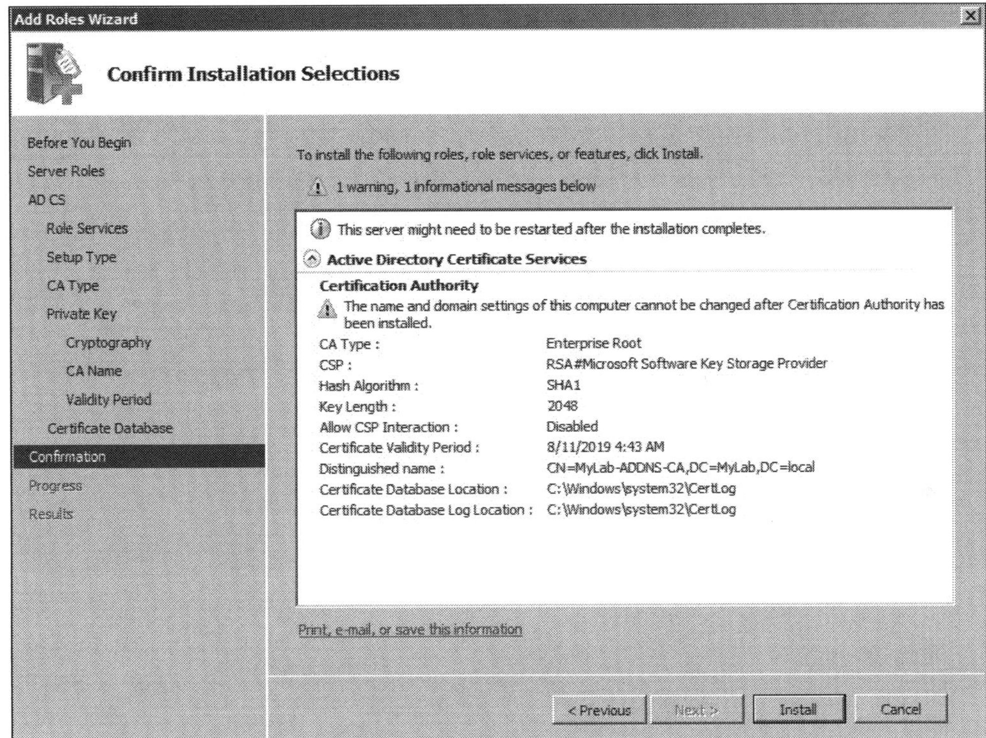

4. After the wizard has finished, open up **Group Policy Manager** and edit **Default Domain Controller Policy**.
5. Navigate to **Computer Configuration** | **Policies** | **Windows Settings** | **Security Settings** | **Public Key Policies** | **Automatic Certificate Request Settings** and then go to **New** | **Automatic Certificate Request Setup**.
6. Finish this wizard again by just clicking on **Next**, which forces the creation of a certificate for your domain controllers.

7. Wait a few minutes or force a policy update on the domain controller using the **gpupdate/force** command.
8. Start the **Certification Authority** tool and check in **Issued Certificates** whether the domain controller was issued with a certificate.
9. To test the SSL configuration connection, we will use Microsoft's **ldp** tool (`C:\Windows\System32\ldp.exe`). Start ldp and connect to the domain controller using SSL (port 636). If this test is successful, continue. If not, check out `http://technet.microsoft.com/en-us/library/cc875810.aspx`.
10. Last but not least, make sure that the Windows firewall allows TCP 389 (with SSL TCP 636) to pass.

Registering AD with Orchestrator

Now, we add AD to Orchestrator:

1. Start the workflow by navigating to **Library** | **Microsoft** | **Active Directory** | **Configuration** | **Configure Active Directory server**.
2. Enter the FQDN of your AD server.
3. Enter the port you are using: `389` without SSL and `636` with SSL.
4. The root is written in the LDAP format, for example, `DC=mylab,DC=local`.
5. Choose whether to use SSL or not. If you are using SSL, you can choose to be asked when importing the certificate.
6. The default domain is written in the `@[FQDN Domain name]` format, for example, `@mylab.local`.
7. If you have configured Orchestrator with SSO, you have to choose a shared session. Enter domain-administrator credentials.

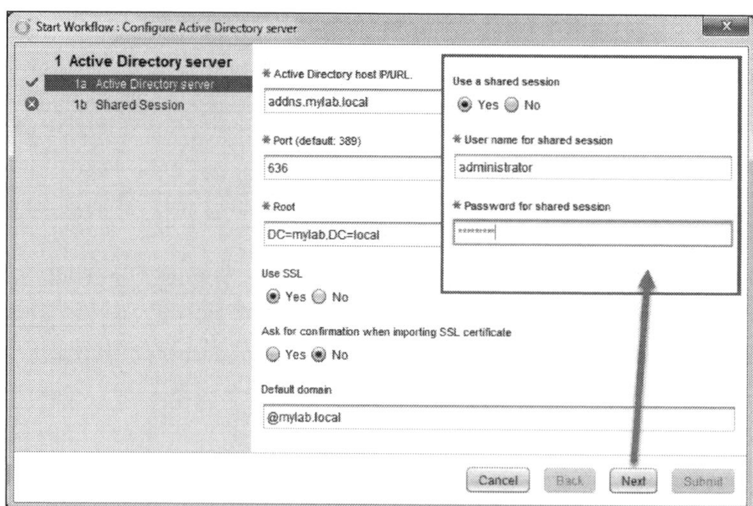

Working with AD

The AD plugin comes with a lot of great workflows that work without a problem. The following table shows you which workflows exist:

Workflow	**Use**
Computer	Create, destroy, disable, and enable a computer
Organizational Unit	Create and destroy
User	Create, destroy, disable, enable, change password, add, and remove from groups
User Groups	Create and destroy groups and add and remove users, computers, and groups to/from groups

As long as you have added the domain controller to your Orchestrator, you can run and integrate all these scripts into your own workflows.

How it works...

The Microsoft plugin is quite easy to use; however, as you may have noticed, setting it up isn't as straightforward. The main issue is using SSL with the domain controller; as soon as this is working, you're home free.

The drawback of an SSO-configured Orchestrator should now be apparent, making it necessary to use a shared session. Some clients have argued that it would make more sense to use an LDAP integration rather than an SSO one, so they can use a session per user. My argument is that SSO integration is the way forward with VMware and that the same customers are happy to use vCloud Director or VMware View with a dedicated user.

Microsoft integration allows for a range of possibilities, user management being the prime target. There are more possibilities that the plugin offers; explore the AD API object.

See also

Refer to the *Managing AD users with vRA* recipe in *Chapter 7, Working with VMware Infrastructure*.

Working with SNMP

This recipe centers on SNMP. Here, you will learn how to use Orchestrator to receive SNMP traps from vCenter/ESXi and use them to trigger workflows.

Getting ready

For this recipe, we need an SNMP source. We will use vCenter and ESXi hosts as SNMP sources.

To prepare vCenter and ESXi servers to send or receive SNMP messages, refer to the *There's more...* section of this recipe.

How to do it...

We will split this recipe into configuring and using SNMP with Orchestrator.

Configuring SNMP devices

To configure Orchestrator to send or receive SNMP messages from SNMP devices, follow these steps for each SNMP device:

1. In the Orchestrator Client, start the workflow by navigating to **Library** | **SNMP** | **Device Management** | **Register an SNMP device**.
2. In **Device address**, enter the IP or FQDN of the device you want to send or receive SNMP messages to/from.
3. **Name** is just a string to identify the SNMP device in the inventory.
4. The **Advanced** function is the configuration that is used to send SNMP messages. Here, you can configure the port, the protocol function, as well as the community string for sending.

Please remember that for vCenter, you just need to configure the hostname, as vCenter won't answer SNMP requests.

Sending a GET query to an ESXi host

Having configured ESXi to send and receive SNMP messages, let's try one out:

1. In the Orchestrator Client, start the workflow by navigating to **Library** | **SNMP** | **Query Management** | **Add a query to an SNMP device**.
2. In **Device**, select the ESXi server and select **GET** in **Type**.
3. In **OID**, enter **1.3.6.1.2.1.1.5.0** (this gets the hostname of the device).
4. In **Name**, enter `Hostname`.
5. Next, run the query by running the workflow; navigate to **Library** | **SNMP** | **Query Management** | **Run an SNMP query**.
6. Select the query underneath the ESXi SNMP device and click on **Submit**. Check the logs for the results.

Refer to the *How it works...* section for more information about OIDs.

Configuring a vCenter alarm to send an SNMP message

vCenter can only send an SNMP message using an alarm configured to send SNMP messages. We will configure an alarm that goes off when a new resource pool is created.

1. Open your vSphere Web Client.
2. Navigate to the object the alarm should be added to, such as a cluster.
3. Click on the **Manage** tab and then click on **Alarm Definitions**.
4. Click on **Add** (the green plus icon).
5. Give the new alarm a name such as `SNMP Example`, opt to monitor **Clusters**, and select **specific event occurring on this object**.
6. Use Add (the green plus icon) to add a trigger. Use the selector to choose **Resource Pool created** and set the status to **Warning**. Click on **Next**.
7. Use Add (the green plus icon) to add an action. Use the selector to choose **Send a notification trap** and click on **Finish**.

To learn more about vCenter alarms, please take a look at the vSphere documentation, or check out this article: `http://www.pearsonitcertification.com/articles/article.aspx?p=1928231&seqNum=6.`

Receiving an SNMP message from vCenter

After you have configured vCenter to send an SNMP alarm, we now use Orchestrator to receive the SNMP message:

1. In Orchestrator, start the workflow by navigating to **Library** | **SNMP** | **Wait for a trap on an SNMP device**.
2. Select the SNMP device you want to listen to. The OID is optional.
3. The workflow will pause until it receives an SNMP message from the selected device.
4. In vCenter, create a new resource pool. This should trigger the configured alarm and send an SNMP message to Orchestrator.
5. Check the logs of the workflow after it has received the SNMP message.

Refer to the *How it works...* section for more information about OID.

Using policies to trap SNMP messages

To use Orchestrator to continually monitor a device for new SNMP messages, follow these steps:

1. Switch Orchestrator to the **Administer** mode.
2. Click on **Policy Templates** (the yellow page with a green border icon).
3. Navigate to **Library | SNMP | SNMP Trap** and select **Apply policy**.
4. Give the new policy a name and description.
5. Select the SNMP device you would like to use and click on **Submit**.
6. Orchestrator automatically switches to the **Run** mode, into the **Policies** section, and onto the policy you have just created. Select **Edit** (the pencil icon).
7. In **Scripting**, expand the subscription and click on **OnTrap**.
8. In the **Script** tab, you will find that there is already a script that will output the SNMP message to the logs.
9. Save and close.

Instead of the existing script, you can create a script or workflow to phrase the SNMP messages. To get to the SNMP message data from the policy event as an array of properties, follow this script:

```
//get the SNMP data out of the Policy
var key = event.getValue("key");
var snmpResult = SnmpService.retrievePolicyData(key);
// convert the SNMPSnmpResult into Array of Property
var data = System.getModule("com.vmware.library.snmp").
processSnmpResult(snmpResult);
```

You can then use the OID number to fork to different workflows to address the issues raised by the SNMP message. A very good example of this can be found at `http://blogs.vmware.com/orchestrator/2013/04/vcenter-operations-integration-with-vcenter-orchestrator-in-5-minutes-or-less.html`

How it works...

SNMP stands for Simple Network Management Protocol and is used to manage and monitor systems by sending or receiving SNMP messages. A system can be monitored or managed by either making it send SNMP messages, or by responding to requests for information.

Each SNMP message can be accompanied by a community string. When an SNMP message is received, the receiver checks the community string against the one defined in the SNMP trap. If the string matches the message, it is accepted. The community string acts as a security measure. The default community string is `public`.

The important thing to understand about vCenter is that vCenter can only send SNMP messages when it starts up or when a triggered alarm is configured to send an SNMP message; it doesn't respond to SNMP requests.

ESXi hosts, however, can not only send messages, but can also react to SNMP requests.

OID and MIB

An **Management Information Base** (**MIB**) is a file that contains descriptions of **Object Identifiers** (**OIDs**). Each vendor defines its own OIDs that are then distributed in MIBs. The VMware MIBs can be downloaded from `kb.vmware.com/kb/1013445`.

A text file that can be downloaded from `kb.vmware.com/kb/2054359` contains all the VMware OIDs in a more readable version.

Working with SNMP return data

The return data of the default SNMP workflows is an array of properties. Each of the array elements contains one OID. Each property contains the following keys:

Key	**Meaning**	**Example key content**
`oid`	The OID identifier	`1.3.6.1.4.1.6876.4.3.306.0`
`type`	The Orchestrator variable type	`String`
`snmpType`	The SNMP variable type	`Octet String`

`value`	The content of the message	`Alarm ResourcePool - Event: Resource pool created (6656)`
		`Summary: Created resource pool asdsadfsad in compute-resource MyCluster in mylab`
		`Date: 16/11/2014 3:07:01 PM`
		`User name: VSPHERE.LOCAL\Administrator`
		`Resource pool: MyCluster`
		`Data center: mylab`
		`Arguments:`
		`    parent.name = Resources`

However, this is produced by the `processSnmpResult` action in the `com.vmware.library.snmp` module. The real SNMP results are stored in a bit more complex variable type, which is `SNMPSnmpResult`. In Orchestrator, it is easier to work with the array of properties, but check out the action and the variable type yourself.

SNMP – port 162 versus port 4000

The default port to send SNMP messages on is TCP 162; however, due to the fact that Linux systems have security restrictions for listening on ports below 1024, the Orchestrator SNMP listener is set to listen on port 4000. This is true for the Orchestrator appliance as well as for the Windows installation.

If you have a device that is not able to send SNMP messages on any port other than 162, here is a way around it (at least with the appliance).

1. Log in to your Orchestrator appliance with the root.
2. Run the following command:

   ```
   iptables -t nat -A PREROUTING -p udp --dport 162 -j REDIRECT --to
   4000
   ```

3. To make this change stick, run the following command:

   ```
   iptables-save
   ```

There's more...

In this section, we take a look at how to configure SNMP on vCenter and on ESXi.

Configuring SNMP for vCenter

For vCenter to be able to send SNMP messages using alarms, we need to configure it first:

1. Open your vSphere Web Client.
2. Navigate to your vCenter and then click on the **Manage** tab.
3. Click on **Settings** and then click on **Edit**.
4. Click on **SNMP receivers**.
5. You can add up to four different SNMP receivers that vCenter can send messages to. For each one you need to specify:
   - The IP or FQDN of the SNMP receiver
   - The port. The default is TCP 162; however, the listener on the Orchestrator appliance is set to TCP 4000
   - The community string (if you're unsure, use the default: `public`)
6. When finished, click on **OK**.
7. Don't forget to configure your firewall to allow TCP 4000 out.

Configuring ESXi servers for SNMP

There are quite a lot of ways to configure SNMP on ESXi hosts. However, they all come down to the same basic method: set SNMP locally for every ESXi, and then open the ESXi firewall. You can use PowerCLI or any other method to interact with the API or use host profiles. In the following steps, we will use the `esxcli` command directly on the ESXi host to configure SNMP v1 and v2. Please note that the default port of the Orchestrator SNMP listener is TCP 4000 not TCP 162:

1. Configure the SNMP target(s):

   ```
   esxcli system snmp set --targets target_address@port/community
   ```

2. Set a different GET port for SNMP (if required):

   ```
   esxcli system snmp set --port port
   ```

3. Enable SNMP:

   ```
   esxcli system snmp set --enable true
   ```

4. Allow SNMP on the ESXi firewall:

   ```
   esxcli network firewall ruleset set --ruleset-id snmp --allowed-all true --enabled true
   esxcli network firewall refresh
   ```

We have used the local `esxcli` commands in this example simply because you could write an SSH workflow to patch all your ESXi hosts based on this example.

To configure SNMP v3 (using authentication and encryption), take a look at the vSphere Monitoring and Performance Guide that is part of the VMware vSphere documentation set.

By default, ESXi SNMP is configured to send SNMP messages for CIM hardware monitoring. This means that you will receive SNMP messages if a hardware component of your ESXi server is alerted.

See also

An example of automating hardening for new VMs is

`http://blogs.vmware.com/vsphere/2012/07/automatically-securing-virtual-machines-using-vcenter-orchestrator.html`

An example showing how to integrate vCOPs into Orchestrator:

`http://blogs.vmware.com/orchestrator/2013/04/vcenter-operations-integration-with-vcenter-orchestrator-in-5-minutes-or-less.html`

`https://solutionexchange.vmware.com/store/products/vco-remediation-workflow-package-for-vcops#.VJF_hXuBxkk`

Working with AMQP

In this recipe, we will learn how to use Orchestrator as a producer and consumer of AMQP message queues, how to create a subscription, and how to use Orchestrator policies to react to messages in the queues.

Getting ready

If you are totally new to AMQP, I suggest you start reading the *How it works...* section first.

An AMQP broker such as RabbitMQ is required. You can download it from `http://www.rabbitmq.com`. You can find a fast and easy Windows installation and configuration for RabbitMQ in the *There's more...* section.

How to do it...

As with SOAP, REST, and a lot of other modules, we can actually use the provided workflows. So in the following sections, we will mostly make use of them.

Adding an AMQP host

To start with AMQP, we first need to add an AMQP broker to Orchestrator:

1. Start the workflow by navigating to **Library** | **AMQP** | **Configuration** | **Add a broker**.
2. Give the connection a name.
3. Add the broker IP or FQDN; the default port is TCP 5672.
4. **Virtual host** (vhost) is always / in a freshly installed AMQP broker.
5. You can use SSL (and probably should) and then enter the username and password that are granted access to the virtual host.
6. After you have submitted the workflow, check out the inventory. Your host should now be visible.

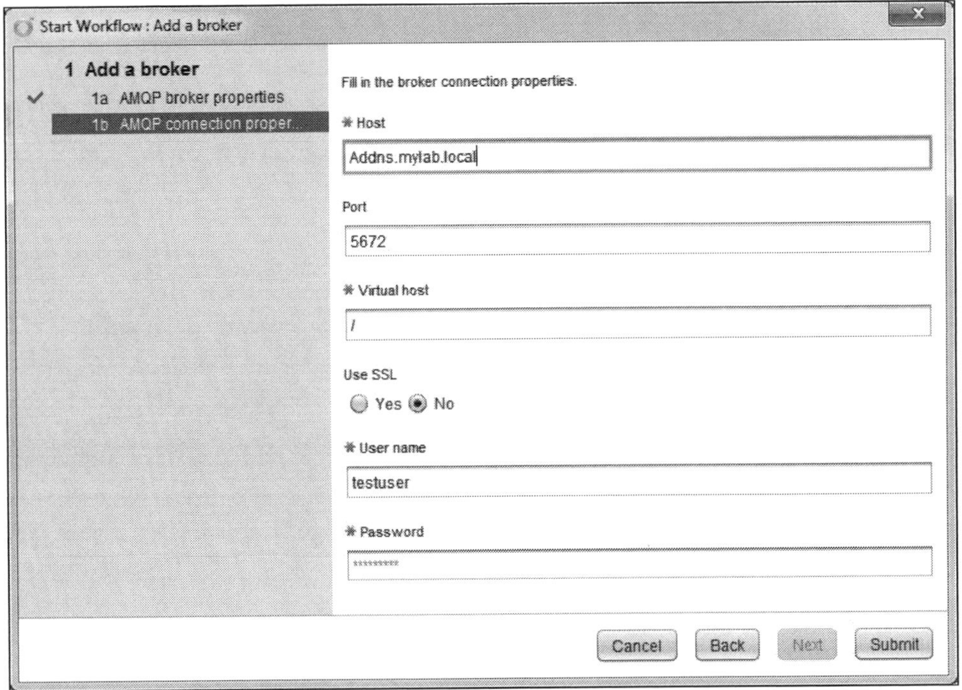

Defining exchanges, queues, and binds

To work with AMQP, we need exchanges and queues, so we will define them now:

1. Run the workflow by navigating to **Library** | **AMQP** | **Declare an exchange**.
2. Select the broker for which you want to add the exchange.
3. Give the exchange a name such as `systemExchange` (this is used by vCloud Director).
4. Select a type of exchange (refer to the *How it works...* section).
5. **Durable** means that messages will be kept in the broker even if it restarts.
6. **AutoDelete** will delete the exchange as soon as there are no more queues bound to it.

Now we will create a queue:

1. Run the workflow by navigating to **Library** | **AMQP** | **Declare an queue**.
2. Select the broker.
3. Name the queue, such as **vco**.
4. Select **Durable**.
5. **Exclusive** means that only one client is allowed for this queue.
6. **Auto Delete** in a queue means that the queue itself will be deleted as soon as there are no more subscribers to it.

Now we will bind the queue to an exchange:

1. Run the workflow by navigating to **Library** | **AMQP** | **Bind**.
2. Select the broker.
3. Select the queue name and the exchange you want to bind it to.
4. Enter a routing key (# is a wildcard for everything).

Sending messages

We will now send a message to the exchange:

1. Run the workflow by navigating to **Library** | **AMQP** | **Send a text message**.
2. Select the broker.
3. Enter the exchange as well as the routing key (at this stage, anything will do).
4. Enter a text message.
5. The message is now stored in the queue until it is read.

Receiving messages

We will now read the message we sent to the queue:

1. Run the workflow by navigating to **Library** | **AMQP** | **Send a text message**.
2. Select the broker.
3. Enter the queue you would like to receive the message from.
4. The message body is in the out-parameter body.

If you are new to AMQP, then I would suggest that you read the *How it works...* section at this stage, where an example of the value of all this is provided.

Subscribing to a queue

Subscribing to a queue means that Orchestrator can use a policy to monitor this queue continually for new messages:

1. Run the workflow by navigating to **Library** | **AMQP** | **Configuration** | **Subscribe to queues**.
2. Enter a name for the subscription by which you can later identify it in the policy.
3. Select the broker.
4. Select the queue(s) you would like to subscribe to, such as **vco**.
5. Your subscription is now visible under the AMQP infrastructure.

Using a policy as trigger

You should be aware of how Orchestrator policies work; refer to the *Working with policies* section in *Chapter 6, Advanced Operations*.

1. Switch Orchestrator to the **Administer** mode.
2. Click on policy templates (the yellow page with the green border icon).
3. Navigate to **Library** | **AMQP** | **Subscription** and select **Apply policy**.
4. Give the new policy a name and description.
5. Select the AMQP subscription you would like to use and click on **Submit**.
6. Orchestrator automatically switches to the **Run** mode, and you are automatically presented with the policy you have just created in the **Policies** section. Select **Edit** (the pencil icon).
7. In the **Scripting** tab, expand the subscription and click on **OnMessage**.
8. In the **Workflow** tab, click on **Choose a workflow** (the magnifying glass icon) and select the workflow to execute when a new message arrives. You can choose the example workflow 4.12.1.
9. Save and close.

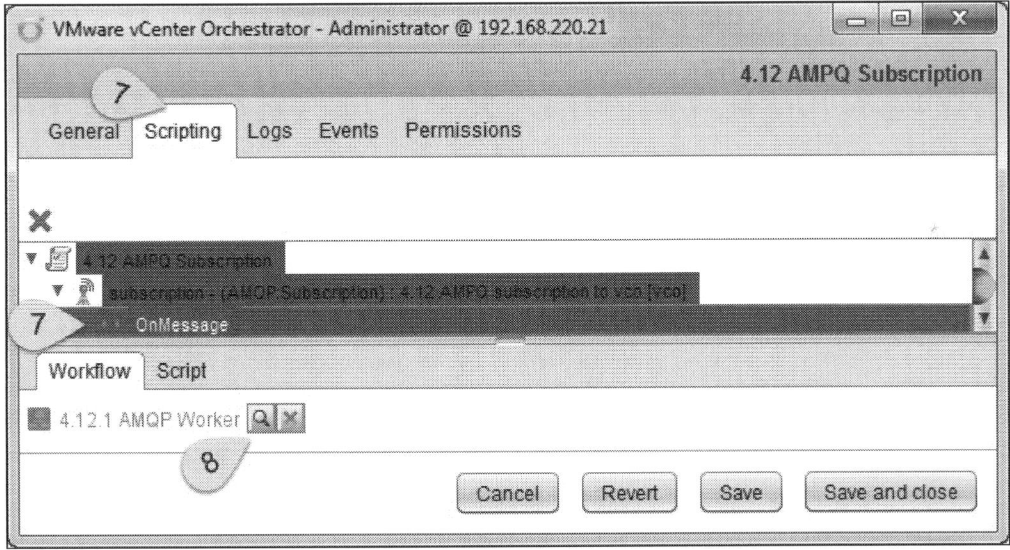

10. Now, start the policy (the green play button).
11. You can use the example workflow 12.4.3 to fill up the queue with messages. Watch the logs in the policy to see the execution happening.

How it works...

A message bus such as RabbitMQ can be compared to a mail server that stores mails until they are taken off the server. The **Advanced Message Queuing Protocol** (**AMQP**) defines a publisher/producer as someone sending messages, a broker (server) as the storage and process host, and a client/consumer as someone who receives messages.

Any message that is sent to the broker will be put in an exchange. The exchange will use the routing key to route the message into a queue. A consumer will read messages from a queue.

AMQP uses a virtual host or vHost (nothing to do with virtualization), which defines authentications, which means that you can have different vHosts that provide access to different users, as you cannot give access rights to exchanges or queues.

Here is a simple example using Orchestrator (example workflows 4.12.1 and 4.12.2):

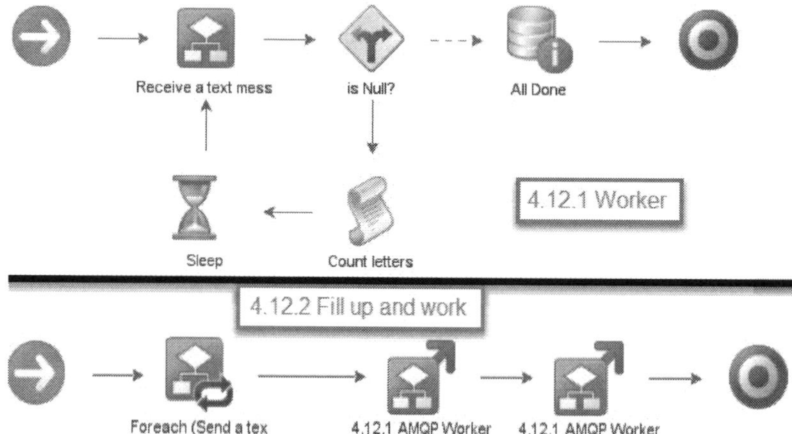

The example workflow 4.12.2 will fill up the `systemExchange` exchange from an attribute (an array of strings) using the # routing key. The # routing key will just forward everything into the `vco` queue. It will then start the workflow example 4.12.1 twice asynchronously. Each of the *Worker* workflows will go and get a message from the queue, check whether the body is defined (not `Null`), and then sleep one second for each letter in the message.

When you run the workflow, you will see how the two worker workflows grab the next message in the queue and work on it until the queue is empty.

To understand routing and exchanges, we need to explain the four different kinds of exchanges:

Exchange type	Description
Direct	This exchange routes messages, depending on their routing key, to a specific queue that is specified by the routing key in the exchange-queue binding.
Fanout	All messages sent to this exchange will be forwarded into all queues that are bound to it.
Headers	This ignores the routing key. It routes messages depending on the sender (as in, mail headers).
Topics	Routing is done using wildcards. There are two wildcards that AMQP understands: * means exactly one word and # means none to many words.

There's more...

Let's take a quick look at how to install and get AMQP going using RabbitMQ.

Installing RabbitMQ

The following steps will install RabbitMQ on a Windows host and configure a user to connect from the outside. Please note that this is a quick-and-dirty installation and configuration that is only okay for labs; however, it gets beginners going:

1. Download RabbitMQ from `http://www.rabbitmq.com` (in this example, we will use the Windows installation).
2. Download OTP from `http://www.erlang.org/download.html`, as RabbitMQ for Windows requires this package.

> Perform all the following steps on the same host. This is important, as RabbitMQ is configured to only accept localhost connections by default.

3. Make sure TCP 5672 and 15672 are open in and outgoing.
4. Install **OTP** with the defaults.
5. Install **RabbitMq** with the defaults.
6. Run the program by navigating to **Start** | **RabbitMQ Server** | **Command Prompt (sbin dir)**.
7. In the console that opens, type `rabbitmq-plugins enable rabbitmq_management`.

8. Open a browser and browse `http://localhost:15672`.
9. The default user is `guest` and the password is `guest`.
10. In the RabbitMQ management, click on **Admin**.
11. Enter a new username (for example, `testuser`) as well as a password. Add the tag **Admin** and click on **Add user**.
12. The user is created. Now, click on the user, as shown in the following screenshot.
13. The details of the user are displayed. Click on **Set permission**.

You now are able to connect from the outside to RabbitMQ and use it.

See also

AMQP basics:

- `https://www.rabbitmq.com/tutorials/amqp-concepts.html`
- `http://www.rabbitmq.com/tutorials/tutorial-one-java.html`

There's an awesome article on how to use AMQP, vCloud director, and Orchestrator together at `http://www.vcoteam.info/articles/learn-vco/179-configure-the-amqp-plug-in.html`

The example workflows are:

- 4.12.1 AMQP Worker
- 4.12.2 Fill up and work
- 4.12.3 Fill

5

Basic Orchestrator Operations

This chapter is dedicated to the typical operations that every Orchestrator admin should know about. In *Chapter 6, Advanced Operations*, we will go deeper and discuss some nifty things that you can do with Orchestrator. However, for the moment, let's look at these:

- Basic Orchestrator operations for Orchestrator elements
- Changing elements in a workflow
- Undelete workflows and actions
- Importing and exporting Orchestrator elements
- Synchronizing Orchestrator elements between Orchestrator servers
- Working with packages
- User management
- User preferences
- Scheduling workflows
- Workflow auto documentation
- Orchestrator and vSphere Web Client

Introduction

This chapter introduces you to some very basic operations that Orchestrator users and admins will find very valuable.

The Orchestrator icons

Let's have a quick look at all the icons of Orchestrator Client:

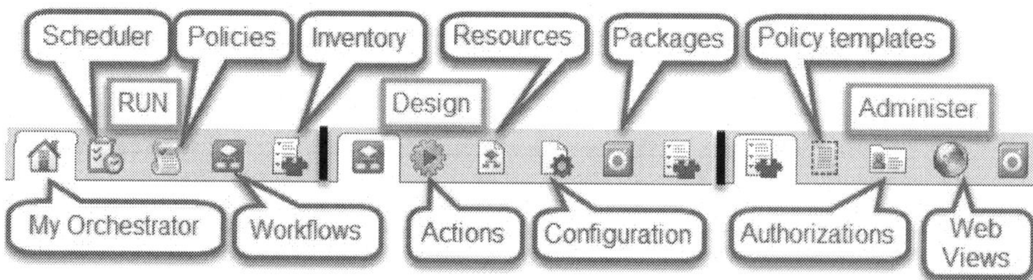

Icon	Used in recipe/chapter	What is covered?
My Orchestrator	*User management*	Overview and non-admin access
Scheduler	*Scheduling workflows*	Management of scheduled workflows
Policies	*Working with policies* in *Chapter 6, Advanced Operations*	A policy is basically an event trigger
Workflows	*Chapter 3, Visual Programming*	Manage everything that has to do with workflows
Inventory	*User preferences* in *Chapter 5, Basic Orchestrator Operations*	Shows all the objects that each plugin has access to
Actions	*Working with actions* in *Chapter 3, Visual Programming*	Manage everything that has to do with actions
Resources	*Working with resources* in *Chapter 6, Advanced Operations*	A resource is a file that can be used from workflows
Configurations	*Working with configurations* in *Chapter 3, Visual Programming*	Configurations are centrally defined attributes that are available to all workflows

Icon	Used in recipe/chapter	What is covered?
Packages	*Working with packages*	A package contains workflows, actions, as well as all other elements to export and import Orchestrator solutions
Policy templates	*Working with resources* in *Chapter 6, Advanced Operations*	Templates for policies
Authorizations	*Introduction* in *Chapter 6, Advanced Operations*	Leftover and not used today anymore (deprecated)
Web Views	*Introduction* in *Chapter 6, Advanced Operations*	Web views are HTTP-based web pages that interact with Orchestrator (deprecated)

More about workflows

This introduction looks at some of the more unknown features of Orchestrator. We start with the **General** section of a workflow.

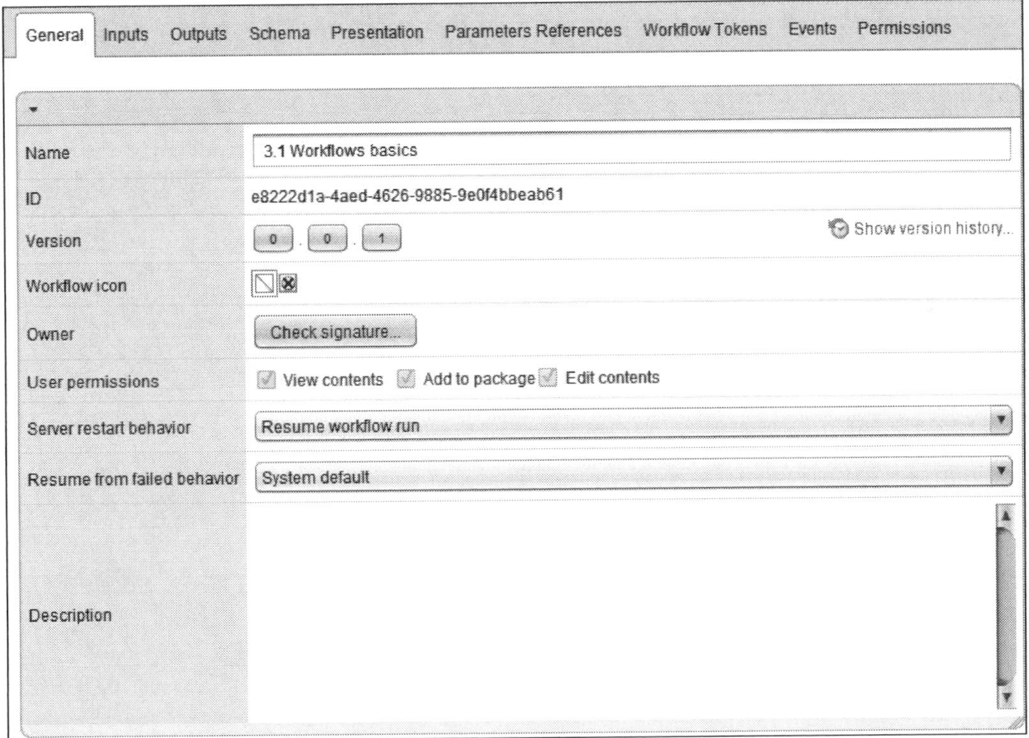

The workflow ID

Underneath the **Name** field in the preceding screenshot, we find a field called **ID**. This is the unique ID (across all Orchestrator installations) that each workflow in Orchestrator has. It is also the ID that is used in the API to interact with a workflow. When you export a workflow and import it to a different Orchestrator Server or synchronize the workflow, the ID will not change. We will work with exports/imports as well as synchronization later in this chapter. Having the same workflow ID is a prerequisite for using Orchestrator clusters, otherwise API calls will start different workflows.

Server restart behavior

The **Server restart behavior** setting determines what happens to a running workflow execution when Orchestrator Server becomes unavailable, for example, when the server is powered off.

You can choose between resuming the workflow runs at the point where Orchestrator Server has become unavailable (**Resume workflow run**) and marking the workflow status as failed (**Do not resume workflow run (set as FAILED)**). The default is resuming the workflow. As already mentioned in the *Resuming failed workflows* recipe in *Chapter 3, Visual Programming*, the checkpoint mechanism plays a vital part here. Before each workflow or subworkflow is executed, a checkpoint is written into the database, making it possible to resume the workflow if it fails.

The workflow icon

You can change the Orchestrator icon that is displayed in front of the workflow. To change the workflow icon, simply edit the workflow and click on the empty window. A selection of the already uploaded icons in Orchestrator is now displayed. Choose one.

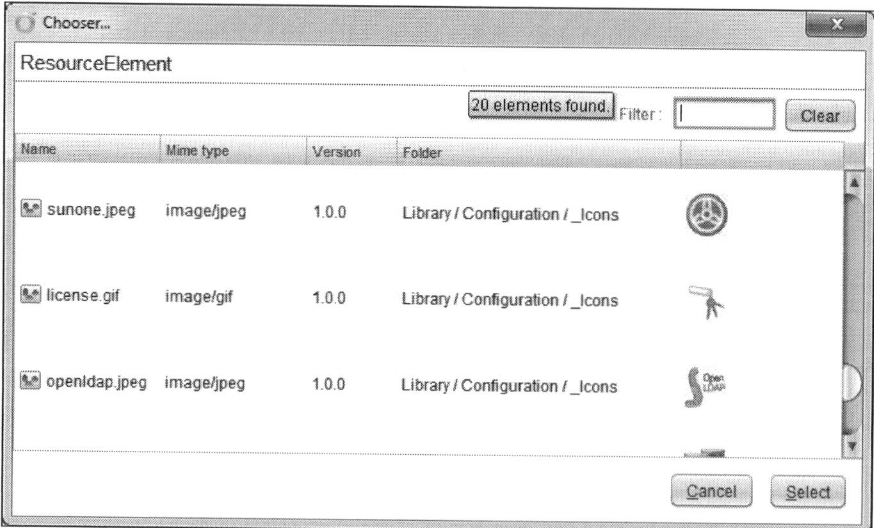

If you want to revert to the default icon, just click on **X** next to the icon in the **General** view. The icon is not only displayed in the workflow tree, but also in the schema of other workflows.

To add a new icon to Orchestrator, you will need to import it into the Orchestrator resources first. In the *Working with resources* recipe in *Chapter 6, Advanced Operations*, we will have a closer look at how to work with resources in Orchestrator.

User permissions

The **User permissions** setting shows permissions any user has regarding changing and reusing this workflow. These permissions are set when you export a package that contains the element. We will have a closer look at this in the *How it works...* section of the *Working with packages* recipe.

Basic Orchestrator operations for Orchestrator elements

In this recipe, we will learn how to duplicate, move, and delete workflows, actions, resources, configurations, and packages.

Getting ready

We need at least one workflow to duplicate, move, and then delete it.

How to do it...

We split this recipe into duplicate, move, and delete sections. We will use a workflow for this example; however, this procedure also works on actions, resources, configurations, and packages.

Duplicate

Duplicating an Orchestrator item, such as a workflow, will only duplicate this item, not its associated subelements.

1. Right-click on the workflow you would like to duplicate and select **Duplicate workflow**.
2. The default name of the new workflow is **Copy of [original workflow name]**. Change the name as needed.
3. The workflow folder displayed is the same as the folder where the original workflow is located. Click on the displayed folder to change the location.
4. If you like, you can copy the history of the original workflow into the new one. This is typically done when you want to keep the revision comments.

5. Click on **Submit** to copy the workflow.

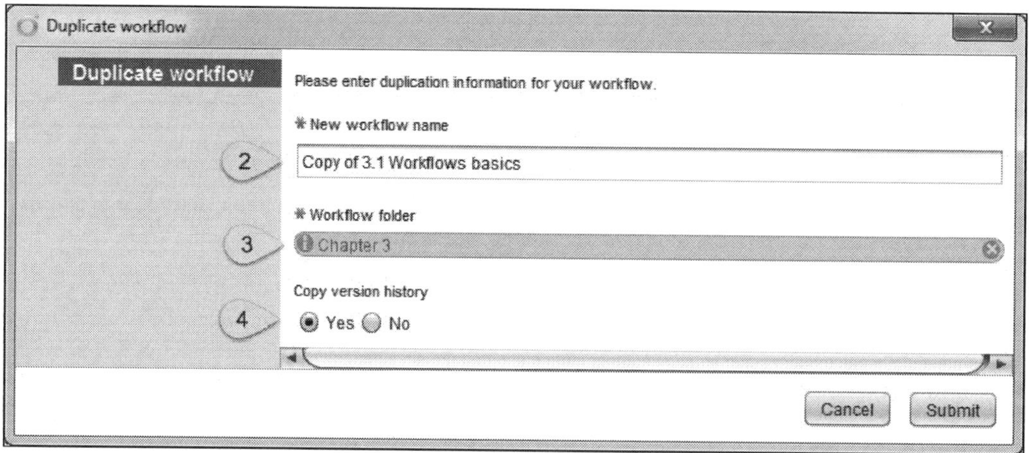

Move

When moving an item, you will only move the current item, not its subelements.

1. Right-click on a workflow and select **Move workflow**.
2. A window will pop up and show you the current workflow tree. Select a new folder and click on **select**.
3. The workflow will now be moved to the selected folder.

> Please note that when moving an action into another module, all workflows that call this action will not work anymore. This is due to the fact that an action is called by its module name. See the *Changing elements in a workflow* recipe in this chapter.

Delete

When deleting an item, you will only delete the current item, not any subelements.

1. Right-click on the object you would like to delete.
2. Some Orchestrator elements have a special right-click choice called **Find elements that use this element**. This function can be used to find Orchestrator elements that depend on the right-clicked element. Before you delete anything, this could come in handy to check whether this element is used by something you need.
3. If you are ready to delete, select **Delete** from the right-click menu.

How it works...

These basic operations are procedures that every Orchestrator admin and programmer needs on a daily basis.

The following Orchestrator elements can be moved or duplicated:

	Workflow	Action	Resource	Configuration	Policy templates
Move	x	x	x	x	x
Duplicate	x	x	-	x	x
Find elements	-	x	x	x	-

Changing elements in a workflow

In this recipe, we will have a closer look at the challenges that changing the workflow elements in a schema pose. Changing the in- and out-parameters as well as moving or renaming actions will be discussed. You will learn how to make these changes as well as what to avoid.

Getting ready

We need a workflow that has an additional workflow as well as an action in its schema.

You can use the example workflows 5.02.1 and 5.02.2 as well as its action `chapter5ChangeMe`.

How to do it...

There are only two major tasks: changing the parameters and renaming/moving the actions.

Changing the parameters of workflows and actions

If you change a subworkflow's in/out-parameters, you will need to synchronize its parameters by following these steps:

1. Make sure that you have a workflow that has a workflow as an element in its schema. You can use the example workflows 5.2.1 subworkflow and 5.2.2 Main-workflow.
2. In the subworkflow, change the name of an out-parameter and add another in-parameter. Then save and exit the subworkflow.
3. In the main workflow, go to the schema and edit the subworkflow element.
4. Click on **Info** and then on **Synchronize parameters**.

5. Now, check the in and out-parameters of the element. You will find a second in-parameter and that the out-parameter isn't bound anymore.

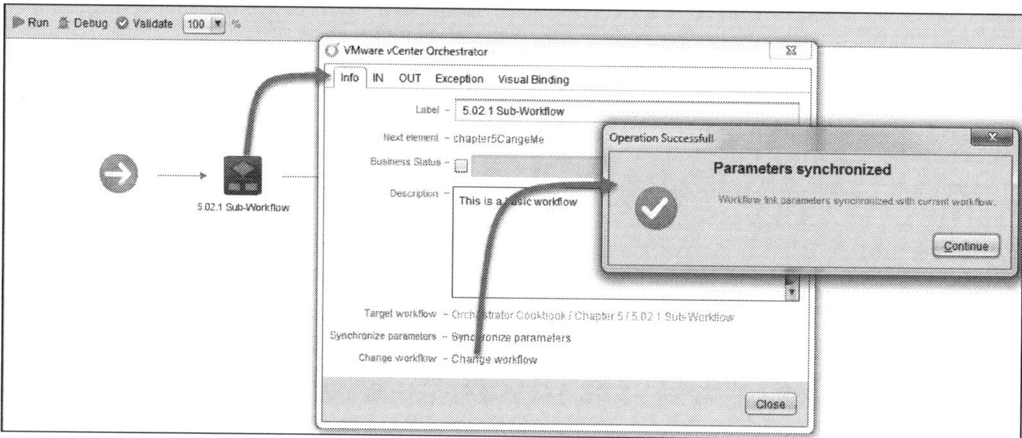

The same method also works for actions.

Renaming and moving actions

Actions are tied into a workflow using their module name and the action name itself. So, if an action is moved to a different module or renamed, you will have to do the following:

1. Make sure that you have a workflow that calls an action either as a scripting task or schema element. You can use the example workflow 5.2.2 Main-workflow and the action `chapter5ChangeMe`.
2. Change the name of the action or move it to another module.
3. In the main workflow, go to the schema and edit the action element.
4. You will see that you can't change the scripting that points to the action, so the only thing you can do is delete the action element and insert it again.

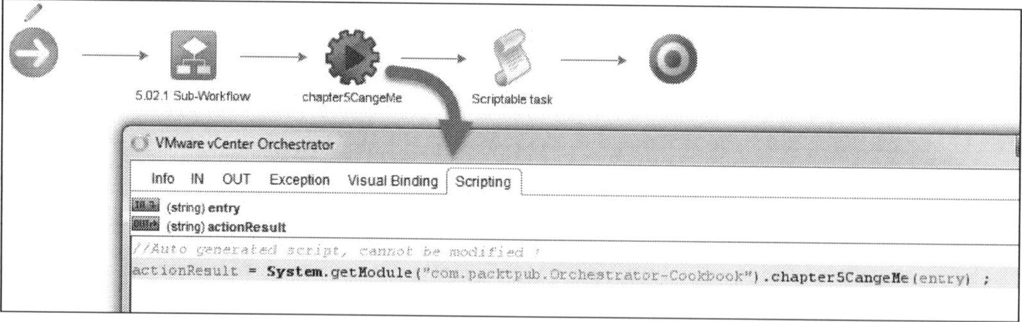

5. If you called the action in a **Scriptable task**, you can change the name or module.

How it works...

Workflows are tied in with each other via their ID (which can't be changed) and not their name. So, renaming or moving a workflow has no impact.

If you add or remove an in/out-parameter from a workflow or action, you can simply synchronize the parameter. When you change the name of an in/out-parameter in a workflow or action and then synchronize, you will have to redefine the binding of that parameter.

An action is always called in the following way:

```
System.getModule([module name]).[action name]([in-parameter],)
```

When you move or rename an action, you will need to adjust this call by either changing the module name (move) or the action name (rename).

If you rename a configuration element or parameter, you will have to bind it again in the workflow. The setting will point to the old configuration element that doesn't exist anymore.

Undelete workflows and actions

This recipe shows how to undelete deleted workflows and actions, as this comes in handy when one deletes something that one shouldn't have.

Getting ready

To undelete a workflow, we need a deleted workflow or action first.

How to do it...

We will use a workflow in this example, as the undelete function for actions works exactly the same:

1. Right-click on a folder (or the root element) and select **Restore deleted workflows**.

2. A popup will display all the workflows or actions that can be restored. Tick all the workflows you would like to restore and click on **Restore**.

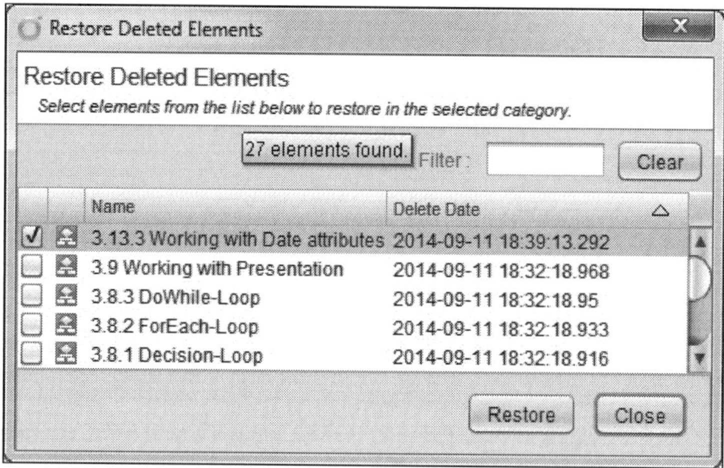

The workflows or actions will now be restored.

How it works...

All workflows and actions are stored in the Orchestrator database and as such, they can be restored. However, you cannot restore a workflow with the same ID that already exists; names of workflows are of no importance in Orchestrator.

Importing and exporting Orchestrator elements

In this recipe, we will learn how to import and export elements from one Orchestrator to another using Orchestrator Client.

Getting ready

We need at least one workflow, action, or other element that we can export, delete, and import. If you have two Orchestrator servers, you can export the element on one and import into the other.

How to do it...

In this example, we will use a workflow to import and export an object. However, the same methods apply to all Orchestrator elements.

Export an object

1. To export a workflow, right-click on it and select **Export workflow**.
2. A window will pop up that shows you your local drives from the computer you are running Orchestrator Client on.
3. Select a directory and a name for the workflow (the default name is the name of the workflow). The default file extension is `.workflow`.
4. You can define a name to encrypt the export with, basically an encryption string. This will make it possible for other importers to import the file, but to not edit it. The name is not a password and Orchestrator will not ask for it; encrypting with name will just create an encrypted file.
5. Click on **Save**.

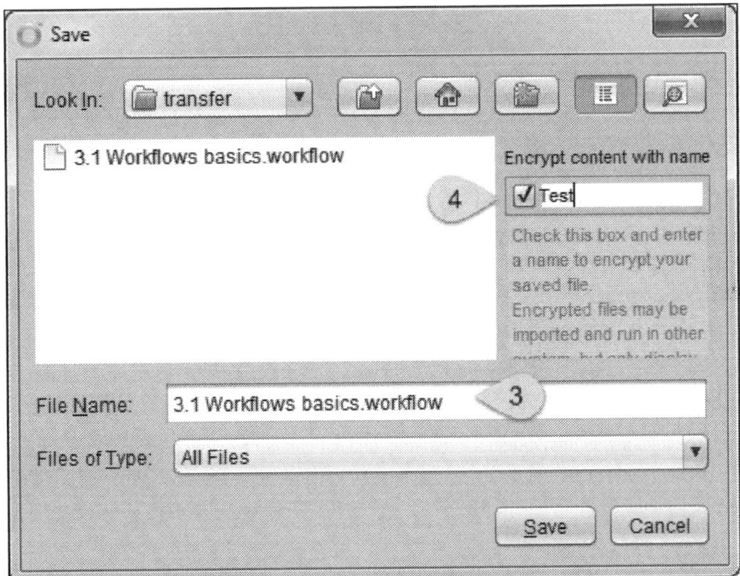

Import an element

1. To import a workflow, right-click on a folder and select **Import workflow**.
2. A window will pop up that shows you your local drives from the computer you are running the Orchestrator Client on.
3. Select a directory and a name for the workflow you would like to import.

> Orchestrator will not ask you to confirm the SSL certificate nor will it import any dependencies that this workflow might have.

4. If the workflow already exists, a warning will be displayed. You can either select **Cancel** or continue the import.
5. The workflow will now be imported into the folder you right-clicked on in step 1.

How it works...

You can import and export single Orchestrator objects. This will import and export only the element and not its subelements or elements the workflow (or action) depends on. You can use a package (see the *Working with packages* recipe in this chapter) to export multiple workflows as well as their dependent elements. As workflows are identified by their IDs and actions by their name and module, it is important to realize that a single workflow export/import might not result in a working configuration.

When you export an object, then it will be exported along with the SSL certificate of the Orchestrator installation (the one we created in the *Creating a Server Package Signing Certificate* section of the *Important Orchestrator base configurations* recipe in *Chapter 1, Installing and Configuring Orchestrator*).

> The elements that can be imported and exported are workflow, action, resource, configuration, package, policy template, and web view.

In addition to this, the element will keep its ID when exported and imported.

See also

Have a look at the *Working with packages* recipe in this chapter and the *Managing remote Orchestrator* recipe in *Chapter 6, Advanced Operations*.

Synchronize Orchestrator elements between Orchestrator servers

This recipe will show how to use synchronizing to update Orchestrator objects between two Orchestrator servers.

Getting ready

We will need at least one workflow, action, or other Orchestrator object that can be synced.

Additionally, we also need two Orchestrator servers; they should not be in a cluster. For test purposes, you can deploy an Orchestrator appliance without any additional configuration.

How to do it...

We will use a workflow in this example. The same method applies to all other Orchestrator elements that can be synchronized.

1. Right-click on a workflow (or a folder) and select **Synchronize**.
2. You will now be asked to enter the IP or FQDN of the other Orchestrator Server as well as some credentials for the connection. Click on **Login**.
3. You will now see a summary of all workflows you have selected for synchronization on both Orchestrator servers.
    - **A**: Here, the version number of a given workflow is shown
    - **B**: You have four options that we will discuss in the *How it works...* section of this recipe
    - **C**: Clicking on the magnifying glass icon will produce a split screen that shows you the difference between the versions (see the *Version control* recipe in *Chapter 3, Visual Programming*)

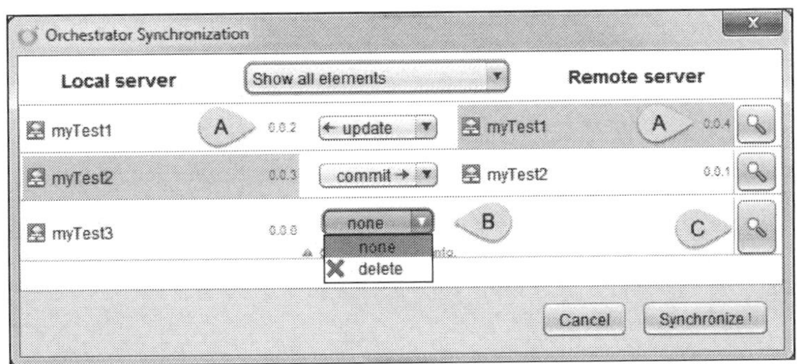

4. Click on **Synchronize !** to synchronize the workflows.

How it works...

Synchronizing Orchestrator objects is one of the easiest ways to make sure that two servers have the same elements. This doesn't work for clusters as both Orchestrators in a cluster share the same database (same workflow IDs). A good example here is a sync between a development environment and a production environment.

The Orchestrator objects that can use synchronizing are workflows, actions, resources, configurations, packages, policy templates, and WebViews.

When synchronizing a local element that doesn't exist on the remote server, Orchestrator will not only create the element but also the folder structure for it. This will make sure that the same structure exists on both servers. Also, the ID of the Orchestrator object will be kept the same when synchronizing.

Please note that depending on from which direction you sync, the options you see might be different.

Action	What it does
None	*This is not what you expect*. This will update the remote version with the local version. If the element doesn't exist on the remote side, it will create it there.
Update	Update will take the version from the remote server and will overwrite the local version.
Commit	This will take the local version and overwrite the remote version.
Delete	If an element doesn't exist on the remote server, you can choose to delete the local version.

See also

The *Managing remote Orchestrator* recipe in *Chapter 6, Advanced Operations*.

Working with packages

In this recipe, you will learn how to create, export, and generally work with packages. Packages are great to ship complete Orchestrator solutions between Orchestrators to customers or for backup.

Getting ready

We need at least one workflow or action to work with in this recipe. Optimally, you have workflows and actions that depend on each other. The package that comes with this book contains a workflow named 5.5 Working with Packages, which you can use to test this recipe.

How to do it...

This recipe has several sections. As an overview, the following screenshot shows all the icons and their usages. To get to the correct section follow these instructions:

1. Using Orchestrator Client, make sure that you are in the **Design** mode.
2. Click on packages (the yellow box with a white circle icon).

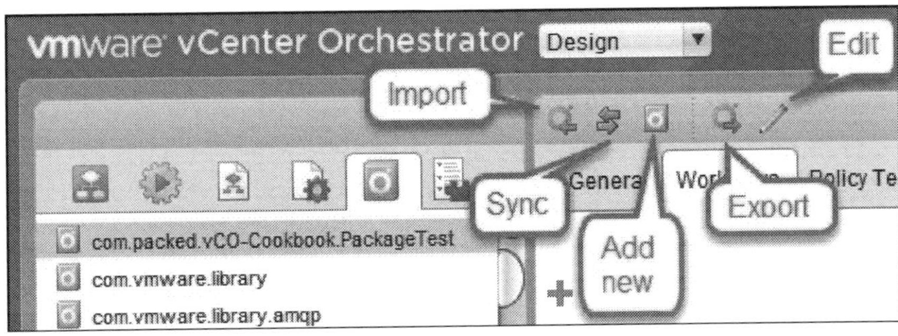

Create a new package

1. Either right-click on the white space below the displayed packages and select **Add package** or select the icon from the right-hand side (the yellow box with a white circle icon).
2. Select a new name for the package; the default is **org.company.mypackage**. A good naming convention is useful.
3. The new package is created; now click on the package and either right-click and select **Edit** or select **Edit** from the right-hand side (the pencil icon).
4. Click on **Workflows**.
5. To add a workflow, you can either select single workflows using **Insert workflow** (the green plus icon) or **Insert workflows** (the folder icon) to insert all workflows of a specific folder. Remember that when Orchestrator shows you an empty selection window, you need to use the filter option (see also the *Gotcha* section in *Chapter 3, Visual Programming*).
6. Choose one option, click on **Select** to add the workflow(s). If your workflow depends on other elements, such as actions, configurations, resources, and so on, these elements will be automatically imported into the package as well.
7. Click on **Save and close** and finish the packaging process.

Export a package

1. Before we export a package, we should make sure that its content is current. To do so, we right-click on the package and select **Rebuild package**. The content of the package will now be updated with the latest versions (and their dependencies) of all elements in the package.
2. After the rebuild has finished, we now export the package by right-clicking on the package and selecting **Export package** or from the menu, as shown in the beginning of this recipe.
3. The export window opens up. Choose an appropriate directory and filename. You also see that there are several options on the right-hand side; we will discuss them in detail in the *How it works...* section of this recipe.

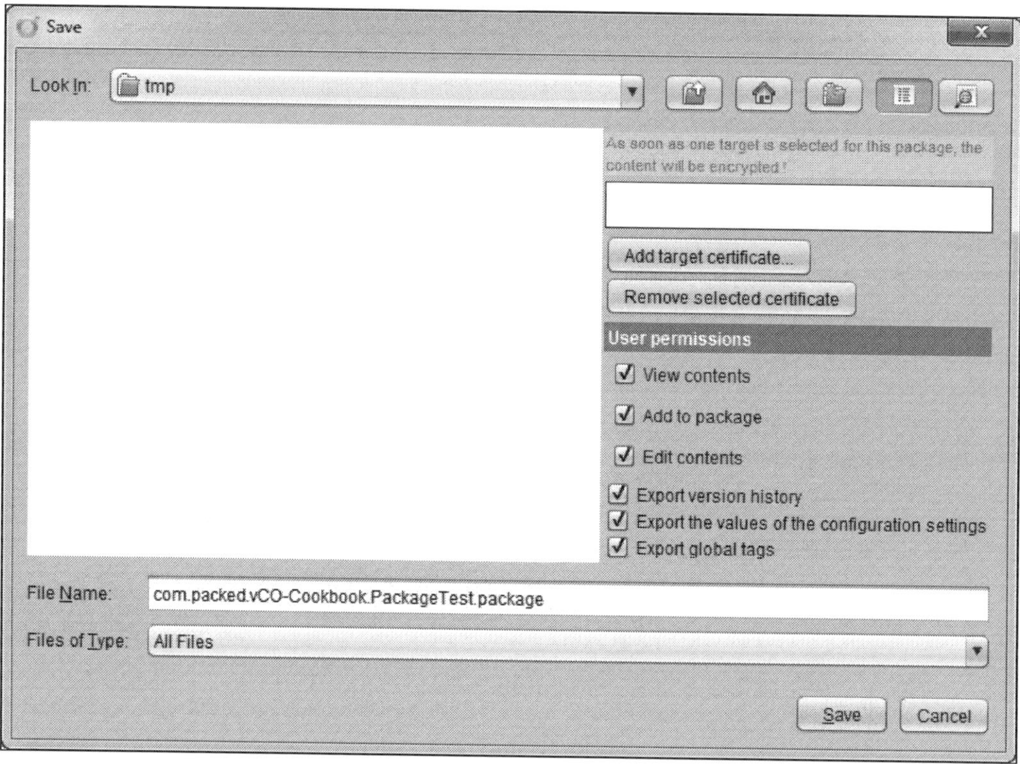

4. Click on **Save**. Your package has now been exported.

Import a package

1. Either right-click on the white space below the displayed packages and select **Import package** or select from the menu, as shown in the beginning of this recipe.
2. Browse to the appropriate directory and select the package you would like to import and click on **Open**.
3. You might now be presented with a request to accept the user certificate of this Orchestrator Server (see also the *Important Orchestrator base configurations* recipe in *Chapter 1, Installing and Configuring Orchestrator*). You can choose to import just the package (**Import once**) or import the package and add the SSL certificate of this user to your trusted certificates (**Import and trust provider**).

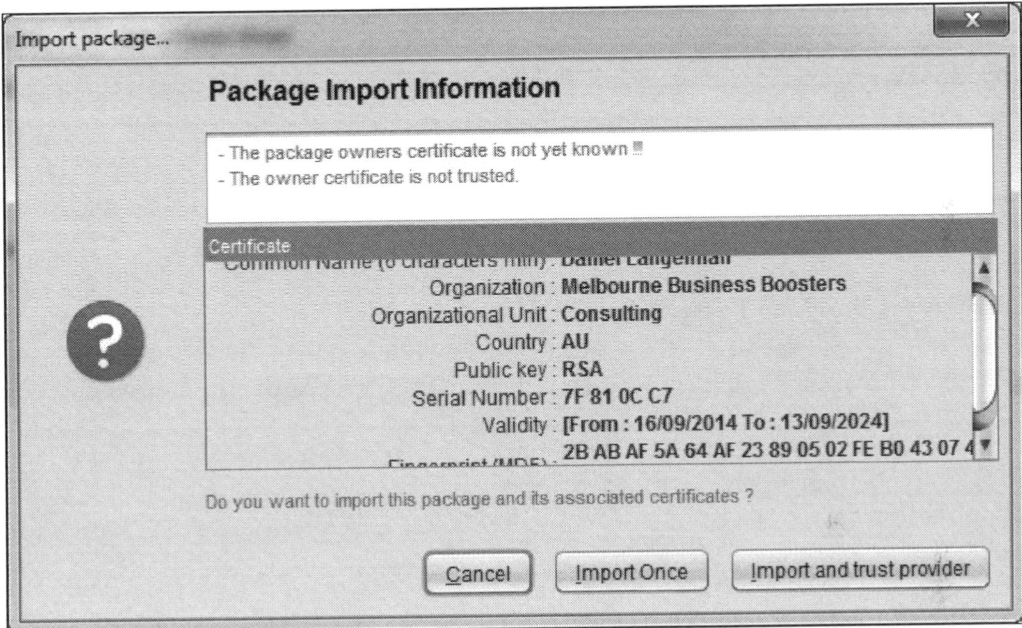

4. Orchestrator will now check the content of your package against what is already installed. The following window will be displayed. Here, you can choose whether an element should be imported or not. You see on the left-hand side the version and name of the element in the package and on the right-hand side the same information for Orchestrator Server (if that element already exists). You can use the magnifying glass icon on the far right to check the version log of your Orchestrator-Server-based element. You can force an import by just ticking the box of the element. Please note that we will discuss the **Import the values of the configuration settings** option in detail in the *How it works...* section of this recipe.

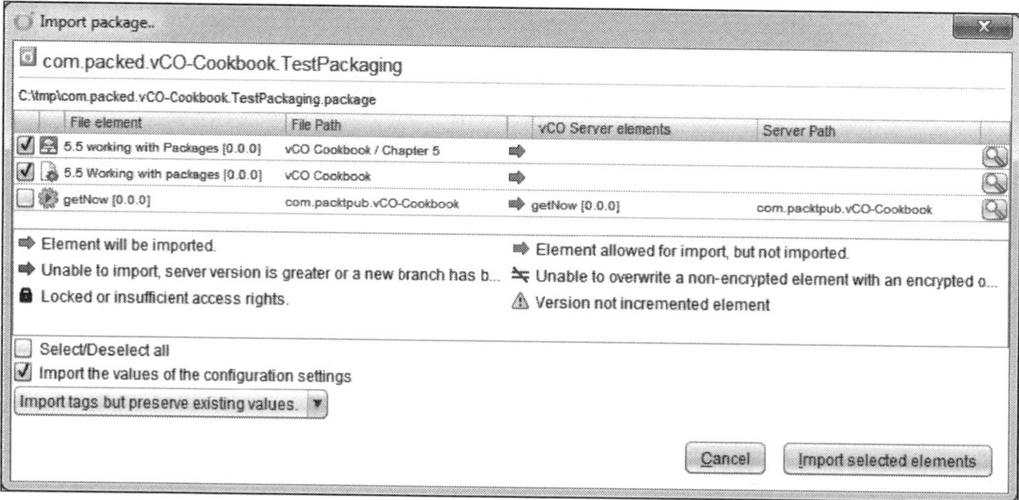

The package will now be imported. Every element that is part of the package will be placed back in its folder or module as it was. This means that the import will also create folders and modules as required.

Deleting a package

When right-clicking on a package, you will see there are two delete options:

Option	**Description**
Delete	This will delete the package only but no content (workflows, actions, and so on) will be deleted
Delete element with content	This not only deletes the package but also its content (workflows, actions, and so on) from Orchestrator

In this example, we will delete the package as well as the content:

1. Right-click on the package and select **Delete element with content**.
2. If you used the example package or have elements in this package that are used by other elements, then you will see the following warning message:

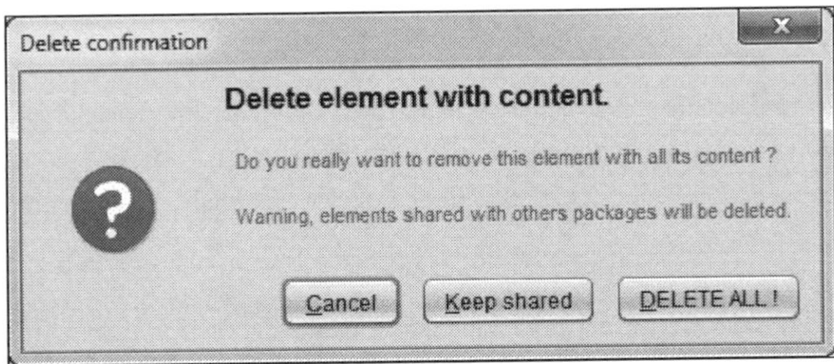

3. If you are not sure, you can **Keep shared** elements or **DELETE ALL!**
4. Your package and its elements will now be deleted.

How it works...

Building packages makes it very easy to transport or publish Orchestrator solutions that have been developed. A package contains all the important elements such as workflows, actions, policy templates, web views, configurations, resources, and plugins used.

Another typical usage for packages is to create a backup.

When your package contains workflows or actions from a plugin, such as vCenter, vCloud Director or such, the plugins and their versions are displayed in the **Used plugin** tab of the package. Orchestrator doesn't display any warnings or messages when you import a package that depends on a certain plugin. It will just import all the elements of this plugin that are part of the package. However, because of the dependencies, you will not be able to execute workflows that depend on this plugin.

Please note that when you export a package that contains AMQP, SNMP, or other Orchestrator plugins, the resource element that contains the server configuration is exported as well. Before delivering this package to a customer, you might want to delete these elements.

Export and import options

When exporting a package, you have several options that you can choose from. When you deselect an option, all elements in this package will inherit the setting.

Option	Description
Add target certificate	We shall discuss this in the *There's more...* section of this recipe.
View Contents	This is not really as restrictive as one would expect. When you deselect this option, you can still see all the normal tabs in the workflow. The only thing that won't work is that you can go to an element by double-clicking on it. For example, if the workflow contains an action, double-clicking on it won't open the action element. However, the action can be accessed normally and you can see the scripting content.
Add to package	Deselecting this option will make it impossible for users to export a package that contains elements from this package. You can still create packages with elements that don't have the **Add to package** flag; however, you will get an error message when trying to export the package.
Edit content	Without this flag, users that import this package will not be able to edit the workflow. This flag is mostly set for all packages that are part of a plugin or to make sure that for support reasons changes are not possible.
Export version history	Deselecting this option will not export the full version history of each element. Instead, the element will be displayed in the latest version with the remark **imported content from package**.
Export values of the configuration settings	Deselecting this section will export the configuration and its attributes; however, it will not export their values.
Export global tags	This will export the global tag of the objects in the package. See the *Working with tags* recipe in *Chapter 6, Advanced Operations*.

When importing a package, you can deselect the **Import the values of the configuration settings** option. This will import the configuration and its attributes but not its values.

The function to switch off editing is extremely important when delivering an Orchestrator solution to a customer. You will want to lock down the customer's ability to edit workflows or actions in order to make it possible to support the solution.

The target server function comes in handy if you want to make sure that Orchestrator packages do not get into the wrong hands. Typical things to mention here are configuration items in Orchestrator that contains sensitive information.

There's more...

As you can see in the import package step, the user certificate we created in the *Important Orchestrator base configurations* recipe in *Chapter 1, Installing and Configuring Orchestrator,* finally has a meaning. Each package that is created is encrypted with this user certificate.

When you import a package, you can choose to trust this certificate. If you do so, it will be stored in the certificate store. You can manage the certificate store by clicking on **Tools** (this is in the top-right corner of Orchestrator Client) and then selecting **Certificate manager**.

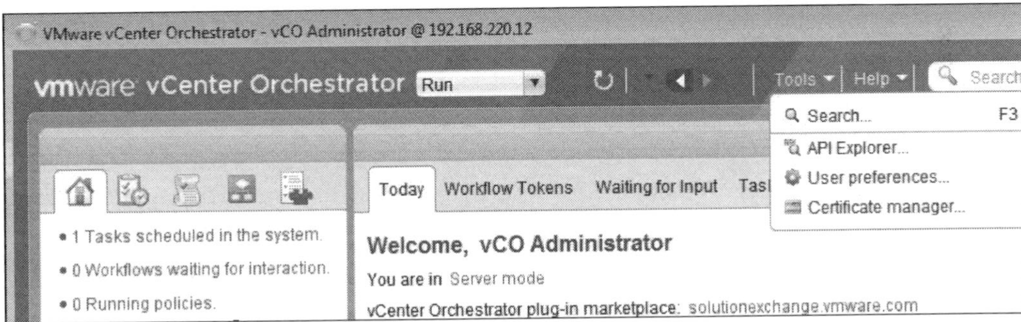

A popup will appear in which the upper part shows your user certificate and the lower part shows all known certificates (you might need to adjust the length of the window). See the following screenshot.

You are able to export your own certificate and also import others or remove others from the certificate store.

When you export a package, you can select the **Add target certificate** option to make sure that the package can only be read by a certain Orchestrator Server. When you add a certificate to the package that is contained in your certificate store, you can make sure that only the Orchestrator Server that is the owner of this certificate can import the package. If you try to import a package that is not intended for you, you will get an error message that says this package is not intended for you. In the example package that comes with this book, I have placed a certificate (in resources) that you can use to test this.

See also

See example workflow 5.5 Working with packages. Also see the *Important Orchestrator base configurations* recipe in *Chapter 1, Installing and Configuring Orchestrator,* and the *Managing remote Orchestrator* recipe in *Chapter 6, Advanced Operations.*

User management

In this recipe, we will see how to control access to Orchestrator. You will learn how to give and control access to users outside the Orchestrator administrator group.

Getting ready

We need a running Orchestrator configured either with SSO, AD, or LDAP.

Also, we need either access to a user management system (LDAP, SSO, or AD) or the existence of other users and groups on a given user management system.

How to do it...

We have three parts to this recipe each for different tasks.

Adding users to the Orchestrator Administrator group

During the configuration of Orchestrator, you specify a user group that is a member of the Orchestrator Administrator group. If you are using the vCenter Orchestrator installation, then this is the Orchestrator administrators group in vsphere.local. To add a user to the Orchestrator Administrator group, follow these steps:

1. Access your user management tool (SSO, AD, or LDAP).
2. Add an additional user to the group you defined as Orchestrator administrators.
3. Open Orchestrator Client.
4. Log in with the new user.

You're now logged in as an Orchestrator administrator.

Giving nonadministrative users access to Orchestrator

As Orchestrator administrators have access to all Orchestrator elements as well as have all the user rights (including delete), you might want to restrict the access that users have. Giving restricted access to users is better than just adding everyone to the Orchestrator administrative group. Please note that you can only add LDAP/AD groups. To grant nonadministrative access to Orchestrator, follow these steps:

1. Log in to Orchestrator Client as an Orchestrator administrator.
2. The **My Orchestrator** (the house symbol) page opens up by default. Select the **Run** mode if not already selected.
3. Click on the **Permissions** tab.

4. Click on **Add access right** (group with green plus).
5. In the **Filter** field, either just press *Enter* to see all existing groups or enter a string to filter for groups and press *Enter*.
6. Select the group you want to add.
7. Select the rights you want this group to have (**View** is the lowest-needed right).
8. Click on **Select**.

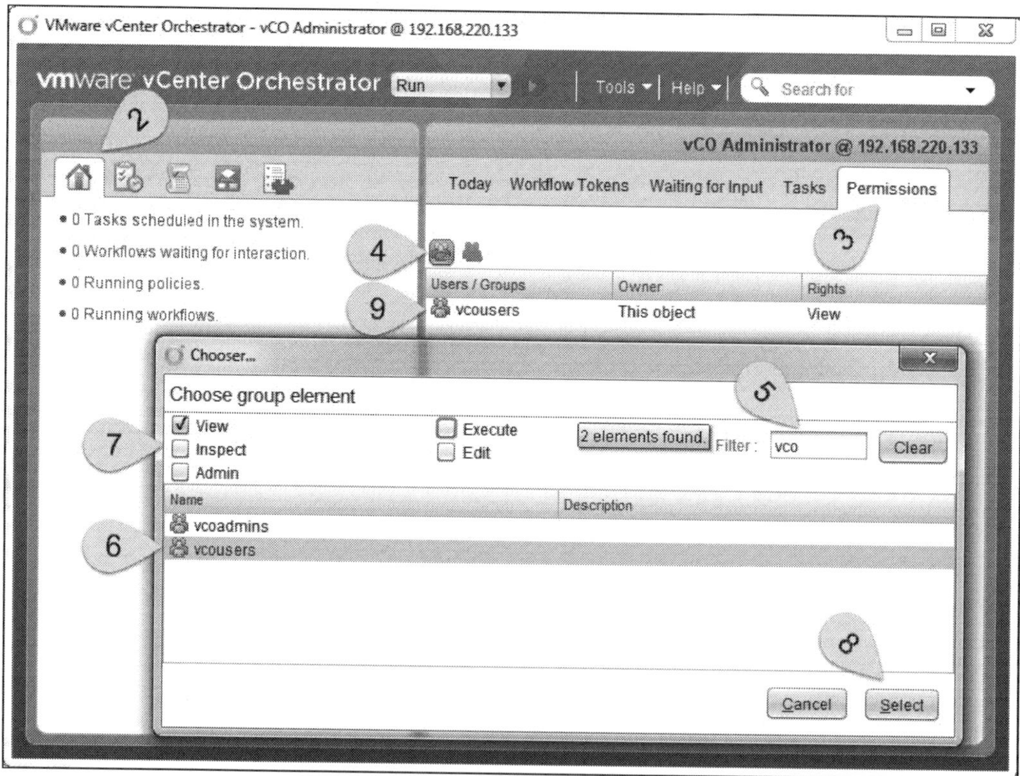

9. The group will now show up in the **Permissions** tab.
10. Close Orchestrator Client (or log out properly).
11. Log in to Orchestrator Client using a user that is a member of the user group you added in step 6.
12. You are now logged in as a nonadministrative user.

Configuring access to Orchestrator elements

After we are granted the nonadministrator access to Orchestrator, we can now modify user rights of other Orchestrator elements.

1. Log in to Orchestrator Client as an Orchestrator Administrator.
2. Select an element (for example, a workflow or folder).
3. Click on **Edit** (the pencil symbol).
4. Click on **Permissions** and then on **Add access right** (group with green plus).
5. In the **Filter** field, either just press *Enter* to see all existing groups or enter a string to filter for groups and press *Enter*.
6. Select the group you want to add.
7. Select the rights you want this group to have (**View** is the lowest-needed right).
8. Click on **Select**.
9. Click on **Save and Close**.
10. Log in and test.

How it works...

The user management in Orchestrator can be a bit tricky, but most problems are caused by the underlying user management system (such as AD). A typical example for this is that you have configured Orchestrator with SSO and used the `vsphere.local:vCOAdministrators` group. To add other AD users or groups to this group, you would have had to add them into the SSO group not to any AD group. Just log in to the vSphere Web Client as an SSO administrator (administrator@vsphere.local) and then add the AD group to the Orchestrator Administrator group.

The best thing is to create a dedicated Orchestrator Administrator group in AD and configure the **Orchestrator SSO Authentication** section with this group. See the *Integrating Orchestrator into SSO and vSphere Web Client* recipe in *Chapter 1, Installing and Configuring Orchestrator*. Add one or more Orchestrator User groups (depending on the access you want to grant them) and add them to AD as well and then, as shown in this recipe, as nonadministrative users to Orchestrator. This will result in a user structure you can manage through AD instead of SSO or Orchestrator.

Right inheritance

The user rights that are given to one Orchestrator element automatically will be inherited by all its child elements. You cannot break the inheritance. However, you can extend or restrict the rights. Because of this, it is prudent to give only the **View** right to a group on the **My Orchestrator** level and extend the rights as needed in the child elements.

To extend or restrict the rights of a user group, just add the same user group to the element again and adjust the rights as required. Have a look at the following screenshot. You find the inherit right (**Parent**) and the current right for this element (**This object**) there. The right of the **This object** element will always overwrite the inheritance. Please note that when you expand or restrict the user rights, all children will again inherit this setting.

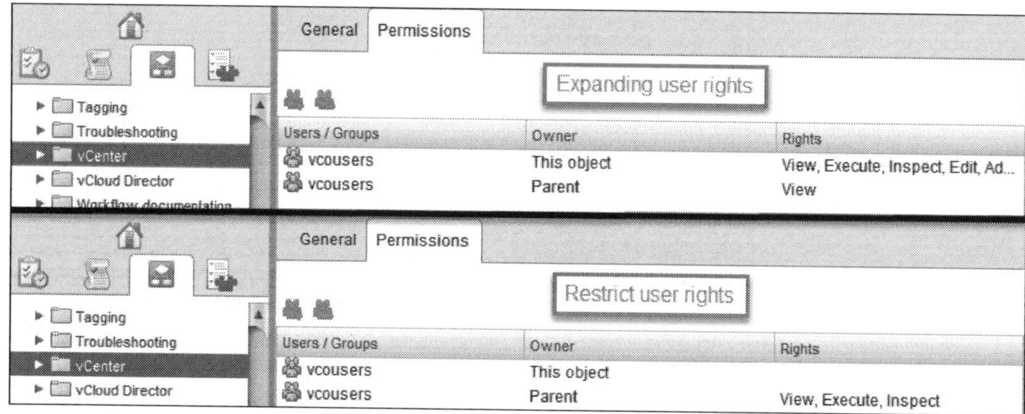

The login format

To log in to Orchestrator, you can use one of the following syntaxes:

- Username (only if you are using the AD or LDAP setup)
- username@FQDN-Domain
- Domain\username

Access right

The following are the Orchestrator user rights:

User right	Description
View	Base access to Orchestrator Client and view elements but not their schema, presentation, script, and parameter references.
Inspect	View schema, presentation, script, and parameter references in elements.
Execute	Able to run a workflow. If this right is not given, every user can still use the **Run As** feature by right-clicking on it. This right also allows you to answer a user interaction.
Edit	Able to edit elements.
Admin	Able to set permissions on elements.

There's more...

Here are some more notes of interest.

Changing the Orchestrator Administrator group

If you have configured Orchestrator with the wrong Orchestrator Administrator group, you can use the Orchestrator configurator to change the setting. See either the *Configuring Orchestrator with an external LDAP or Active Directory* or *Integrating Orchestrator into SSO and vSphere Web Client* recipe in *Chapter 1, Installing and Configuring Orchestrator* for details. Don't forget to restart Orchestrator Server after changing the Orchestrator Administrator group.

Typical error messages

This is a list of the most typical login error messages:

- **[002] User [username] is not authorized**: Here, the user is not a member of the Orchestrator Administrator group or doesn't have the **View** right in **My Orchestrator**.
- **Smart client connection is disabled by server security**: Here, nonadministrative access to Orchestrator has been disabled.
- **Invalid user/password**: This is one of those error messages that can mean a lot. Starting from the obvious typo in the username or password to the fact that the user doesn't exist.

  A typical problem here is that a user exists and has access rights to Orchestrator. In this case, this message means that the user management system can't find him, indicating that something in the LDAP/SSO/AD system is going wrong.

Disabling nonadministrative access to Orchestrator

If you want to turn off the possibilities for any nonadministrative access to Orchestrator by editing the `vmo.properties` file, have a look at the following:

1. Log in to the operation system where Orchestrator is installed.
2. Locate the `vmo.properties` file.

Operating system	Path
Windows	`[install_dir]\VMware\Orchestrator\app-server\conf`
Linux	`/etc/vco/app-server/`

3. Add the `com.vmware.o11n.smart-client-disabled = true` line to the `vmo.properties` file.
4. Restart Orchestrator Server.

User preferences

In this recipe, we will have a look at how to configure the behavior of Orchestrator Client. You will learn how to manipulate the coloring of scripts, the start-up behavior, and much more.

Getting ready

We need a running Orchestrator installation as well as an Orchestrator account that we can log in to.

How to do it...

1. Log in to Orchestrator Client.
2. Click on **Tools** (in the top-right corner of Orchestrator) and select **User preferences**.

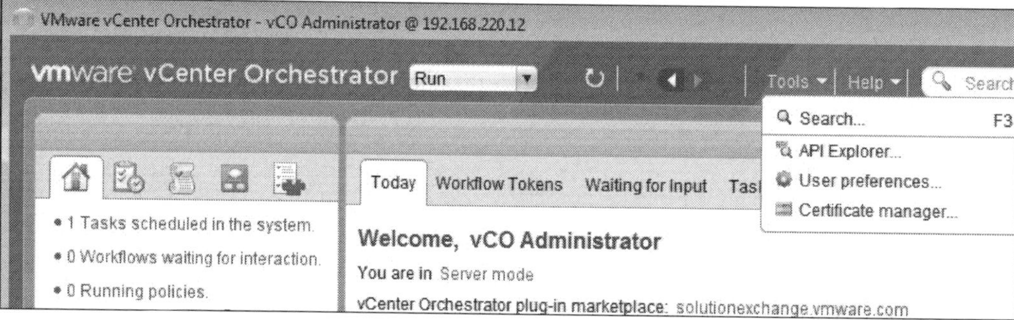

3. The **User Preferences** window will open.
4. Configure the settings as you like.
5. Click on **OK**.

The user preferences have four areas of configuration: **General**, **Workflow**, **Inventory**, and **Script Editor**.

How it works...

The user preferences can only be set by Orchestrator administrators as they determine how Orchestrator Client behaves.

The user preference settings are specific for each user and are stored in the `vmware-vmo.cfg` file that is located in the local Orchestrator Client directory. If you are using Java Web Start (from the Orchestrator home page), the settings are stored in the hidden folder `.vmware` in your local user profile. This means that if you are logging in from the same computer or with the same Windows user account (even when using different Orchestrator users), the settings will be shared.

There are four sections that can be configured: general, workflow, Inventory, and script editor.

General

The general section contains the settings for the general behavior of Orchestrator Client. You can set the following items:

Item	Options	Default	Meaning
Auto-edit new inserted	[Yes|NO]	Yes	A new object will open automatically in the edit mode
Script compilation delay	[ms]	2000	How often will input be check by the editor
Show decision scripts	[Yes|NO]	No	Shows the script that is the base of a decision object
Delete non empty folder permitted	[Yes|NO]	No	Able to delete nonempty folders
Size of run logs	[lines]	300	Amount of lines displayed in the workflow log
Server log fetch limit	[lines]	100	Amount of lines displayed in the **Events** tab of an element
Finder maximum size	[items]	20	Amount of elements returned in a search
Check usage when deleting an element	[Yes|NO]	No	Check whether an element is used by another element before deleting
Check OGNL expression	[Yes|NO]	Yes	Not supported anymore since vCO 5.1

The typical setting you might like to change is **Finder maximum size** as a higher number will return a higher number of search results in a search box, which can be helpful, for example, if you are searching for get actions.

Workflow

The workflow settings alter how Orchestrator workflows behave. Most of the settings are switched on (except three display settings) and configured for a production environment. Changing these settings should be considered carefully. Changing them won't damage Orchestrator but can impact the visual presentation of your work. An extremely cool feature is the **Edit workflow items in a pop-up window** option. This will allow you to edit workflow elements directly without clicking on the edit icon. This feature is switched on by default in vRO and off in vCO.

Inventory

There is only one option available, that is, **Use contextual menu in inventory** (by default, this is switched on in version 5.5). The function automatically displays all workflows that can be used with a selected object in the inventory. For example, right-clicking on the cluster in the vCenter Server inventory will display all the workflows that are available for a cluster.

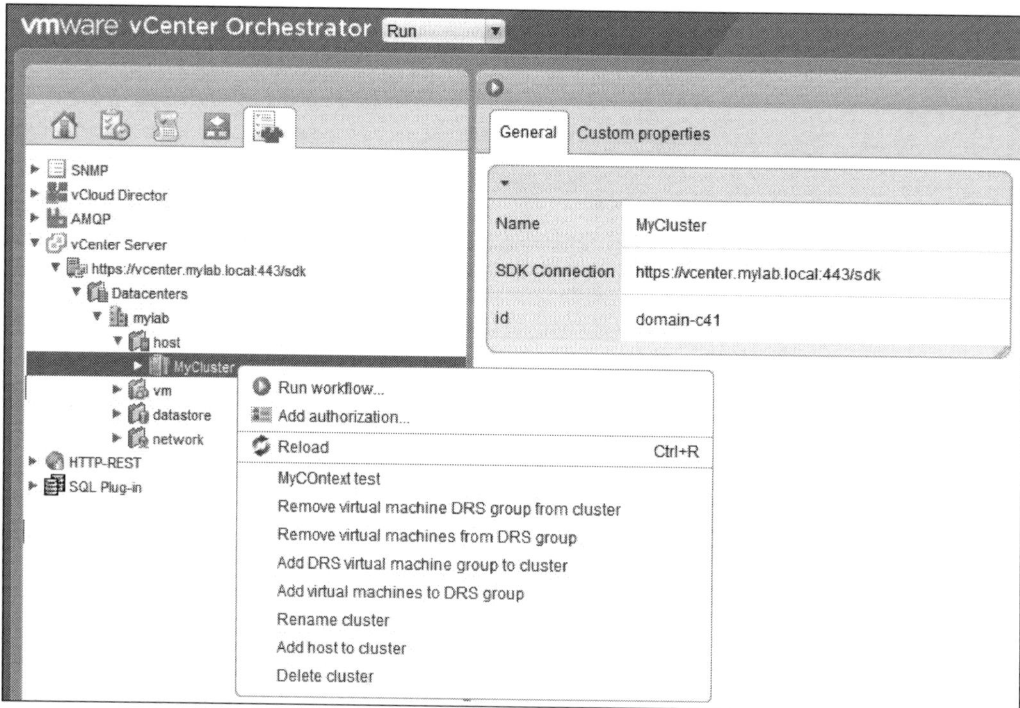

To make this work, you will need to assign the workflow presentation property **Show in Inventory** to an in-parameter of a particular type (for example, `VC:ClusterComputeResource`). Also see the *Working with presentations* recipe in *Chapter 3, Visual Programming*.

Script editor

In the script editor section, you can choose how a script element behaves when you enter the JavaScript code.

Item	Options	Default	Meaning
Enable code assist	[Yes | NO]	Yes	Code assist allows the use of *Ctrl* + Space bar to see properties or methods of the object.
Highlight selected line	[Yes | NO]	Yes	This highlights the current line you selected.

Item	Options	Default	Meaning
Highlight brackets	[Yes|NO]	Yes	When the cursor is on a bracket (any type), it will display its corresponding partner.
Display EOL	[Yes|NO]	No	This displays the end of line of a given line of code.

The rest of the choices are about color and how elements (such as strings and comments) are color coded. You can use the default or create a color scheme that resembles other code editors you use.

Scheduling workflows

In this recipe, you will learn how to schedule workflows. Scheduled workflows will automatically run at given times and intervals.

Getting ready

We need at least one workflow we can schedule. The workflow should not contain a user interaction.

How to do it...

1. Right-click on the workflow you would like to schedule and choose **Schedule workflow**.
2. Select **Task name**. By default, the task name is set to be the workflow name. A good naming standard comes in handy here, especially if you schedule reoccurring tasks.
3. Set a start date and time.
4. If this task has been scheduled in the past, you can still run the workflow. This setting is useful if a task had been scheduled but during the planned execution time, Orchestrator Server was not available (for example, powered off). The task will then start as soon as Orchestrator Server is available again.
5. You can create a recurring task. You have the base setting for every minute, hour, day, week, and month. Except for the week setting, you can schedule multiple executions by clicking on the green **+** sign. So, you can, for example, set a task that runs every day at 9 A.M. and 9 P.M.
6. Last but not least, you can set a stop date and time at which the recurring task will stop.
7. Click on **Next** to get to the in-parameters for this workflow. Fill them out as required and when finished, click on **Submit**.

8. Orchestrator will now automatically jump into the **Run** | **Scheduler** view and show you the scheduled task.

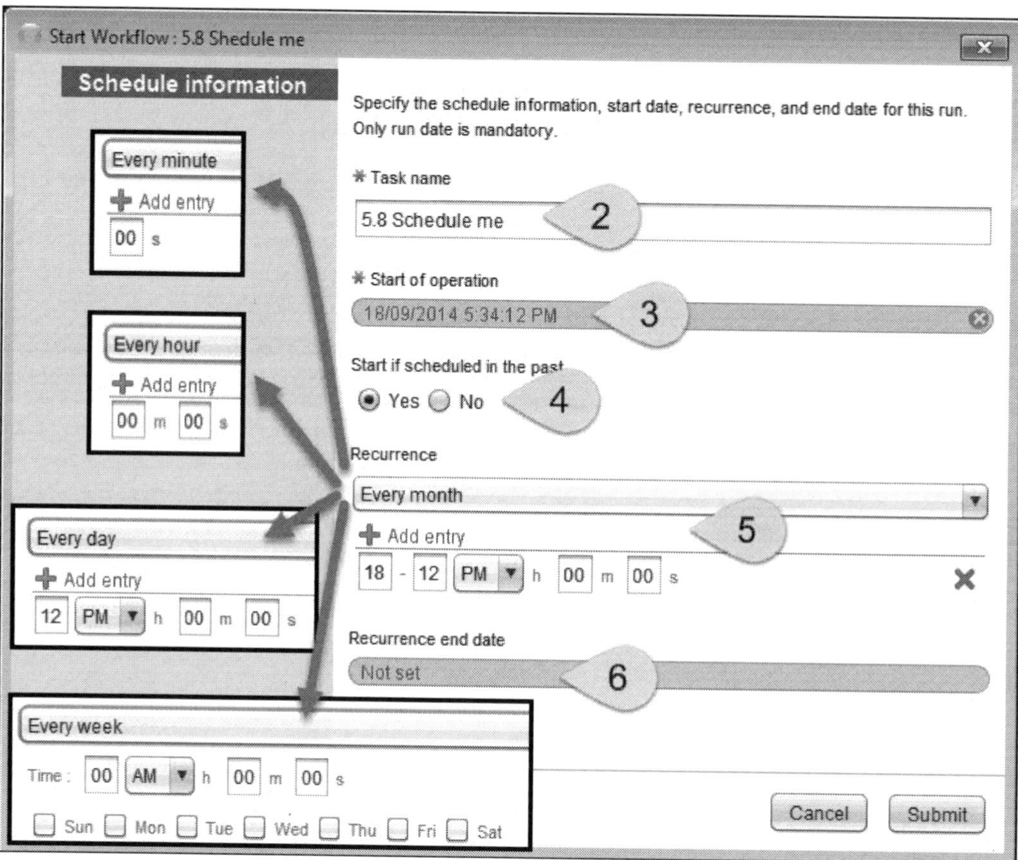

How it works...

Using the Orchestrator scheduler allows you to make sure certain tasks are running at a specific time. There are multiple examples. There is a maintenance task that is scheduled to run every evening to disconnect all CD-ROM drives from VMs or a provisioning/decommissioning task that you want to enact at a certain time.

You can manage all scheduled tasks from the **Run** | **Scheduler** view. Here, you can review all relevant information for all scheduled tasks. The information provided includes: what workflow it is currently running, when the last run was made, and when it will run next, and you also see the in-parameters (**Parameters**) you have supplied to the workflow. By right-clicking on the task, you can suspend and resume it as well as cancel/delete and edit it. When editing the task, you can change all settings with regard to the scheduling, however, you cannot change the workflow you have scheduled or the in-parameters you entered when you scheduled the task.

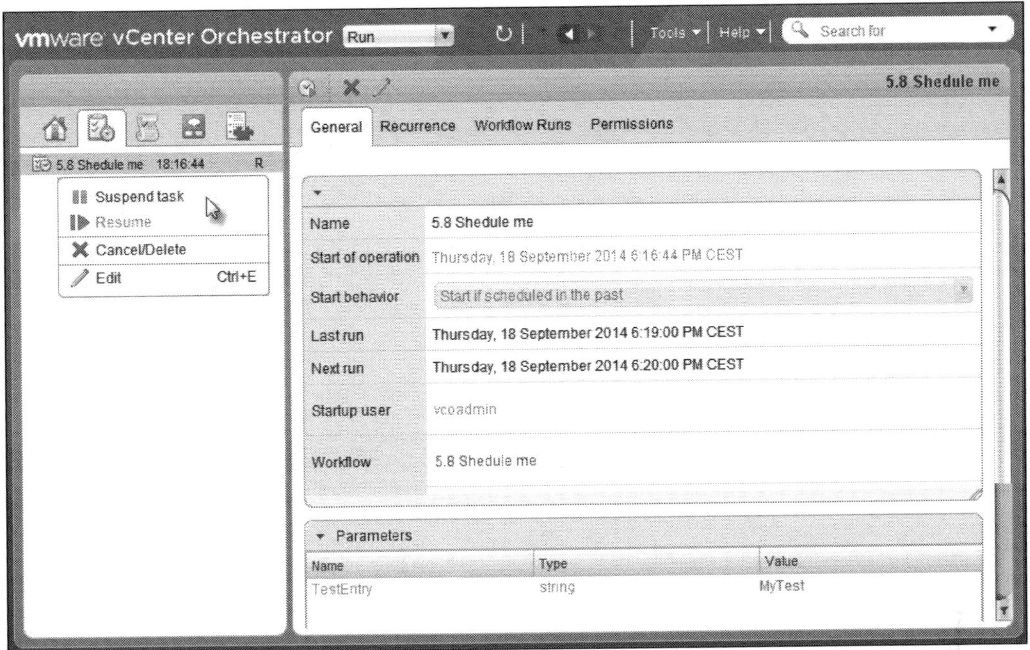

Clicking on the **Workflow runs** tab, you can see all the information for each run. You see the start and end time as well as the workflow state (waiting, failed, completed, cancelled, running). If the workflow is currently running, you can see which element of the workflow is currently running (**Current item**) as well as its business state.

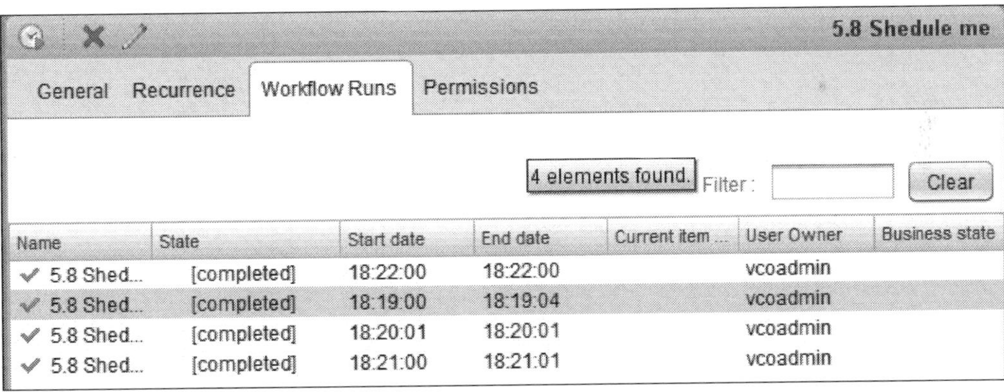

Name	State	Start date	End date	Current item ...	User Owner	Business state
5.8 Shed...	[completed]	18:22:00	18:22:00		vcoadmin	
5.8 Shed...	[completed]	18:19:00	18:19:04		vcoadmin	
5.8 Shed...	[completed]	18:20:01	18:20:01		vcoadmin	
5.8 Shed...	[completed]	18:21:00	18:21:01		vcoadmin	

In addition to this, you can also schedule and monitor a scheduled task from vCenter. In the vCenter Web Client, click on **vCenter Orchestrator** and then on **Scheduled workflows**.

There's more...

You can interactively schedule a workflow using a workflow. A typical example for this is a workflow that requests a VM but then schedules the actual provisioning at a later date and time. To do this, just use the schema element **Schedule workflow** that you find in the **Generic** section. This element only schedules tasks once; it doesn't allow recurring tasks.

You can schedule workflows using JavaScript. Using the two methods `Workflow.schedule()` and `Workflow.scheduleRecurrently()`, you can now schedule this workflow. Have a closer look into the schema element **Schedule workflow**; the `Workflow.schedule()` method is used there.

See also

See example workflow 5.8.1 Schedule me! and 5.8.2. Automatic schedule.

Workflow auto documentation

This recipe will showcase the automatic documentation ability of Orchestrator. We will learn what Orchestrator documents and how it documents workflows.

Getting ready

We need at least one workflow for this recipe that we can document. A good example workflow would be one that contains other workflows, actions, and scriptable tasks.

How to do it...

1. Right-click on a workflow or a folder and select **Generate Documentation**.
2. Select a directory and give the file a name.
3. A PDF with the documentation is now created.

How it works...

The documentation that is created isn't that flashy, however, it is quite useful. The created PDF document contains the following sections:

Section	Description
Versions	This is a summary of all existing versions this workflow has, including the create date, create user, and any comments you have made in regards to this version.
Inputs	This contains a list of all in-parameters of the workflow as well as their type and description.
Outputs	This contains a list of all out-parameters of the workflow as well as their type and description.
Attributes	This contains a list of all attributes of the workflow as well as their type and description. It does not contain any values.
Parameter presentation	This shows all properties of all in-parameters that are defined in the presentation of this workflow.
Workflow schema	This is a picture of the workflow that shows the elements of the schema.
Workflow items	This is a tabular overview of all existing elements in the workflow schema.
Source code for the used actions	This lists every script that was used in an action, scriptable task, log element, and so on.

If you are running the documentation feature from a folder, each workflow in this folder will be documented.

Orchestrator and vSphere Web Client

In this recipe, we further explore the Orchestrator integration into vSphere Web Client. You will learn how to run Orchestrator workflows using vSphere Web Client as well as how to configure workflows so that they work with it.

Getting ready

You find the base information on how to integrate Orchestrator into the vSphere Web Client in the *Integrating Orchestrator into SSO and vSphere Web Client* recipe in *Chapter 1, Installing and Configuring Orchestrator*.

For this recipe, we need Orchestrator integrated into vSphere Web Client.

How to do it...

This recipe is made up of two parts the configuration and the passing along of information between the web client and Orchestrator.

Configure workflows for the Web Client

We now configure workflows for the usage with the vSphere Web Client:

1. Open the vSphere Web Client in a web browser.
2. You have to use a user account that has the `View` and `Executive` rights in Orchestrator. The best option is to log in with a user that is part of the Orchestrator Administrator group.
3. Click on **vCenter Orchestrator** and wait until the web client has finished loading all information. You should now see at least one Orchestrator Server registered.
4. Click on **Manage** and then on **Context Actions**. You can now see all workflows that have been configured to be used with the right-click menu from vSphere Web Client.

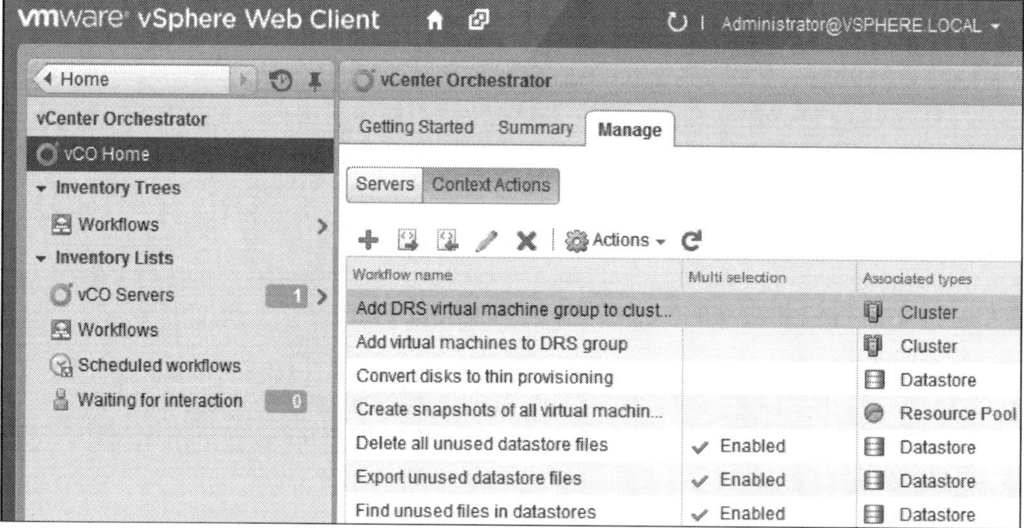

5. To configure a new workflow for use with the Web Client, click on **Add** (the green plus sign).
6. Select a workflow from the list of available workflows (choose the workflow **Rename virtual machine** from **Library** | **vCenter** | **Virtual Machine Management** | **Basic**, as this workflow can be used without extra configuration).

7. Select the type of vSphere object this workflow should be available to (such as a VM).
8. **Multi selection** lets you choose not only one but multiple instances of the same vSphere object, for example, not only one VM but multiple VMs. For this to work, you also have to make sure that the workflow has an in-parameter of the `Array of [VC:object]` type.
9. Click on **OK**.

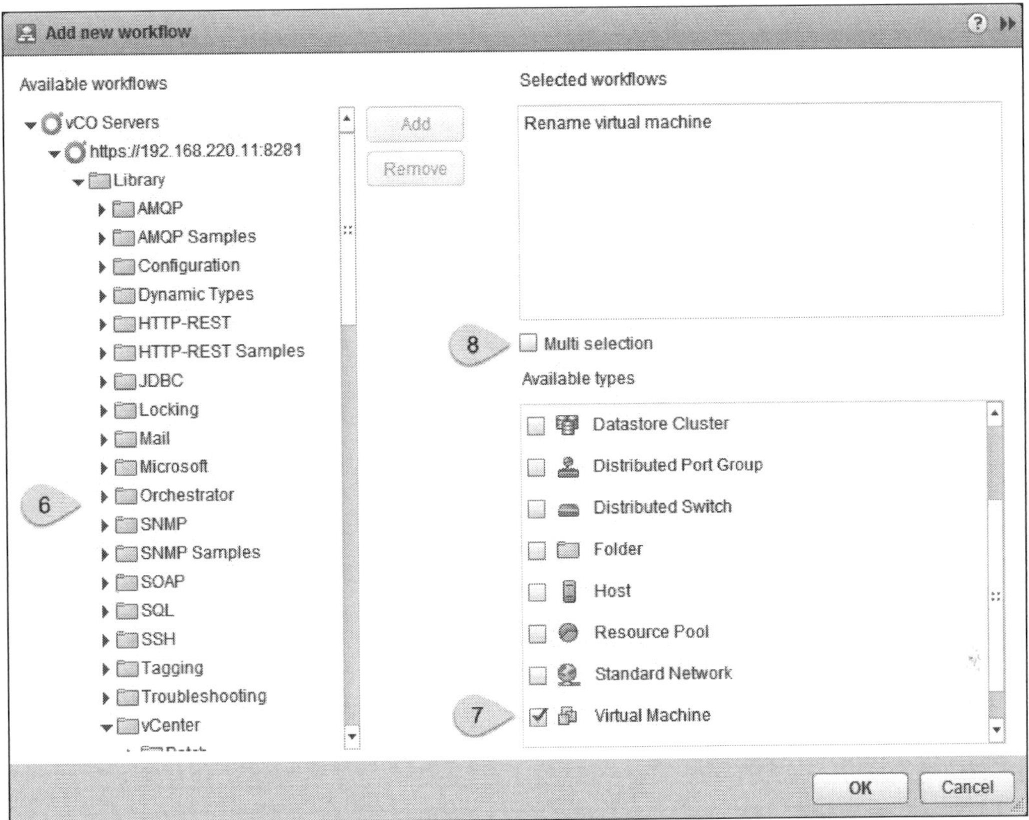

10. To run the **Rename Virtual Machine** workflow from our example, navigate in the Web Client to a VM, then right-click on the VM, and navigate to **All vCenter Orchestrator Actions** | **[name of the workflow]**.

11. Enter a new name for the VM and click on **Submit**.

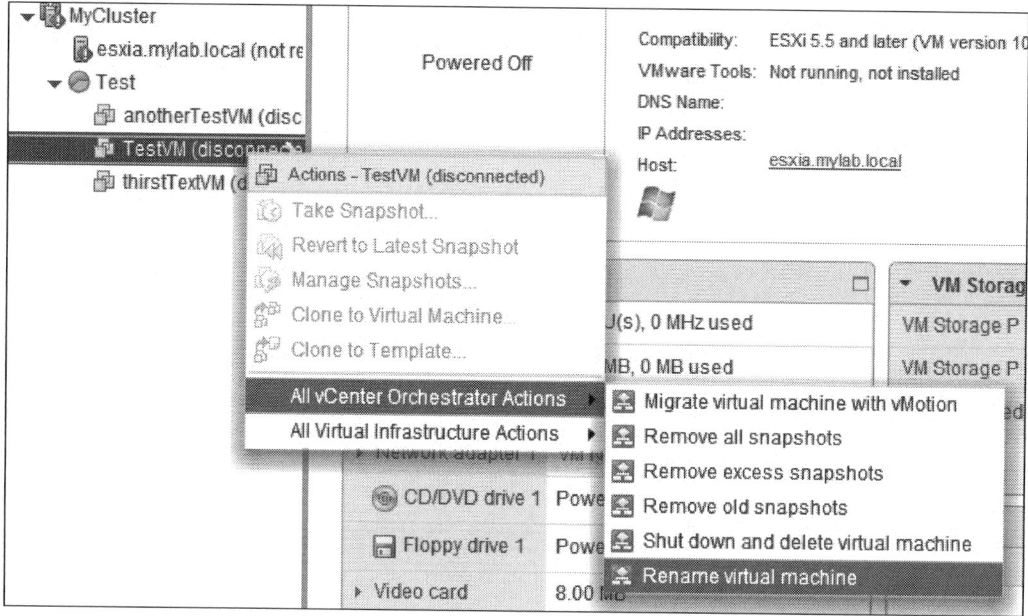

Writing workflows for web integration

When running a workflow from the Web Client, you might want to pass some information to the workflow in Orchestrator, for instance, the vSphere object you are running the workflow on.

1. Open the workflow you want to use with the Orchestrator Client in the edit mode.
2. Make sure that you have a workflow in-parameter of the type you want to associate with in the vSphere Web Client, for example, `VC:VirtualMachine`. If you plan to use the **Multi selection** option, make sure that you use an `Array of VC:VirtualMachine`.
3. In **Presentation**, assign the **Show in Inventory** property to the workflow in-parameter. If this property is assigned to more than one in-parameter, only one parameter at a time is used. For example, you have an in-parameter for a VM and for a cluster, both have the **Show in Inventory** property assigned to them. When starting the workflow from a VM, the VM ID will be used and the cluster ID will not be transferred to the workflow. When starting the workflow from a cluster, the cluster ID will be used and the VM ID will be ignored.
4. Save the workflow.

How it works...

The vSphere integration of Orchestrator into the vSphere Web Client allows you to easily use workflows that you have created.

You can also start all workflows from the Web Client by clicking on **vCenter Orchestrator** | **Inventory Trees** | **Workflows**. The Orchestrator Workflow tree you know from Orchestrator Client will appear and you can select and then start the workflow.

It's also possible to schedule workflows; just click on the workflow that you would like to run and then click on the right window onto **Schedule workflow**. This works the same as in Orchestrator Client. You can monitor all scheduled workflows by clicking on **vCenter Orchestrator** | **Inventor List** | **Scheduled workflows**.

The last and most important thing is that you can also interact with workflows that are waiting for interaction. Just click on **vCenter Orchestrator** | **Inventor List** | **Waiting for interaction** to see all workflows that is currently waiting for interaction.

There's more...

As you need to define **Context Actions** (right-click on the menu), it is rather important that you are able to back up or restore these settings.

By clicking on **vCenter Orchestrator** | **Manage** | **Context Actions**, you can use the export action (the white paper icon with the blue right arrow) to export all current settings into an XML file. Using import (the white paper icon with the green left arrow), you can import these settings into Web Client again. Please note that the export contains the workflow ID, so make sure that the workflows on another Orchestrator Server have the same ID (see the *Synchronize Orchestrator element between Orchestrator Servers* and *Working with packages* recipes in this chapter).

See also

- Recipe *Integrating Orchestrator into SSO and vSphere Web Client* in *Chapter 1, Installing and Configuring Orchestrator*.
- Recipe *Working with user interaction* in *Chapter 3, Visual Programming*
- Recipe *Working with presentations* in *Chapter 3, Visual Programming*
- Recipe *Language packs (localization)* in *Chapter 6, Advanced Operations*

6

Advanced Operations

In this chapter, we will be looking at the following recipes:

- Accessing the Orchestrator API via REST
- Working with resources
- Working with tags
- Working with locks
- Language Packs (localization)
- Working with policies
- Managing remote Orchestrator

Introduction

In this chapter, we will look at the more advanced operations you can perform with Orchestrator.

This chapter could have been longer and should have contained a recipe about creating WebViews and some more details about authentication; however, here is the bad news about these two features.

WebViews

WebViews are disappearing from Orchestrator. As an alternative to WebViews, Wavemaker can be used. Wavemaker is a great tool, but to get it working involves a bit more work and requires a lot of extra information and skills. Therefore, I decided to leave it out of this book.

To make a start with Wavemaker, have a look at the following links:

- `www.wavemaker.com`
- `http://labs.vmware.com/flings/wavemaker-integration-for-vcenter-orchestrator`

Authorizations

Authorizations are leftovers in Orchestrator from the Dunes times, and they have lost their importance since VMware integrated plugin authentication and permissions with the product. What you could do with them was to create authorizations towards resource elements (plugins), especially role-based WebViews. However, there is no workable example that would be usable in any real-world environment. All the more so since WebViews are about to go.

Accessing the Orchestrator API via REST

In this recipe, we will see how one can interact with the Orchestrator's REST interface and run workflows.

Getting ready

We need a working Orchestrator and a REST client. We will use Firefox with the REST client; Firefox can be downloaded from `https://addons.mozilla.org/en-US/firefox/addon/restclient/`.

You might think it is odd to use a web browser to connect to and use a REST host; however, there is method to this madness. A REST implementations in PHP, Python, or .NET might not expose all the features that one needs or wants. Using a web browser enables you to experiment with all the available features you might need.

How to do it...

We will divide this recipe into:

- Establishing a connection
- Getting information
- Running a workflow

Establishing a connection

The first thing we need to do is establish a connection to the Orchestrator REST interface:

1. Open Firefox; if you have not accepted the Orchestrator SSL certificate, please browse to `https://[IP or FQDN Orchestrator]:8281/vco/api/` and accept the certificate.
2. In Firefox, click on the REST client (see the next screenshot).
3. Switch **Method** to **GET**.
4. Click on **Authentication** and enter a user that has access to Orchestrator. After clicking on **OK**, you will find that **Headers** now show an authentication item.
5. Enter the `https://[IP or FQDN Orchestrator]:8281/vco/api/` URL and click on **SEND**.
6. **Response Headers** shows the general return code such as the return code whereas **Response Body (Preview)** shows the content that has been returned.

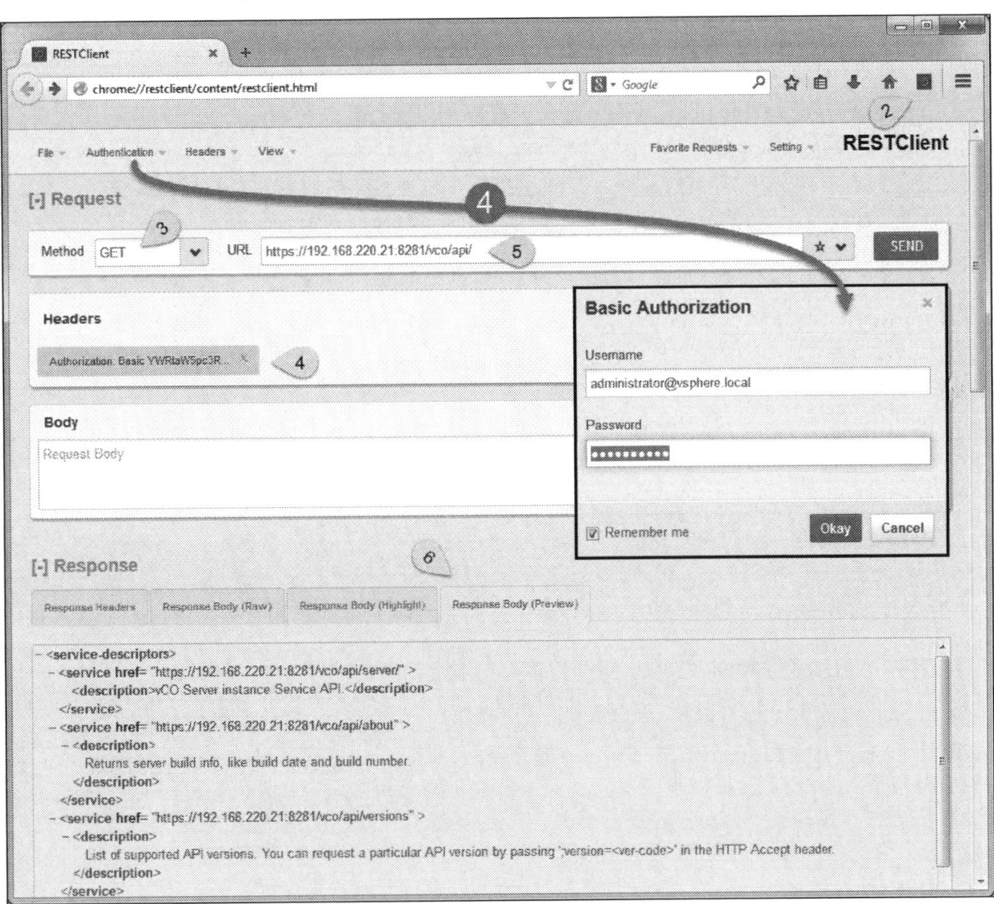

Getting information

Now that we have established a connection to the API, let's pull some information from it:

1. We'll start from where we left off in the last section. Scroll down in **Response Body (Preview)** and look for **workflows**.
2. Click on the hyperlink provided. The URL is now automatically changed to `https://[IP or FQDN Orchestrator]:8281/vco/api/workflows`.
3. Click on **Send**. It might take a moment, as the response contains all existing workflows. Have a scroll.
4. As this is a bit too much information, let's filter the results. Add `?conditions=name=3.01%20Workflow%20basics` to the **URL** after `/workflows/`.
5. Click on **Send** and you will be able to see a single workflow `3.01 Workflow basics` from the example pack. We just had to replace the spaces with `%20`, as with any good HTML.
6. The response will show you some basic information about the workflow as well as its link, as shown in the following screenshot:

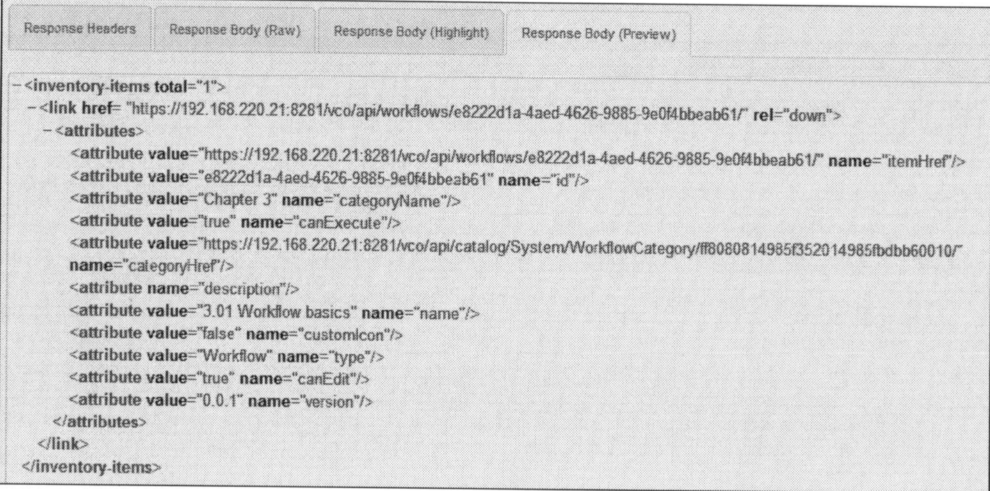

7. Click on the hyperlink provided in `<link href="` and click on **Send**.
8. You are now taken to the workflows interaction page.

```
- <workflow customized-icon="false" href= "https://192.168.220.21:8281/vco/api/workflows/e8222d1a-4aed-4626-9885-9e0f4bbeab61/" >
  - <relations>
      <link href= "https://192.168.220.21:8281/vco/api/inventory/System/Workflows/Orchestartor%2BCookbook/Chapter%2B3/" rel="up"/>
      <link href= "https://192.168.220.21:8281/vco/api/workflows/e8222d1a-4aed-4626-9885-9e0f4bbeab61/executions/" rel="executions"/>
      <link href= "https://192.168.220.21:8281/vco/api/workflows/e8222d1a-4aed-4626-9885-9e0f4bbeab61/presentation/" rel="presentation"/>
      <link href= "https://192.168.220.21:8281/vco/api/workflows/e8222d1a-4aed-4626-9885-9e0f4bbeab61/tasks/" rel="tasks"/>
  A   <link href= "https://192.168.220.21:8281/vco/api/workflows/e8222d1a-4aed-4626-9885-9e0f4bbeab61/icon/" rel="icon"/>
      <link href= "https://192.168.220.21:8281/vco/api/workflows/e8222d1a-4aed-4626-9885-9e0f4bbeab61/schema/" rel="schema"/>
      <link href= "https://192.168.220.21:8281/vco/api/workflows/e8222d1a-4aed-4626-9885-9e0f4bbeab61/permissions/" rel="permissions"/>
      <link href= "https://192.168.220.21:8281/vco/api/workflows/e8222d1a-4aed-4626-9885-9e0f4bbeab61/interactions/" rel="interactions"/>
    </relations>
    <id>e8222d1a-4aed-4626-9885-9e0f4bbeab61</id>
  - <input-parameters>
      <parameter type="string" name="input"/>   B
    </input-parameters>
  - <output-parameters>
      <parameter type="string" name="output"/>   C
    </output-parameters>
    <name>3.01 Workflow basics</name>
    <version>0.0.1</version>
  </workflow>
```


Here, you find all the methods that can be worked on the Workflow (marked as A in the preceding screenshot) as well as the input (B) and output (C) variables for this workflow.

Running a workflow

To start a workflow using the API, follow these steps:

1. Let's continue from where we left off in the last section; click on the hyperlink in the **link** tag that has the **rel** tag **executions** at the end.
2. The responses you see are the workflow runs that have taken place (if the response is empty, don't worry, we will come back to this step).
3. To run the workflow, we need to switch to **POST**. This will start the workflow you are currently in (ID in the URL).
4. We also need an additional header. Navigate to **Headers** | **Custom Header** and enter `Content-Type` under **Name** and `application/xml` under **Value**.
5. In **Body**, enter the variable content you would like to use in the following form:

```
<execution-context xmlns="http://www.vmware.com/vco">
    <parameters>
        <parameter type="string" name="input" scope="local">
            <string>Entry String</string>
        </parameter>
    </parameters>
</execution-context>
```

6. Click on **Send** to run the workflow.

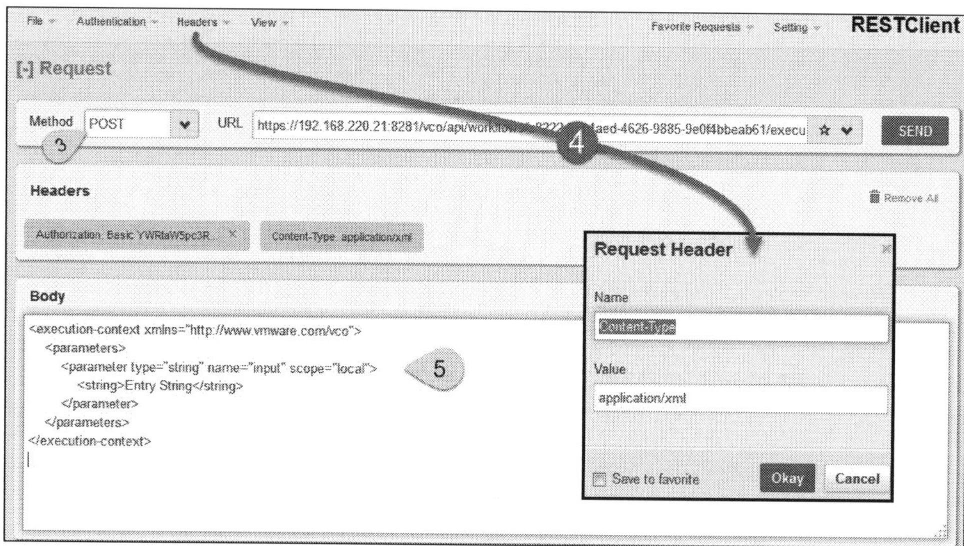


```
<execution-context xmlns="http://www.vmware.com/vco">
  <parameters>
    <parameter type="string" name="input" scope="local">
      <string>Entry String</string>
    </parameter>
  </parameters>
</execution-context>
```

7. Check out **Response Header**. If everything went right, you should see **202 Accepted**.
8. Switch **Method** to **GET** and click on **Send**. You now see the execution of the workflow again.
9. Click on the hyperlink provided in `<link href="` and click on **Send**.
10. You now see the output of the workflow execution:

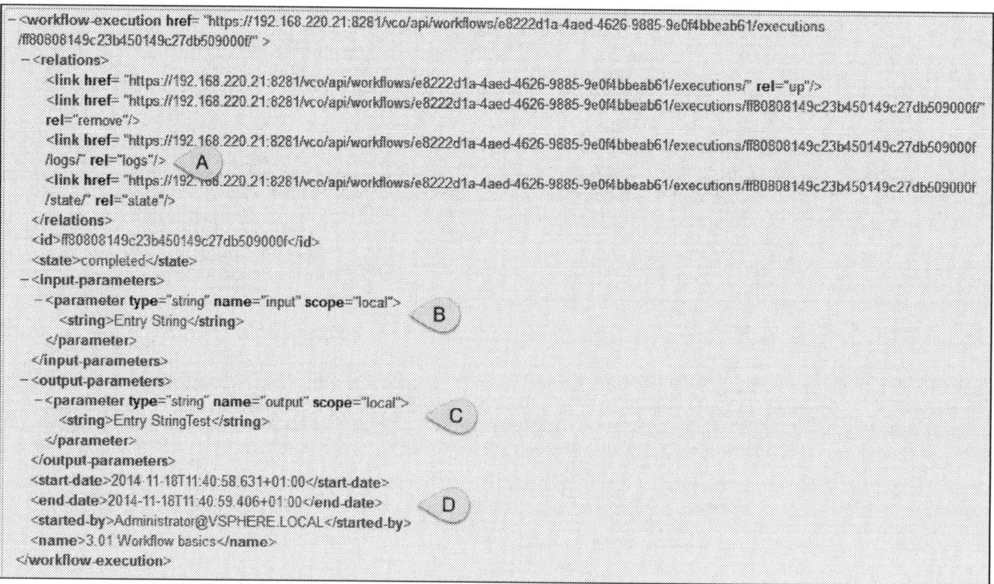


```
- <workflow-execution href= "https://192.168.220.21:8281/vco/api/workflows/e8222d1a-4aed-4626-9885-9e0f4bbeab61/executions/ff80808149c23b450149c27db509000f/" >
  - <relations>
      <link href= "https://192.168.220.21:8281/vco/api/workflows/e8222d1a-4aed-4626-9885-9e0f4bbeab61/executions/" rel="up"/>
      <link href= "https://192.168.220.21:8281/vco/api/workflows/e8222d1a-4aed-4626-9885-9e0f4bbeab61/executions/ff80808149c23b450149c27db509000f/" rel="remove"/>
      <link href= "https://192.168.220.21:8281/vco/api/workflows/e8222d1a-4aed-4626-9885-9e0f4bbeab61/executions/ff80808149c23b450149c27db509000f/logs/" rel="logs"/>
      <link href= "https://192.168.220.21:8281/vco/api/workflows/e8222d1a-4aed-4626-9885-9e0f4bbeab61/executions/ff80808149c23b450149c27db509000f/state/" rel="state"/>
    </relations>
    <id>ff80808149c23b450149c27db509000f</id>
    <state>completed</state>
  - <input-parameters>
    - <parameter type="string" name="input" scope="local">
        <string>Entry String</string>
      </parameter>
    </input-parameters>
  - <output-parameters>
    - <parameter type="string" name="output" scope="local">
        <string>Entry StringTest</string>
      </parameter>
    </output-parameters>
    <start-date>2014-11-18T11:40:58.631+01:00</start-date>
    <end-date>2014-11-18T11:40:59.406+01:00</end-date>
    <started-by>Administrator@VSPHERE.LOCAL</started-by>
    <name>3.01 Workflow basics</name>
</workflow-execution>
```

The execution contains a link to the logs (marked as A in the preceding screenshot), the input (B), output (C) as well as some basic information (D).

How it works...

REST is the current interface of choice for most applications. Orchestrator has a SOAP interface as well; however, VMware plans to retire this at some stage. The other important point is that the REST interface provides a lot more functionality. To see the difference, check out the *Working with SOAP* recipe in *Chapter 4, Working with Plugins*.

You can see that REST uses XML extensively; after this little example, this probably makes a lot of sense as you can see that the information is formed and encapsulated very readably.

You can find all the Orchestrator-relevant REST documentation at `https://[IP or FQDN Orchestrator]:/vco/api/docs/`.

See also

- See the *Working with REST* recipe in *Chapter 4, Working with Plugins*. A more detailed walk-through can be found at `http://www.vcoteam.info/articles/learn-vco/268-how-to-use-the-rest-api-to-start-a-workflow.html`.

Working with resources

In this recipe, we will work with resources. We will see how we can integrate files with Orchestrator and use them in workflows and for other purposes, such as storing configuration information.

Getting ready

We need a functional Orchestrator. We also need a text file. One is part of the example workflow package named `textFile.txt`.

How to do it...

This recipe contains multiple parts, each dealing with different aspects of resources.

Adding resources manually

Let's start by adding a resource to Orchestrator manually:

1. Switch Orchestrator to **Design** mode.
2. Click on **Resources** (white page with a blue symbol on it).

3. Create a new folder where you can store your resources by right-clicking the highest element in the tree and selecting **New folder**.
4. Right-click on the new folder and select **Import resources**.
5. Select a file such as an image or text file from your local folder and click on **Open**. The new resource is now available under the folder you created.
6. Click on the resource and browse through the tabs that are presented.
7. Please note that **Description** automatically contains the location from where you imported it. Also, if the file is a picture or text file, you can view it in the **Viewer** tab.

You can also update (reupload a file) and download (save to a file) resources in Orchestrator.

Using resources in workflows

To add a resource to a workflow, we need to add it as an attribute. This is shown as follows:

1. Create a new workflow and add a new attribute.
2. Rename the attribute to `textFile`.
3. Change the type of the attribute to **ResourceElement**.
4. Now click on **Value**. You can now search the existing resources and select one.
5. Add a scriptable task to the schema and edit it.
6. Bind the `textFile` attribute as a parameter and add the following script:

```
System.log("Name :"+textFile.name);
System.log("MimeType :"+textFile.mimeType);
System.log("Resource Category :"+textFile.
getResourceElementCategory().name);
System.log("Description :"+textFile.description);
System.log("Version :"+textFile.version);
System.log("Size :"+textFile.contentSize);
//get the content as MimeAttachment
Attachment = textFile.getContentAsMimeAttachment();
// get string content from MimeAttachment
Content = attachment.content;
System.log("Content: \n"+content);
```

7. Save and run the workflow.

In the logs, we output all the possible properties of `resourceElement`. The most important one is its content.

Creating a new resource element

Instead of manually uploading a resource element, you can dynamically add new resource elements to Orchestrator.

1. Create a new workflow and add the following variables:

Name	Type	Section	Use
`name`	String	IN	This is the name of the resource
`resourceFolder`	ResourceElementCategory	IN	This is where the resource should be stored
`textContent`	String	IN	This is the plain text that the resource should contain

2. Add a scripting task to the schema and bind all variables.
3. Add the following script:

```
//initialize a mime attachment object
var attachment = new MimeAttachment();
//fill it
attachment.name = name;
attachment.mimeType = "text/plain";
attachment.content = textContent;
//create the resource element form the Mime attachment
Server.createResourceElement(resourceFolder,name,attachment);
```

4. Save and run the workflow.

When the workflow runs, select a resource folder you would like to store it in. After the workflow has finished, check the resource folder and its content.

Updating a resource

We can also update existing resources. To do this perform the following steps:

1. Create a new workflow and add the following variables:

Name	Type	Section	Use
`resource`	ResourceElement	IN	This is the resource element that should be updated
`newTextContent`	String	IN	This is the new text content

2. Add a scripting task to the schema and bind all variables.
3. Add the following script:

```
//prepare for update
var attachment = new MimeAttachment() ;
//set new content
attachment.content = newTextContent;
//use old settings
attachment.name = resource.name;
attachment.mimeType = resource.mimeType;
//update
resource.setContentFromMimeAttachment(attachment);
//overwrite the description
resource.description="Updated";
```

4. Save and run the workflow.

When you run the workflow, select a resource to update, preferably one you have created before. After the workflow has finished, check the resource and its content.

How it works...

Resource elements have many uses. First of all, you can use a small picture as an icon for Orchestrator workflows. Secondly, you can use them to send e-mail attachments (see the *Working with mails* recipe in *Chapter 4, Working with Plugins*). There is also a method of storing information as a resource element. Orchestrator uses this method to store the configuration for the SOAP, REST, and multinode plugins. The stored information is the configuration for each SOAP, REST, or Orchestrator server. Go have a look!

Last but not least, you can use the resource elements to store templates. For example, you can store a text template for an e-mail you want to send to customers. You can write variables in the text such as `"Dear {name}..."` and use the string method `replace` to substitute the variables before sending the e-mail, for example `ResourceContent.replace("{name}",sendToName);`.

Any kind of file can be used as a resource element, but typically one uses XML, plain text, or pictures as resource elements.

There's more...

You can do more with resources. Some examples are as follows.

Accessing resources directly

You don't need to actually add a resource as an attribute to a workflow to access it, you can directly access them.

You can get all existing resource element categories with `Server.getAllResourceElementCategories()`. To get resource elements from a given category, use `ResourceElementCategory.resourceElements`. Use `ResourceElementCategory.subCategories` to get all sub categories from a given category.

Have a look at example workflow 6.02.4 for a guide.

Saving and loading resources

You can also write a resource to the local filesystem or load one from it.

To save a resource, use `resourceElement.writeContentToFile(file);`. To load a resource element, use `newResource.setContentFromFile(file,mimeType);`. Have a look at the example workflow 6.02.5 as a reference. Also, a useful idea would be to upload a resource from the local computer using the mimeAttachment type as an input. Please note that Orchestrator will need access to the local filesystem, see the *Configuring access to the local filesystem* recipe in *Chapter 2, Optimizing Orchestrator Configuration*.

See also

The following are some example workflows:

- 6.02.1 Use Resources
- 6.02.2 Create Resources
- 6.02.3 Update a Resource
- 6.02.4 Access Resources directly
- 6.02.5 Save and load Resources

Working with tags

Let's explore the tagging of workflows. Tagging introduces the same kind of tagging you're familiar with from vCenter Server 5.5. Tagging allows you to add tags to Orchestrator objects and search for them.

Getting ready

You will need Orchestrator version 5.5.1 or higher. We need some workflows we can tag. You can use the example workflow if you want.

How to do it...

Tagging involves the following elements.

Tagging a workflow

Let's start by setting a tag on a workflow:

1. Start the workflow by navigating to **Library** | **Tagging** | **Tag workflow**.
2. Select the workflow you would like to tag.
3. Enter a tag and a value.
4. Select whether you would like this tag to be global or not. A global tag is visible to all users whereas nonglobal (private) tags are only visible to the user who places the tag.

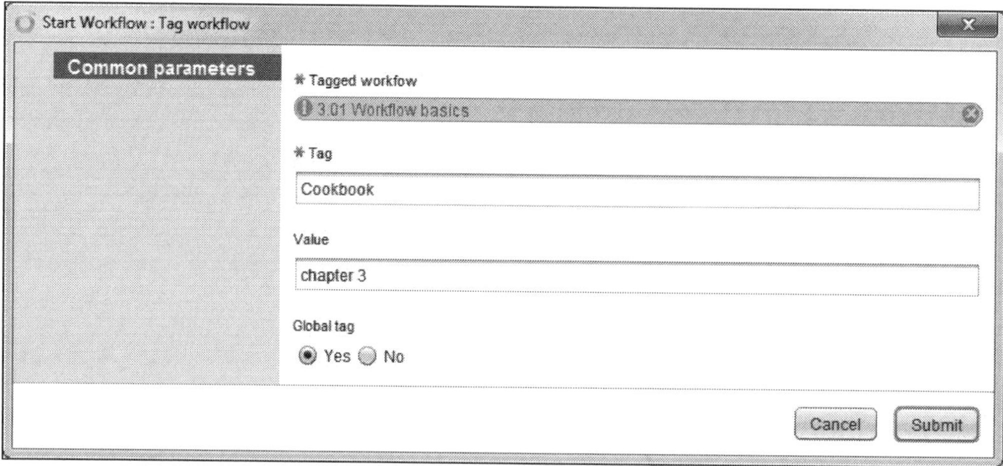

5. Submit the workflow.

Viewing all tags in a workflow

1. Start the workflow by navigating to **Library | Tagging | List Workflow tags**.
2. Select the workflow you would like to see a list of all its tags.
3. After submitting the workflow, check the logs. All tags and their values will be listed.

Finding workflows by tags

1. Start the workflow by navigating to **Library** | **Tagging** | **Find objects by tag**.
2. Enter only a tag or a tag and its value.
3. Select whether this tag is global or private and submit the workflow.
4. The output is an array of workflows.

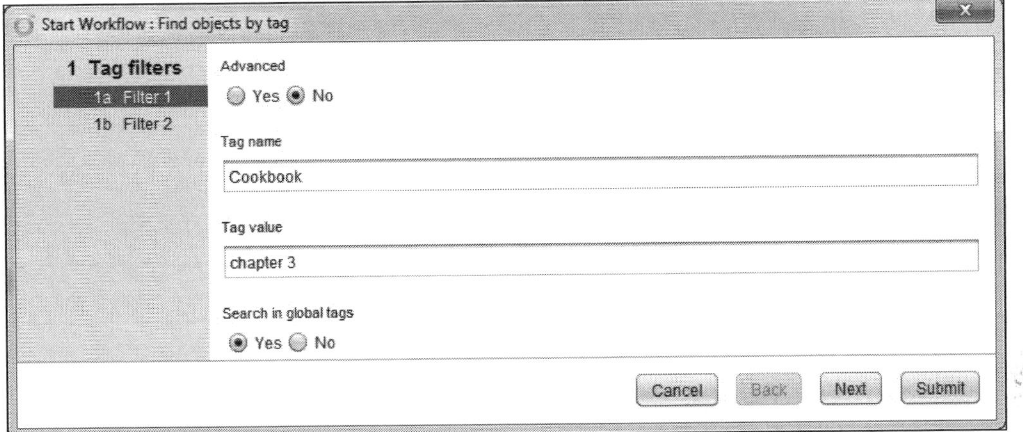

How it works...

Tags are new since version 5.5.1 and VMware announced that they will be more integrated with newer versions of Orchestrator. Currently, tags are only usable and visible via the workflows or the API. However, they align very well with VMware's tags in vSphere, vCloud Director, and other products.

There are two type of tags: global tags and private tags. A global tag is visible to all users whereas nonglobal (private) tags are only visible to the user who places the tag.

Tags are not stored with the workflows. Importing and exporting a workflow to a different Orchestrator will not preserve the tags; however, several websites state that this is the case.

The existing tag workflows that we had a look at only work on workflows, but any Orchestrator object can be tagged using the JavaScript implementation.

There's more...

The JavaScript behind the tags is straightforward:

JavaScript tags	Function
`Server.tagGlobally(taggedObject, tagName, tagValue );`	This allows tagging an object with a global tag
`Server.tag(taggedObject, tagName, tagValue );`	This allows tagging an object with a private tag
`Server.findGlobalTagsForObject(taggedObject);`	This allows listing an object's global tags
`Server.findTagsForObject(taggedObject);`	This allows listing an object's private tags
`Server.queryByTags(tagQuery, null);`	This allows finding an object by its tags
`Server.untagGlobally(taggedObject,  tags);`	This allows untagging a global tag from an object
`Server.untag(taggedObject, tags);`	This allows untagging a private tag from an object

Working with locks

There are two types of locks in Orchestrator: Workflow Locking and **LockingSystem**. We will learn how to lock and unlock objects using both mechanisms.

Getting ready

For Workflow Locking, we need a workflow that we can use to lock, primarily, a workflow that calls other actions or workflows. If you don't have one at hand, use the example workflow 3.15.1 Using Asynchronous Workflows - First.

For LockingSystem, we need a resource, such as a VM or an Orchestrator resource.

How to do it...

We will have a quick look at Workflow Locking before we address the locking system in the *There's more* section.

Locking workflows

To lock a workflow, action, or package, follow these steps:

1. Right-click on a workflow, action, or package.
2. Navigate to **Locking** | **Lock** or **Locking** | **Lock with dependencies**. Lock with dependency will lock all subworkflows and subactions that are used in this workflow.

Notice the little lock icon on the item you have locked; you will no longer be able to edit this workflow. However, you are still able to run it.

Unlocking workflows

Unlocking should be obvious now. However, please note that there is no unlock with dependencies, which means that you have to unlock each element by itself:

1. Right-click on a locked workflow, action, or package.
2. Navigate to **Locking** | **Unlock**.

How it works...

Locking locks the edit mode of a workflow, which marks it as not accessible. Everyone with the **Admin** right can place or lift a lock.

A lock disables **Edit**, **Delete**, **Synchronize**, and **Move**. Locks cannot be exported.

Workflow Locking actually has nothing to do with LockingSystem. Workflow Locking locks workflows and actions, whereas the LockingSystem locks resources.

Locks (workflow and LockingSystem) can be useful in a cluster situation or a production environment, where one wants to make sure that an important production workflow can't be altered.

There's more...

Orchestrator has an internal locking mechanism. It enables you to lock any resource item (such as VMs). You set a lock with `LockingSystem.lock(resourceID, owner)`. Using the `LockingSystem.lockAndWait(resourceID, owner)` method with the same `resourceID` string will pause the workflow until the `resourceID` is unlocked with `LockingSystem.unlock(resourceID, owner)`.

Please note that the object isn't really locked; only a lock entry is set. The lock is just a flag and nothing else. If you want to use the locking system, you will need to check for the locking entry. You can check all locking entries with LockingSystem.retrieveAll(), which returns an array of strings where each string represents `resourceID,owner`.

You can release all locks with `LockingSystem.unlockAll()`.

In the example packages, there are three examples on how to use the locking system.

See also

The following are some example workflows:

- 6.04.1 Locking an object
- 6.04.2 Wait for lock
- 6.04.3 Check for locks

Language packs (localization)

This recipe will look into the possibility of creating localized language packs for workflows. Localization enables users to see workflow presentations in their local language.

Getting ready

We just need an Orchestrator and the ability to edit text files. Additionally, you might want to know a foreign language (or use Google Translate).

How to do it...

We will now create a language pack for the example workflow 3.0.1 Workflow basics:

1. Navigate to the workflow you want to create localization on.
2. Right-click on the workflow and navigate to **Localization** | **create localization resources**.
3. Navigate to the Orchestrator resources. You will notice that new `ResourceElementCategory` folders have been created along with `ResourceElements` for English, Japanese, French, German, and Korean.

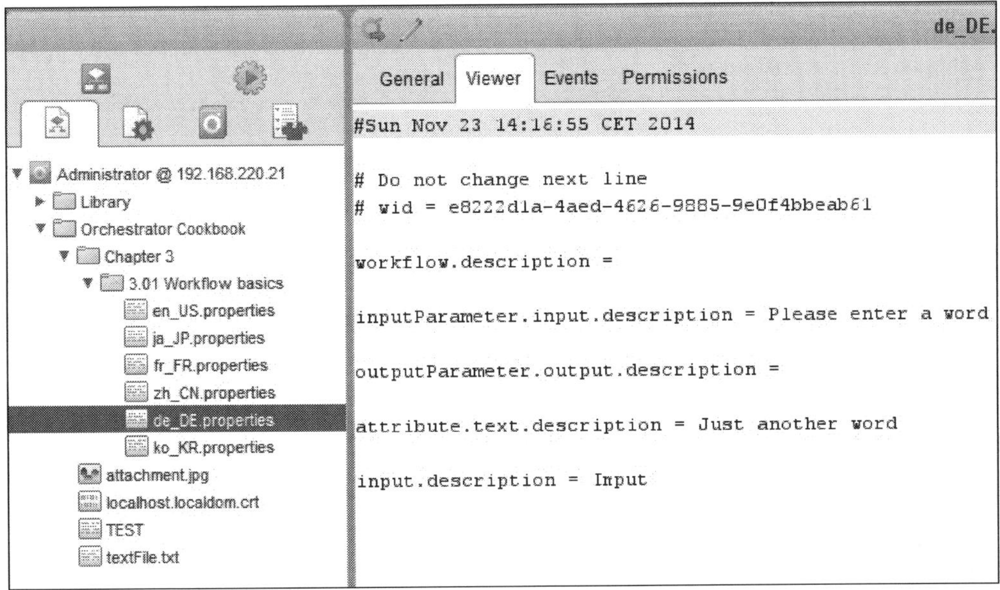

4. Right-click on the workflow again, navigate to **Localization** | **export localization bundle**, and save it onto a local file.
5. Switch to your local file system and unzip the localization bundle.
6. Edit one of the language files and replace the text with a local language.
7. Rezip the file and then upload the bundle by right-clicking on the workflow and navigating to **Localization** | **import localization bundle**.
8. Check `ResourceElement` to see the updates.
9. To check the result, switch the language of a web browser to the language you specified—for example, **De-DE** (not just **de**). Please note that this is case-sensitive.

10. Now start vSphere Web Client and then the workflow (see the *Orchestrator and vSphere Web Client* recipe in *Chapter 5, Basic Orchestrator operations*).

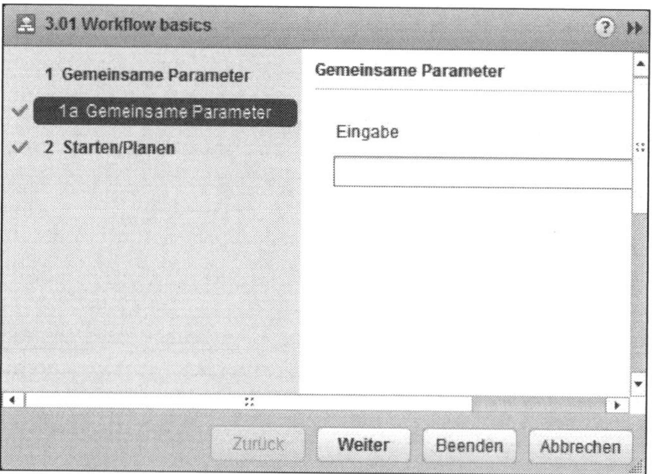

How it works...

Localization works with any application that pulls the REST API using an `Accept-Language` header to transport the language code, such as `de-DE`. Orchestrator Client doesn't support this feature.

vRealize Automation (**vRA**) (formerly vCAC) supports localization from version 6.2 onwards.

Working with policies

In this recipe, we will look into policies. We will learn how to create and use policies to react automatically to events that occur outside Orchestrator.

Getting ready

For this recipe, we need something that we can monitor for events. We already had a look at policies with the *Working with SNMP* and *Working with AMQP* recipes in *Chapter 4, Working with Plugins*.

In this example, we will monitor vCenter Server.

How to do it...

We will create a simple policy that will monitor a VM by performing the following steps:

1. In Orchestrator client, switch to the **Run** mode and click on **Policies**.
2. Click on **Create a new Policy** (scroll down; you will see an icon with a plus sign).
3. After you give the policy a name, you will find a new policy in the policy list. Right-click on **New policy** and select **Edit** (the pencil icon).

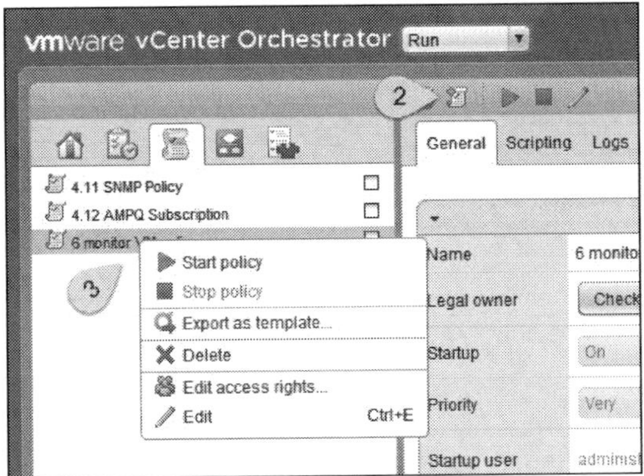

4. In the **General** tab under **Startup**, choose whether the policy should be started with the Orchestrator service or not. This is used when Orchestrator is powered down.
5. **Priority** regulates how multiple policies determine priorities about each other.
6. The **Startup user** credential is used to run the policy.

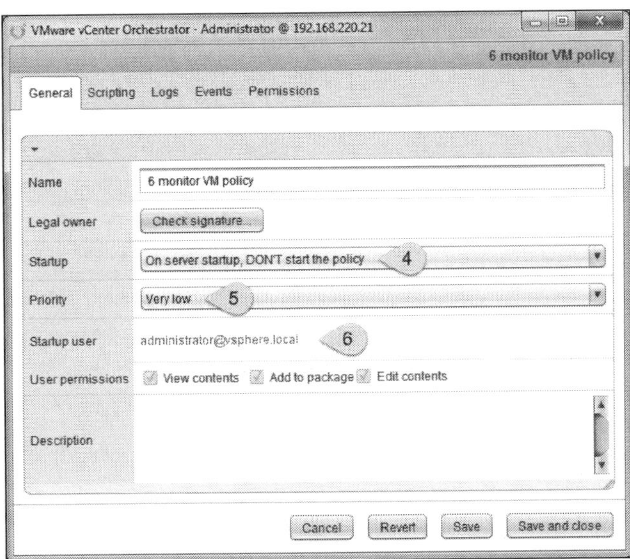

7. Switch to the **Scripting** tab.
8. Click on the top element (scroll icon) and then select **Add policy element** (scroll down; you will see an icon with a plus sign).
9. Select a policy element (choose **VC:VirtualMachine**) and click on **OK**. Then, select a VM that you would like to monitor (I selected a VM called **OrchestratorVM** which is just a plain VM, not the Orchestrator itself).
10. Right-click on the new policy (called tag-0) and then **Add trigger event**. From the pop-up, select **OnStateChanged**. This trigger will monitor the VM for changes in its power state.

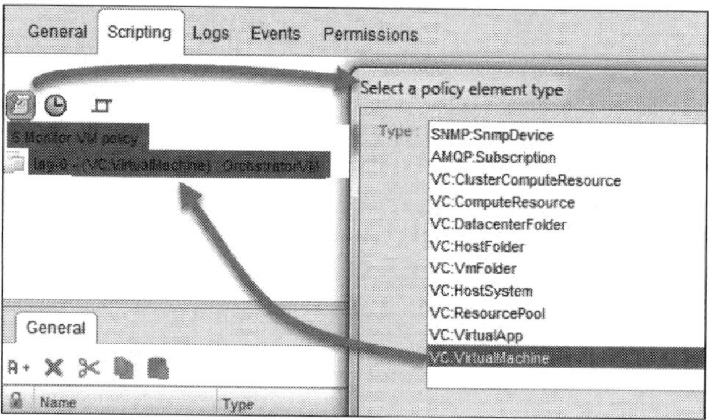

11. Click on the **OnStateChanged** trigger and then select a workflow or write a script that is executed. I wrote the following script:

```
System.log("VM changed state");
```

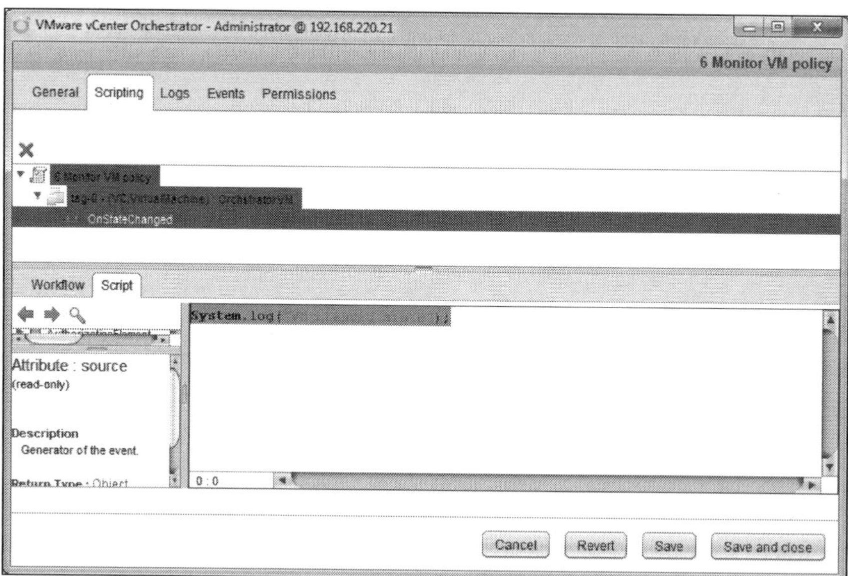

12. Click on **Save** and then **Close**.
13. Now start the policy by clicking on the play button. Go to vCenter Server and start or stop the VM you are monitoring. If you have used the same script as mine, you should see a message.

How it works...

Policies are constant monitoring programs that check whether a monitored event has been triggered. The VMware documentation about policies is really nonexistent. You will find some more information regarding policies in the upcoming sections.

As a supplement to this recipe, have a look at the *Working with SNMP* and *Working with AMQP* recipes in *Chapter 4, Working with Plugins*. In these recipes, we use policies.

Policy Templates

Let's start by defining the difference between **Polices** and **Policy Templates**. If you repeat the same recipe as described earlier, under the **Policy Templates** tab you will find that you wouldn't be able to define which VM you would like to monitor. This is what templates are about; you define the raw layout, triggers, and script, and so on. If you then want to apply the template, you can choose **Apply Policy** (scroll down, you will see a green right arrow icon) from either the template in the **Template** tab or the **Policy** tab.

Triggers

Triggers are implemented by plugins and can be used to build policies. There are three basic elements that can be added to policies:

Icon	Name	Function
	Policy Element	This monitors an element such as a VM or SNMP device
	Periodic Task	This is a workflow or script that will be executed on a given timescale
	Trigger	This is a trigger that starts a script or workflow

Each element can have special triggers. A trigger can either start a workflow or run a script, but not both. In the following tables, you will find detailed information on which trigger is available with what element. The `OnInit` and `OnExit` triggers can be added to any element. The `OnInit` and `OnExit` triggers are actually quite important—for example, when you need to write a script that checks whether all conditions that the policy requires (such as whether an `AMQP` queue exists or a VM exists) are met.

Element	Trigger element	Threshold
`Periodic task`	`OnExecute`	NA
`SNMP:SnmpDevice`	`OnTrap`	NA
`AMQP:Subscription`	`OnMessage`	NA
`VC:ClusterComputerResource`	`OnOverallStatusChanged`	NA
`VC:ComputerResource`	`OnOverallStatusChanged`	NA
`VC:DatacenterFolder`	`OnOverallStatusChanged`	NA
`VC:HostFolder`	`OnOverallStatusChanged`	NA
`VC:VmFolder`	`OnOverallStatusChanged`	NA

`VC:HostSystem`	`OnOverallStatusChanged`
	`OnConnectionStateChanged`
	`OnInMaintenanceModeChange`
		`NumMksConnections`
		`RealtimeCpuUsage`
		`RealtimeMemoryUsage`
		`RealtimeDiskUsage`
		`RealtimeNetworkUsage`

`VC:ResourcePool`	`OnOverallStatusChanged`	NA
`VC:VirtualApp`	`OnOverallStatusChanged`	NA

`VC:VirtualMachine`	`OnOverallStatusChanged`
	`OnStateChanged`
	`OnConnectionStateChanged`
		`NumMksConnections`
		`RealtimeCpuUsage`
		`RealtimeMemoryUsage`
		`RealtimeDiskUsage`
		`RealtimeNetworkUsage`

Here is an explanation of all triggers:

Trigger	Meaning
`OnInit`	This is triggered when the policy is started
`OnExit`	This is triggered when a policy is stopped
`OnExecute`	This is triggered when a periodic task is triggered
`OnTrap`	This is triggered when a new SNMP message was trapped
`OnMessage`	This is triggered when a new AMQP message is in the queue
`OnOverallStatusChanged`	This is triggered when the health of the object changes
`OnConnectionStateChanged`	This is triggered when a VM/host is not available for management; for example, VM is disconnected due to ESXi failure or a host is switched off
`OnInMaintenanceModeChange`	This is triggered when a host is entering/exiting the maintenance mode

Trigger	Meaning
`OnStateChanged`	This is triggered when the power state of a VM changes
`NumMksConnections`	This is triggered when the amount of console session towards a VM/host is below or above a set value
`RealtimeXXXUsage`	This is triggered when a CPU, memory, disk, or network is below or above a set value; all values are in percentage

The event variable

The event variable is almost not documented and any information is hard to find. The following are the known event properties and methods:

Variable	Function
`event.when`	Gets the date as a number
`event.source`	An object that contains the source of the event
`event.getValue("agent")`	Receives the SNMP source
`event.getValue("key")`	Retrieves the SNMP message
`self.retrieveMessage(event)`	Retrieves an AMQP message

See also

- See the *Working with SNMP* and *Working with AMQP* recipes in Chapter 4, Working with Plugins

Managing remote Orchestrator

This recipe centres on using the multinode plugin. As this plugin is mostly used for operations and than for programming, it finds its place in this chapter. We will learn how to manage other Orchestrator installations.

Getting ready

We need at least two Orchestrator installations. You need to make sure that the SSL certificate of the server matches the hostname. If you have used the Orchestrator appliance and changed its IP or hostname, you will need to generate a new SSL certificate (see the *Configuring the Orchestrator Service SSL certificate* recipe in *Chapter 2, Optimizing Orchestrator Configuration*).

It is also quite important that both Orchestrator instances are compatible with each other. You will not be able to link a vCO 5.1 to a vRO (5.5.2.1 and higher), as the interface that is used is the REST interface. The REST interface was introduced in vCO 5.5.

The plugin that is required is the multinode plugin that is installed automatically with the 5.5 version.

Please note that a SSO-based connection isn't fully working, see `kb.vmware.com/kb/2095701` for solutions.

How to do it...

We will call the first Orchestrator installation (the main or original one) local Orchestrator, and the one we add will be called remote Orchestrator.

Adding an Orchestrator server

First, we need to add remote Orchestrator to local Orchestrator by performing the following steps:

1. Log in to local Orchestrator using the Orchestrator client, then start the workflow by navigating to **Library** | **Orchestrator** | **Server Configuration** | **Add a vCO Server**.
2. The workflow will ask you for URL or just host:port for non-HTTPS SSL services. What it really asks for is the URL to the SSL certificate of the remote Orchestrator's API. Enter the URL `https://[IP or FQDN of remote Orchestrator]:8281`.
3. The **Yes/No** question next asks you whether you would like to accept certificates even if they are not signed without further asking (choose **Yes**).
4. Now, enter the FQDN or IP for remote Orchestrator. The default settings are OK, and don't choose to create proxy workflows yet; we will do it in the next section.

5. As the remote Orchestrator is not SSO enabled, we will choose **SSO enabled:No** and **Shared:Yes** and enter `vcoadmin` with the password `vcoadmin`.

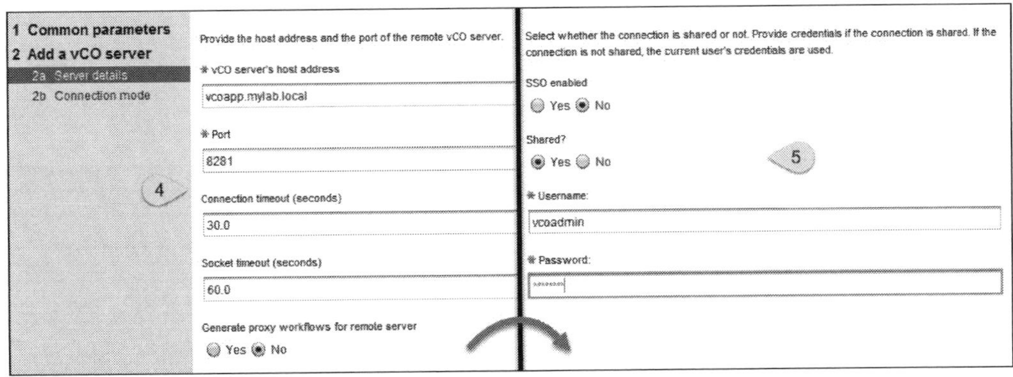

6. Submit the workflow.

Navigate to **Resources** | **Library** | **VCO** | **Configuration** and **Inventory** | **vCO Multi-node**; you should now see the new entries there.

Creating proxy workflows

We declined in the section before to create proxy workflows, because we will now do it here:

1. Using the local Orchestrator client, start the workflow by navigating to **Library** | **Orchestrator** | **Remote Executions** | **Server Proxies** | **Create proxy workflows for a vCO server**.
2. Choose the remote Orchestrator and click on **Next**.
3. Choose to create proxy workflows that are executed synchronous (**Yes**) or asynchronous (**No**). Synchronous means that Orchestrator will wait until the workflow is executed completely (use the default, which is **Yes**).

4. Wait until the workflow has finished. Then, check whether the new folder has been created in the workflow tree called **VCO@[IP or FQDN Orchestrator]:8281** as well as the workflows under it. See the following collage:

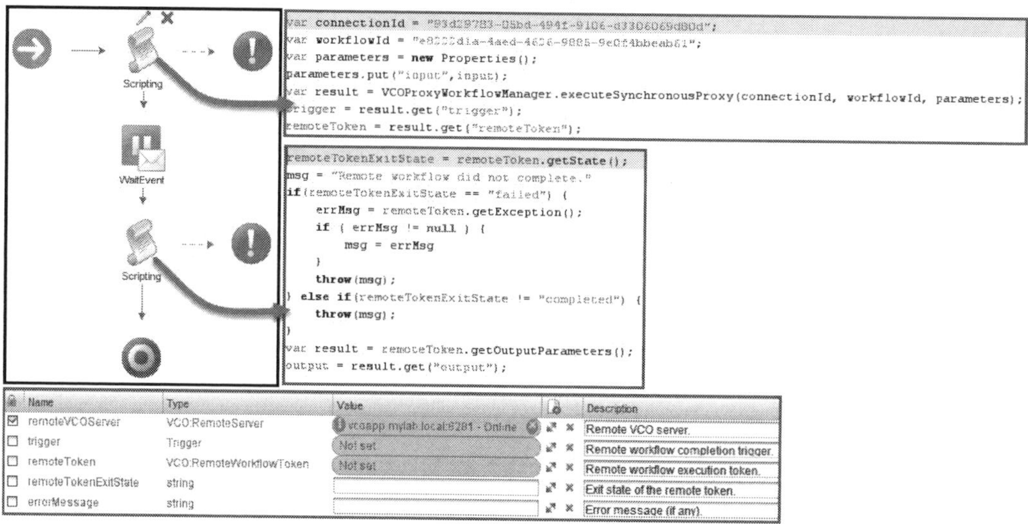

5. Now, execute one of the proxy workflows. When finished, check on both Orchestrators; you will find that the proxy workflow will have executed on both sides. However, log messages and variable tracking will only be in place on the remote server.

Instead of just creating proxies for all workflows of remote Orchestrator, you can also choose a single workflow by navigating to **Library** | **Orchestrator** | **Remote Executions** | **Create a proxy workflow** or a workflow folder **Library** | **Orchestrator** | **Remote Executions** | **Create proxy workflows from a folder**.

Also, note that you can refresh the proxy workflows. This will make sure that changes in the input or output variable are synced to the proxy workflows.

Deploying packages to remote Orchestrator

Another useful function is the ability to deploy packages to remote servers. Perform the following steps:

1. Using the local Orchestrator client, start the workflow by navigating to **Library** | **Orchestrator** | **Remote Management** | **Deploy a package from a local server**.
2. Select the package you would like to deploy from local Orchestrator to remote Orchestrator.
3. When selecting the remote server, you are actually able to choose multiple remote Orchestrators. An array window will open; select **Insert Value**. An additional pop-up will show up here; select remote Orchestrator and click on **Add**.

4. The chosen package is now installed on remote Orchestrator.

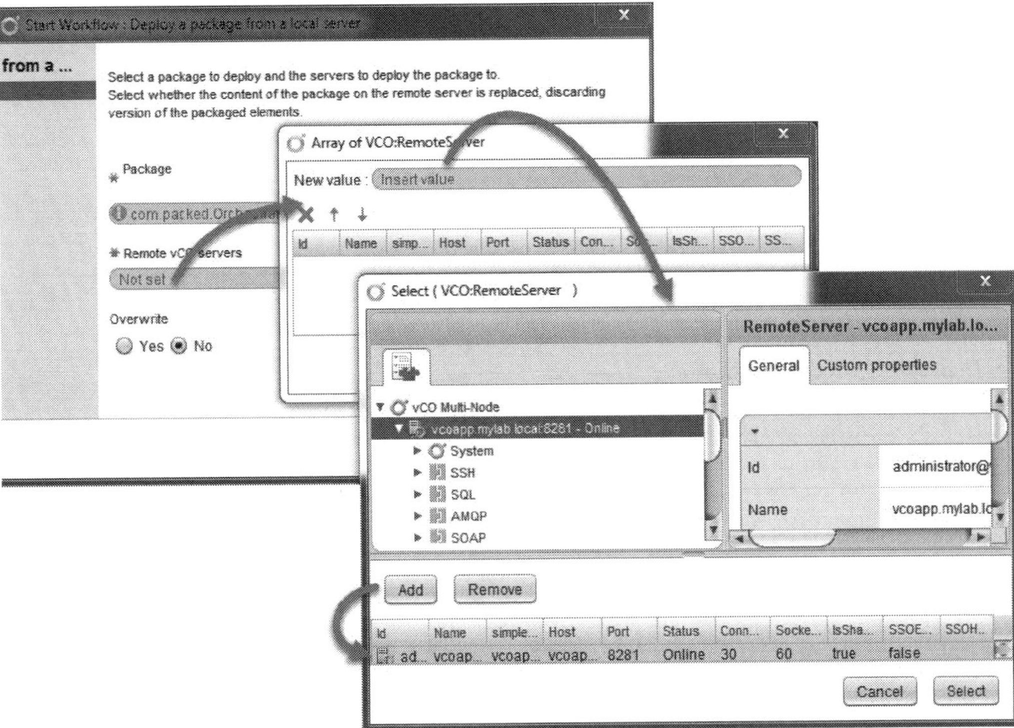

How it works...

The multinode plugin can be used in quite a lot of situations. The first and foremost is to manage remote servers that are in a cluster. In the *Creating an Orchestrator cluster* recipe in *Chapter 2, Optimizing Orchestrator Configuration*, we already discussed how to create a cluster. Using the multinode plugin, we can now feed an Orchestrator cluster with workflows.

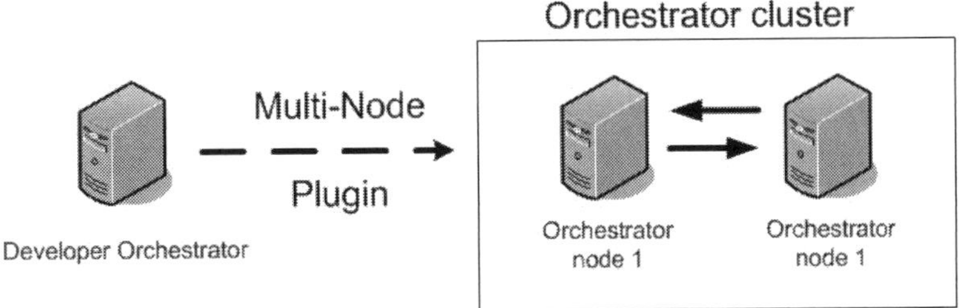

The use of geographically dispersed Orchestrators is common in large companies. Here, a central Orchestrator instance executes workflows on remote environments. The amount of bandwidth used to execute a workflow remotely (using the multinode plugin) is much less than the amount that would be needed to run the workflows directly. This is especially true when a lot of input variables have to be collected to run the workflow.

Another good idea is to make sure that workflows, or basically any other Orchestrator element (by building a specific workflow), are replicated between Orchestrator installations. For example, for load balancing or audit reasons, you have multiple Orchestrator servers and you need to make sure that elements are the same on all of them.

A very common usage of the multinode plugin is for maintenance work, such as cleaning out all finished workflows from remote Orchestrators.

Last but not least, you can execute workflows from a different Orchestrator. For example, you can write a workflow that automatically configures a new Orchestrator installation.

Please note that you can create a task from a workflow (see the *Scheduling workflows* recipe in *Chapter 5, Basic Orchestrator Operations*) and thus create an automated push or pull update from a cluster.

Explore the workflows that come with the multinode plugin, as there is quite a lot you can do. The following are examples:

Proxy workflows	Create, delete, update, create one workflow, create from folder
Packages	Delete, delete by name, deploy from local, deploy from remote, deploy multiple from local
Workflows	Delete all finished, delete remote, deploy from local, deploy from remote Start in series, start in parallel
Server	Add, update, delete
Tasks	Create, create recurring

As a last note, when you delete an Orchestrator server using the workflow by navigating to **Library** | **Orchestrator** | **Server Configuration** | **Delete a vCO Server**, all proxy workflows of remote Orchestrator will also be deleted from local Orchestrator.

See also

- See the *Creating an Orchestrator cluster* recipe in *Chapter 2, Optimizing Orchestrator Configuration*

7

Working with VMware Infrastructure

In this chapter, we will take a closer look at how Orchestrator interacts with vCenter Server and vRealize Automation (vRA—formerly known as vCloud Automation Center, vCAC). vRA uses Orchestrator to access and automate infrastructure using Orchestrator plugins. We will take a look at how to make Orchestrator workflows available to vRA.

We will investigate the following recipes:

- Unmounting all the CD-ROMs of all VMs in a cluster
- Provisioning a VM from a template
- An approval process for VM provisioning
- Working with the vCenter API (to change VM's HA settings)
- Standard vSwitch and Distributed Switch ports
- Executing a program inside a VM
- Configuring a vRA instance in Orchestrator
- Configuring an external Orchestrator in vRA
- Adding an Orchestrator endpoint
- Integrating Orchestrator workflows in vRA
- Managing AD users with vRA

Introduction

There are quite a lot of plugins for Orchestrator to interact with VMware infrastructure and programs:

- vCenter Server
- vCloud Director (vCD)
- vRealize Automation (vRA—formally known as vCloud Automation Center, vCAC)
- Site Recovery Manager (SRM)
- VMware Auto Deploy
- Horizon (View and Virtual Desktops)
- vRealize Configuration Manager (earlier known as vCenter Configuration Manager)
- vCenter Update Manager
- vCenter Operation Manager, vCOPS (only example packages)

VMware, as of writing of this book, is still renaming its products. An overview of all plugins and their names and download links can be found at `http://www.vcoteam.info/links/plug-ins.html`.

There are quite a lot of plugins, and we will not be able to cover all of them, so we will focus on the one that is most used, vCenter. Sadly, vCloud Director is earmarked by VMware to disappear for everyone but service providers, so there is no real need to show any workflow for it.

We will also work with vRA and see how it interacts with Orchestrator.

vSphere automation

The interaction between Orchestrator and vCenter is done using the vCenter API. Here is the explanation of the interaction, which you can refer to in the following figure.

A user starts an Orchestrator workflow (**1**) either in an interactive way via the vSphere Web Client, the Orchestrator Web Operator, the Orchestrator Client, or via the API. The workflow in Orchestrator will then send a job (**2**) to vCenter and receive a task ID back (type VC:Task). vCenter will then start enacting the job (**3**). Using the `vim3WaitTaskEnd` action (4), Orchestrator pauses until the task has been completed. If we do not use the wait task, we can't be certain whether the task has ended or failed. It is extremely important to use the `vim3WaitTaskEnd` action whenever we send a job to vCenter. When the wait task reports that the job has finished, the workflow will be marked as finished.

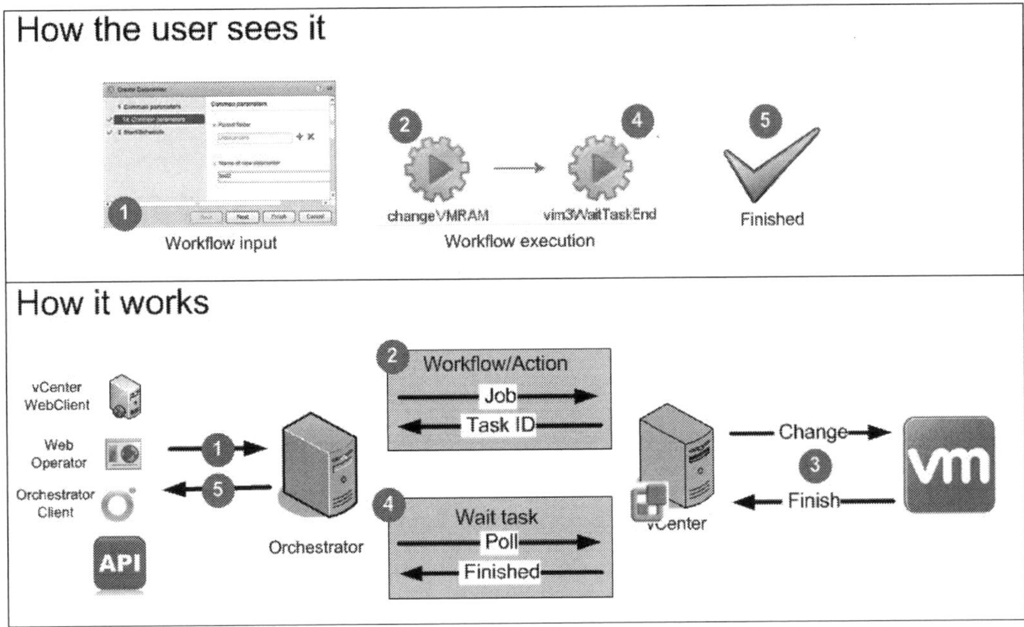

The vCenter MoRef

The **MoRef** (Managed Object Reference) is a unique ID for every object inside vCenter. MoRefs are basically strings; some examples are shown here:

VM	Network	Datastore	ESXi host	Data center	Cluster
vm-301	network-312 dvportgroup-242	datastore-101	host-44	data center-21	domain-c41

The MoRefs are typically stored in the attribute `.id` or `.key` of the Orchestrator API object. For example, the MoRef of a vSwitch Network is `VC:Network.id`. We will make use of them in the recipe *Standard vSwitch and Distributed Switch ports* in this chapter.

To browse for MoRefs, you can use the Managed Object Browser (MOB), documented at `https://pubs.vmware.com/vsphere-55/index.jsp#com.vmware.wssdk.pg.doc/PG_Appx_Using_MOB.20.1.html`.

The vim3WaitTaskEnd action

As already said, `vim3WaitTaskEnd` is one of the most central actions while interacting with vCenter. The action has the following variables:

Category	Name	Type	Usage
IN	vcTask	VC:Task	Carries the reconfiguration task from the script to the wait task
IN	progress	Boolean	Write to the logs the progress of a task in percentage
IN	pollRate	Number	How often the action should be checked for task completion in vCenter
OUT	ActionResult	Any	Returns the task's result

The wait task will check in regular intervals (`pollRate`) the status of a task that has been submitted to vCenter. The task can have the following states:

State	Meaning
Queued	The task is queued and will be executed as soon as possible.
Running	The task is currently running. If the progress is set to `true`, the progress in percentage will be displayed in the logs.
Success	The task is finished successfully.
Error	The task has failed and an error will be thrown.

Other vCenter wait actions

There are actually five waiting tasks that come with the vCenter Server plugin. Here's an overview of the other four:

Task	Description
`vim3WaitToolsStarted`	This task waits until the VMware tools are started on a VM or until a timeout is reached.
`Vim3WaitForPrincipalIP`	This task waits until the VMware tools report the primary IP of a VM or until a timeout is reached. This typically indicates that the operating system is ready to receive network traffic. The action will return the primary IP.
`Vim3WaitDnsNameInTools`	This task waits until the VMware tools report a given DNS name of a VM or until a timeout is reached. The in-parameter `addNumberToName` is not used and can be set to `Null`.
`WaitTaskEndOrVMQuestion`	This task waits until a task is finished or if a VM develops a question. A vCenter question is related to user interaction.

vRealize Automation (vRA)

Automation has changed since the beginning of Orchestrator. Before, tools such as vCloud Director or vCloud Automation Center (vCAC)/vRealize Automation (vRA), Orchestrator was the main tool for automating vCenter resources.

With version 6.2 of vCloud Automation Center (vCAC), the product has been renamed vRealize Automation.

Now vRA is deemed to become the central cornerstone in the VMware automation effort. vRealize Orchestrator (vRO), is used by vRA to interact with and automate VMware and non-VMware products and infrastructure elements.

Throughout the various vCAC/vRA interactions, the role of Orchestrator has changed substantially. Orchestrator started off as an extension to vCAC and became a central part of vRA.

- In vCAC 5.x, Orchestrator was only an extension of the IaaS life cycle. Orchestrator was tied in using the stubs
- vCAC 6.0 integrated Orchestrator as an XaaS service (Everything as a Service) using the Advanced Service Designer (ASD)
- In vCAC 6.1, Orchestrator is used to perform all VMware NSX operations (VMware's new network virtualization and automation), meaning that it became even more of a central part of the IaaS services.
- With vCAC 6.2, the Advance Service Designer (ASD) was enhanced to allow more complex form of designs, allowing better leverage of Orchestrator workflows.

As you can see in the following figure, vRA connects to the vCenter Server using an infrastructure endpoint that allows vRA to conduct basic infrastructure actions, such as power operations, cloning, and so on. It doesn't allow any complex interactions with the vSphere infrastructure, such as HA configurations.

Using the Advanced Service Endpoints, vRA integrates the Orchestrator (vRO) plugins as additional services. This allows vRA to offer the entire plugin infrastructure as services to vRA. The vCenter Server, AD, and PowerShell plugins are typical integrations that are used with vRA.

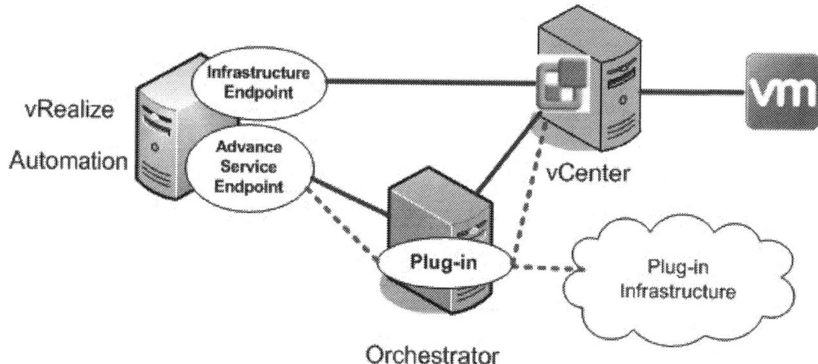

Using Advance Service Designer (ASD), you can create integrations that use Orchestrator workflows. ASD allows you to offer Orchestrator workflows as vRA catalog items, making it possible for tenants to access any IT service that can be configured with Orchestrator via its plugins. The following diagram shows an example using the Active Directory plugin. The Orchestrator Plugin provides access to the AD services. By creating a custom resource using the exposed AD infrastructure, we can create a service blueprint and resource actions, both of which are based on Orchestrator workflows that use the AD plugin. In the *Managing AD Users with vRA* recipe, we will showcase all of these features.

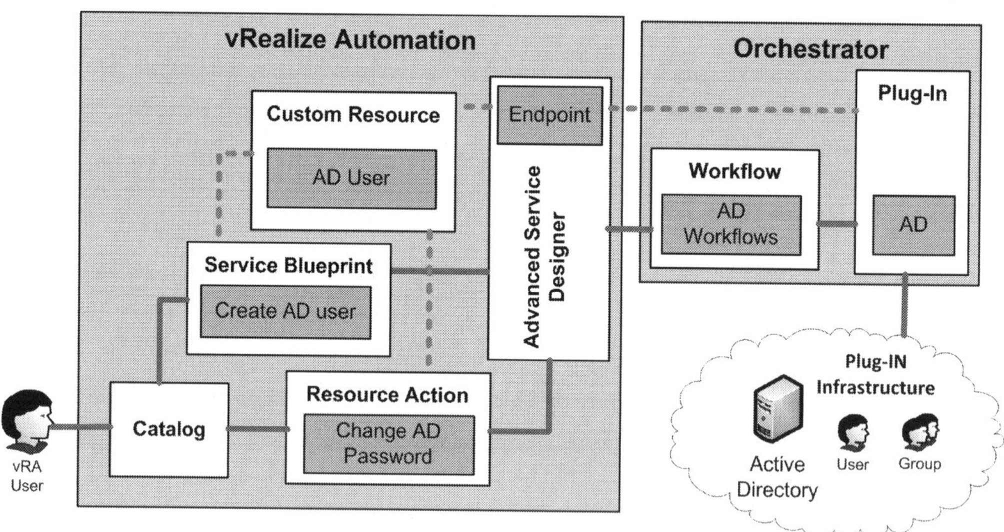

The other method of integrating Orchestrator into the IaaS life cycle, which was predominately used in vCAC 5.x was to use the stubs. The build process of a VM has several steps; each step can be assigned a customizable workflow (called a **stub**). You can configure vRA to run an Orchestrator workflow at these stubs in order to facilitate a few customized actions. Such actions could be taken to change the VMs HA or DRS configuration, or to use the guest integration to install or configure a program on a VM.

Installation

How to install and configure vRA is out of the scope of this book, but take a look at `http://www.kendrickcoleman.com/index.php/Tech-Blog/how-to-install-vcloud-automation-center-vcac-60-part-1-identity-appliance.html` for more information.

If you don't have the hardware or the time to install vRA yourself, you can use the VMware Hands-on Labs, which can be accessed after clicking on **Try for Free** at `http://hol.vmware.com`.

The vRA Orchestrator plugin

Due to the renaming, the vRA plugin is called `vRealize Orchestrator vRA Plug-in 6.2.0`, however the file you download and use is named `o11nplugin-vcac-6.2.0-2287231.vmoapp`. The plugin currently creates a workflow folder called **vCloud Automation Center**.

vRA-integrated Orchestrator

The vRA appliance comes with an installed and configured vRO instance; however, the best practice for a production environment is to use a dedicated Orchestrator installation, even better would be an Orchestrator cluster. We will configure an external Orchestrator for vRA in the *Configuring an external Orchestrator in vRA* recipe.

Dynamic Types or XaaS

XaaS means Everything (X) as a Service. The introduction of Dynamic Types in Orchestrator Version 5.5.1 does exactly that; it allows you to build your own plugins and interact with infrastructure that has not yet received its own plugin.

Take a look at this article by Christophe Decanini; it integrates Twitter with Orchestrator using Dynamic Types at `http://www.vcoteam.info/articles/learn-vco/282-dynamic-types-tutorial-implement-your-own-twitter-plug-in-without-any-scripting.html`.

Read more...

To read more about Orchestrator integration with vRA, please take a look at the official VMware documentation.

Please note that the official documentation you need to look at is about vRealize Automation, and not about vCloud Automation Center, but, as of writing this book, the documentation can be found at `www.vmware.com/support/pubs/vcac-pubs.html`.

- The document called **Advanced Service Design** deals with vRO and Advanced Service Designer
- The document called **Machine Extensibility** discusses customization using subs

Unmounting all the CD-ROMs of all VMs in a cluster

This is an easy recipe to start with, but one you can really make it work for your existing infrastructure. The workflow will unmount all CD-ROMs from a running VM. A mounted CD-ROM may block a VM from being vMotioned.

Getting ready

We need a VM that can mount a CD-ROM either as an ISO from a host or from the client.

Before you start the workflow, make sure that the VM is powered on and has an ISO connected to it.

How to do it...

1. Create a new workflow with the following variables:

Name	**Type**	**Section**	**Use**
`cluster`	VC:ClusterComputerResource	IN	Used to input the cluster
`clusterVMs`	Array of VC:VirtualMachine	Attribute	Use to capture all VMs in a cluster

2. Add the `getAllVMsOfCluster` action to the schema and assign the `cluster` in-parameter and the `clusterVMs` attribute to it as **actionResult**.
3. Now, add a `Foreach` element to the schema and assign the workflow **Disconnect all detachable devices from a running virtual machine**.

4. Assign the `Foreach` element `clusterVMs` as a parameter (refer to the *Working with loops* recipe in *Chapter 3, Visual Programming*).

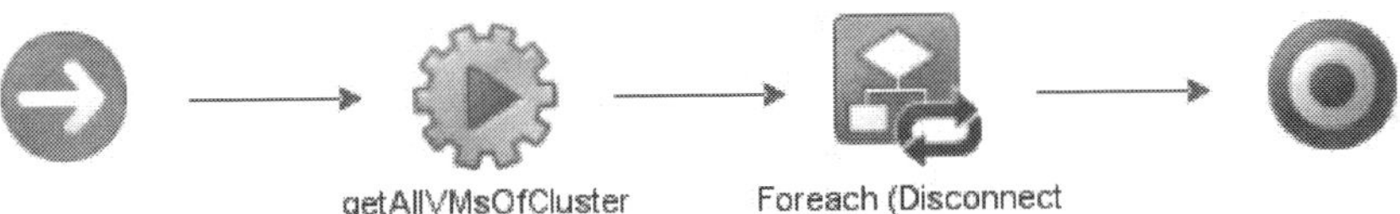

5. Save and run the workflow.

For real-life usage, you can schedule this workflow as shown in the *Scheduling workflows* recipe in *Chapter 5, Basic Orchestrator Operations*.

How it works...

This recipe shows how fast and easily you can design solutions that help you with everyday vCenter problems. The problem is that VMs that have CD-ROMs or floppies mounted may experience problems using vMotion, making it impossible for them to be used with DRS. The reality is that a lot of admins mount CD-ROMs and then forget to disconnect them.

Scheduling this script every evening just before the nighttime backups will make sure that a production cluster is able to make full use of DRS and is therefore better load-balanced.

You can improve this workflow by integrating an exclusion list.

See also

Refer to the example workflow, 7.01 UnMount CD-ROM from Cluster.

Provisioning a VM from a template

In this recipe, we will build a deployment workflow for Windows and Linux VMs. We will learn how to create workflows and reduce the amount of input variables.

Getting ready

We need a Linux or Windows template that we can clone and provision.

How to do it...

We have split this recipe in two sections. In the first section, we will create a configuration element, and in the second, we will create the workflow.

Creating a configuration

We will use a configuration for all reusable variables. If you need help to create a configuration element, take a look at the *Working with configurations* recipe in *Chapter 3, Visual Programming*.

Build a configuration element that contains the following items:

Name	Type	Use
`productId`	String	This is the Windows product ID—the licensing code
`joinDomain`	String	This is the Windows domain FQDN to join
`domainAdmin`	Credential	These are the credentials to join the domain
`licenseMode`	VC:CustomizationLicenseDataMode	Example, perServer
`licenseUsers`	Number	This denotes the number of licensed concurrent users
`inTimezone`	Enums:MSTimeZone	Time zone
`fullName`	String	Full name of the user
`orgName`	String	Organization name
`newAdminPassword`	String	New admin password
`dnsServerList`	Array of String	List of DNS servers
`dnsDomain`	String	DNS domain
`gateway`	Array of String	List of gateways

Creating the base workflow

Now we will create the base workflow:

1. Create the workflow as shown in the following figure by adding the given elements:
    - **Clone, Windows with single NIC and credential**
    - **Clone, Linux with single NIC**
    - **Custom decision**

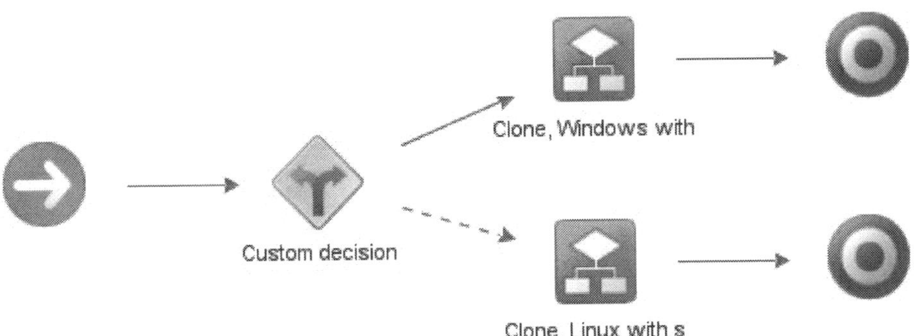

2. Use the **Clone, Windows...** workflow to create all variables. Link up the ones that you have defined in the configuration as attributes, as shown in the *Working with configurations* recipe in *Chapter 3, Visual Programming*. The rest are defined as follows:

Name	Type	Section	Use
`vmName`	String	IN	This is the new virtual machine's name
`vm`	VC:VirtualMachine	IN	Virtual machine to clone
`folder`	VC:VmFolder	IN	This is the virtual machine folder
`datastore`	VC:Datastore	IN	This is the datastore in which you store the virtual machine
`pool`	VC:ResourcePool	IN	This is the resource pool in which you create the virtual machine
`network`	VC:Network	IN	This is the network to which you attach the virtual network interface
`ipAddress`	String	IN	This is the fixed valid IP address
`subnetMask`	String	IN	This is the subnet mask
`template`	Boolean	Attribute	For value No, mark new VM as template
`powerOn`	Boolean	Attribute	For value Yes, power on the VM after creation
`doSysprep`	Boolean	Attribute	For value Yes, run Windows Sysprep
`dhcp`	Boolean	Attribute	For value No, use DHCP
`newVM`	VC:VirtualMachine	OUT	This is the newly-created VM

3. The following sub-workflow in-parameters will be set to special values:

Workflow	**In-parameter**	**value**
Clone, Windows with single NIC and credential	`host`	Null
	`joinWorkgroup`	Null
	`macAddress`	Null
	`netBIOS`	Null
	`primaryWINS`	Null
	`secondaryWINS`	Null
	`name`	`vmName`
	`clientName`	`vmName`
Clone, Linux with single NIC	`host`	Null
	`macAddress`	Null
	`name`	`vmName`
	`clientName`	`vmName`

4. Define the in-parameter `VM` as input for the **Custom decision** and add the following script. The script will check whether the name of the OS contains the word `Microsoft`:

```
guestOS=vm.config.guestFullName;
System.log(guestOS);
if (guestOS.indexOf("Microsoft") >=0){
  return true;
} else {
  return false
}
```

5. Save and run the workflow.

This workflow will now create a new VM from an existing VM and customize it with a fixed IP.

How it works...

As you can see, creating workflows to automate vCenter deployments is pretty straightforward. Dealing with the various in-parameters of workflows can be quite overwhelming. The best way to deal with this problem is to hide away variables by defining them centrally using a configuration, or define them locally as attributes.

Using configurations has the advantage that you can create them once and reuse them as needed. You can even push the concept a bit further by defining multiple configurations for multiple purposes, such as different environments.

While creating a new workflow for automation, a typical approach is as follows:

1. Look for a workflow that you need.
2. Run the workflow normally to check out what it actually does.
3. Either create a new workflow that uses the original or duplicate and edit the one you tried, modifying it until it does what you want.

A fast way to deal with a lot of variables is to drag every element you need into the schema and then use the binding to create the variables as needed. This is shown in the introduction to *Chapter 3, Visual Programming*.

You may have noticed that this workflow only lets you select vSwitch networks, not distributed vSwitch networks; this can be easily remedied by following the *Standard vSwitch and Distributed Switch ports* recipe in this chapter.

You can improve this workflow with the following features:

- Read the existing Sysprep information stored in your vCenter Server
- Generate different predefined configurations (for example DEV or Prod)

There's more...

We can improve the workflow by implementing the ability to change the vCPU and the memory of the VM. Follow these steps to implement it:

1. Move the out-parameter `newVM` to be an attribute.
2. Add the following variables:

Name	Type	Section	Use
`vCPU`	Number	IN	This variable denotes the amount of vCPUs
`Memory`	Number	IN	This variable denotes the amount of VM memory
`vcTask`	VC:Task	Attribute	This variable will carry the reconfiguration task from the script to the wait task
`progress`	Boolean	Attribute	Value NO, `vim3WaitTaskEnd`
`pollRate`	Number	Attribute	Value 5, `vim3WaitTaskEnd`
`ActionResult`	Any	Attribute	`vim3WaitTaskEnd`

3. Add the following actions and workflows according to the next figure:
    - **shutdownVMAndForce**
    - **changeVMvCPU**
    - **vim3WaitTaskEnd**
    - **changeVMRAM**
    - **Start virtual machine**

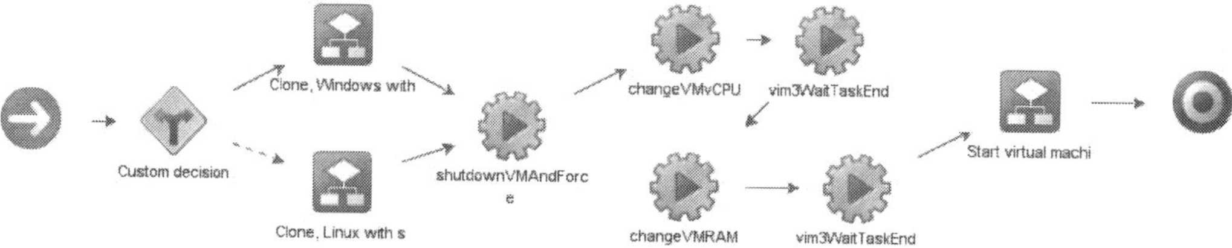

4. Bind `newVM` to all the appropriate input parameters of the added actions and workflows.
5. Bind `actionResults` (VC:tasks) of the change actions to `vim3WaitTasks`.

See also

Refer to the example workflows, 7.02.1 Provision VM (Base), 7.02.2 Provision VM (HW custom), as well as the configuration element, 7 VM provisioning.

An approval process for VM provisioning

In this recipe, we will see how to create a workflow that waits for an approver to approve the VM creation before provisioning it. We will learn how to combine mail and external events in a workflow to make it interact with different users.

Getting ready

For this recipe, we first need the provisioning workflow that we have created in the *Provisioning a VM from a template* recipe. You can use the example workflow, 7.02.1 Provision VM (Base).

Additionally, we need a functional e-mail system as well as a workflow to send e-mails. Refer to the *Working with mails* recipe in *Chapter 4, Working with Plugins*. You can use the example workflow, 4.02.1 SendMail as well as its configuration item, 4.2.1 Working with e-mail.

We will also work with events as discussed in the *Sending and waiting for custom events* recipe in *Chapter 3, Visual Programming*.

How to do it...

We will split this recipe in three parts. First, we will create a configuration element then, we will create the workflow, and lastly, we will use a presentation to make the workflow usable.

Creating a configuration element

We will use a configuration for all reusable variables. If you need help to create a configuration element, take a look at the *Working with configurations* recipe in *Chapter 3, Visual Programming*.

Build a configuration element that contains the following items:

Name	Type	Use
templates	Array/VC:VirtualMachine	This contains all the VMs that serve as templates
folders	Array/VC:VmFolder	This contains all the VM folders that are targets for VM provisioning
networks	Array/VC:Network	This contains all VM networks that are targets for VM provisioning
resourcePools	Array/VC:ResourcePool	This contains all resource pools that are targets for VM provisioning
datastores	Array/VC:Datastore	This contains all datastores that are targets for VM provisioning
daysToApproval	Number	These are the number of days the approval should be available for
approver	String	This is the e-mail of the approver

Please note that you also have to define or use the configuration elements for **SendMail**, as well as the **Provision VM** workflows. You can use the examples contained in the example package.

Creating a workflow

1. Create a new workflow and add the following variables:

Name	Type	Section	Use
`mailRequester`	String	IN	This is the e-mail address of the requester
`vmName`	String	IN	This is the name of the new virtual machine

Name	Type	Section	Use
`vm`	VC:VirtualMachine	IN	This is the virtual machine to be cloned
`folder`	VC:VmFolder	IN	This is the virtual machine folder
`datastore`	VC:Datastore	IN	This is the datastore in which you store the virtual machine
`pool`	VC:ResourcePool	IN	This is the resource pool in which you create the virtual machine
`network`	VC:Network	IN	This is the network to which you attach the virtual network interface
`ipAddress`	String	IN	This is the fixed valid IP address
`subnetMask`	String	IN	This is the subnet mask
`isExternalEvent`	Boolean	Attribute	A value of `true` defines this event as external
`mailApproverSubject`	String	Attribute	This is the subject line of the mail sent to the approver
`mailApproverContent`	String	Attribute	This is the content of the mail that is sent to the approver
`mailRequesterSubject`	String	Attribute	This is the subject line of the mail sent to the requester when the VM is provisioned
`mailRequesterContent`	String	Attribute	This is the content of the mail that is sent to the requester when the VM is provisioned

Name	Type	Section	Use
`mailRequesterDeclinedSubject`	String	Attribute	This is the subject line of the mail sent to the requester when the VM is declined
`mailRequesterDeclinedContent`	String	Attribute	This is the content of the mail that is sent to the requester when the VM is declined
`eventName`	String	Attribute	This is the name of the external event
`endDate`	Date	Attribute	This is the end date for the wait of external event
`approvalSuccess`	Boolean	Attribute	This checks whether the VM has been approved

2. Now add all the attributes we defined in the configuration element and link them to the configuration.
3. Create the workflow as shown in the following figure by adding the given elements:
   - **Scriptable task**
   - **4.02.1 SendMail** (example workflow)
   - **Wait for custom event**
   - **Decision**
   - **Provision VM** (example workflow)

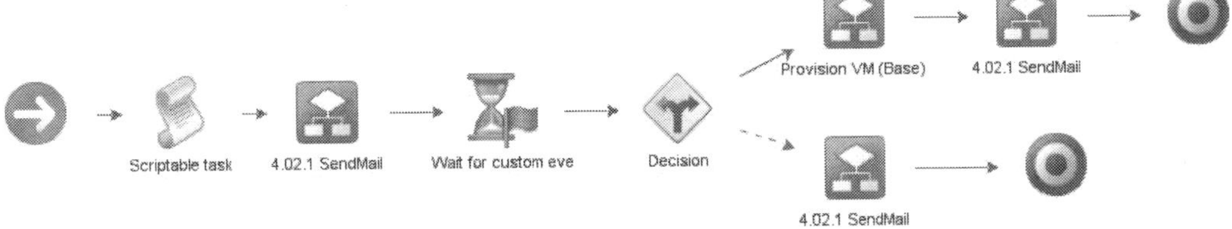

4. Edit the scriptable task and bind the following variables to it:

In	Out
vmName	mailApproverSubject
ipAddress	mailApproverContent
mailRequester	mailRequesterSubject
template	mailRequesterContent
approver	mailRequesterDeclinedSubject
days to approval	mailRequesterDeclinedContent
	eventName
	endDate

5. Add the following script to the scriptable task:

```
//construct event name
eventName="provision-"+vmName;
//add days to today for approval
var today = new Date();
var endDate = new Date(today);
endDate.setDate(today.getDate()+daysToApproval);
//construct external URL for approval
var myURL = new URL() ;
myURL=System.customEventUrl(eventName, false);
externalURL=myURL.url;
//mail to approver
mailApproverSubject="Approval needed: "+vmName;
mailApproverContent="Dear Approver,\n the user "+mailRequester+"
would like to provision a VM from template "+template.name+".\n To
approve please click here: "+externalURL;
//VM provisioned
mailRequesterSubject="VM ready :"+vmName;
mailRequesterContent="Dear Requester,\n the VM "+vmName+" has been
provisioned and is now available under IP :"+ipAddress;
//declined
mailRequesterDeclinedSubject="Declined :"+vmName;
mailRequesterDeclinedContent="Dear Requester,\n the VM "+vmName+"
has been declined by "+approver;
```

6. Bind the out-parameter of **Wait for customer event** to `approvalSuccess`. Configure the **Decision** element with `approvalSuccess` as `true`.
7. Bind all the other variables to the workflow elements.

Improving with the presentation

We will now edit the workflow's presentation in order to make it workable for the requester. To do so, follow the given steps:

1. Click on **Presentation** and follow the steps given in the *Working with presentations* recipe from *Chapter 3, Visual Programming* to alter the presentation, as seen in the following screenshot:

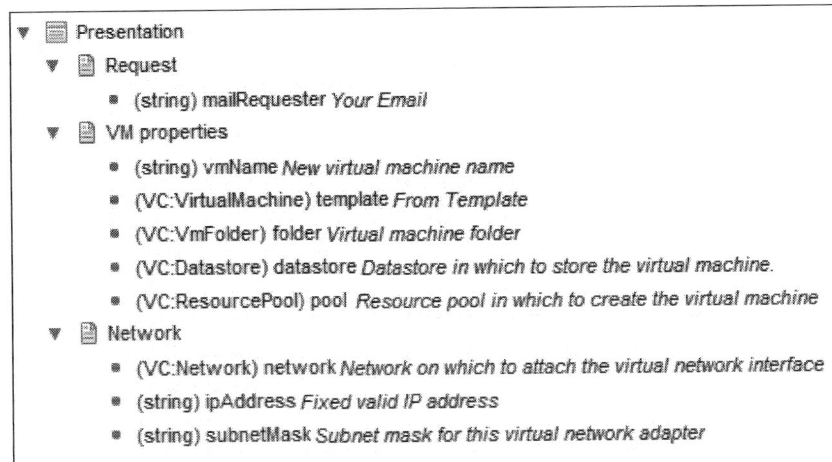

2. Add the following properties to the in-parameters:

In-parameter	Property	Value
`template`	Predefined list of elements	#templates
`folder`	Predefined list of elements	#folders
`datastore`	Predefined list of elements	#datastores
`pool`	Predefined list of elements	#resourcePools
`network`	Predefined list of elements	#networks

3. You can now use the **General** tab of each in-parameter to change the displayed text.
4. Save and close the workflow.

How it works...

This is a very simplified example of an approval workflow to create VMs. The aim of this recipe is to introduce you to the method and ideas of how to build such a workflow.

This workflow will only give a requester the choices that are configured in the configuration element, making the workflow quite safe for users that have only limited knowhow of the IT environment. When the requester submits the workflow, an e-mail is sent to the approver. The e-mail contains a link, which when clicked, triggers the external event and approves the VM. If the VM is approved it will get provisioned, and when the provisioning has finished an e-mail is sent to the requester stating that the VM is now available. If the VM is not approved within a certain timeframe, the requester will receive an e-mail that the VM was not approved.

To make this workflow fully functional, you can add permissions for a requester group to the workflow and Orchestrator so that the user can use the vCenter to request a VM.

Things you can do to improve the workflow are as follows:

- Schedule the provisioning to a future date as discussed in the *Scheduling workflows* recipe in *Chapter 5, Basic Orchestrator Operations*.
- Use the resources for the e-mail and replace the content as discussed in the *Working with resources* recipe in *Chapter 6, Advanced Operations*.
- Add an error workflow in case the provisioning fails as discussed in the *Error handling in workflows* recipe in *Chapter 3, Visual Programming*.
- Use AD to read out the current user's e-mail and full name to improve the workflow. Refer to the *Working with Active Directory* recipe in *Chapter 4, Working with Plugins*.
- Create a workflow that lets an approver configure the configuration elements that a requester can chose from. Refer to the *Working with configurations* recipe in *Chapter 3, Visual Programming*.
- Reduce the selections by creating, for instance, a development and production configuration that contains the correct folders, datastores, networks, and so on.
- Create a decommissioning workflow that is automatically scheduled so that the VM is destroyed automatically after a given period of time.

See also

Refer to the example workflow, 7.03 Approval and the configuration element, 7 approval.

Working with the vCenter API (to change a VM's HA settings)

This recipe will showcase how to derive a function for a more complicated feature. We will be configuring the HA setting for a single VM. In this recipe, we will primarily focus on how to work with the vCenter API.

Getting ready

For this recipe, we will need a vCenter cluster that is configured for HA, as well as a VM which has a HA (VMware High Availability) restart priority that we can change.

For this recipe, you should understand the content of the *Working with the API* recipe in *Chapter 4, Working with Plugins*, as well as the introduction to JavaScript in *Chapter 3, Visual Programming*.

How to do it...

We will use the API and find out how to set VM's HA restart priority. This recipe requires you to take a close look at each of the objects that we will visit and read its properties and its external documentation. It is best to follow this step by step using the API browser.

1. Create a new workflow and create the following variables:

Name	**Type**	**Section**	**Use**
`priority`	String	IN	This variable denotes the HA priority. It can have the values `clusterRestartPriority`, `disabled`, `high`, `medium`, and `low`. It can also use the presentation property `Predefined answers`.
`VM`	VC:VirtualMachine	IN	This is the VM we will be working with.
`cluster`	VC:ClusterComputeResource	IN	This is the cluster the VM is in.
`vcTask`	VC:Task	Attribute	This variable will carry the reconfiguration task from the script to the wait task.
`progress`	Boolean	Attribute	The default value is `false`, It shows the progress of a task.
`pollRate`	Number	Attribute	The default value is 5 (seconds). It shows how often should be checked for task completion.

2. Add a scriptable task to the schema and edit it.
3. Use the API browser to search for the word **restart**.
4. Check the results. You should find `VcClusterDasVmConfigInfo.restartPriority` and `VcClusterDasVmSettings.restartPriority`. Click on the first one and open it in the API browser.
5. Then, click on **External documentation**. Your web browser will open and bring you to the vCenter API documentation. Take a look, the things we need are marked as **Deprecated**, meaning they are of no use to us. They still work, but, it's not a good idea to use functions that are about to be removed.

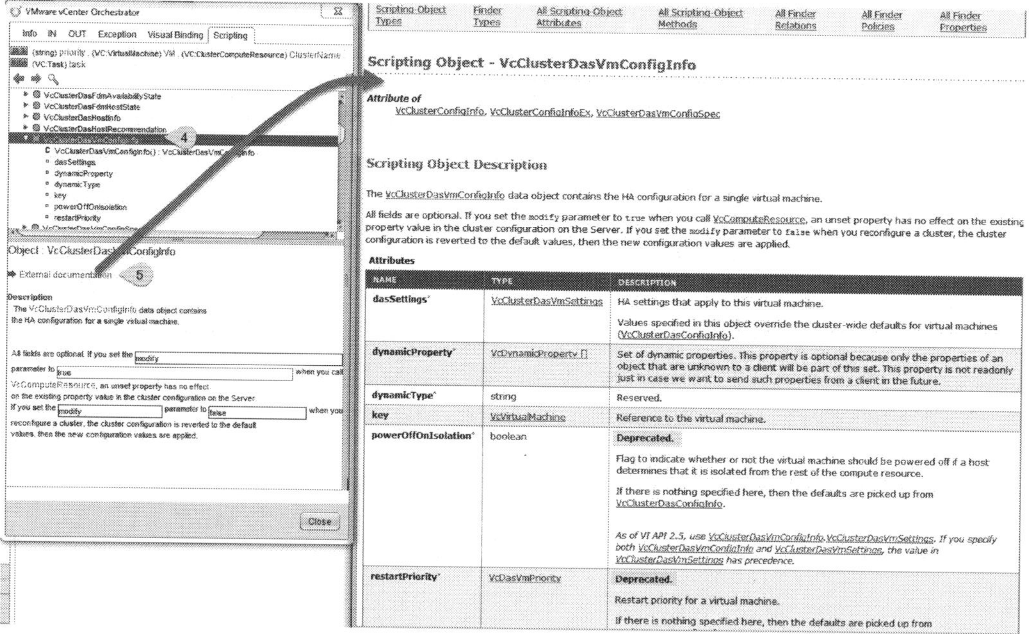

6. Do the same with the second choice. You will find that there are no deprecated functions, meaning we can use them. Let's start adding some lines to our script. First, we need the constructor. We will copy and paste `VcClusterDasVmSettings`, which results in:

```
var myVcClusterDasVmSettings = new VcClusterDasVmSettings();
```

7. Then, we need to add the `restartPriority` attribute to it. Clicking on the `restartPriority` attribute tells us that it is of the type `VcClusterDasVmSettingsRestartPriority`, so take a look at that. We will use the value directly as shown in this line:

```
myVcClusterDasVmSettings.restartPriority=VcClusterDasVmSettingsRes
tartPriority.fromString(priority);
```

8. Next, we need to think about changing the configuration. The external documentation also tells us that `VcClusterDasVmSettings` is a property of `VcClusterDasVmConfigInfo`. Taking a look at this object, we find that the attribute `.key` is a VM object, and that the `.dasSettings` attribute will take our `myVcClusterDasVmSettings`.

9. Now, we will add the constructor of `VcClusterDasVmConfigInfo` to our script as well as the rest of the lines:

```
var myVcClusterDasVmConfigInfo = new VcClusterDasVmConfigInfo();
myVcClusterDasVmConfigInfo.key=VM;
myVcClusterDasVmConfigInfo.dasSettings=myVcClusterDasVmSettings;
```

10. Again, we need to go higher in the API tree. Looking at the parent of `VcClusterDasVmConfigInfo`, we find `VcClusterDasVmConfigSpec`. This has a `.info` attribute, which will take a value of `VcClusterDasVmConfigInfo`. However, a closer look at the external documentation shows us that we need to define the `.operation` attribute. We know this because all the other attributes come with * saying that they do not need to be present, meaning the operation has to be there. So we will add that as well:

```
var myVcClusterDasVmConfigSpec = new VcClusterDasVmConfigSpec();
myVcClusterDasVmConfigSpec.operation = VcArrayUpdateOperation.add;
myVcClusterDasVmConfigSpec.info = myVcClusterDasVmConfigInfo;
```

11. We will still need to go higher. The parent of `myVcClusterDasVmConfigSpec` is `vcClusterConfigSpecEX`. It has a `.dasVmConfigSpec` attribute, which will take a value of `VcClusterDasVmConfigSpec`; but further inspection reveals that it needs an array of `VcClusterDasVmConfigSpec`. So let's do that:

```
var myVcClusterDasVmConfigSpecArray = new Array() ;
myVcClusterDasVmConfigSpecArray.push( myVcClusterDasVmConfigSpec
);
var myVcClusterConfigSpecEx = new VcClusterConfigSpecEx() ;
myVcClusterConfigSpecEx.dasVmConfigSpec =
myVcClusterDasVmConfigSpecArray;
```

12. The next part isn't documented, but results from trial and error. We need to define the `.dasConfig` attribute: (try the finished script and comment the next two lines out, and you will get an error message telling you that you need `VcClusterDasConfigInfo`)

```
var myVcClusterDasConfigInfo = new VcClusterDasConfigInfo() ;
myVcClusterConfigSpecEx.dasConfig = myVcClusterDasConfigInfo;
```

13. We are almost there, one more step and we are done. Check out the `VcClusterConfigSpecEx` object, which tells us that it can be used with a cluster, so let's look the other way around. Search for **Cluster** and take a closer look at `ClusterComputeResource`. It has a method called `reconfigureCluster_Task()`, which will take our `VcClusterConfigSpecEx`. So, let's use this:

```
vcTask=cluster.reconfigureComputeResource_Task(
myVcClusterConfigSpecEx, true );
```

14. The return value of this attribute is a vCenter task. We will define the Boolean of the method as `true`, as only the changes to the cluster are needed. If we set it to `false`, it will apply all the changes defined in `VcClusterDasConfigInfo`.

15. Our little script is finished and looks like this:

```
var myVcClusterDasVmSettings = new VcClusterDasVmSettings();
myVcClusterDasVmSettings.restartPriority=VcClusterDasVmSettingsRes
tartPriority.fromString(priority);

var myVcClusterDasVmConfigInfo = new VcClusterDasVmConfigInfo();
myVcClusterDasVmConfigInfo.key=VM;
myVcClusterDasVmConfigInfo.dasSettings=myVcClusterDasVmSettings;

var myVcClusterDasVmConfigSpec = new VcClusterDasVmConfigSpec() ;
myVcClusterDasVmConfigSpec.operation = VcArrayUpdateOperation.add;
myVcClusterDasVmConfigSpec.info = myVcClusterDasVmConfigInfo;

var myVcClusterDasVmConfigSpecArray = new Array() ;
myVcClusterDasVmConfigSpecArray.push( myVcClusterDasVmConfigSpec
);
var myVcClusterConfigSpecEx = new VcClusterConfigSpecEx() ;
myVcClusterConfigSpecEx.dasVmConfigSpec =
myVcClusterDasVmConfigSpecArray;
var myVcClusterDasConfigInfo = new VcClusterDasConfigInfo() ;
myVcClusterConfigSpecEx.dasConfig = myVcClusterDasConfigInfo;

vcTask=cluster.reconfigureComputeResource_Task(
myVcClusterConfigSpecEx, true );
```

16. As the last step, we will add the action `vim3WaitTaskEnd` to the workflow:

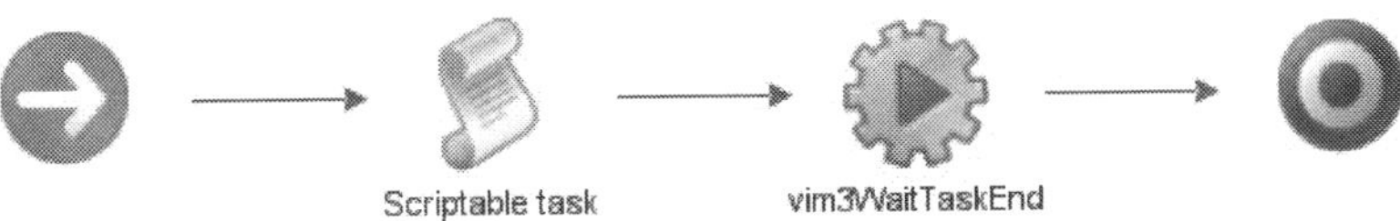

How it works...

This recipe has probably caused a bit of a headache to you, but it is also extremely important to understand how to create workflows that use properties that are not implemented in the existing library. Working through the API, finding the items, and putting them together is a vital part of advanced programming skills in Orchestrator.

The method shown here is a difficult one, but, if you already know to which object a setting belongs, you can also move from the top down. In this case, you will have to drill down from `ClusterComputeResource`. If you like, give it a try. Have a go at the DRS setting for a VM. It basically follows the same route.

There is another way to generate this kind of scripts. Check out the Onyx project at `labs.vmware.com/flings/onyx`.

Onyx integrates itself between vSphere Client and vCenter Server and translates the actions in a script. However, it is always better to understand what actually happens, and how to search and find it.

There's more...

To make the workflow work better, we will apply a few presentation properties to it. We looked at them in the *Working with presentations* and *Linking actions in presentations* recipes in *Chapter 3, Visual Programming*:

1. Add to the presentation of the in-parameter **priority**, the **Predefined answers** property. The correct answers are found in the `VcClusterDasVmSettingsRestartPriority` object. This will only show the correct values that should be entered.
2. Add to the presentation of the in-parameter VM, the **Predefined list of elements** property.

3. Click on the purple puzzle piece (It helps us to create an action call), and in the pop-up search for **Cluster**, select the only return action called `getAllVMsOfCluster` and assign it to the input of the cluster.

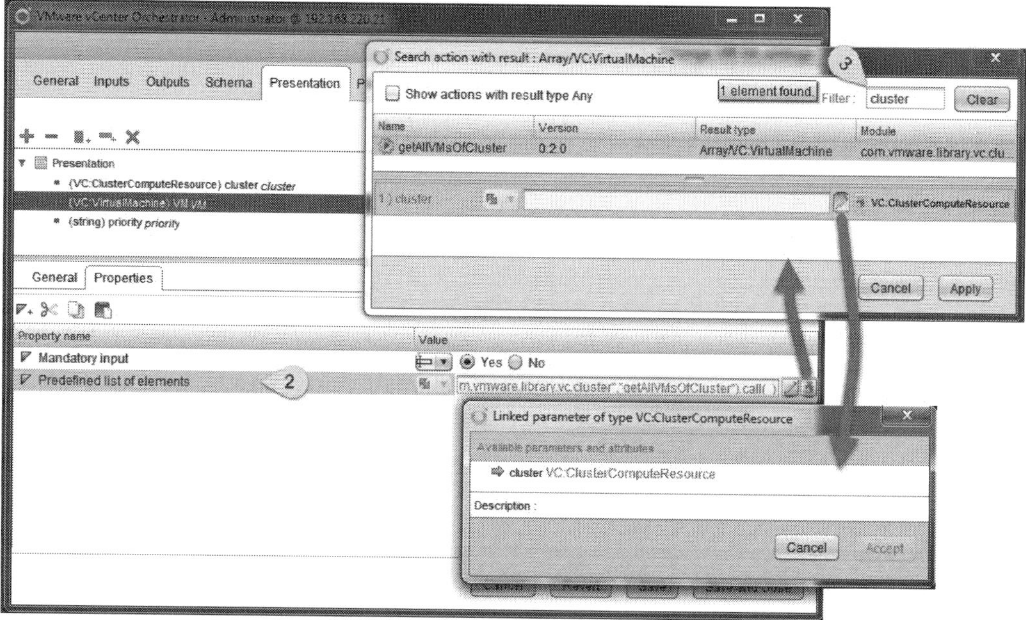

See also

Refer to the example workflow, 7.05.1 Change VM HA settings and 7.05.2 Change VM DRS settings.

Standard vSwitch and Distributed Switch ports

Here, we will discuss the problems that arise in vCenter from the difference between vSwitch and Distributed Switch ports in vCenter. We will learn how to bypass these problems, and create a workflow that will connect a VM to a Standard vSwitch or Distributed Switch port.

Getting ready

We need a vSphere environment that has at least one vSwitch as well as at least one Distributed Switch configured, each with at least one VM Network port group. For this recipe, it is not necessary that the switches are actually connected to any NICs; they can be implemented as blind switches.

To understand the creation of the action, you should understand how to use the vCenter API, as showcased in the *Working with the vCenter API (to change a VM's HA settings)* recipe.

We also need a VM with a virtual network card.

How to do it...

We will split this recipe into three parts, building an action, building a workflow that uses the action, and the final piece, to make it work the way we want it to.

Create an action

We will create a new action that will connect a VM to any network. I derived the code for this action from the existing vCenter Server plugin actions `connectVmNicNumberToVirtualDistributedPortgroup` and `createVirtualEthernetCardNetworkConfigSpec`. Take a look at their source code. To create an action, follow the given steps:

1. Create a new action and name it `connectVmToNetwork`.
2. Define the following variables:

Name	Type	Section	Use
vm	VC:VirtualMachine	IN	This variable contains the VM that should be changed
network	VC:Network	IN	This variable defines the new network which you connect to
startConnected	Boolean	IN	This variable denotes whether the network should be connected at the start of the VM
connected	Boolean	IN	This variable denotes whether the network should be connected
	VC:Task	Return	The return value of the action that contains the vCenter task ID

3. Enter the following script:

```
//connection settings
var connectInfo = new VcVirtualDeviceConnectInfo();
connectInfo.allowGuestControl = false;
connectInfo.connected = connected;
connectInfo.startConnected = startConnected;
//check if this is a distributed switch?
if (network.id.indexOf("dvport")>=0){
```

```
    //backing for distributed switch
    var netBackingInfo = new
VcVirtualEthernetCardDistributedVirtualPortBackingInfo();
    var port = new VcDistributedVirtualSwitchPortConnection();
    var dvSwitch = VcPlugin.convertToVimManagedObject(network,
network.config.distributedVirtualSwitch);
    port.switchUuid = dvSwitch.uuid;
    port.portgroupKey = network.key;
    netBackingInfo.port = port;
} else {
    //backing for vSwitch
    var netBackingInfo = new
VcVirtualEthernetCardNetworkBackingInfo();
    netBackingInfo.deviceName = network.name;
}
//Devicespecs are arrays
var nicArray = new Array();
//constructor for VM configuration
var vmspec = new VcVirtualMachineConfigSpec();
//constructor for the device configuration
var devicespec = new VcVirtualDeviceConfigSpec();
//get existing configuration
var devices = vm.config.hardware.device;
//go through all devices to find NIC
for( var i in devices){
// is it a NIC?
    if (System.getModule("com.vmware.library.vc.vm.network").
isSupportedNic(devices[i])) {
        devicespec.device = devices[i];
        //edit the exiting configuration
        devicespec.operation = VcVirtualDeviceConfigSpecOperation.
edit;
        //attach new backing
        devicespec.device.backing = netBackingInfo;
        //attach new connection setting
        devicespec.device.connectable = connectInfo;
        //make array
        nicArray.push(devicespec);
    }
}
//build config
vmspec.deviceChange = nicArray;
//enact change on VM
return vm.reconfigVM_Task(vmspec);
```

4. Save and close the action.

Please note that this is a simplified version that will connect all virtual network cards of a VM to the new network. Please refer to the original action, `connectVmNicNumberToVirtualDistributedPortgroup` for pointers on how to select a single network card.

Creating the workflow

Now, we will create the workflow:

1. Create a new workflow and define the following variables:

Name	Type	Section	Use
vm	VC:VirtualMachine	IN	This contains the VM that should be changed
network	VC:Network	IN	This is the new network which you connect to
task	VC:Task	Attribute	This transports the vCenter Task ID
progress	Boolean	Attribute	Value `False`. Show progress in percent
pollRate	Number	Attribute	Value 5. Interval for task check

2. Add the following actions to the schema:
   - `connectVmToNetwork`
   - `vim3WaitTaskEnd`

3. Bind all the parameters.
4. Run the workflow. You will see that at the moment, you can only select vSwitch ports. Distributed Switch ports cannot be selected.

Make it work with presentation

Now, we will make the workflow function for distributed port groups:

1. Edit the workflow and go to presentation.
2. Add the following properties to the network in-parameter:

Property	Value
Predefined list of elements	GetAction("com.vmware.library.vc.network","getNetworkForResourcePoolHostVm").call(null , null , #vm)
Select value as	list

3. Save and run the workflow.

Now when you select the network, you will be presented with a list of all the existing networks (vSwitch and Distributed Switch).

How it works...

There isn't much magic here, what we have used is a deeper understanding of the API. VMware introduced the Distributed Switch back in vSphere 4, and before that, only normal switches (vSwitch) existed. So, VMware has added new types for the Distributed Switch. A vSwitch port group is of the `VC:Networks` type, while a distributed port group is of the `VC:DistributedVirtualPortGroup` type. Take a look at each of these types in the API browser, and you will find that they have the same structure. Both types are more or less interchangeable.

Let's discuss how this workflow functions in more detail:

- We will use the property in the presentation to display all the available vSwitch and Distributed Switch ports.
- We will then push either `VC:Network` or `VC:DistributedVirtualPortGroup` in a `VC:Network` in-parameter. As both are the same, this works. We will use `VC:Network` because of the existing action that we used in the presentation.
- In the action, we will check the ID of the network object. The ID is the MoRef (Managed Object Reference—refer to the *Introduction* section of this chapter) string that each object in vCenter has. The MoRef of `VC:Network` begins with **network** and that of `VC:DistributedVirtualPortGroup` starts with **dvport**.
- We will then either use the method for vSwitches or for Distributed Switches to define V`cVirtualEthernetCardNetworkBackingInfo`.
- The rest is more or less a straightforward copy of the action, `connectVmNicNumberToVirtualDistributedPortgroup`.

If you take a closer look at the script, you will see the difference in how the vSwitch and the Distributed Switch ports are connected. Both use the `BackingInfo` type to build the connection. Please note that they are actually different types, but, they are interchangeable.

The vSwitch port uses a `netBackingInfo` instance, `var netBackingInfo = new VcVirtualEthernetCardNetworkBackingInfo();`, and then simply connects the network name to it, like this:

```
netBackingInfo.deviceName = network.name;
```

For the Distributed Switch, we will also use a `netBackingInfo` instance; however, we will use a slightly different one:

```
var netBackingInfo = new
VcVirtualEthernetCardDistributedVirtualPortBackingInfo();
```

We need to define a port connection:

```
var port = new VcDistributedVirtualSwitchPortConnection();
```

The port connection requires the UUID of the Distributed Switch:

```
var dvSwitch = VcPlugin.convertToVimManagedObject(network, network.
config.distributedVirtualSwitch);
port.switchUuid = dvSwitch.uuid;
```

Instead of the name, we will connect the network using its key (MoRef):

```
port.portgroupKey = network.key;
```

Now, we can build the connection:

```
netBackingInfo.port = port;
```

Independent of the vSwitch or Distributed Switch, we will use the `backinginfo` variable to alter the device settings of the VM:

```
devicespec.device.backing = netBackingInfo;
```

See also

Refer to the example workflow, 7.05.1 Connect VM to Network and the action connectVmToNetwork.

Executing a program inside a VM

In this recipe, we will take a look at how to use Guest Operations (formally called VIX) with Orchestrator. Guest Operations is a method by which vCenter can transfer files and execute programs inside a VM using VMware Tools. This method is of interest in DMZs, where security reduces the amount of possible automation.

Getting ready

We will need a running VM of any OS flavor you are happy with. This VM also needs to have VMware Tools installed. In this example, we will use a Windows VM.

We also need a program to install in the operating system. In this example, we will use Java for Windows. The silent install instructions can be found at `https://www.java.com/en/download/help/silent_install.xml`.

You will need to upload this file to the Orchestrator in a directory that is accessible to Orchestrator. Refer to the *Configuring access to the local filesystem* recipe in *Chapter 2, Optimizing Orchestrator Configuration*. In this example, we will upload the file to the Orchestrator appliance in the `/var/run/vco/` directory.

You need a user that has local administrator rights on the VMs operating system.

How to do it...

We will divide this recipe into two steps first, building the two necessary workflows, and second conducting a test run.

Create a wait workflow

When we want to run a program on a VM, we need to know when it has finished. So, let's build a waiting workflow first:

1. Create a new workflow and name it as `waitUntilProgramInstalled`.
2. Define the following variables:

Name	Type	Section	Use
`vmUsername`	String	IN	This variable denotes the local VM user
`vmPassword`	SecureString	IN	This variable denotes the local VM user password
`vm`	VC:VirtualMachine	IN	This variable denotes the VM to run on
`processID`	Number	IN	This variable denotes the process ID of the program that is running

Name	Type	Section	Use
`sleepTime`	Number	IN	This variable denotes the time to wait between polls in seconds
`counter`	Number	Attribute	The default value of this variable is 0
`errorCode`	String	Attribute	This variable denotes the error code

3. Create the workflow as shown in the following figure by adding the given elements:
    - **Sleep**
    - **Get process from guest**
    - **Custom decision**
    - **Decision**
    - **Increase counter**
    - **Scriptable task**
    - **Throw exception**

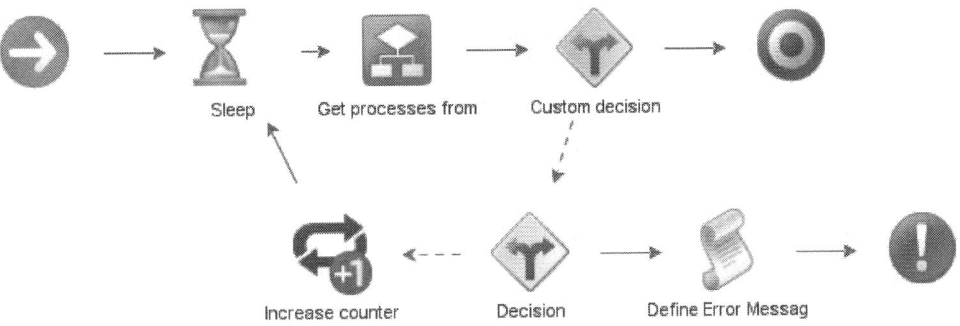

4. Edit the **Get process from guest** element and bind the **result** out-parameter as an attribute. We will do this because **result** is a composite type and is too complicated to create manually.
5. In the **Custom decision** element, select **processID** and **result** (defined in the last step) as in-parameters. Add the following script:

```
var finished=true;
for each (value in result) {
    if (value.pid == processID) {
        finished=false;
        System.log(processID+" still running");
    }
}
return finished;
```

6. In the **Decision** element, set `counter, greater or equal, 9`.
7. In the **Increase counter** element, set `counter` as `in-parameter` and `out-parameter`.
8. In the **Scriptable task** element, add the following parameters:

In-parameters	`vm`, `sleepTime`, `counter`, and `processID`
Out-parameters	`errorCode`
Script	`time=sleepTime*counter;` `errorCode="PID:"+processID+" on VM "+vm.name+" still running after "+time;`

9. Bind `errorCode` to **Throw exception**.
10. Save and close the workflow. Proceed to the next section.

Create an installation workflow

We will now build a workflow that will copy a file to the VM, install a program, and perform clean up.

1. Create a new workflow and define the following variables:

Name	Type	Section	Use
`vmUsername`	String	IN	This variable denotes the local VM user
`vmPassword`	SecureString	IN	This variable denotes the local VM user password
`vm`	VC:VirtualMachine	IN	This variable denotes the VM to run on
`programFileName`	String	IN	This variable denotes the name of the file to run
`arguments`	String	IN	This variable denotes the install arguments
`dirPath`	String	Attribute	This variable denotes the path directory on VM
`createParents`	Boolean	Attribute	This variable denotes whether to create parent folders

Name	Type	Section	Use
`result`	Boolean	Attribute	This variable is set to true if the directory is created successfully
`vcoPath`	String	Attribute	This variable denotes the path on the vCO server
`guestFilePath`	String	Attribute	This variable denotes the path on the VM
`overwrite`	Boolean	Attribute	This variable allows to overwrite a file if it exists
`interactiveSession`	Boolean	Attribute	This variable enables interactive session for the program running on the VM
`ProcessID`	Number	Attribute	This variable denotes the process ID of the running program
`recursive`	Boolean	Attribute	This variable allows deletion of the directory content recursively
`sleepTime`	Number	Attribute	This variable denotes the time between the polls
`errorCode`	String	Attribute	This variable denotes the error code

2. Now, we need to assign some values to all the attributes. The attributes that are not mentioned in the following table do not require a start value:

`dirPath`	`c:\OrchestratorInstall`
`createParents`	`False`
`vcoPath`	`/var/run/vco`
`overwrite`	`True`
`interactiveSession`	`False`
`recursive`	`True`
`sleepTime`	`90`
`errorCode`	`nothing`

3. Create the workflow as shown in the following figure by adding the given elements:
    - **Scriptable task**
    - **Create directory in guest**
    - **Copy file from vCO to guest**
    - **Run program in guest**
    - **waitUntilProgramInstalled**
    - **Kill process in guest**
    - **Delete directory in guest**
    - **Decision**
    - **Throw exception**

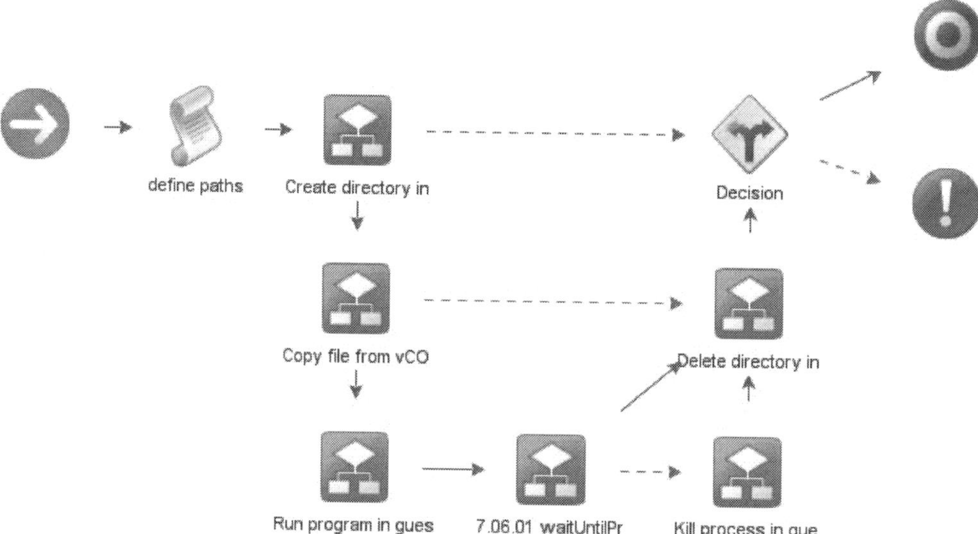

4. In the **Scriptable task** element, add the following parameters:

In-parameters	`programFileName`, `vcoPath`, and `dirPath`
Out-parameters	`vcoPath` and `guestFilePath`
Script	`vcoPath=vcoPath+"/"+programFileName;` `guestFilePath=dirPath+"\\"+programFileName;`

Please note the double backslashes `\\`. We need to escape the `\` for Windows.

5. In the **Decision** element, set `errorCode`, `equal`, and `nothing`.
6. Bind all the other parameters to all the other workflow elements.

An example run

Now, let's play through an example run of the workflows:

1. Copy the Java installation file (`jre-8u25-windows-i586.exe`) to the Orchestrator appliance in the directory `/var/run/vco`. You may need to change the access rights with `chmod 555 jre-8u25-windows-i586.exe`.
2. Make sure that your test VM is ready, has VMware Tools installed, and that you have access to it as a local administrator. Creating a snapshot at this stage isn't a bad idea either.
3. Run the workflow, **Install program on VM** (the second workflow that you created).
4. Select the VM on which you want to execute the program, and enter the credentials for the local administrator.
5. The value of `programFileName` is `jre-8u25-windows-i586.exe`.
6. The input for **Arguments** is `/s` (refer to Java's silent install options).
7. Submit the workflow.
8. The workflow will now create a directory `C:\OrchestratorInstall` in the VM and copy the Java install file from the Orchestrator to the VM via the VMware Tools. If any of these actions fail, the program will clean up and exit with error.

The program will now be executed, and the process ID is piped to the wait workflow (the first workflow that you built).

1. In the wait workflow, we will first wait a bit before we get all the processes that run on the VM. We will check whether the process ID exists, and if so, we will go back to waiting. To make sure that we can break out of this loop, we will only run the loop 10 times.
2. If the wait task finishes with an error, we will kill the install process on the VM, clean up, and exit with error.
3. If the installation finishes, we will delete the directory that we created.
4. If no error has occurred, `errorCode` will still contain the start value "nothing"; so, we will check whether this is the case, and if so, we will exit successfully. Otherwise, if an error exists, `errorCode` will throw an error.

How it works...

In this recipe, we used the Guest Operations system, which is implemented with the VMware Tools in the VMs. This allows us to directly work inside the Guest OS, without the need for network connectivity between the VM and Orchestrator. Guest Operations is useful for a lot of functions:

- VMs that are in a DMZ and can't be accessed via a network by Orchestrator.
- VMs that have no network connection. Typically, you do this when you want to configure the VM first before connecting it to a network. A good example is to reconfigure an SQL server you have just cloned.
- You can also configure VMs that are hardened and do not allow a network log in to the OS.

There's more...

A way to optimize this workflow is by:

- Creating a configuration element to store the central configuration elements
- Adding decisions to choose between Linux and Windows VMs and to adjust the guestPath accordingly
- Copying the file to be installed from a central shared directory onto the Orchestrator first
- Checking whether the program has installed correctly

See also

Refer to the example workflows, 7.06.01 waitUntilProgramInstalled and 7.06.2 Install program on VM.

Configuring a vRA instance in Orchestrator

Not only can vRA use Orchestrator to access vCenter or other plugins, but you can also automate your vRA instance using Orchestrator. In this recipe, we will show you how to do the first steps.

Getting ready

Please make sure that you read the introduction of vRA at the beginning of this chapter. We need a functional and configured vRA. We also need the vRA plugin for Orchestrator installed.

How to do it...

Make sure that the vRA (vCAC) plugin is installed in Orchestrator. To configure the vRA plugin, perform the following steps:

1. Log in to the Orchestrator Client.
2. Run the workflow **vCloud Automation Administration** | **Configuration** | **Add an IaaS host**.
3. Enter the FQDN of the VM that the IaaS component of vRA is installed on.
4. Enter the HTTPS URL of the IaaS component of the vRA installation.
5. Agree to install the SSL certificates.
6. Leave the connection variables at their default and click on **Next**.
7. Choose **Shared session** and enter an vRA **Infrastructure Admin** account.
8. Click on **Submit** and wait till the workflow has finished.

Check the Orchestrator inventory. You should now see all the vRA items.

How it works...

Now, you have hooked up Orchestrator to vRA and are able to do a lot of things. You can configure vRA by configuring workflow stubs, endpoints, and properties.

You can, for example, use the workflows in **vCloud Automation Center** | **Extensibility** | **Installation** | **Install vCO customization** to create an interaction between vRA and Orchestrator when certain subs are triggered.

There is a nice example on how to use Orchestrator to configure vRA in order to use Orchestrator at a certain stage of the provisioning process at `http://www.virtualnebula.com/blog/2014/1/24/running-vco-workflows-from-vcac-during-the-provisioning-of-a-virtual-machine`.

Configuring an external Orchestrator in vRA

vRA comes with an installed and configured Orchestrator, but, the best practice is to use an external Orchestrator, or better yet, an Orchestrator cluster. In this recipe, we will show you how to do this.

Getting ready

Please make sure you read the introduction of vRA at the beginning of this chapter. We need a functional and configured vRA. We also need the vRA plugin for Orchestrator.

How to do it...

This recipe has three parts. First, we will configure the Orchestrator, bind it to vRA, and then, we will clean up the vRA appliance.

Building and configuring an external Orchestrator

To attach an external Orchestrator, we first need an Orchestrator that we can connect to:

1. Install the Orchestrator appliance (refer to the *Deploying the Orchestrator appliance* recipe in *Chapter 1, Installing and Configuring Orchestrator*).
2. Configure Orchestrator with an external DB (refer to the *Configuring an external database* recipe in *Chapter 1, Installing and Configuring Orchestrator*).
3. Configure the appliance for SSO and connect it to vCenter (refer to the *Integrating Orchestrator into SSO and vSphere Web Client* recipe in *Chapter 1, Installing and Configuring Orchestrator*).
4. Install the vRA plugin (refer to the *Plugin basics* recipe in *Chapter 2, Optimizing Orchestrator Configuration*).This will install the plugins: **vCAC Infrastructure Administration** and **vCloud Automation Center** (VMware still needs to finish renaming everything).
5. Tune the appliance by disabling LDAP and the local DB (refer to the *Tuning the appliance* recipe in *Chapter 2, Optimizing Orchestrator Configuration*).

If you want to build an Orchestrator cluster, follow the *Creating an Orchestrator cluster* recipe in *Chapter 2, Optimizing Orchestrator Configuration*.

Configuring vRA

Next, we need to attach Orchestrator to vRA:

1. Log in to vRA as an **Infrastructure** or **Tenant** admin.
2. Click on **Administration** | **Advanced Services** | **Server Configuration** and select **Use an external Orchestrator server**.

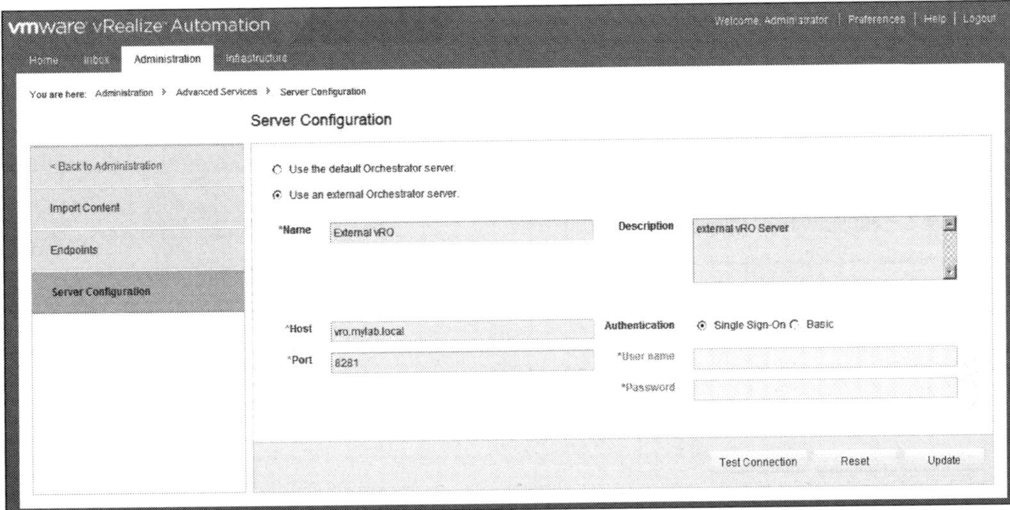

3. Select a name under which you would like to store this configuration and description.
4. In the **Host** field, enter the FQDN or IP of the Orchestrator or the Orchestrator cluster.
5. The default port is **8281**.
6. You should use **Single Sign-On** to archive a higher level of integration. This requires vRA, vCenter, and Orchestrator to be configured to the same SSO. The **Basic** authentication option works by using a username and password only, and it acts as a shared configuration.
7. Test the connection, and when successful, click on **Update**.
8. After the update, you can be notified that the existing endpoints will be deleted. These are the existing Orchestrator endpoints. Accept and then add new endpoints. Follow the *Adding an Orchestrator endpoint* recipe.

Tuning vRA

Now that we are using an external Orchestrator, we can give the vRA appliance some space.

1. Log in to the vRA appliance as root.
2. Run the following script, line by line:

```
chkconfig vco-server off
service vco-server stop
chkconfig vco-configurator off
service vco-configurator stop
```

This will stop and disable the services for Orchestrator and the Orchestrator Configurator.

How it works...

The vRA appliance has Orchestrator installed on it, the same way as in the Orchestrator appliance. The initial configuration of vRA is done to use the internal Orchestrator, but VMware's best practice for production environments dictates that an external Orchestrator or Orchestrator cluster should be used. It is best to reconfigure vRA for external Orchestrator usage before adding Orchestrator endpoints.

There's more...

You can define a workflow folder per tenant. This enables you to expose different workflows to different tenants. You can use the base folder for this purpose.

1. Navigate to **Administration** | **Advanced Services** | **Default Orchestrator Folder**.
2. Select the tenant you want to assign a base folder to and click on **Edit**.
3. Browse to the Orchestrator workflow folder and then click on **Add**.

Adding an Orchestrator endpoint

Before you can use any Orchestrator plugins in vRA, you need to define them as endpoints. In this recipe, we will show you how to do this.

Getting ready

For this recipe, you will need a working and configured vRealize Automation installation. Please refer to the introduction of this chapter.

You can either use the vRA integrated Orchestrator or an external Orchestrator.

In this example, we will add an Active Directory endpoint. Please note that if you want to add users or change passwords, you will need to enable SSL for AD, refer to the *Working with Active Directory* recipe in *Chapter 4, Working with Plugins*.

How to do it...

1. Log in to vRA as an **Infrastructure** admin.
2. Navigate to **Administration** | **Advanced Services** | **Endpoints**.
3. Click on **Add** (green plus sign) and select the plugin that you would like to configure as an endpoint, such as the Active Directory plugin.
4. Give the endpoint a name, such as `ActiveDirectory`.
5. Follow the *Working with Active Directory* recipe in *Chapter 4, Working with Plugins*, to configure this endpoint. What you are basically doing is running the configuration workflow.

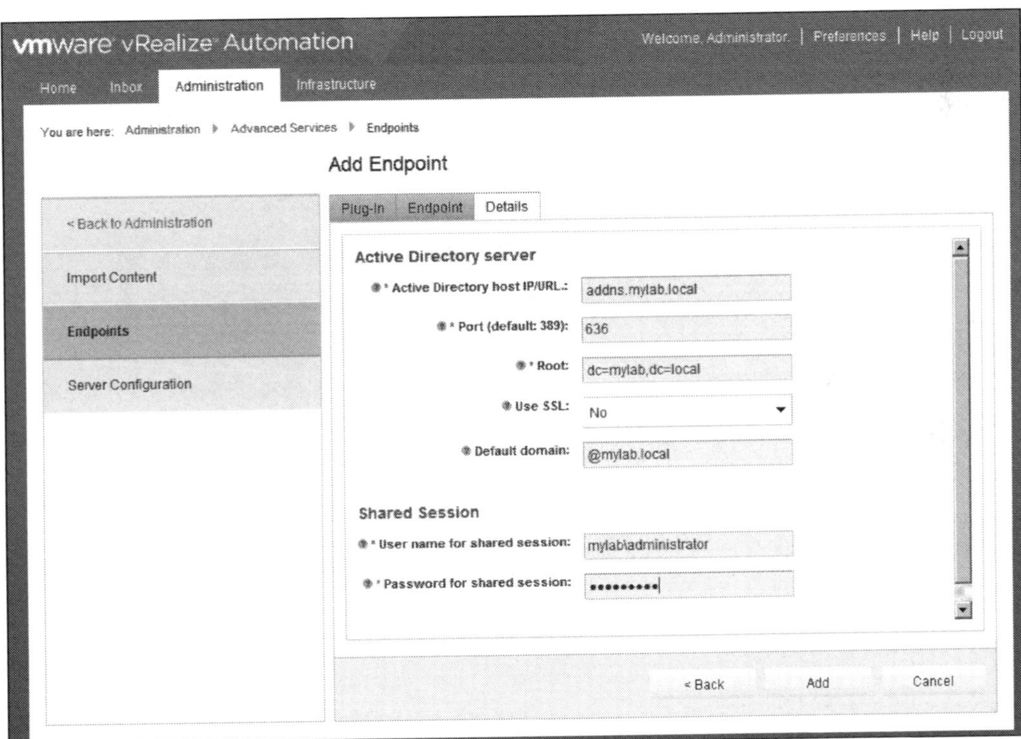

6. Click on **Add** to add the endpoint.

How it works...

As discussed in the introduction to this chapter, endpoints are essentially the connection points between vRA and plugin-driven infrastructures.

Using the vRA integrated Orchestrator, you can add the following endpoints out of the box. The following table contains the recipes in which the plugin is discussed, and a quick overview of the prerequisites for using the plugin.

Plugin	**Recipe/chapter**	**Prerequisite**
Active Directory	*Working with Active Directory* recipe in *Chapter 4, Working with Plugins*	AD SSL Certs, SSL Cert import
HTTP-REST	*Working with REST* recipe in *Chapter 4, Working with Plugins*	SSL Cert import
PowerShell	*Working with PowerShell* recipe in *Chapter 4, Working with Plugins*	WinRM and Kerberos configurations
SOAP	*Working with SOAP* recipe in *Chapter 4, Working with Plugins*	SSL Cert import
vCenter Server	*Integrating Orchestrator into SSO and vSphere Web Client* recipe in *Chapter 1, Installing and Configuring Orchestrator*	SSL Cert import

Integrating Orchestrator workflows in vRA

We will now showcase how to integrate Orchestrator workflows in vRealize Automation. We will learn how to create a vRA Catalog item that will run a workflow when requested.

Getting ready

In order to use an Orchestrator workflow as a vRA Catalog item, you should have the following vRA items configured:

- Entitlements
- Services
- Business groups

To configure these items, please refer to the link shown in the introduction of this chapter or take a look at the official VMware documentation of vRA.

We will use the example workflow 3.01 Workflow basics to add to the vRA catalog. Refer to the *Workflow basics* recipe in *Chapter 3, Visual Programming*.

How to do it...

This recipe is divided into three parts.

Activate the advanced services tab

By default, the advanced services tab is not visible, so the first step is to make it appear:

1. Log in to vRA as an **Infrastructure** admin.
2. Navigate to **Administration** | **Users & Groups** | **Custom Groups**.
3. Click on **Add**.
4. Give the group a name and then assign it the role of **Service Architect**.

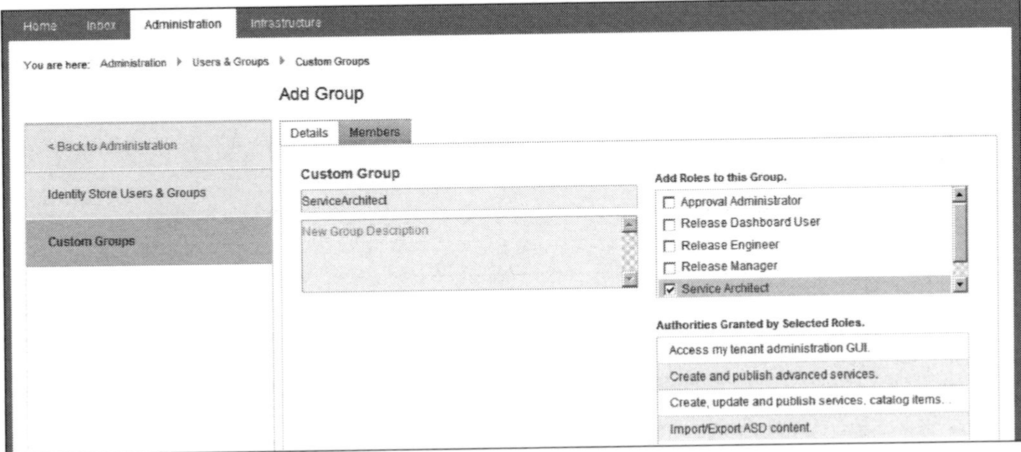

5. Click on **Next** and select a group or user to assign to this group.
6. Log out and log in with the user that you specified in step 5.

The **Advanced Services** tab should now be visible.

Adding a service blueprint

We will now add a simple Orchestrator workflow as a vRA Catalog item. We will add the example workflow 3.01 Workflow basics.

1. Log in to vRA with a user that is a service architect.
2. Navigate to **Advanced Services** | **Service Blueprints** and click on **Add**.

3. Select the workflow 3.01 Workflow basics. On the left-hand side, you will see all in- and out-parameters of the workflow. Click on **Next**.

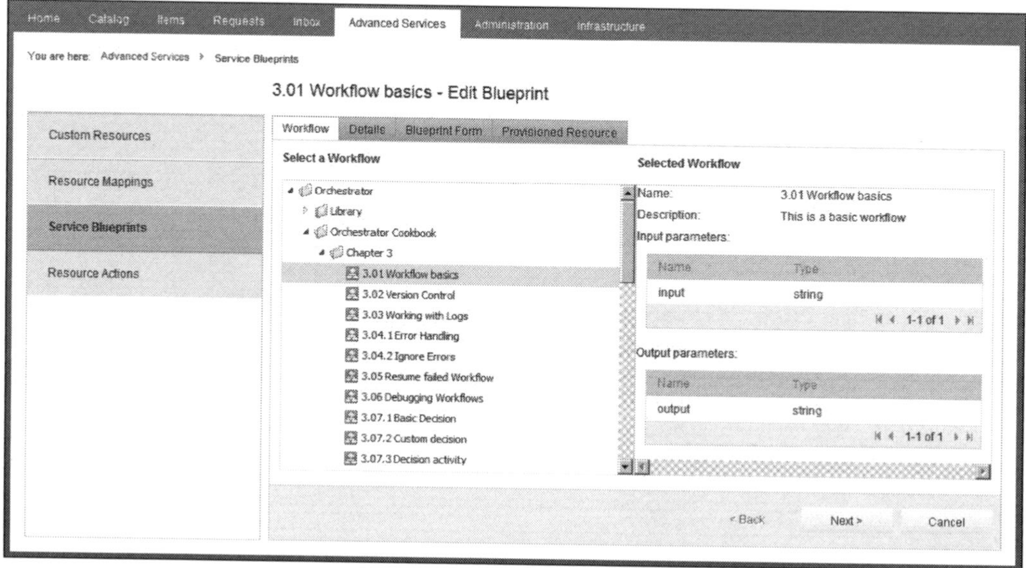

4. You can now change the display name of the workflow as well as modify the **Description** and the **Version** fields. Click on **Next**.
5. The blueprint form allows you to modify the presentation screen. We will discuss this in the *There's more...* section of this recipe. For now, just click on **Next**.
6. You are now asked what you would like to provision. As we did not define any custom resources, you can only choose **No provisioning**. Click on **Add**.

Publishing and adding the workflow to the catalog

We will now publish this workflow and then add it to the catalog:

1. Navigate to **Advanced Services** | **Service Blueprints** and click on the service blueprint you created in the last section, and then select **Publish** (a green-colored tick).
2. Now, navigate to **Administration** | **Catalog Management** | **Catalog Items**. The service blueprint can now be seen. Click on it and select **Configure** (a grey gear icon).
3. You can now change the icon that will be displayed with the Catalog item. This icon will always be an Orchestrator Item, and it has no connection to the workflow item in the Orchestrator Client.
4. Select the **Status** as **Active** to make it usable in the catalog.
5. Select a service to attach and then click on **Update**.

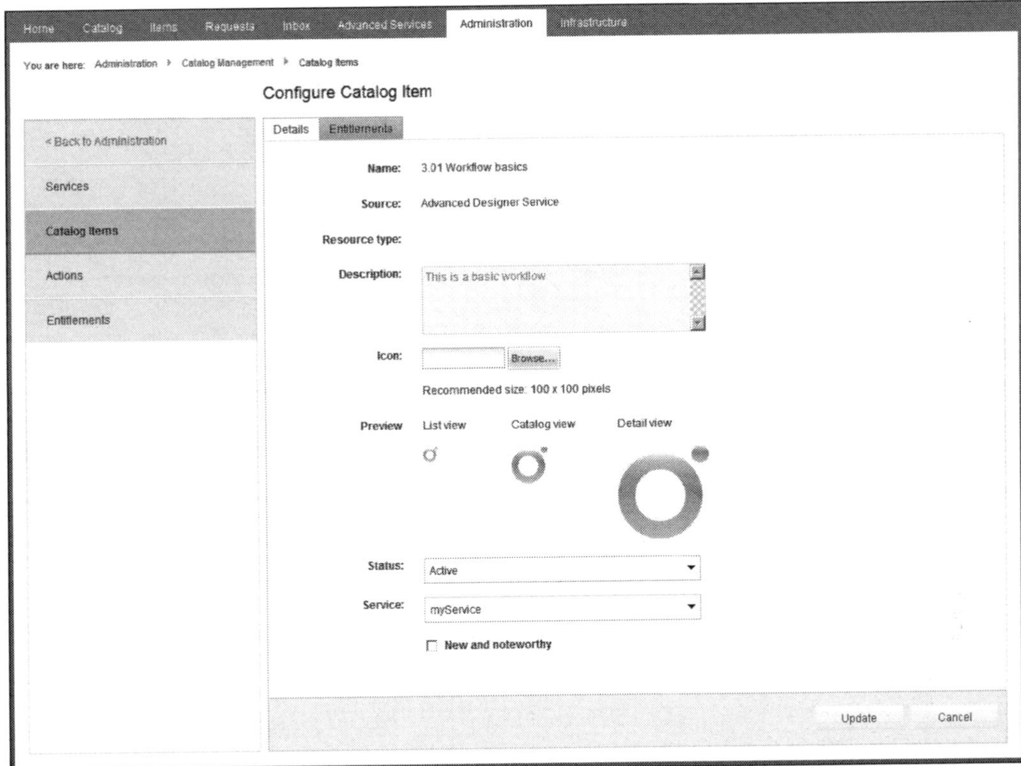

6. Now, go to the **Catalog** tab and take a look at the result:

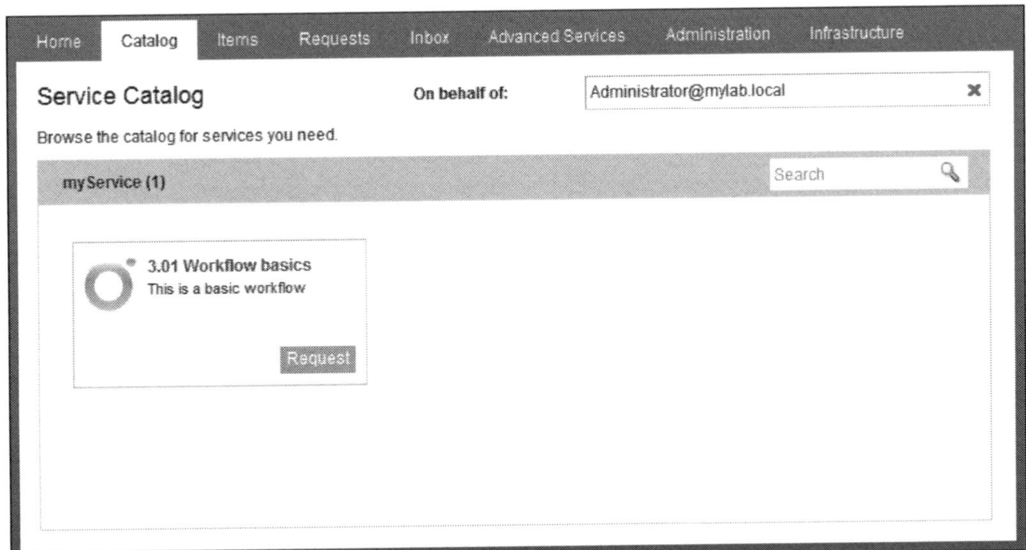

You can now **Request** this Catalog Item, which results in the workflow being executed. Check the Orchestrator Client for the result.

How it works...

This is a very simple integration of a workflow with vRA, but it shows the power of the whole concept and the possibilities.

In this example, we have just used a simple workflow that doesn't interact with any infrastructure. In the *Manage AD users with vRA* recipe, we will use a more elaborate setup; however, the principle is the same for all of the workflow interactions.

If the workflow you are executing uses a customer interaction, you can find and start the interaction by clicking on your inbox.

There's more...

The Blueprint Designer is a tool that helps you design the form that vRA users interact with. The Blueprint designer uses the settings of the workflow presentation and can enhance the visualization inside the vRA web engine.

You can change and move all the text headers and in-parameters around. Properties such as default values or integrations will be kept, whereas HTML tags and the variable integration in the description are not kept.

The following figure shows the workflow presentation as well as the Blueprint designer of the example workflow, 3.09 Working with Presentation:

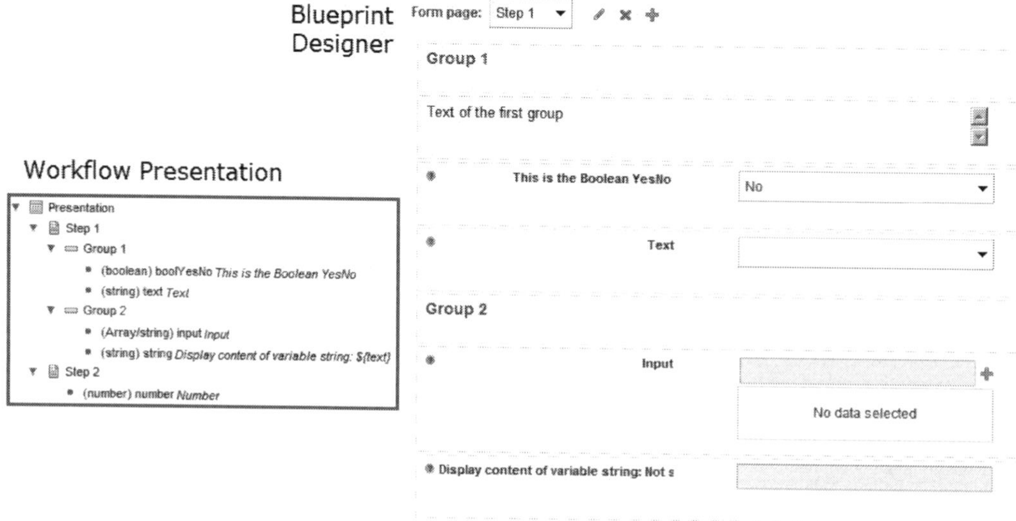

Managing AD users with vRA

In this recipe, we will explore the full spectrum of an Orchestrator/vRA integration. You will learn how to create custom resources and actions, and how to integrate and use them.

Getting ready

In order to add an Orchestrator workflow as a vRA Catalog item, you should have the following vRA items configured:

- Entitlements
- Services
- Business groups

To configure these items, please refer to the link shown in the introduction of this chapter or take a look at the official VMware documentation of vRA.

The **Advanced Services** tab must be activated as shown in the *Integrating Orchestrator workflows in vRA* recipe.

You also have to add the AD endpoint as shown in the *Adding an Orchestrator endpoint* recipe in this chapter, and the AD endpoint needs to be configured with SSL for this recipe to work.

How to do it...

We have split this recipe into multiple sections. Work though them one after another.

Creating a custom resource

We will first need to create a custom resource, which makes it possible for vRA users to manage their resources:

1. Log in to vRA with a user that is an **Service Architect**.
2. Navigate to **Advanced Services** | **Custom Resources** and click on **Add**.
3. Start typing `AD:User` in the **Orchestrator Type** field. You will see how the field's selection is reduced. Click on **AD:User**. This is the Orchestrator variable type we will add to vRA.

4. Give this resource a name under which it will be shown in vRA, such as **AD User**, then click on **Next**.

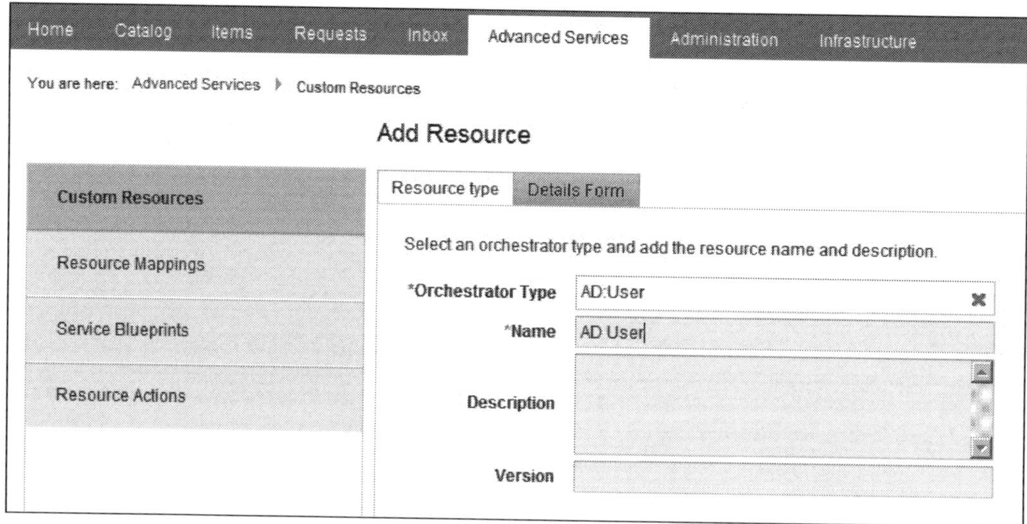

5. The **Details Form** shows all attributes of the variable type we just defined. We need to delete the attribute **Category name** as it can't be used in vRA. Hover the mouse to the right on the **Category Name** field and click on the red X sign.
6. Finish the setup by clicking on **Add**.

Creating the service blueprint

Next, we will create the service blueprint to create a new AD user:

1. Follow the *Integrating Orchestrator workflows in vRA* recipe to add a service blueprint with the following changes.
2. Use the workflow by navigating to **Library** | **Microsoft** | **Active Directory** | **User** | **Create a user with a password in a group**.

3. In the **Provisioned Resource** tab, select the custom resource (**AD User**) that you created.

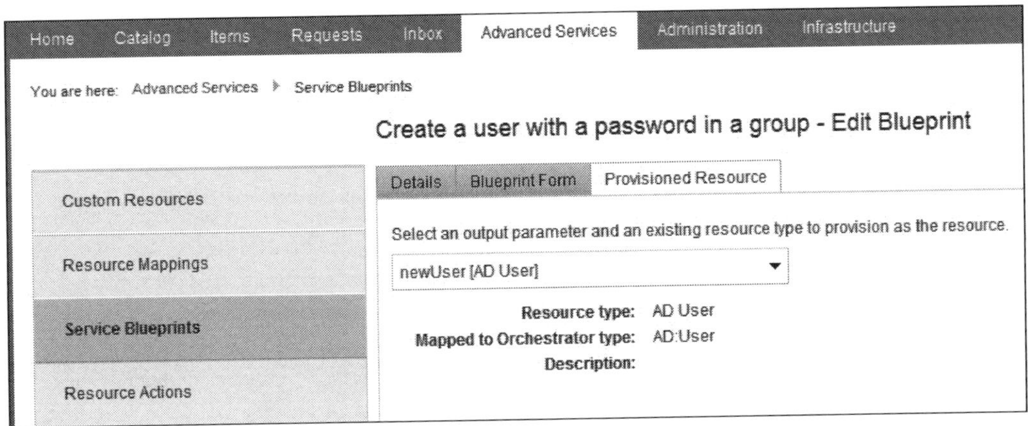

Don't forget to add the blueprint to the catalog.

Creating a resource action

We will now create a resource action and bind it to an entitlement:

1. Navigate to **Advanced Services** | **Resource Actions** and click on **Add**.
2. Select the workflow by navigating to **Library** | **Microsoft** | **Active Directory** | **User** | **Change a user password** and click on **Next**.
3. As **Resource type**, select the custom resource that you created, and as **Input parameter**, select **user**.
4. In the **Details** screen, you can just accept the default settings by clicking on **Next**.
5. You can now change the form with which a user will interact. Click on **Add** and finish creating this action.
6. Now, publish this action by clicking on **Publish**.
7. Navigate to **Administration** | **Catalog Management** | **Entitlements**.
8. Click on your entitlement and edit it.

9. Under **Items & Approvals** in **Entitled Actions**, add the custom action you just created. Click on update when finished.

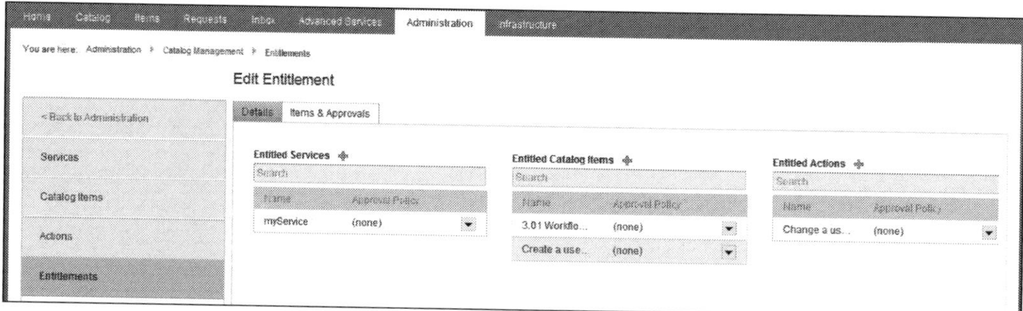

Conducting a test run

We will now start a test run to see what we have achieved and how it works:

1. Go to your vRA catalog and request the service blueprint you have created.
2. Wait a minute until it is finished.
3. Click on **Items** and you will find a new item—the user you just created.
4. Click on the user and select **Actions**. You will find the custom action you created here.

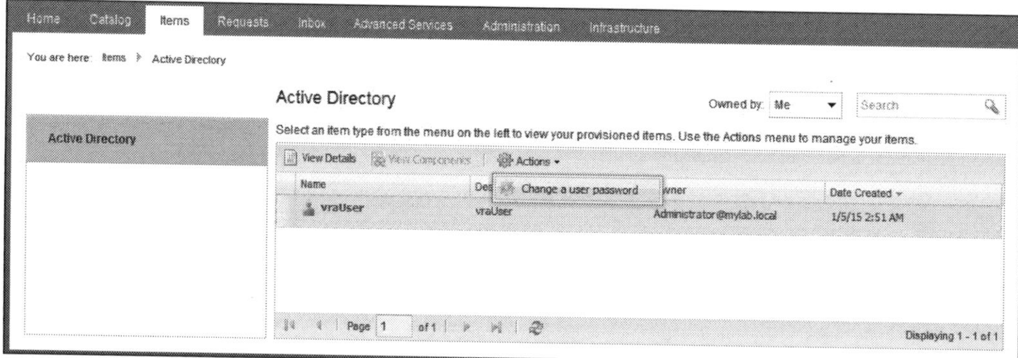

How it works...

This example shows how powerful the Orchestrator integration in vRealize Automation has become.

A custom resource is nothing but an Orchestrator plugin type that you reuse as a resource, and that can be managed and worked with using custom actions. Please note that the request/approval mechanism of vRA can also be used to regulate the use of custom actions and blueprints.

You can leverage any Orchestrator plugin type to manage its life cycle from vRA, or create your own type using the Orchestrator Dynamic Types.

Index

A

B

C

D

E

F

G

H

P

T

U

V

W

X

Thank you for buying VMware vRealize Orchestrator Cookbook

About Packt Publishing

Packt, pronounced 'packed', published its first book, *Mastering phpMyAdmin for Effective MySQL Management*, in April 2004, and subsequently continued to specialize in publishing highly focused books on specific technologies and solutions.

Our books and publications share the experiences of your fellow IT professionals in adapting and customizing today's systems, applications, and frameworks. Our solution-based books give you the knowledge and power to customize the software and technologies you're using to get the job done. Packt books are more specific and less general than the IT books you have seen in the past. Our unique business model allows us to bring you more focused information, giving you more of what you need to know, and less of what you don't.

Packt is a modern yet unique publishing company that focuses on producing quality, cutting-edge books for communities of developers, administrators, and newbies alike. For more information, please visit our website at `www.PacktPub.com`.

About Packt Enterprise

In 2010, Packt launched two new brands, Packt Enterprise and Packt Open Source, in order to continue its focus on specialization. This book is part of the Packt Enterprise brand, home to books published on enterprise software – software created by major vendors, including (but not limited to) IBM, Microsoft, and Oracle, often for use in other corporations. Its titles will offer information relevant to a range of users of this software, including administrators, developers, architects, and end users.

Writing for Packt

We welcome all inquiries from people who are interested in authoring. Book proposals should be sent to `author@packtpub.com`. If your book idea is still at an early stage and you would like to discuss it first before writing a formal book proposal, then please contact us; one of our commissioning editors will get in touch with you.

We're not just looking for published authors; if you have strong technical skills but no writing experience, our experienced editors can help you develop a writing career, or simply get some additional reward for your expertise.

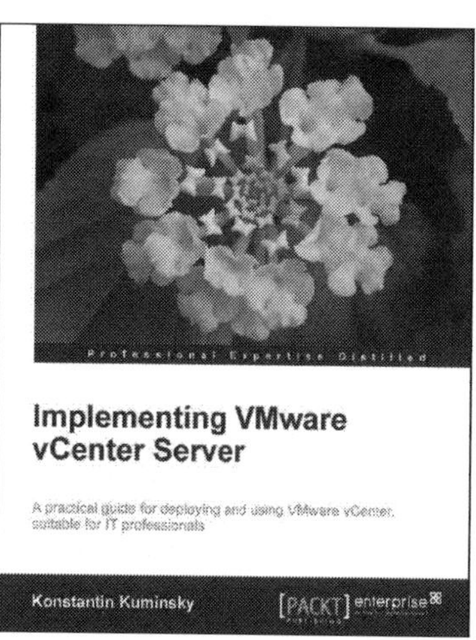

Implementing VMware vCenter Server

ISBN: 978-1-84968-998-4 Paperback: 324 pages

A practical guide for deploying and using VMware vCenter, suitable for IT professionals

1. Gain in-depth knowledge of the VMware vCenter features, requirements, and deployment process.
2. Manage hosts, virtual machines, and learn storage management in VMware vCenter server.
3. Overview of VMware vCenter Operations Manager and VMware vCenter Orchestrator.

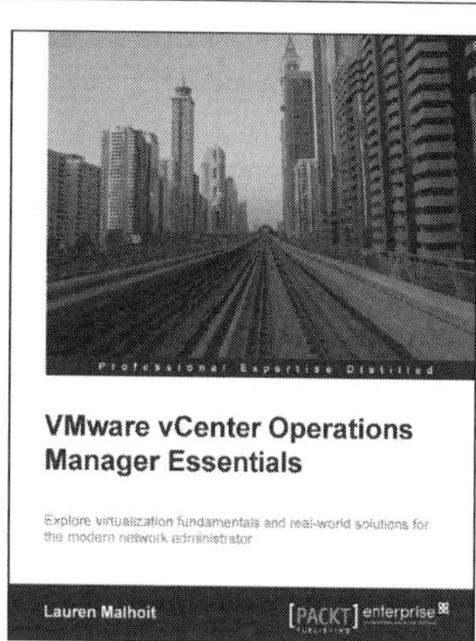

VMware vCenter Operations Manager Essentials

ISBN: 978-1-78217-696-1 Paperback: 246 pages

Explore virtualization fundamentals and real-world solutions for the modern network administrator

1. Written by VMware expert Lauren Malhoit, this book takes a look at vCenter Operations Manager from a practical point of view that every administrator can appreciate.
2. Understand, troubleshoot, and design your virtual environment in a better and more efficient way than you ever have before.
3. A step-by-step and learn-by-example guide to understanding the ins and outs of vCenter Operations Manager.

Please check **www.PacktPub.com** for information on our titles

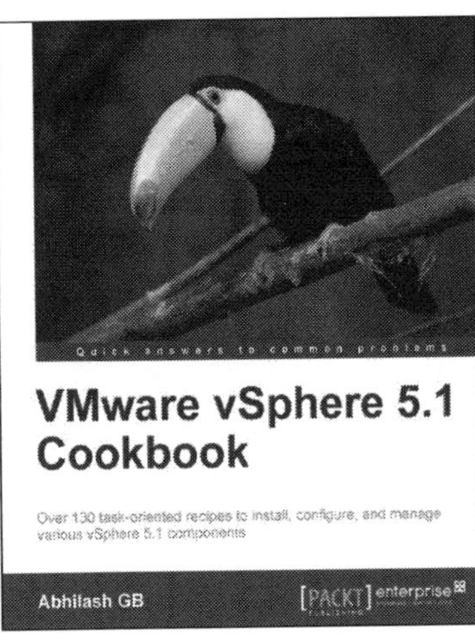

VMware vSphere 5.1 Cookbook

ISBN: 978-1-84968-402-6 Paperback: 466 pages

Over 130 task-oriented recipes to install, configure, and manage various vSphere 5.1 components

1. Install and configure vSphere 5.1 core components.
2. Learn important aspects of vSphere such as administration, security, and performance.
3. Configure vSphere Management Assistant(VMA) to run commands/scripts without the need to authenticate every attempt.

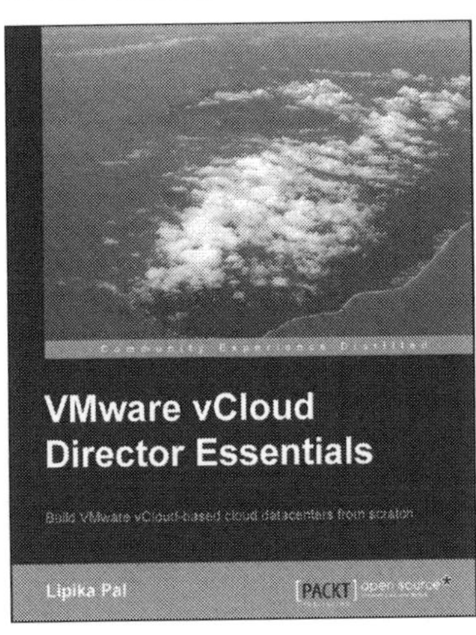

VMware vCloud Director Essentials

ISBN: 978-1-78398-652-1 Paperback: 198 pages

Build VMare vCloud-based cloud datacenters from scratch

1. Learn about DHCP, NAT, and VPN services to successfully implement a private cloud.
2. Configure different networks such as Direct connect, Routed, or Isolated.
3. Configure and manage vCloud Director's access control.

Please check **www.PacktPub.com** for information on our titles